Minority Self-Government in Europe and the Middle East

Studies in International Minority and Group Rights

VOLUME 15

The titles published in this series are listed at *brill.com/imgr*

Minority Self-Government in Europe and the Middle East

From Theory to Practice

Edited by

Olgun Akbulut
Elçin Aktoprak

BRILL
NIJHOFF

LEIDEN | BOSTON

The Library of Congress Cataloging-in-Publication Data is available online at http://catalog.loc.gov

Typeface for the Latin, Greek, and Cyrillic scripts: "Brill". See and download: brill.com/brill-typeface.

ISSN 2210-2132
ISBN 978-90-04-40544-8 (hardback)
ISBN 978-90-04-40545-5 (e-book)

This book is printed on acid-free paper and produced in a sustainable manner.

Contents

Preface VII
Contributors XI

PART 1
Theoretical Perspectives

1 The Right of Self-Determination in International Law 3
Gudmundur Alfredsson

2 Nations, Territorial Minorities, Democratic Theory and National Self-Determination 32
Ephraim Nimni

3 The Multiple Paths to Territorial Autonomy: Examples and Conceptual Underpinnings 62
Sia Spiliopoulou Åkermark

4 Distribution of Legislative Powers in a Sub-state Context – a Comparison of Double Enumerations in Federal and Autonomy Settings 83
Markku Suksi

5 Autonomous Communities and Environmental Law: The Basque Case 106
Daniele Conversi and Xabier Ezeizabarrena

PART 2
European and Middle Eastern Perspectives

6 Territorial Autonomy and Minority Self-Government in Spain: Catalonia and the Basque Country 133
Eduardo J. Ruiz Vieytez

7 Territorial and Cultural Self-Governance in Italy: Strengths and Challenges of South Tyrol's Autonomy 154
Andrea Carlà and Sergiu Constantin

8 Self-Determination, Federalism and Autonomy in the Middle-East 183
Thomas Schmidinger

9 Democratic Confederalism in Syria: The Nation-State, the Kurds, and International Law 201
Thomas James Phillips

10 Legal Background of Autonomy Arrangements in Turkey from Historical Perspectives 228
Olgun Akbulut

11 Unpacking the 'Democratic Confederalism' and 'Democratic Autonomy': Proposals of Turkey's Kurdish Movement 246
Cengiz Gunes

Index 269

Preface

In September 2016, we organized a workshop on the concept of autonomy examined both from theoretical and practical perspectives at the Liverpool Law School, the UK. Those scholars who presented papers or participated in discussions indicated that only a few research materials could be reached in the English language which focused on the self-governing territories and related discussions in the Middle East. This fact encouraged us to further concentrate on the possibility of enriching workshop presentations and turning them into an edited volume, an idea to which the contributing scholars responded positively. The Raoul Wallenberg Institute of Human Rights and Humanitarian Law from Lund/Sweden supported the workshop and the preliminary works of this book project.

The theory and practice of self-determination, autonomy models and minority accommodation have been an enduring topic of politics and scholarship for more than two centuries. Although materials written in English about the autonomy arrangements are fast growing, this volume is novel from several perspectives. First, it combines theory with facts on the ground, going beyond legal perspectives without neglecting existing laws and their implementation. Second, theoretical discussions transcend examining existing autonomy models in certain regions. It offers new models in the field, discussing such critical themes as environmentalism. Third, traditional concepts such as self-determination and, well-known successful autonomy examples, including the Åland Islands, Basque and Catalonian models, are examined from different perspectives by the contributing authors, who are experts on different dimensions of these themes. Fourth, some chapters of this volume focus on certain regions (including Turkey, Syria and, Iraq) which have only recently received scholarly attention. As can be expected, all chapters complement one another in terms of their theoretical inputs and outputs from the field, laying the groundwork for future studies.

In Chapter 1 Prof. Alfredsson classifies and distinguishes between some of the distinct socio-political contexts in which claims to the right of self-determination have thus far been brought.

In Chapter 2 Ephraim Nimni argues national self-determination and expands the concept by taking the autonomy discussions to non-territorial autonomy concept through focusing on national minorities who are not fairly represented in a system based on the idea of 'one person one vote'. His criticisms are crucially important for the discussion of national self-determination within the nation-state and are related to the on-going discussions on different autonomy models in Europe and in the Middle East. For developing democracies, Nimni argues that democratic theory must break with this residue of the nation-state and understand democracy not as a single body but as a plurality of constituent democracies.

In Chapter 3 Sia Spiliopoulou Åkermark provides a competent background for on-going territorial autonomy discussions in the different parts of the world. Instead of constricting territorial autonomy discussions in a strict legal approach, she shows the inadequateness of this approach of conceptualizing territorial autonomy in a particular moment and a particular context, searching for a broader, or rather a more *longue dureé* type of reflection. Spiliopoulou Åkermark examines how we end up having concepts and institutions of 'territorial autonomy' today by studying the legally reflected justificatory chains behind territorial autonomy by and basing her analyses on historical developments since early 19th century.

In Chapter 4 Markku Suksi follows the theoretical discussions on autonomy and self-determination with practical cases from Canada, Finland and Denmark by focusing on the distribution of legislative powers, which is a vital issue for developing autonomy discussions in the Middle East. He examines typical federation and typical autonomy cases, especially dwelling on a third option for distributing legislative powers, where both national law-makers and sub-state law-makers have enumerated powers based on separate lists of competences. This is the situation in a number of cases, some of which are normally considered federations (e.g., Canada and its provinces) and some of which are normally considered autonomy arrangements (Finland and the Åland Islands, but also Denmark and the Faroe Islands, as well as France and New Caledonia). Suksi explores the three ways of distributing legislative competence within a state and focuses in particular on the third category, the double enumeration, which has so far not been studied much from a comparative perspective.

In Chapter 5 Daniele Conversi and Xabier Ezeizabarrena focus on a newly developing issue in the self-determination and autonomy debates: environmentalism. They firstly argue the historical connection between nationalism and environment, and then reply the question of recent years: Do regional governments controlled by sub-state nationalist parties have a better record of implementing robust environmental policies and effective sustainable development, while fighting climate change at the same time? After briefly exploring the exemplary cases, Conversi and Ezeizabarrena analyze the case of the Basque autonomous community in Spain, with occasional reference to the broader national territory envisioned by Basque nationalists, Euskal Herria, and other meso-level institutions.

While the first section of this collection gives a theoretical background for self-determination and autonomy discussions with a special emphasis on developing issues like environmental issues and evolving legislative competence;

the second section of the book presents autonomy cases and prospected models from Europe and the Middle East.

The first case from Europe is Spain, which has been a model for decentralization for decades although recently facing disputes with autonomous communities. In Chapter 6, Eduardo Javier Ruiz Vieytez examines territorial autonomy and minority self-government issues in Spain with highlighting Catalonia and Basque Country. He argues that the real debate in the Spanish constitutional system is not about autonomy, but about the recognition of the 'pluri-national' character of the country and the political asymmetry. In this framework he refers to the debate on the multinational character of the Spanish Kingdom to describe the constitutional framework (1978) dealing with territorial diversity. He is further analysing the tensions raised by the evolution of this very system in the last 20 years and evaluating the Catalan and Basque cases by dwelling on his main argument about political asymmetry.

In Chapter 7 Andrea Carlà and Sergiu Constantin present South Tyrol as an example of successful conflict resolution and minority protection through territorial and cultural self-governance; underlining at the same time the idea of copying and reproducing the entire set of South Tyrol's mechanism and institutions into a different cultural, politico-economic context. They explore South Tyrol's autonomy arrangements, focusing on strengths and challenges by providing a thorough analysis of South Tyrolean institutions and mechanisms of self-governance and minority protection. They also highlight the several challenges at regional, national and European level that the autonomous system face and provide.

Catalonia, Basque Country and South Tyrol provides significant lessons for a better understanding of minority accommodation and different autonomy models from Europe before moving to the Middle East cases and prospected models for autonomy. On the other hand, Thomas Schmidinger's chapter on self-determination, federalism and autonomy in the Middle East displays that autonomy discussions and practices are not recent phenomena in the region as it has been widely suggested by the general public opinion, but cases from Europe could be useful for the development of the discussions on the issue.

In Chapter 8 Schmidinger examines historical and contemporary concepts, realities of autonomies and federalism in the Middle East. He also deals with the difficulties to establish federalist structures that are also accepted by central governments by giving examples of the Democratic Federation of Northern Syria (DFNS) – Rojava and the Kurdistan Region of Iraq providing insights on these issues. Finally, he discusses the special cases of Palestine and the United Arab Emirates.

In Chapter 9 Thomas Phillips elaborates on Schmidinger's analyses, studying the organizational program of the multi-ethnic DFNS, formerly known as

Rojava, and its relationship with the internal aspect of the right of all peoples to self-determination. Phillips examines the DFNS program in terms of its political and economic aims, arguing that one can plausibly interpret the right of self-determination as a participatory norm that is concerned with relationships between various groups and segments of society in the example of Rojava.

In Chapter 10 Olgun Akbulut analyses autonomy discussions in Turkey with an emphasis on the Lausanne Treaty of 1923 and related domestic legislation. Legal discussions on autonomy arrangements in Turkey can be approached from both historical and current perspectives. Research which focuses on the current unavoidably encounters a legal deadlock, but a historical perspective often provides a higher vantage point wherefrom autonomy in the Turkish context may be better evaluated. For many autonomy discussions in the Turkish context focus on the existing constitutional rules and the judgments of the Turkish Constitutional Court as the main stumbling blocks. This chapter stresses the significance of the historical perspective.

In Chapter 11 Cengiz Gunes analyses 'democratic confederalism' and 'democratic autonomy' demands of the Kurdish movement in Turkey. By examining the key texts through which these proposals have been articulated, he firstly unpacks what democratic confederalism and democratic autonomy entail and then examines the specific demands for minority groups. Gunes evaluates these two concepts in detail as a proposed solution to the Kurdish question in the light of a decentralised and democratised vision of the Middle East. He is also building bridges with Nimni's chapter referencing non-territorial autonomy.

We wish to thank all the contributors for their invaluable time and scholarship as well as for their endurance for supporting this project for more than two years. We, as two human rights scholars from Turkey, went through difficult times over this period. It was our contributors who encouraged us all the way through to complete the work. We owe them a lot.

We would like to express our gratitude to Brill series editors Gudmundur Alfredsson and Kristina Henrard, who worked hard to catch up the time we lost when editing the series. Without their invaluable advice this volume could not have been completed. Our thanks also go to Lindy Melman and Bea Timmer (Brill Publishers) and Sindhuja Vijayabaskaran (Spi Global) for all kinds of editorial and practical work rendered in the preparation of the publication.

We hope that the volume would be beneficial for all students of autonomy and autonomy related subjects.

Olgun Akbulut & Elçin Aktoprak
Istanbul & Ankara, 22 February 2019

Contributors

Olgun Akbulut
is a constitutional and human rights scholar at Kadir Has University, Faculty of Law (Istanbul/Turkey). His research interests address human rights, minority rights and comparative constitutional law. He was a post-doc visiting scholar at Harvard Law School (2012–2013) and a doctoral researcher at the Raoul Wallenberg Institute of Human Rights and Humanitarian Law (Lund/Sweden, 2004–2007). He has published in human rights and constitutional law in various academic journals both in Turkey and abroad. In addition to his first book, titled *Legal Basis for Living Together in Peace*, Akbulut's second published monograph is entitled *Religious Pluralism from Constitutional Perspectives*.

Elçin Aktoprak
was an Assistant Professor at the Faculty of Political Sciences, Ankara University. She was dismissed as per an emergency decree in February 2017 because of signing a peace petition. She is the author of *States and Their Nations: Nationalism and Minority Issues in Western Europe* (2010), co-editor of *Nationalism in the 21st century: Theory and Practice* (2016) and co-editor of *Democratic Representation in Plurational States: The Kurds in Turkey* (2018). Her research interests are theories of nationalism, minority issues in Europe, the Kurdish question, conflict resolution and peace studies.

Gudmundur Alfredsson
(SJD, Harvard Law School, 1982) is Law Professor at the University of Akureyri and at the China University of Political Science and Law in Beijing. He has also held teaching positions at the University of Greenland, the University of Lund, the University of Strasbourg and American University in Washington DC. He was Director of the Raoul Wallenberg Institute of Human Rights in Lund (1995–2006), staff member with the UN Secretariat (1983–95), member of the UN Sub-Commission for the Promotion and Protection of Human Rights (2004–06), and Chairman of the UN Working Group on Minorities (2006). He chaired the expert meetings that drafted the Lund Recommendations on the Effective Participation of National Minorities in Public Affairs (OSCE 1998–99). He is Editor-in-Chief of the *Yearbook of Polar Law* (with Timo Koivurova) and of the International Journal on Minority and Group Rights (both published by Brill).

Andrea Carlà
(PhD in Politics, New School for Social Research, New York – Postgraduate studies in Diplomacy and International Relations, University of Bologna) is Senior Researcher at the Institute for Minority Rights, EURAC Research, Italy. His research focuses on ethnic politics, management of diversity, migration issues and their interplay with security issues. He co-edited the volume *Migration in Autonomous Territories. The Case of South Tyrol and Catalonia* (Brill 2015).

Sergiu Constantin
is a researcher at the Institute for Minority Rights of EURAC Research (Italy). He holds a law degree from University of Bucharest (Romania) and a Master in European Studies from University of Graz (Austria). His research deals with legal protection of national and ethnic minorities focusing on language rights, political participation and autonomy systems. He co-edited the volume *Autonomy Arrangements Around the World – A Collection of Well and Lesser Known Cases* (ISPMN 2014).

Daniele Conversi
a Research Professor at the University of the Basque Country and Ikerbasque, the Basque Foundation for Science. He received his PhD at the London School of Economics. He taught at the Government and History Departments at Cornell and Syracuse Universities, as well as at the Central European University, Budapest and University of Lincoln, UK. His first book, *The Basques, the Catalans, and Spain* has been reviewed in over forty international journals. His volume, *Ethnonationalism in the Contemporary World*, is a collection of essays by some of the top international scholars entirely devoted to explore the relationship between nationalism and modernity.

Cengiz Gunes
completed his PhD at the Ideology and Discourse Analysis Research Programme, the Department of Government, University of Essex, UK. He is the author of *The Kurdish National Movement in Turkey: From Protest to Resistance* (Routledge 2012) and co-editor of *The Kurdish Question in Turkey: New Perspectives on Violence, Representation, and Reconciliation* (Routledge 2014). His main research interests are in the areas of peace and conflict studies, the Kurds in the Middle East, the international relations of the Middle East and Turkish politics. Currently he works as an associate lecturer at the Open University, UK.

Ephraim Nimni
taught at the Universities of Keele, New South Wales in Sydney, and Queen's University Belfast. His teaching areas are comparative ethnic conflict, theories

of ethnicity and nationalism, national cultural autonomy and minority rights, extra-territorial self-determination, multiculturalism, the Israeli Palestinian Conflict. His research interests follow two interrelated directions. First direction is comparative ethnic conflicts, theories of nationalism and minority rights, models of national self-determination that do not require separate nation states, multiculturalism and the applicability of the national cultural autonomy model to contemporary multination states. Second direction is the Israeli Palestinian conflict from the perspective of conflict resolution.

Thomas James Phillips
is a lecturer in law at Liverpool John Moores University. His PhD thesis considers the right of self-determination as it applies to the Kurds in Turkey, with a particular focus on political participation and linguistic rights. His research interests include minority rights, group rights, Kurdish rights and Kurdish studies more generally.

Xabier Ezeizabarrena Saenz
is a lawyer based in San Sebastian, Basque Country (PhD Law, University of the Basque Country) and a lecturer on Administrative and Environmental Law at the University of the Basque Country and at Deusto University. He is a member of the IUCN World Commission on Environmental Law and Director of the Environmental Law Master of the University of the Basque Country.

Thomas Schmidinger
is a political scientist as well as a social and cultural anthropologist. He has a lecturing position at the Vienna University's Institute for Political Science and at the Universities of Applied Sciences Vorarlberg and Upper Austria. He is affiliated researcher of the Institute for the Sociology of Law and Criminology. Schmidinger is secretary general of the Austrian Association for Kurdish Studies and Co-Editor of the Vienna Kurdish Studies Yearbook and in the Editorial Review Board of the international peer-reviewed journal *Kurdish Studies*. He works on Syrian and Iraqi Kurdistan as well as on Jihadism and State failure.

Sia Spiliopoulou Åkermark
is Associate Professor in International Law, Director of the Åland Islands Peace Institute (www.peace.ax). She focuses on diversity, autonomy, demilitarization, the use of force and international law and its institutions. She has worked in several universities, research institutions and non-governmental organisations around the world. She has been an expert member of the *Advisory Committee on the Framework Convention on National Minorities of the Council of Europe* (2002–2006 and 2010–2014) and served for two years as the

Committee's President. She is currently heading a project entitled "Demilitarisation in an Increasingly Militarized World: International Perspectives in a Multilevel Framework".

Markku Suksi
is Professor of Public Law at Åbo Akademi University, Finland. He has authored several books and articles about autonomy issues, such as *Sub-State Governance through Territorial Autonomy* (Springer 2011) and edited the volume *Autonomy – Applications and Implications* (Kluwer Law 1998).

Eduardo J. Ruiz Vieytez
is a professor of Constitutional Law at University of Deusto (Bilbao), where he acts as dean of the Faculty of Social and Human Sciences, and previously as director of the Human Rights Institute. He has been legal adviser of the Basque Ombudsman and the president of an NGO working in the promotion of immigrants' rights in the Basque Country (1993–1999). He has also been a member of the Spanish Council for Integration of Migrants, and participated in several country missions of the Council of Europe concerning linguistic and national minorities. His fields of research are integration policies, national conflicts, minority rights and the relation between human rights and religious, linguistic and cultural diversity.

PART 1

Theoretical Perspectives

CHAPTER 1

The Right of Self-Determination in International Law

Gudmundur Alfredsson

1 Introduction

From 1945 till today, the number of UN Member Sates has grown from 51 to 193, and much of that increase is linked to the exercise of the right of self-determination. That process has not been completed, and many legitimate and other less likely self-determination demands are pending as frequently seen in the news. Colonial situations still persist – the United Nations continues to maintain a list of non-self-governing territories under Chapter XI of its Charter, still other territories may qualify as colonies although they may be disguised as 'integrated' territories. And worldwide many indigenous peoples and minorities are restless often for good reasons.

In Europe and in its neigbourhood, for a variety of reasons and in different circumstances, today one sees external or internal self-determination demands, moves and/or concrete steps taken by, amongst others, the Basques, the Berbers, Catalonians,[1] Corsicans, Faroe Islanders,[2] Greenlanders,[3] Karelians, Kosovars,[4]

1 There are plenty of academic and other writings on all of the mentioned territories; only a few samples follow in the subsequent footnotes. For a recent contribution on Catalonia, *see* Anne Peters, 'Populist International Law? The Suspended Independence and the Normative Value of the Referendum on Catalonia' (12 October 2017) Blog of the European Journal of International Law, *see* https://www.ejiltalk.org/populist-international-law-the-suspended-independence-and-the-normative-value-of-the-referendum-on-catalonia/.

2 Gudmundur Alfredsson, 'The Faroese People as a Subject of Public International Law' (2001) 1(1) *Føroyskt Lógar Rit – Faroese Law Review* 45–57.

3 Gudmundur Alfredsson, 'Greenland and the Law of Political Decolonization' (1982) 25 *German Yearbook of International Law* 290–308; and 'The Greenlanders and their Human Rights Choices', in M. Bergsmo (ed), *Human Rights and Criminal Justice for the Downtrodden, Essays in Honour of Asbjörn Eide* (Martinus Nijhoff Publishers 2003) 453–459.

4 Accordance with International Law of the Unilateral declaration in respect of Kosovo, Advisory Opinion of the International Court of Justice, delivered on 22 July 2010. *See* also John Dugard, *The Secession of States and Their Recognition in the Wake of Kosovo* (Pocketbooks of the Hague Academy of International Law 2013).

 | DOI:10.1163/9789004405455_002

Kurds,[5] the Quebecois,[6] Palestinians, the Scots and South Tyrolians.[7] And it is not so long ago that Czechoslovakia, the Soviet Union and Yugoslavia broke up into old and new components.

Hundreds if not thousands of additional peoples and groups from around the world have expressed the desire to exercise the right of self-determination. Their histories and circumstances vary widely: colonization of overseas possessions, disguised colonialism, recently occupied territories, histories of past glory, oppressed minorities and indigenous peoples, and so on. Some of the claims are firmly rooted in legal arguments which, in a very broad and general sense, will be examined below.

This article is divided into two main parts, addressing external and internal self-determination. The labels may be similar but the bottomline is fundamentally different. External self-determination is about peoples deciding on their international juridical status, with independence as the most frequent choice. Internal self-determination is about self-governance of groups within a State, without the interruption of sovereignty and of the territorial integrity of the States concerned. Federal arrangements and political participation at the national and local levels will also enter the picture. Some contents may relate to both the external and internal dimensions, like the ownership and control of natural resources.

Within each of the two parts, a survey will be conducted of the sources of the applicable international law instruments. This article relies first and foremost on the primary sources of law and the existing practice of States and international organizations. An abundance of academic literature addresses the right of self-determination, and the divergent views illustrate that both the identification of beneficiaries (who) and the contents (what) of both external and internal self-determination are often both unclear and uncertain.

5 For views on the Kurds and the right of self-determination, *see* Israel T. Naamani, 'The Kurdish Drive for Self-Determination' (1966) 20(3) *Middle East Journal* 279–295; Ove Bring, 'Kurdistan and the Principle of Self-Determination' (1992) 35(1) *German Yearbook of International Law* 157–169; Gunnar M. Karlsen, Conflict Dynamics and Human Rights Problems (1996), *Norwegian Institute of Human Rights, Human Rights Report* no. 6; and Albertus Jacobus Meintjes, 'The Complications of Kurdish Independence' (2018) 8(1) *Open Journal of Political Science* 1–11. *See* also *Documentation of the International Conference on Human Rights in Kurdistan* (The Initiative for Human Rights in Kurdistan, 1989).

6 *See* Reference re Secession of Quebec, judgement of the Supreme Court of Canada, 20 August 1998, https://scc-csc.lexum.com/scc-csc/scc-csc/en/item/1643/index.do. This case is often quoted for its fine overview and analysis of self-determination issues.

7 In the present volume, *see* the article by Andrea Carlà and Sergiu Constantin entitled 'Territorial and cultural self-governance in Italy: strengths and challenges of South Tyrol's autonomy'.

After looking at the law sources, the Why, the Who, the What, the When and the How will be examined in an attempt to determine, at least in part and by way of an overview, in which situations peoples/groups can make and realize their claims to the right of self-determination and when the surrounding world should consider accepting such claims.[8] Apart from occasional references to actual situations for explanatory purposes, the article does not focus on particular claims or specific situations.

II External Self-Determination

External self-determination is about peoples deciding their international juridical status. As to the Who, the main beneficiaries of the right of external self-determination are peoples under colonial rule or recent occupation, with possible expansion to minorities and indigenous peoples if and when they are denied representation and their human rights are otherwise severely violated. The What refers to independence, free association and integration or other solutions chosen by the people concerned.

II.A *Sources of Relevant International Law*

There are plenty of references to the right of self-determination in the external sense in international instruments, both treaties and declarations, as well as in the case-law and the practice of States and international organizations. Some of the main sources will now be outlined.[9]

Articles 1, paragraph 2, and 55 of the United Nations Charter, on the purposes, principles and roles of the Organization, mention friendly relations among na-

8 This author has on prior occasions tried to distinguish between the various contents and forms of self-determination, *see* Gudmundur Alfredsson, 'Different Forms of and Claims to the Right of Self-Determination' in D. Clark and R. Williamson (eds), *Self-Determination. International Perspectives* (MacMillan Press & St. Martin's Press 1996) 58–86 (collection of essays from a symposium at the University of Saskatchewan in memory of Martin Ennals); and 'Access to International Monitoring Procedures: Choices between Self-Determination and the Human Rights of Groups' in M.C. van Walt van Praag and O. Seroo (eds), *The Implementation of the Right to Self-Determination as a Contribution to Conflict Prevention. Report of the 1998 International Conference of Experts on the Right to Self-Determination* (UNESCO Centre of Catalonia 1999), 197–209.

9 For the history and early evolution of the right of self-determination, *see* two studies carried out under the auspices of the UN Sub-Commission for the Prevention of Discrimination and Protection of Minorities, by H. Gros Espiell, *The Right to Self-Determination*, U.N. Doc. E/CN.4/Sub.2/405/Rev.1, UN Sales No. E.79.XIV.5 (1980), and A. Cristescu, *The Right to Self-Determination*, U.N. Doc. E/CN.4/Sub.2/404/Rev. 1, UN Sales No. E.80.XIV.3 (1980).

tions based on 'respect for the principle of equal rights and self-determination of peoples' in the context of universal peace. Self-determination is also implicit in the provisions of chapters XI and XII of the Charter on the treatment of non-self-governing and trust territories, in particular articles 73 and 76. These are further elaborated by the 1960 UN Declaration on the Granting of Independence to Colonial Countries and Peoples[10] which contains strong self-determination language: '2. All peoples have the right to self-determination; by virtue of that right they freely determine their political status and freely pursue their economic, social and cultural development'.

Along with the 1960 Decolonization Declaration, the UN General Assembly adopted resolution 1541 (XV)[11] which in an annex sets forth twelve principles for guiding colonizing States in determining when to submit information about their colonies under article 73e of the Charter. According to principle III, 'The obligation to transmit information under Article 73e of the Charter constitutes an international obligation and should be carried out with due regard to the fulfilment of international law'. Resolution 1541 (XV) also spells out the avenues for a colony reaching a full measure of self-government as required by article 73e, that is through independence, free association or integration with an independent State (see below under What).

Articles 1 of the two International Covenants on Civil and Political Rights (ICCPR) and on Economic, Social and Cultural Rights are key sources on self-determination: '1. All peoples have the right of self-determination. By virtue of that right they freely determine their political status and freely pursue their economic, social and cultural development'. And in paragraphs 2 and 3, the right of self-determination is also clearly linked to natural resources and decolonization. A general comment adopted by the Human Rights Committee, the monitoring body for the ICCPR, offers further clarification.[12]

---

10 Adopted by General Assembly resolution 1514 (XV) of 14 December 1960. This and other UN system instruments, ratification lists, monitoring reports, court or treaty body cases and studies quoted in this article are, in April and May 2018, available at www.un.org, www.ohchr.org, www.icj-cij.org/en, www.ilo.org and www.unesco.org.

11 'Principles which should Guide Members in Determining whether or not an Obligation Exists to Transmit the Information called for under Article 73e of the Charter', Resolution No 1541 (XV), UN Doc. A/4684 (1960), Adopted on 15 December 1960. The principles in 1541 (XV) built on the lists of factors annexed to prior GA resolutions, the last one being 742 (VIII) of 1953.

12 General Comment No. 12 concerning self-determination. For the history of article 1 and its use before and after the adoption of the ICCPR, *see* Jakob Th. Möller and Alfred de Zayas in *United Nations Human Rights Committee Case Law 1977–2008. A Handbook* (N.P. Engel Publisher 2009) 120–123; and Manfred Nowak, 'U.N. Covenant on Civil and Political Rights' *CCPR Commentary*, 2nd revised edition (N.P. Engel 2005) 5–26.

Another key instrument is the UN Declaration on Principles of International Law concerning Friendly Relations and Cooperation among States in accordance with the Charter of the United Nations.[13] In paragraph 3, the Declaration stipulates that the 'principles of the Charter which are embodied in this Declaration constitute basic principles of international law'. Self-determination is one of these principles. Beyond decolonization, as to the Who and the availability for the rest of the content categories, the answer may sometimes be positive, often unclear and on other occasions negative.

II.B *The Why*

The UN Charter and other instruments have already been quoted to the effect that respect for the principle of equal rights and self-determination of peoples serves universal peace. It flows from these texts that the reason behind and the purpose of the right of external self-determination is the correction of injustice and the prevention of violent conflicts through the termination of colonial rule and of occupation. Addressing serious human rights violations and the non-representation of minority and indigenous groups may be the next front.

A chapter in the Friendly Relations Declaration is entitled 'The principle of equal rights and self-determination of peoples', and borrowing much of the language from the UN Charter it reads: 'By virtue of the principle of equal rights and self-determination of peoples ... all peoples have the right freely to determine, without external interference, their political status and to pursue their economic, social and cultural development'. It is added that 'every State has the duty to respect this right in accordance with the provisions of the Charter. Every State has the duty to promote, through joint and separate action, realization of the principle of equal rights and self-determination of peoples, ... and to render assistance to the United Nations in carrying out the responsibilities entrusted to it by the Charter regarding the implementation of the principle, in order' to promote friendly relations and co-operation among States and to bring a speedy end to colonialism, having due regard to the freely expressed will of the peoples concerned.

The Friendly Relations Declaration goes on, in the context of self-determination, to say that

> subjection of peoples to alien subjugation, domination and exploitation constitutes a violation of the principle, as well as a denial of fundamental human rights, and is contrary to the Charter. Every State has the duty

13 The Declaration was adopted in 1970 by General Assembly resolution 2625 (XXV).

> to promote through joint and separate action universal respect for and observance of human rights and fundamental freedoms in accordance with the Charter.

Furthermore, the door is opened to indigenous peoples and minorities who are not represented in the government of the country in which they live:

> Nothing in the foregoing paragraphs shall be construed as authorizing or encouraging any action which would dismember or impair, totally or in part, the territorial integrity or political unity of sovereign and independent States conducting themselves in compliance with the principle of equal rights and self-determination of peoples as described above and thus possessed of a government representing the whole people belonging to the territory without distinction as to race, creed or colour.

The peace connection is underlined in preambular paragraphs of the Declaration on Friendly Relations which read:

> Convinced that the subjection of peoples to alien subjugation, domination and exploitation constitutes a major obstacle to the promotion of international peace and security; Convinced that the principle of equal rights and self-determination of peoples constitutes a significant contribution to contemporary international law, and that its effective application is of paramount importance for the promotion of friendly relations among States, based on respect for the principle of sovereign equality; Convinced in consequence that any attempt aimed at the partial or total disruption of the national unity and territorial integrity of a State or country or at its political independence is incompatible with the purposes and principles of the Charter.

There is also a broader human rights connection. The monitoring body for the ICCPR, the Human Rights Committee, in 1984 adopted General Comment No. 12 on article 1. In paragraph 1, the Committee observed that

> The right of self-determination is of particular importance because its realization is an essential condition for the effective guarantee and observance of individual human rights and for the promotion and strengthening of those rights. It is for that reason that States set forth the right of self-determination in a provision of positive law … and placed this

provision as article 1 apart from and before all of the other rights in the two Covenants.[14]

II.C *The Who*

Practically all the instruments quoted above refer to 'peoples' as the holders of the right of external self-determination. Peoples, as with many other terms relating to the collective beneficiaries of human rights, like also minorities and indigenous peoples, written and formally adopted definitions of the relevant terms are missing. Still, there are plenty of indications in the international instruments, in case-law and in the practice of States and international organizations which identify all or most of the content elements of the relevant terms.

Which collectivities or groupings qualify as 'peoples'? It has been suggested that the term 'peoples' stands for the population, irrespective of its ethnic or linguistic composition, of a territory that is accepted by the international community.[15] The clearest example relates to political decolonization, or the right of colonized peoples to external self-determination, which is by now a binding rule under international law. The International Court of Justice (ICJ) has said as much in advisory opinions on Namibia and Western Sahara and in the East Timor case.[16] Gradually new case law will further clarify the existing coverage; a request for an advisory opinion on the legal consequences of the 1965 separation of the Chagos Archipelago from Mauritius, which was submitted pursuant to General Assembly resolution 71/292 (22 June 2017), is currently pending before the ICJ.

The limitations on who can pursue self-determination claims can appear in relation to both substance and procedure. For example, article 1 can be relevant for interpreting other articles of the ICCPR, like article 25 on political participation. In the Gillot v France case (no. 932/2000), the Human Rights Committee considered that 'it would not be unreasonable to limit participation in' self-determination referenda to persons concerned by the future of the territory in question (New Caledonia). Furthermore, as repeatedly stated by

---

14 *See* note 12 above.

15 *See* Gudmundur Alfredsson, 'Peoples' in Ruediger Wolfrum (ed), *The Max Planck Encyclopedia of Public International Law* VIII (Max-Planck-Gesellschaft and OUP 2012) 240–245.

16 For a survey of these opinions/cases *see* Daniel Thuerer and Thomas Burri, 'Self-Determination' in Ruediger Wolfrum (ed), *The Max Planck Encyclopedia of Public International Law* IX (Max-Planck-Gesellschaft and OUP 2012) 113–128. The opinions/cases are all available on the ICJ website at www.icj-cij.org/en/decisions.

the Committee, in the Lubicon Lake Band v Canada (no. 167/1984) and the A.B. et al. v Italy (no. 413/1990, about South Tyrol) cases, the Optional Protocol to the ICCPR allows only 'individuals' to file complaints about violations of the Covenant while the right of self-determination in article 1 belongs to 'peoples';[17] in this context, for reasons of obvious self-interest, States are and will be keen to maintain strict limits on the access of peoples and groups to justice.

The Friendly Relations Declaration says in regard to decolonization that a colony 'has, under the Charter, a status separate and distinct from the territory of the State administering it'. This separate and distinct status exists until the people of the colony has exercised the right of self-determination in accordance with the Charter, and it continues as a matter of course if the people concerned chooses indpendence or free asociation. The colonized territory thus has integrity of its own. The Permanent Court of International Justice relied in part on Greenland's insular integrity in the Eastern Greenland Case already in 1933.

II.C.1 Overseas Colonized Territories

The primary example of the right of external self-determination concerns political decolonization. This flows from the UN Charter, the 1960 Declaration on the Granting of Independence to Colonial Countries and Peoples, and the two International Human Rights Covenants. As pointed out above, it is in this context that the majority of new States created during the UN lifetime have come into being.

In principle I of GA resolution 1541 (XV), it is stated that the authors of the Charter 'had in mind that Chapter XI should be applicable to territories which were then known to be of the colonial type. An obligation exists to transmit information under Article 73e of the Charter in respect of such territories whose peoples have not yet attained a full measure of self-government'. In principle II, it says that 'the Charter embodies the concept of Non-Self-Governing Territories in a dynamic state of evolution and progress towards a full measure of self-government. As soon as a territory and its peoples attain a full measure of self-government, the obligation ceases'. Principles X, XI and XII contain further technical regulation of the reporting requirements.

The decolonization rule is confirmed in common articles 1, paragraph 3, of the two International Covenants on Civil and Political Rights and on Economic, Social and Cultural Rights: The States Parties, 'including those having

17 *See* the explanation by Möller and de Zayas, 'United Nations Human Rights Committee Case Law 1977–2008' 524–525.

responsibility for the administration of Non-Self-Governing and Trust Territories, shall promote the realization of the right of self-determination, and shall respect that right, in conformity with the provisions of the Charter of the United Nations'.

The drive towards political decolonization continues; some 17 colonial countries and peoples remain on the UN list of non-self-governing territories.[18] And the UN General Assembly has declared the period 2011–2020 the Third International Decade for the Eradication of Colonialism.[19]

In addition to the territories on the UN list, there are still several disguised colonies. These are overseas possessions which have been incorporated by traditional colonial powers like Denmark, France and the United Kingdom without fully and properly providing the peoples concerned with the democratic exercise of free and informed choices extending to independence or integration or something in between.

The so-called overseas element of decolonization appears in principle IV of GA resolution 1541 (XV): '*Prima facie* there is an obligation to transmit information in respect of a territory which is geographically separate and is distinct ethnically and/or culturally from the country administering it'. The element of geographic separation has also been referred to as the blue water thesis or the salt-water theory. An attempt to expand the reach to geographically contiguous territories, the so-called Belgian thesis aimed mainly at extending decolonization to republics of the Soviet Union, failed at the United Nations in the 1950s. The element of ethnic and/or cultural distinctness does not mean that the people concerned has to be homogenous; there is still space for groups within and belonging to the 'people'.

Under principle V, when it has been established that a *prima facie* case of geographical and ethnical or cultural distinctness of a territory exists, other elements may be brought into consideration. 'These additional elements may be, *inter alia,* of an administrative, political, juridical, economic or historical nature. If they affect the relationship between the metropolitan State and the territory concerned in a manner which arbitrarily places the latter in a position or status of subordination, they support the presumption that there is an obligation to transmit information under Article 73 e of the Charter'.

18 For the largest of these territories, the Centre for Human Rights at the University of Pretoria organized in February 2017 a forum entitled 'Self-determination delayed: The Sahrawi Arab Democratic Republic (Western Sahara)'; *See* http://www.chr.up.ac.za/index.php/centre-news-a-events-2017/1745-invitation-discussion-forum-self-determination-delayed-the-sahrawi-arab-democratic-republic.html.

19 *See* http://www.un.org/en/decolonization/nonselfgovterritories.shtml.

II.C.2 Territories Subject to Alien Subjugation and Recent Occupation

In addition to and apart from decolonization, the international instruments refer to alien subjugation, domination and/or exploitation as grounds for the exercise of the right of external self-determination. Occupation brought about after the UN Charter's ban on the use of force also qualifies as grounds; instead of 1945 one could also look at the 1928 Kellogg-Briand Pact[20] as a timeline for unlawful occupation.

With the demise of the Soviet Union, some of the so-called socialist republics which had been sovereign States before they were occupied by force and annexed without consent in 1940, that is after the adoption of the Kellogg-Briand Pact, such as the three Baltic States, took the opportunity and restored their independence.[21]

As to recent occupation, one can look at Palestine and repeated resolutions by UN bodies, such as this language from the General Assembly: 'Urges all States and the specialized agencies and organizations of the United Nations system to continue to support and assist the Palestinian people in the early realization of their inalienable human rights, including their right to self-determination' in light of fifty years of occupation and the continued denial and violation of human rights.[22]

II.C.3 Non-represented Groups and Massive Human Rights Violations

The language on the right of self-determination in the UN Friendly Relations Declaration and the 1993 Vienna Declaration and Plan of Action adopted at the 2nd UN World Conference on Human Rights contain similar texts indicating that minority and indigenous groups may obtain the right of external self-determination if their representation and human rights are denied in some serious ways.

The Friendly Relations Declaration thus states that

> Nothing in the foregoing paragraphs shall be construed as authorizing or encouraging any action which would dismember or impair, totally or in part, the territorial integrity or political units of sovereign and independent States conducting themselves in compliance with the principle of equal rights and self-determination of peoples as described above and

20 *See* http://avalon.law.yale.edu/20th_century/kbpact.asp.

21 Ineta Ziemele, *State Continuity and Nationality: The Baltic States and Russia. Past, Present and Future as Defined by International Law* (Martinus Nijhoff Publishers 2005).

22 Operative paragraph 16 of General Assembly resolution 72/87 of 7 December 2017.

> thus possessed of a government representing the whole people belonging to the territory without distinction as to race, creed or colour.

This language, about complying with equal rights and a government representing everyone belonging to the territory without distinction, can be construed as going beyond decolonization. Minorities and indigenous peoples stand to benefit from this approach. A case in point could be Kosovo where autonomy had been withdrawn and where serious human rights violations took place, violations that have even been confirmed by an international criminal tribunal. This type of scenario has also been referred to as remedial secession; in its advisory opinion on Kosovo the ICJ does not close the door on this argument.[23]

This formulation about non-representation and human rights violations has much in common with the third preambular paragraph of the 1948 Universal Declaration of Human Rights: 'Whereas it is essential, if man is not to be compelled to have recourse, as a last resort, to rebellion against tyranny and oppression, that human rights should be protected by the rule of law'. Respect for human rights helps keeping the peace, and this language acknowledges that non-respect can lead to rebellion. It may not authorize rebellion but acknowledges its inevitability in light of history.

The absence of international fora and procedures which peoples and minorities can access for determining whether they have a valid and viable claim to exercise the right of self-determination is the sad part of the this story. In some situations, the missing fora may lead collectivities to take up arms and use violence as the sole method available for attracting the attention of and getting law-based reaction from international organizations and foreign governments.

II.C.4 Agreed Separation

If a central government agrees that a part of the country can break away and establish its own State, the international community is unlikely to raise objections. Thus, when the Soviet Union and Czechoslovakia broke up and when territories broke away from Ethiopia and the Sudan, restored and newly created States that came about as a result were quickly recognized by other States and admitted or readmitted to membership in international organizations.

The same is true for Canada and the UK allowing Quebec and Scotland to vote on independence; if the peoples concerned had voted in favor of independence and been allowed to create new States, undoubtedly Quebec and Scotland would have been able to rapidly join the international community. On the other hand, Catalonia has so far been stuck with a Spanish refusal; in any case,

23 Dugard, note 4 above, 140–153.

it is noteworthy that none of the territories mentioned in this paragraph have gained prior support from other States or endorsements from international organizations. As mentioned above, most States see it in their own interest to maintain a small and charmed club of peoples, thus limiting the number of possible breakaways.

Maybe it is wrong to designate this process of agreed separation as part and parcel of the right of external self-determination; it is not much of a right if it is entirely up to an administering State to agree or not to agree to the release. Nevertheless, common items on the watch list presumably include the procedural methods and the substantive choices.

II.D *The What*

The substantive contents or the What of external self-determination is about determining the external status of peoples, with emphasis on the options of independence, free association and integration. These choices are provided in principle VI of General Assembly resolution 1541 (XV): 'A Non-Self-Governing Territory can be said to have reached a full measure of self-government by: (a) Emergence as a sovereign independent State; (b) Free association with an independent State; or (c) Integration with an independent State'.

In this respect, the Friendly Relations Declaration reiterates the language of the 1960 Declaration: 'The establishment of a sovereign and independent State, the free association or integration with an independent State or the emergence into any other political status freely determined by a people constitute modes of implementing the right of self-determination … ' Most of the peoples which have had the opportunity to exercise the right of external self-determination have chosen independence and statehood.

Principle VII of resolution 1541 (XV) elaborates on the contents of the free association option:

> (a) Free association should be the result of a free and voluntary choice by the peoples of the territory concerned expressed through informed and democratic processes. It should be one which respects the individuality and the cultural characteristics of the territory and its peoples, and retains for the peoples of the territory which is associated with an independent State the freedom to modify the status of that territory through the expression of their will by democratic means and through constitutional processes.
>
> (b) The associated territory should have the right to determine its internal constitution without outside interference, in accordance with due constitutional processes and the freely expressed wishes of the people.

> This does not preclude consultations as appropriate or necessary under the terms of the free association agreed upon.

A few former colonies have chosen free association. They include the Cook Islands associated with New Zealand, and the Marshall Islands, Micronesia, the Palau Islands and Puerto Rico associated with the USA. Unlike a territory which would have chosen integration, freely associated territories continue to have the right of self-determination, including the gaining of independence and full sovereignty if these have not already been achieved, as evidenced by repeated referenda in Puerto Rico,[24] or taking over powers retained by the former administering country. The outcome of negotiations about free association may vary considerably, concerning for example membership of intergovernmental organizations and the powers and functions kept by the former administering power.

In principle VIII of resolution 1541 (XV), there is an elaboration of the integration option. There should be complete equality between the erstwhile colonized peoples and the peoples of independent countries with which they are integrated:

> The peoples of both territories should have equal status and rights of citizenship and equal guarantees of fundamental rights and freedoms without any distinction or discrimination; both should have equal rights and opportunities for representation and effective participation at all levels in the executive, legislative and judicial organs of government.

As to the What in the context of natural resources, relating to both external and internal self-determination, peoples may draw economic and cultural strength and vitality from the land and its natural resources. The United Nations, in General Assembly resolution 1803 (XVII), has proclaimed the 'right of peoples and nations to permanent sovereignty over their natural wealth and resources', and common articles 1, paragraph 2, of the two International Covenants state that 'All peoples may, for their own ends, freely dispose of their natural wealth and resources without prejudice to any obligations arising out of international economic co-operation, based upon the principle of mutual benefit, and international law. In no case may a people be deprived of its own means of subsistence'.

24 *See* https://www.theguardian.com/world/2017/jun/11/puerto-rico-51st-state-referendum-voting.

II.E *The When*

When the right of external self-determination is in place, the people concerned can exercise the right without delay, unless the instruments refer or the parties agree to a possible postponement. Article 73 of the UN Charter thus talks about the self-governance steps to be taken on the decolonization road. Once these steps have been taken, the 1960 Decolonization Declaration prescribes that '3. Inadequacy of political, economic, social or educational preparedness should never serve as a pretext for delaying independence'.

II.F *The How*

In line with article 21 of the Universal Declaration of Human Rights which refers to the will of the people as the foundation of government, it is for the people to self-determine. The people should have the choice, as a minimum, between the options of independence, free association and integration. The decisions should be made in a free and informed manner, by referenda or in elections. If a people has the right of external self-determination, like in the cases of the decolonization of an overseas territory or the liberation of an oppressed and non-represented minority or indigenous group, the exercise of the right of self-determination leads to secession; the human rights argument would be that an administering State cannot and should not be able to stop or block that process by referring to its own sovereignty or territorial integrity.

Under principle VII (a) of resolution 1541 (XV), 'Free association should be the result of a free and voluntary choice by the peoples of the territory concerned expressed through informed and democratic processes'. And according to principle IX, the integrating territory should have attained an advanced stage of self-government with free political institutions, so that its peoples would have the capacity to make a responsible choice. In addition, integration should have come about as the result of the freely expressed wishes of the peoples concerned, 'acting with full knowledge of the change in their status, their wishes having been expressed through informed and democratic processes, impartially conducted and based on universal adult suffrage'. When appropriate, the United Nations should be able to supervise these processes.

Furthermore, it is stipulated in the Friendly Relations Declaration that every State has the duty to refrain from any forcible action which deprives colonized peoples of their right to self-determination and freedom and independence. 'In their actions against, and resistance to, such forcible action in pursuit of the exercise of their right to self-determination, such peoples are entitled to seek and to receive support in accordance with the purposes and principles of the Charter'. According to the 1960 Decolonization Declaration,

> 4. All armed action or repressive measures of all kinds directed against dependent peoples shall cease in order to enable them to exercise peacefully and freely their tight to complete independence, and the integrity of their national territory shall be respected.

As to the transition, under the Decolonization Declaration, immediate steps shall be taken, in colonies which have not yet attained independence, 'to transfer all powers to the peoples of those territories, without any conditions or reservations, in accordance with their freely expressed will and desire, without any distinction as to race, creed or colour, in order to enable them to enjoy complete independence and freedom'.

III Internal Self-Determination

Internal self-determination is about States delegating functions to autonomies of minorities or indigenous peoples, both as a matter of equal enjoyment of human rights and/or as a tool for the handling of violent conflicts. One must remember that the State is there for its entire population, that is the people, and not just for the national or ethnic or religious majority.

The term internal self-determination is from time to time used in other contexts, from democracy to patient rights to the human rights of women and other equal and participatory rights issues, but these may go beyond the very concept of external and internal self-determination as drafted and adopted by States in international fora. Democracy and the right to political participation should not been as part and parcel of internal self-determination; rather it can and should be counterargued that such issues have been and are covered by other instruments.

III.A *Sources of Relevant International Law*

There are a few direct and more often indirect or implicit and sometimes ambiguous references to internal self-determination in global and regional instruments and in the practices of States and international organizations. Some of these texts are formulated as rights, others are introduced as tools for the prevention, management and resolution of violent conflict, and on still other occasions the two are interrelated.

In article 3 of the UN Declaration on the Rights of Indigenous Peoples (UNDRIP),[25] it says that 'Indigenous peoples have the right to self-determination.

25 Adopted in 2007 by General Assembly resolution 61/295.

By virtue of that right they freely determine their political status and freely pursue their economic, social and cultural development'. This sounds like external self-determination with language borrowed from the International Covenants. In the preamble, UNDRIP also affirms 'that indigenous peoples are equal to all other peoples' and it expresses concern 'that indigenous peoples have suffered from historic injustices as a result of, inter alia, their colonization and dispossession of their lands, territories and resources…'.

When the above-mentioned preambular paragraph and article 3, however, are read in conjunction with other substantive provisions of the UNDRIP, it would seem that the overall approach is about internal self-determination. Indeed, if article 3 was about the right of external self-determination, many of the Declaration's subsequent articles would be superfluous; if an indigenous people had successfully exercised the right and chosen independence and statehood of its own, the internal dimension is hardly necessary.

With three other operative articles of UNDRIP dealing expressly with internal self-determination, it would seem clear that the introduction of autonomy has been the intention of the States which drafted and adopted the UNDRIP. The two of them read:

> Article 4: Indigenous peoples, in exercising their right to self-determination, have the right to autonomy or self-government in matters relating to their internal and local affairs, as well as ways and means for financing their autonomous functions.
>
> Article 5: Indigenous peoples have the right to maintain and strengthen their distinct political, legal, economic, social and cultural institutions, while retaining their right to participate fully, if they so choose, in the political, economic, social and cultural life of the State.

Furthermore, in article 46, paragraph 1, of UNDRIP, as is common in instruments concerning minority and indigenous rights, it says that nothing in the Declaration may be interpreted as implying for any State, people, group or person the right to authorize or encourage 'any action which would dismember or impair, totally or in part, the territorial integrity or political unity of sovereign and independent States'.

The ILO Convention no. 169 concerning Indigenous and Tribal Peoples in Independent Countries from 1989 refers neither to self-determination nor self-government. However, some of its provisions, like articles 5–8 and 13–18, mention the role of indigenous institutions and clearly imply indigenous representation in the self-management of lands and resources.

Likewise, the 1960 UNESCO Convention against Discrimination in Education does not expressly refer to internal self-determination or self-government. However, in article 5, it says that 'It is essential to recognize the right of members of national minorities to carry on their own educational activities, including the maintenance of schools and … the use or the teaching of their own language …' subject to certain conditions. Maintaining such minority schools will as a matter of fact and law require some degree of autonomy.[26]

The Lund Recommendations on the Effective Participation of National Minorities in Public Life (in short the Lund Recommendations), contain much more instructive language on the political rights of minorities and the forms of minority participation in the governance of States. These Recommendations build on prior OSCE texts, beginning with principle VII of the 1975 Helsinki Final Act which emphasized the link between respecting the legitimate interests and rights of persons belonging to national minorities and the maintenance of peace and stability. This link has been underlined in a number of other basic OSCE documents named after conferences sites in, amongst others, Copenhagen, Geneva, Lisbon, Madrid, Paris and Vienna.

The Lund Recommendations draw on autonomy references in OSCE texts, such as paragraph 35 of part IV of the Document from the 1990 Copenhagen Meeting of the OSCE Conference on the Human Dimension. There it says that the participating States must give persons belonging to minorities sufficient opportunity to participate in public affairs and to protect and promote their identity. Furthermore, in the same paragraph, States

> note the efforts undertaken to protect and create conditions for the promotion of the ethnic, cultural, linguistic and religious identity of certain national minorities by establishing, as one of the possible means to achieve these aims, appropriate local or autonomous administrations corresponding to the specific historical and territorial circumstances of such minorities in accordance with the policies of the State concerned.

The Lund Recommendations were drafted and adopted by expert meetings convened in 1998–99 under the auspices of the High Commissioner on National Minorities, an institution of the Organization of Security and Co-Operation

26 For comparison, it is interesting to read the 1935 Advisory Opinion of the Permanent Court of Justice on Minority Schools in Albania, *see* http://www.worldcourts.com/pcij/eng/decisions/1935.04.06_albania.htm.

in Europe (OSCE).[27] The High Commissioner at that time was Max van der Stoel. In addressing autonomy, the Lund Recommendations employ the term self-governance; there is no reference to internal self-determination and that omission was intentional.

The conceptual division within the Lund Recommendations is about (1) participation in governance of the State as a whole at national and local levels, (2) self-governance over certain local or internal minority affairs and this self-governance can be either non-territorial or territorial, and (3) guarantees for implementation and remedies in case of non-implementation. For this article, the self-governance stipulations are highly relevant.

III.B *The Why*

The reasoning behind internal self-determination has to do with (1) the respect for human rights, with an emphasis on the political rights of minorities and indigenous peoples, in particular the elimination of discrimination and the achievement of equal rights, together with special measures when necessary, and (2) the prevention, management and/or resolution of violent conflicts. The combination of both may of course also occur. If minority and indigenous rights in general are about keeping the groups happy within States, autonomy is certainly one of the best guarantees a group can wish for, and many States have successfully put it in place.

As already noted, the connection between minority rights and the prevention of violent conflict is a strong element the OSCE instruments and even the motivating factor for the Organization's involvement. This link between minority rights and peace and stability is also expressed in the preamble to the 1992 UN Declaration on Minorities and in a number of UN reports and resolutions.[28]

While dozens of countries have autonomy arrangements in place, under a variety of labels, other countries resist autonomy arrangements for the usual reasons of either non-concern for human rights and minority rights or more likely for fear of separatism and secession, or both. The non-adoption of a draft Convention on Self-Determination through Self-Administration,[29] submitted by Liechtenstein to the UN General Assembly in the 1990s, may be indicative of exactly that.

27 *See* http://www.osce.org/hcnm/32240.

28 *See* f.ex. An Agenda for Peace, in UN document A/47/277 – S/24111, 17 June 1992.

29 Arthur Watts, 'The Liechtenstein Draft Convention on Self-Determination through Self-Administration: A Commentary' in Wolfgang F. Danspeckgruber (ed) *The Self-Determination of Peoples: Community, Nation, and State in an Interdependent World* (Lynne Rienner Publishers 2002) 365–392.

III.C *The Who*

As far as autonomy is concerned, the main beneficaries of internal self-determination would be indigenous peoples, tribal peoples[30] and minorities.[31] Indigenous peoples with treaty relations raise especially intriguing questions.[32]

Like with the term 'peoples' in relation to external self-determination, definitions of the terms 'indigenous peoples', 'tribal peoples' and 'minorities' have not been adopted by the international organizations. Nevertheless, many or most of the elements of all of these definitions are known from practice and literature and much of the time one can say which group is what.[33]

The definition elements in relation to minorities are (a) objective characteristics, that is national, ethnic, linguistic and/or religious characteristics that are different from the majority, (b) the subjective element based on self-identification, that is whether the members wish to identify with the group, (c) the numerical element, that is their numbers should be less than one half of a country's population, and (d) the time element, that is whether they have been living long enough in the country concerned, presumably at least one or two generations, to qualify as a minority group rather than as migrant workers, refugees or other recent arrivals for whom other instruments of human rights protection have been adopted. For indigenous peoples, the definition elements are mostly the same with additional considerations, namely stronger cultural distinctness, greater vulnerability, and longer history (the time element) as the rights holders are usually the original inhabitants of the land on which they live.

30 This term appears in ILO Convention no. 169 and in the World Bank Operational Manual; the term is not used by the United Nations.

31 For bibliographic references on indigenous peoples and external and internal self-determination, *see* James Anaya, *Indigenous Peoples in International Law*, 2nd edition, (OUP 2004); John B. Henriksen, 'Sami self-determination. Scope and implementation', (2008) 2 *Gáldu Čala – Journal of Indigenous Peoples Rights* available at http://galdu.custompublish.com/getfile.php/3131428.2388.rdccarxpsb/2_2008_sami_selfdetermination_eng.pdf; and Benedict Kingsbury, 'Indigenous Peoples', in Ruediger Wolfrum (ed), *The Max Planck Encyclopedia of Public International Law* V (Max-Planck-Gesellschaft and OUP 2012) 116–133.

32 Gudmundur Alfredsson, 'Indigenous Peoples, Treaties with', in Ruediger Wolfrum (ed), *The Max Planck Encyclopedia of Public International Law* V (Max-Planck-Gesellschaft and OUP 2012) 133–136.

33 Kristin Henrard, the entry on 'Minoritles, International Protection' in Ruediger Wolfrum (ed), *The Max Planck Encyclopedia of Public International Law* VII (Max-Planck-Gesellschaft and OUP 2012) 253–270; and Gudmundur Alfredsson, 'Minorities, Indigenous and Tribal Peoples, and Peoples: Definitions of Terms as a Matter of International Law' in Nazila Ghanea and Alexandra Xhantaki (eds) *Minorities, Peoples and Self-Determination. Essays in Honour of Patrick Thornberry* (Brill 2004) 163–172.

III.D *The What*

The What of internal self-determination is primarily about the autonomy of minorities and indigenous peoples. Other suggested contents relate to the enjoyment of the right to choose the form and system of their constitution or government, federation,[34] democracy and political participation, but the latter may or may not fall under the self-determination umbrella, not least as they are adequately addressed in other instruments.[35]

III.D.1 Autonomy

The autonomy labels differ from country to country. Also used are self-government, self-governance, tribal or traditional government, self-management, self-administration, home rule, or the delegation of powers to a municipal or local authority with an expanded set of functions. The label does not matter much as long as a central government agrees to delegate and/or share power in a meaningful way and to leave significant local issues in the hands of group representatives.[36]

Respect for the political rights of minority and indigenous groups is an essential aspect of their rights, in regard to both representation and participation in regard to their own local and internal affairs and not least the assertion of other rights. In order to overcome discrimination and achieve equal rights with other parts of society, autonomy can be seen as a set of special measures which are necessary to guarantee equal enjoyment of political rights. States again are said to have a choice between a variety of measures, but the aim and result must be approximately equal enjoyment of human rights including political rights.

Autonomous institutions would usually involve an elected assembly and an executive; the political and legislative processes have a crucial bearing on the

34 In the present volume *see* the chapter by Thomas Schmidinger entitled 'Self-determination, federalism and autonomy in the Middle-East'.

35 *See* note 12 above on General Comment no. 12 by the Human Rights Committee.

36 There is plenty of autonomy literature, *see* for example Louis B. Sohn, 'The Concept of Autonomy in International Law and the Practice of the United Nations' (1980) 15 *Israel Law Review* 180–190; Markku Suksi (ed), *Autonomy: Applications and Implications* (Kluwer Law International 1998); Hurst Hannum, Documents on Autonomy and Minority Rights (Martinus Nijhoff Publishers 1993); Asbjörn Eide, 'From Prevention of Discrimination to Autonomy and Self-Determination' in R. Dunbar-Ortiz et. al. (eds), *Indigenous Peoples' Rights in International Law. Emergence and Application* (Gáldu and IWGIA 2015) 98–120; and Peter Hilpold (ed), *Autonomy and Self-determination. Between Legal Assertions and Utopian Aspirations* (Edward Elgar Publishing 2018). In the present volume, *see* also the chapter by Sia Spiliopoulou Åkermark entitled 'The Multiple Paths to Territorial Autonomy: Examples and Conceptual Underpinnings'.

respect for other minority rights, including and maybe especially those relating to initiative and control over language, education, diverse customs and other issues that may affect the dignity, the identity and the destiny of a group. These are also often the subject of delegation to group autonomies.

Like is the case with several provisions in UNDRIP, special measures can include the requirement that governments obtain consent from or engage in meaningful consultations with minority and indigenous groups about matters affecting them, constitutional or legislative recognition of group customs and laws and their application by the groups; guaranteed seats or observer status for the groups in legislative and municipal assemblies and other public institutions, and proportional numbers of appointed and elected officials. Solutions must also be sought for small groups that do not have the necessary numbers for running an effective autonomy or for national representation.

It is pointed out in paragraph 15 of the Lund Recommendations on the political rights of minorities that the central authorities will generally be in charge of 'defense, foreign affairs, immigration and customs, macro-economic policy and monetary matters', while a number of other functions may be managed by minorities or territorial administrations or shared with the central authorities.

In the self-governance part of the Lund Recommendations, under the heading of Self-Governance, paragraphs 14–21 are of central interest to this article. The opening paragraphs read:

> 14) Effective participation of minorities in public life may call for non- territorial or territorial arrangements of self-governance or a combination thereof. States should devote adequate resources to such arrangements.
>
> 15) It is essential to the success of such arrangements that governmental authorities and minorities recognize the need for central and uniform decisions in some areas of governance together with the advantages of diversity in others....

In paragraph 16 it is spelled out that institutions of self-governance must be based on democratic principles to ensure that they genuinely reflect the views of the affected population. And autonomous authorities must respect and ensure the human rights of all persons, including the rights of any minorities within minorities that come under their jurisdiction.

Especially noteworthy in the Lund Recommendations is the distinction between non-territorial and territorial arrangements, including the indicative lists of minimum functions in paragraphs 18 and 20 that each type of autonomy could take over. Non-territorial autonomies are listed first and should be seen as particularly attractive to States as they come without the internal borders that could encourage or facilitate the demands of separatists. This avenue is thus likely to reduce the fear of separatism and secession as internal borderlines are not necessary.

If a group's members are spread over a large area and/or are intermixed with other population groups, non-territorial or personal/cultural autonomy, meaning membership of and participation in the group's political institutions and processes regardless of residence, is a legitimate and workable solution that may benefit all the parties. The arrangements are described in paragraphs 17 and 18 of the Lund Recommendations.

Without internal borders, they would generally have jurisdiction over fellow minority persons throughout the country concerned as long as they are associated with the group for which the autonomy is designed. Thus covering all members of a group, irrespective of whether they live in traditional minority territory or elsewhere in the country, this type of arrangement can be seen as attractive to minorities and useful for maintaining and developing the identity and culture of minorities.

The issues often regulated by the non-territorial arrangements and so listed in the Lund Recommendations include 'education, culture, use of minority language, religion, and other matters crucial to the identity and way of life of national minorities', such as the determination and enjoyment of their own symbols and other forms of cultural expression. Also included is the right of individuals and groups to use their names in the minority language and obtain official recognition of their names.

Furthermore, minority institutions should be able to determine curricula for teaching of minority languages, cultures and history, while governmental authorities set overall educational standards. Shifting certain legislative and executive functions from the central to the minority level, beyond mere decentralization and drawing on the principle of subsidiarity, the devolution of powers improves the opportunities of minorities to exercise authority over matters affecting them.

Territorial autonomy arrangements are more common and certainly more visible than the non-territorial ones. Functions over which territorial administrations have assumed primary or significant authority, so listed in paragraph 20 of the Lund Recommendations, include education, culture, use of minority language, the environment, local planning, natural resources, economic development, local policing functions, and housing, health, and other social services. Functions that are often shared by central and regional authorities include taxation, the administration of justice, tourism, and transport.

The Lund Recommendations indicate certain flexibility in designing autonomous arrangements. Under paragraph 20, 'appropriate local, regional, or autonomous administrations that correspond to the specific historical and territorial circumstances of national minorities may undertake a number of functions in order to respond more effectively to the concerns of these minorities'. In the last sentence of paragraph 15, it says that 'Functions may be allocated asymmetrically to respond to different minority situations within the same State'. Differences in the delegation of functions, however, may run counter to the rule of law, they are likely to lead to claims of discrimination, and they may create problems in terms of the dissatisfaction among groups that get the shorter straw.

Most of the other law sources on internal self-determination as listed above do not provide many details on powers or institutions. State practices also differ widely, in terms of the powers delegated and the institutions created. The same is true for the reasons (the Why) for the establishment of autonomies that can be traced back to concerns about either rights or violent conflicts or both.

Has autonomy for either minorities or indigenous peoples, or both, emerged as binding or recognized international law? The instruments are likely to be seen as too soft, but what about customary law? Dozens of States have minority and indigenous autonomies in place, but the practices of these States vary considerably when it comes to the autonomous institutions and delegated functions. Even within one and the same State, there is often massive in consistency between the autonomies established for different groups, thus weakening the argument behind a customary law approach. In Finland, for example, the Swedish minority on the Aaland Islands enjoys strong autonomous institutions with broad powers originally set up for conflict prevention purposes while, without any obvious justifications, the indigenous Sami have a much weaker human rights oriented setup.

On top of it, contrary to the Finnish setup, the indigenous peoples' claim to autonomy may be stronger than the minority one. Certainly, UNDRIP has stronger human rights language than the minority rights texts. After all, as original inhabitants of the land they have history on their side, and their cultural distinctness and vulnerabilities are usually greater than those faced by minority groups. And the minority claim may be less firmly rooted in the human rights instruments and more based on conflict prevention and resolution.

III.D.2 Control of Natural Resources

Land and resources often have significant economic value, and as a result they are exploited by States for national development and/or by business communities for profit. Such exploitation often results in major changes to the living environment and the ways of life and traditional economic activities of the peoples and groups whose land is being used. In a way, it is about economic, social and cultural self-determination.

Above, in respect of external self-determination, reference was made to General Assembly resolution 1803 (XVII) on the 'right of peoples and nations to permanent sovereignty over their natural wealth and resources' and articles 1, paragraphs 2, of the two International Covenants with the statement that 'All peoples may, for their own ends, freely dispose of their natural wealth and resources…'.

As to internal self-determination, the control, management and, in most cases, possession of land and other natural resources on and in the land can be of crucial importance to groups or communities in their struggle to maintain rights related to identities, cultures, ways of life and autonomy. This has special importance in regard to indigenous peoples whose traditional bond with and reliance on the land and the natural environment is especially strong; hence the provisions on land and resources rights in UNDRIP and ILO Convention No. 169.

III.D.3 Political Participation and Democracy

Internal self-determination is sometimes also said to encompass political participation and democracy. That is about trying to place everything under a popular umbrella, but political rights are already covered in several human rights instruments, and most of them are also individual rather than collective rights.

The Universal Declaration of Human Rights in article 21 provides that 'the will of the people shall be the basis of the authority of government', and article 25 of the International Covenant on Civil and Political Rights contains a similar statement. The Human Rights Committee in a General Comment has observed that

'The rights under article 25 are related to, but distinct from, the right of peoples to self-determination. By virtue of the rights covered by article 1(1), peoples have the right to freely determine their political status and to enjoy the right to choose the form of their constitution or government. Article 25 deals with the right of individuals to participate in those processes which constitute the conduct of public affairs. Those rights, as individual rights, can give rise to claims under the first Optional Protocol'.[37]

37 Paragraph 2 of General Comment No. 25, entitled The right to participate in public affairs, voting rights and the right of equal access to public service, adopted by the Human Rights Committee in 1996.

Likewise, according to article 2, paragraphs 2 and 3, of the 1992 UN Declaration on Minorities, '[p]ersons belonging to minorities have the right to participate effectively in [...] public life' and 'the right to participate effectively in decisions on the national and, where appropriate, regional level concerning the minority to which they belong or the regions in which they live'. And article 15 of the Council of Europe's 1994 Framework Convention for the Protection of National Minorities offers even less: 'The Parties shall create the conditions necessary for the effective participation of persons belonging to national minorities in cultural, social and economic life and in public affairs, in particular those affecting them'. These provisions are distinctly different from the right of self-determination.

III.D.4 Other Configurations

The rights of patients to self-determination, the rights of women to self-determination and other similar configurations seem to fit an umbrella approach to a popular concept. They represent real issues and valid demands, but they do generally not relate to external or internal self-determination as we know the concepts from the UN Charter and subsequent standard-setting and State practices.

III.E *The When*

Like with other political rights, when it comes to implementation of internal self-determination, there should not be talk about a step-by-step approach and progressive achievement. If there is a group and if there is a right, it should be implemented as soon as possible.

III.F *The How*

Autonomy is by its very nature a group phenomenon. The minority or indigenous entity claims the right, enjoys it and through its institutions runs the local administration. In exercising its powers, the group regime must be created and managed with respect for democratic principles and universal human rights. This includes referenda and elections for respecting the will as well as other human rights of all the persons concerned.

Human rights may result in impositions on minority and indigenous autonomies; cultural practices may have to give way to human rights on issues like representative leadership, equality of the sexes and the best interests of the child. In a territorial autonomy, the group should protect not only the rights of its own members but also those of other individuals and groups that may come under its jurisdiction. Autonomy must also be exercised in a manner consistent with other principles of international law relating to, for example, the sovereignty, national unity and territorial integrity of States and the maintenance of international peace and security.

IV Concluding Remarks

There has been considerable evolution and expansion of the right of self-determination since 1945. In part it has been based on progressive and ongoing development and in part it has relied on codification of international law. As a result, strengthened rules relating to external self-determination have emerged, in particular concerning political decolonization. Inroads have also been made in situations involving minorities and indigenous peoples when massive human rights violations and non-representation have occurred. Internal self-determination and autonomy have been clearly established as far as indigenous peoples' rights are concerned.

On the other side, there remains much work to be done on clarifying, demarcating and consolidating the concepts and terms involved. It is likely that the ongoing work will continue and it would not be surprising if the terms and concepts will see further expansion albeit in a gradual and probably slow process. And one must hope that this expansion will take place in a peaceful manner; after all the furtherance of clear rules and fora for dealing with self-determination rights should serve as tools for preventing violent conflicts.

As a matter of justice, a number of stateless minority and indigenous groups, not least those with a history of prior statehood, ought to have the chance of exercising the right of external self-determination. Following the example of Kosovo, some groups like f.ex. the Kurds could claim the right of self-determination with independence as an option as a result of massive human rights violations, including instances of chemical weapons use and aerial bombardments in some of the countries in which they live; the governments concerned should be worried. Another argument in favour of external self-determination could be based on reclaiming, not independence which they may never have enjoyed, but the promises made to the Kurds by departing colonial powers.

As to internal self-determination, as a matter of both human rights and conflict prevention/management/resolution, many more minority and indigenous groups than is currently the case should be able to govern their own internal and local affairs by way of autonomy. In situations with serious tensions, non-territorial autonomy could be seen as an advantageous option, for both the States and the groups and individuals concerned.

As the preceding survey has demonstrated, even if the right of external self-determination is brought up in a number of treaties and declarations and employed in international case law and in the practice of States and international organizations, the right is firmly established only with regard to political decolonization. For good reasons, the granting of external self-determination rights in cases of serious human rights violations and denials of representation comes close. The clarity in respect of other contents and applicability desired has not been fully achieved.

This failure of the international lawmakers is remarkable, as the absence of clear rules and corresponding procedures and institutions is in itself conflict-generating. It is, however, not a surprising failure, as States are reluctant to address issues so close to and so imposing on their sovereignty and territorial integrity. Needless to say, academic writing has not done much to improve on the picture – one can find literature to support or oppose practically every argument and position related to the right of external and internal self-determination.

Bibliography

Akbulut, Olgun & Aktoprak, Elçin (eds), *Autonomy as a Model for Minority Self Government: From Theory to European and Middle Eastern Perspectives* (Brill 2019).

Alfredsson, Gudmundur, 'Greenland and the Law of Political Decolonization' (1982) 25 *German Yearbook of International Law*.

Alfredsson, Gudmundur, 'Different Forms of and Claims to the Right of Self-Determination' in D. Clark & R. Williamson (eds), *Self-Determination. International Perspectives* (MacMillan Press & St. Martin's Press 1996).

Alfredsson, Gudmundur, 'Access to International Monitoring Procedures: Choices between Self-Determination and the Human Rights of Groups' in M.C. van Walt van Praag and O. Seroo (eds), *The Implementation of the Right to Self-Determination as a Contribution to Conflict Prevention. Report of the 1998 International Conference of Experts on the Right to Self-Determination* (UNESCO Centre of Catalonia 1999).

Alfredsson, Gudmundur, 'The Faroese People as a Subject of Public International Law' (2001) 1(1) *Føroyskt Lógar Rit – Faroese Law Review*.

Alfredsson, Gudmundur, 'The Greenlanders and their Human Rights Choices', in M. Bergsmo (ed), *Human Rights and Criminal Justice for the Downtrodden, Essays in Honour of Asbjörn Eide* (Martinus Nijhoff Publishers 2003).

Alfredsson, Gudmundur, 'Minorities, Indigenous and Tribal Peoples, and Peoples: Definitions of Terms as a Matter of International Law' in Nazila Ghanea and Alexandra Xhantaki (eds), *Minorities, Peoples and Self-Determination. Essays in Honour of Patrick Thornberry* (Brill 2004).

Alfredsson, Gudmundur, 'Peoples' in Ruediger Wolfrum (ed), *The Max Planck Encyclopedia of Public International Law* VIII (Max-Planck-Gesellschaft and OUP 2012).

Anaya, James, *Indigenous Peoples in International Law*, 2nd edition, (OUP 2004).

Bring, Ove, 'Kurdistan and the Principle of Self-Determination' (1992) 35(1) *German Yearbook of International Law*.

Carlà, Andrea & Constantin, Sergiu, 'Territorial and Cultural Self-governance in Italy: Strengths and Challenges of South Tyrol's Autonomy' in Olgun Akbulut and Elçin Aktoprak (eds), *Autonomy as a Model for Minority Self Government: From Theory to European and Middle Eastern Perspectives* (Brill 2019).

Cristescu, A., *The Right to Self-Determination*, U.N. Doc. E/CN.4/Sub.2/404/Rev. 1, UN Sales No. E.80.XIV.3 (1980).

Documentation of the International Conference on Human Rights in Kurdistan (The Initiative for Human Rights in Kurdistan 1989).

Dugard, John, *The Secession of States and Their Recognition in the Wake of Kosovo* (Pocketbooks of the Hague Academy of International Law 2013).

Eide, Asbjörn, 'From Prevention of Discrimination to Autonomy and Self-Determination' in R. Dunbar-Ortiz et al. (eds), *Indigenous Peoples' Rights in International Law. Emergence and Application* (Gáldu and IWGIA 2015).

Espiell, H. Gros, *The Right to Self-Determination*, U.N. Doc. E/CN.4/Sub.2/405/Rev.1, UN Sales No. E.79.XIV.5 (1980).

Hannum, Hurst, Documents on Autonomy and Minority Rights (Martinus Nijhoff Publishers 1993).

Henrard, Kristin, The Entry on 'Minorities, International Protection' in Ruediger Wolfrum (ed), *The Max Planck Encyclopedia of Public International Law* VII (Max-Planck-Gesellschaft and OUP 2012).

Henriksen, John B., 'Sami self-determination. Scope and implementation', (2008) 2 *Gáldu Čala – Journal of Indigenous Peoples Rights*, available at http://galdu.custompublish.com/getfile.php/3131428.2388.rdccarxpsb/2_2008_sami_selfdetermination_eng.pdf.

Hilpold, Peter (ed), *Autonomy and Self-determination. Between Legal Assertions and Utopian Aspirations* (Edward Elgar Publishing 2018).

Karlsen, Gunnar M., Conflict Dynamics and Human Rights Problems, *Norwegian Institute of Human Rights, Human Rights Repor*t (1996) 6.

Kingsbury, Benedict, 'Indigenous Peoples', in Ruediger Wolfrum (ed), *The Max Planck Encyclopedia of Public International Law* V (Max-Planck-Gesellschaft and OUP 2012).

Meintjes, Albertus Jacobus, 'The Complications of Kurdish Independence' (2018) 8 *Open Journal of Political Science*.

Möller, Jakob Th. & Zayas, Alfred de, *United Nations Human Rights Committee Case Law 1977–2008. A Handbook* (N.P.Engel Publisher 2009).

Naamani, Israel T., 'The Kurdish Drive for Self-Determination' (1966) 20(3) *Middle East Journal*.
Nowak, Manfred, 'U.N. Covenant on Civil and Political Rights' *CCPR Commentary*, (N.P.Engel, 2nd revised edition, 2005).
Permanent Court of Justice, *Advisory Opinion on Minority Schools in Albania*, [1935], http://www.worldcourts.com/pcij/eng/decisions/1935.04.06_albania.htm.
Peters, Anne, 'Populist International Law? The Suspended Independence and the Normative Value of the Referendum on Catalonia' (12 October 2017) Blog of the European Journal of International Law, see https://www.ejiltalk.org/populist-international-law-the-suspended-independence-and-the-normative-value-of-the-referendum-on-catalonia/.
Schmidinger, Thomas, 'Self-determination, Federalism and Autonomy in the Middle-East', in Olgun Akbulut and Elçin Aktoprak (eds), *Autonomy as a Model for Minority Self Government: From Theory to European and Middle Eastern Perspectives* (Brill 2019).
Sohn, Louis B., 'The Concept of Autonomy in International Law and the Practice of the United Nations' (1980) 15 *Israel Law Review*.
Suksi, Markku (ed), *Autonomy: Applications and Implications* (Kluwer Law International 1998).
Supreme Court of Canada, Reference re Secession of Quebec, Judgement, 20 August 1998, https://scc-csc.lexum.com/scc-csc/scc-csc/en/item/1643/index.do.
Thuerer, Daniel & Burri, Thomas, 'Self-Determination' in Ruediger Wolfrum (ed), *The Max Planck Encyclopedia of Public International Law* IX (Max-Planck-Gesellschaft and OUP 2012).
United Nations, General Assembly, 'Declaration on the Granting of Independence to Colonial Countries and Peoples', Resolution No 1514 (XV), UN Doc. A/RES/1514(XV) (1960), Adopted on 14 December 1960.
United Nations, General Assembly, 'Principles which should Guide Members in Determining whether or not an Obligation Exists to Transmit the Information called for under Article 73e of the Charter', Resolution No 1541 (XV), UN Doc. A/4684 (1960), Adopted on 15 December 1960.
Watts, Arthur, 'The Liechtenstein Draft Convention on Self-Determination through Self-Administration: A Commentary' in Wolfgang F. Danspeckgruber (ed) *The Self-Determination of Peoples: Community, Nation, and State in an Interdependent World* (Lynne Rienner Publishers 2002).
Ziemele, Ineta, *State Continuity and Nationality: The Baltic States and Russia. Past, Present and Future as Defined by International Law* (Martinus Nijhoff Publishers 2005).
Åkermark, Sia Spiliopoulou, 'The Multiple Paths to Territorial Autonomy: Examples and Conceptual Underpinnings', in Olgun Akbulut and Elçin Aktoprak (eds), *Autonomy as a Model for Minority Self Government: From Theory to European and Middle Eastern Perspectives* (Brill 2019).

CHAPTER 2

Nations, Territorial Minorities, Democratic Theory and National Self-Determination

Ephraim Nimni

1 Introduction: Shifting Democratic Theory and National Self Determination

> The national state claims to treat all citizens as equal members of the nation, this fair principle only serves to disguise the tyranny of one group over another. The nation must be, all its citizens must be, animated with the same spirit. Differences are divisive and therefore treasonable.[1]

The mainstream concept of National Self Determination (NSD), as officially recorded in international law and enshrined in UN resolutions, and, as normatively argued in mainstream liberal democratic theories,[2] is the principle that nations have the right to freely choose their sovereignty and international political status with no external compulsion or external interference. In this doctrine, nationhood and territorial sovereignty are inextricably linked, for nations are a constitutive element of the configuration of states in the age of Modernity. It need not be so, and it was not so before Modernity. Nevertheless, the linkage between nation and state became constitutive and normatively hegemonic, to the point that it became counterintuitive to think otherwise. This all-encompassing hegemonic understanding of National Self-determination is thus applied to states and to cultural communities that can build a sovereign state that does not clash with a world system of sovereign states.[3]

1 Elie Kedourie, *Nationalism* (Hutchinson 1960) 127.

2 I call mainstream liberal democratic theories, what Warren calls Standard liberal democracy. These theories differ on many matters, but they commonly assume that democracy is an instrumental value for protecting and realizing the rights of atomised individuals. *See* Mark Warren, 'Democratic Theory and Self-Transformation' (1992) 86(1) *The American Political Science Review* 9. From a different angle, *see* Otto Bauer's notion of the centralist atomist character of the modern state, in Otto Bauer, *The Question of Nationalities and Social Democracy* (Series ed Ephraim Nimni) (University of Minnesota Press 2000) 30.

3 Douglas J Sylvester, 'International Law as Sword or Shield–Early American Foreign Policy and the Law of Nations' (1999–2000) 32(1) *New York University Journal of International Law and Politics* 10–11.

 | DOI:10.1163/9789004405455_003

The above is certainly not the only way to understand national self-determination, and even less so, democracy, as both terms are polysemic and multifaceted. But by virtue of being hegemonic, the interpretation above is the most common and the most dangerous. It has the proclivity to sacrifice cultural minorities in the High Altar of nation building, to securitize cultural communities, and, ominously, to conflate Ethnos with Demos. This is by no means a recent development, but one that goes back to earliest modern expressions of Republican egalitarianism, and is in more than one way, a constitutive failure of the modern nation state. Consider the statements of radical Jacobins:

> The language of a free people must be one and the same for all. (...) Federalism and superstition speak low Breton, emigration and hatred of the Republic speak German, the counterrevolution speaks Italian and fanaticism speaks Basque. Lets break these instruments damage and error (...) Among the ancient idioms, Welsh<sic> (Cymraeg), Gascon, Celtic, Visigoths, Phoenicians or oriental nuances that make communications in various countries and citizens forming the territory of the Republic. We observed (and reports of representatives meet on this point with those of various agents sent into the departments), that the idiom called low-Breton, Basque idiom, the German and Italian languages have perpetuated the reign of fanaticism and superstition, ensured the domination of priests, nobles and practitioners, prevented the entry of the revolution into nine important departments and could help the enemies of France.[4]

4 Bertrand Barère de Vieuzac, *Rapport du Comité de salut public sur les idiomes* (*Report of the Committee of Public Health on Languages*) – 8 pluviôse an II: 27 January 1794 <http://www.tlfq.ulaval.ca/axl/francophonie/barere-rapport.htm> accessed 12 December 2012. *La langue d'un peuple libre doit être une et la même pour tous.* (...) *Le fédéralisme et la superstition parlent bas-breton; l'émigration et la haine de la république parlent allemand; la contre-révolution parle italien et le fanatisme parle basque. Brisons ces instruments de dommage et d'erreur*(...) *Parmi les idiomes anciens, welches, gascons, celtiques, wisigoths, phocéens ou orientaux, qui forment quelques nuances dans les communications des divers citoyens et des pays formant le territoire de la République, nous avons observé* (*et les rapports des représentants se réunissent sur ce point avec ceux des divers agents envoyés dans les départements*) *que l'idiome appelé bas-breton, l'idiome basque, les langues allemande et italienne ont perpétué le règne du fanatisme et de la superstition, assuré la domination des prêtres, des nobles et des praticiens, empêché la révolution de pénétrer dans neuf départements importants, et peuvent favoriser les ennemis de la France* (translated by the author).

Here you have a splendid example of securitization of minorities, two hundred and ten years before the term was coined! Securitization is not a contemporary innovation as many International Relations users of securitization argue[5] (let's stop re-inventing wheels), but a by-product of the historical conflation of nations, popular sovereignty and territorial states. In whatever way one defines national-popular sovereignty, it is a concept dependent upon the definition of cultural- territorial boundaries, which inexorably creates outsiders and cultural insiders.

To be sure, this argument is not a peculiarity of French Republicanism, far from it. It is also present in the works of the founding father of Anglo liberalism. Consider John Stuart Mill well known assertion that: *Free institutions are next to impossible in a country made up of different nationalities.... Among people without fellow-feeling, especially if they speak different languages, the united public opinion, necessary to the working of representative government cannot exist.*[6]

For this reason, securitization of minorities is in many ways, a constitutive deficiency of a model of political organization that became hegemonic over the last three hundred years, and generated what Michael Mann calls in an important work, 'The Dark Side of Democracy'; its propensity for ethnic cleansing.[7] I will here immediately qualify Mann's generalisation of the process he so eloquently and incisively describes with one important consideration. Ethnic cleansing is not the dark side of democracy, for the later has forms that roundly escape this cruel imposition – Democracy must not be exclusively conflated with popular sovereignty and liberal democratic representative democracy in nation states. What Mann refers to is the dark side of the sovereign, popular democratic nation state, and the likely by-product of the exercise of national (territorial) self-determination in areas of mixed populations. In these cases, when two or more national communities reside in *the same* territorial space, when it is not possible to territorially disentangle one from the other, popular national sovereignty and territorial national self-determination becomes a zero sum game. The gain of one is unavoidably, the loss of the other. For this

5 Olav F. Knudsen, 'Post-Copenhagen Security Studies: Desecuritizing Securitization' (2001) 32 *Security Dialogue* 358.

6 J. S Mill (1862) *Considerations of Representative Government* in H.B. Acton (eds) *Utilitarism, On Liberty and Considerations on Representative Government* (J.M. Dent & Sons 1976).

7 Michael Mann, *The Dark Side of Democracy: Explaining Ethnic Cleansing* (Cambridge University Press 2005 and four reprints).

reason, ethno-national conflicts in mixed areas are bloody, extremely violent and protracted, for full victory for one means the expulsion or destruction of the other. Consider the Nakbah, the paradox of a national community being cleansed from its homeland by a contemporary ethnocracy[8] wanting to secure its ethnic homogeneity, and claiming to act on behalf of the victims of the most murderous European genocide, which, incidentally, was carried out by a different type of technocratic state claiming to act to secure the racial homogeneity of its own citizens. To be sure, these are two extreme and fortunately rare examples, both of them superficially appear to contradict the egalitarian spirit of the liberal democratic states. Disturbingly, even if they contradict the egalitarian spirit of liberal democracies, they are not unrelated to the popular sovereign nation state in what Ludwig Wittgenstein calls a 'family resemblance' (*Familienähnlichkeit*).[9]

From here, and fortunately in a much less extreme fashion, family resemblances notwithstanding, out of the concurrence of French Republicanism and English Liberalism, the model of a democratically sovereign monocultural state over which one nation (titular) exercises its right to self-determination, became the imprint of the modern process of liberal democratic national emancipation. It was used in the colonial settler states of the Americas and Oceania to politically preserve and protect the newly created colonial settler nations in lands illegitimately taken from indigenous peoples, who were

8 Ethnocracy is a model of government where the various institutions of governance exclusively represent a particular ethnic group, and use mechanisms of power and governance to enshrine the dominance of this group. Its main characteristic is the systematic use of legal, institutional, and physical instruments of power to secure ethnic dominance. An Ethnocracy normally is a political regime which citizenship is instituted on the basis of qualified rights and with ethnic affiliation (defined in terms of ethnicity, descent or religion) as the fundamental principle. The aim is to secure the most important instruments of state power in the hands of a dominant ethnic collectivity. For this reason, Ethnocracies are considered to be non-democratic. From a different direction, an Ethnocracy could be considered also a radical and extreme exaggeration of the European nation-state model. *See* Oren Yiftachel, *Ethnocracy Land and Identity Politics in Israel/Palestine* (Penn University Press 2006) and Oren Yiftachel, 'The Israeli Regime and the Question of Democracy' in C. Rubenberg (eds) *Encyclopedia of the Israeli-Palestinian Conflict* (Lynne Reiner Publishers 2011) 691–699.

9 Ludwig Wittgenstein, *Philosophical Investigations* (John Wiley & Sons 2010) 250, ff92 clarification of the editors. Wittgenstein suggests that concepts may not be connected by one essential common feature, but may in fact be connected by a series of overlapping similarities, with no one feature common to all. He rejects definitions based on sufficient and necessary conditions ("craving for generality" as he calls it). In contrast, he points to 'family resemblance' as the more suitable analogy for the way of connecting particular uses of

then subjected to ethnic cleansing and genocide. Make no mistake, whatever other reasons are invoked; most of the European inspired nation states of the Americas and Oceania were born under the original sin of genocide and ethnic cleansing. When the equality of all citizens is conflated with the equality for all members of the nation under the guise of an egalitarian liberal democracy in nascent colonial settler societies, these societies are at their most murderous, for they create a community of insiders that must destroy their local outsiders (which often outnumber the new nation), if the new born liberal nation-state is to expand and survive.[10] In colonial settler societies, the concomitant destruction of indigenous peoples and other injustices to those culturally different from the dominant nation became hidden under the seductive rhetoric of the discourse of liberal Modernisation.

In whatever way one understands liberal democratic national-popular sovereignty, the demos is always defined by mechanisms of inclusion and exclusion, mechanisms that by virtue of its inescapable national dimension, are always cultural. National-popular sovereignty cannot be by definition coterminous with the whole of humanity, so there has to be an explicit definition of insiders and outsiders. Sovereignty is thus the prerogative of a titular nation,[11] a culturally defined democratic polity that sits uncomfortably with universal claims of democracy and liberalism. Consider that liberal democracies are predicated on the principle of formal equality between citizens. This principle is then subverted by the linguistic and cultural privileges of the titular nation. Minorities of different kind and sorts are often invited to assimilate to the ways of the titular nation with equality as compensation. This is invitation is often couched in the language of modernization, integration and Affirmative Action. In many cases, this procedure intensifies ethno-cultural injustices and generates alienation, for in the eyes of many members of minority communities, the procedure violates the egalitarian ethos of liberal democracy that the state purports to defend. The standard accusation is *we are only equals if*

---

the same concept. Family resemblance also serves to exhibit the lack of boundaries due to unavoidable interpretations, and the subsequent imprecise uses of the same concept. In this regard, as the nation state when subverted by different interpretations of democracy, sovereignty and nation, might not share a common essence, but a family resemblance in the overlapping characteristic of conflating ethnos with demos.

10 Mann, *op. cit.*, 4.

11 The term 'titular nation' is taken from the terminology of the former Soviet Union, but it is applicable to most liberal democratic nation states. It refers to a governing ethno-national community in the state, usually the majority of the population, typically after which the state is named.

we partake in the cultural behaviour of the majority. The issue touches many dimensions (the vast majority of liberal democratic nation states are not culturally homogeneous) , and this is convincingly shown in an example by Paul Stratham in relation to the debate over asylum seekers: he claims that the issue of asylum ...*opens up a particular contradiction within liberal nation-states: it puts the universal principle that they should respect and protect human rights by offering asylum to aliens fleeing persecution in direct competition with the principle that they should primarily serve the interests of the national community of people from whom sovereignty derives–a group with a self-image of common descent and ethnicity enshrined in a shared nationhood.*[12] Hannah Arendt, in different but important twist of this argument, in an case that has some parallels (and many differences) from the one developed here, also explains that in the cruel logic of the declining nation state, the human being that is stateless and a refugee can only be recognized as a human being when s/he has been recognized as citizens of other nation-states.[13]

When understood in the manner above, the doctrines of popular nation-state sovereignty and national self-determination are monistic, not democratic, and are neither pluralist nor inclusive. Here I part ways with Arendt, for the problem does not result from the decline of the nation state, the emergence of imperialism, or the emergence of what she calls 'Totalitarianism'. As argued earlier, the securitization of minorities was present since the early days of the French Revolution, long before imperialism and 'totalitarianism' had any relevance. The key problem is ingrained in the likely conflation of ethnos with demos in the monist architecture of an exemplary nation state. Popular nation-state sovereignty runs the serious risk of fusing the dominant ethnos with sovereign demos, for the most common manner of exercising popular sovereignty is through the regime of one nation in one state. It is important to note here that the conflation of ethnos with demos might not be in some circumstances dangerous: in the form of collective rights and community representation for example. Like in many deadly explosives, in isolation the ingredients are harmless; even it could be argued that in the case of collective rights, the conflation of ethnos with demos might offer a positive contribution to the expansion of democracy to alienated or subordinated communities. The argument here is that the formula becomes unstable and dynamite like when it incorporates

12 Paul Stratham, 'Understanding Anti-Asylum Rhetoric: Restrictive Politics or Racist Publics?' (August 2003) 74 Supplement s1 *The Political Quarterly* 165.

13 Hannah Arendt, *The Origins of Totalitarianism*, Ch 9, (Meridian Books 1962) 280.

ethnos as the foundation for the demos, and as an equivalent to popular territorial sovereignty in a single monist mixture. This is particularly so when other cultural communities are present in the territory of the state. In this explosive mix, national self-determination and territorial sovereignty legitimises the governance of only a minority of nations, the titular ones. It threatens others with disappearance in most cases through forceful assimilation, or thankfully in a small number of cases, through ethnic cleansing and genocide. In this way, this type of sovereign self-determination contradicts the democratic, universally egalitarian values that laid the original foundation of its principles.[14] Fortunately, this established doctrine of national self-determination is being frontally challenged by the demands of territorial minorities,[15] first and foremost indigenous peoples, both territorially scattered and concentrated, and in this way, they, (the territorial minorities) act as facilitators for an historical paradigm shift taking place on the meaning of national self-determination, and whose importance goes well beyond self-determination demands and revises well established notions in democratic theory.

Consider the following: a conservative estimate puts the number of nations in this world to well above 3,000, while with the admission of South Sudan in July 2011, there are 193 states represented in the UN. Fewer than 20 states are ethnically homogeneous in the sense that cultural minorities account for less than 5% of the population.[16] Nation-states in the proper sense of the term are only a handful, and titular nations (nations that have states) are only a

14 In a dissenting view, Allen Buchanan shows clearly the serious limitations of international law's line of reasoning when he argues that *International law should recognize a remedial right to secede, but not a general right of self-determination that includes the right to secede for all peoples or nations. From the standpoint of international law, the unilateral right to secede – the right to secede without consent or constitutional authorization – should be understood as a remedial right only, as a last resort response to serious injustices.* Allen Buchanan, *Justice, Legitimacy, and Self-Determination: Moral Foundations for International Law* (Oxford University Press 2004) 331. Even if this were the case, for the right to NSD to be exercised in this way it requires a territorial majority exercising territorial sovereignty, thus rendering this principle ineligible for territorial minorities such as indigenous peoples.

15 I mean by territorial minorities, cultural communities that are a minority of the population in the predefined territorial space. In most cases, the limits of these territories are arbitrarily predefined. Consider the case of the Aaland Islands, a historical landmark in international law established by the League of Nations. If the territory is the Aaland Islands, there is no doubt that Swedish speakers are the vast majority. If the territory is Finland, the opposite is true.

16 Michael E. Brown, *Ethnic Conflict and International Security* (Princeton University Press 1993) 6.

small fraction of all nations, and it is not an exaggeration to say that the term 'nation state' – understood as one (cultural) nation in one state – is a misnomer.[17]

While the overwhelming majority of states represented in the UN are not culturally homogeneous, the configuration of their political institutions often gives the impression they are, trapping indigenous peoples and other cultural minorities that have *different symbols and memories* into at best, ambiguity and at worst, alienation, subordination, and in worst case scenario, ethnic cleansing. For make no mistake, if the term ethnic cleansing is a by-product of the Modernity of the monist popular-sovereign nation state, and like the latter, it was invented in Europe, and spread across the world and scattered minorities are its appointed victims. Michael Mann is his authoritative 'Dark Side of Democracy'[18] meticulously substantiates this argument.

II The Centralist Atomist Principle and the Limits of Liberal Democracies

Otto Bauer, in his 1907 seminal work, argues that the liberal democratic state is an imperfect democracy because it is organised according to the 'centralist-atomist' principle. In the genesis of the modern nation state, Bauer argues, one of its most important characteristics, its centralisation of power, was in fact initially developed by the absolutism. This centralisation completed in a democratic mode, through Abolition of guilds, estates, and other segmental organizations. This had the effect of reducing recognised political actors to their smallest parts, Bauer call these 'atoms', i.e. to single individual citizens. For Otto Bauer and Karl Renner, a constitutional jurist, the legal representative order knows only two units. On the one hand, state sovereignty and on the other hand the sovereignty of the individual citizen.[19]

On this point Bauer sees no difference between Rousseau and Hobbes. With the hegemonic victory of modern liberal democracy, the work of absolutism was roundly completed. Constitutionally, in nation state liberal democracies, there are two recognised sovereign politico-juridical entities, the atomised citizen and the collective totality. This logic is also applicable to federal

17 Trudy Govier, *Social Trust and Human Communities* (McGill-Queen's University Press 1997) 269.

18 Mann, *op. cit.*

19 Bauer, *op. cit.*, 232.

territorial states with some adjustments to cater for the division of competences between the central state and the provinces. In both cases, the juridical political entities are atomised individuals and the sovereign will of the undivided collective. This is what Bauer calls the centralist-atomist structure of modern liberal democratic nation-states. This organizational characteristic expels all intermediate communitarian locations from the arena of representative politics. While there can be no doubt (in Bauer's mind also) that in some important cases this lead to the expansion of democracy through the irrevocable abolition of sectarian political privilege, in the form of castes, feudal guilds, landlords, etc. It simultaneously threw the new born democratic baby through the bath water, for it impoverished the quality of the nascent democracy. This is because it also abolished and made impossible mechanisms of representation of different, territorially scattered national and ethnic minorities which are left at the mercy of governmental bureaucracies and worse, of the tyranny of the majority; a less that adequate form of democracy.

The citizens of the modern state are nationally identified with the state through residence and citizenship, irrespectively of ethnic and national affiliations. Most states represented in the UN are thus seen as nation-states whether or not they are ethnically or nationally homogeneous. In the liberal democratic nation-state the cultural practice of the dominant nation (the 'titular nation' or if you prefer, the official ethnicity of the state) is disguised by a procedural practice that claims neutrality but is derived from the cultural and historical experiences of the dominant national community. Following the logic of this argument, Atomistic states, however much consideration they might show for individual and democratic rights, and however equalitarian their practices, are averse to recognising collective representation mechanisms for its cultural minorities. These demands are effectively suppressed with what are apparently 'democratic instruments', via the tyranny of the majority.

In a very paradoxical way, this situation makes de-facto, but not de-jure multination states inherently unstable, for there are non-actionable legal mechanisms to represent national minorities. Both, majorities and minorities are faced with an increasingly difficult dilemma: coercively assimilate cultural minorities through the famous Friedrich Engels' slogan of assimilation of minorities to more 'energetic' and 'vital' nations with 'democracy as compensation',[20] or, to alternatively split the de-facto multination state along national lines. Both strategies have been tried with catastrophic results, for there is no democratic

20 Ephraim Nimni, *Marxism and Nationalism Theoretical Origins of a Political Crisis* (2nd edn, Pluto Press 1994) 43.

gain the coerced assimilation of minorities, and because the other solution, partition, often exhibits the 'Matrioshka (Russian doll) syndrome', when you pull one out, there is another one inside.[21]

III Expansive Democracy and Human Rights

In a dissenting discussion to mainstream liberal democratic theories, liberal democratic models that attach a positive normative value to democracy – the ones that argue that democracy has more than an instrumental value to liberalism, are often referred as expansive liberal democratic theories. Expansive democracy refers to the effects of institutions in increasing individuals' control over self-governance, self-determination and self-development.[22] The idea (supported in this paper) is that democracy is much more than instrument for the preservation of liberty. Collective democratic participation is a normative value in itself, one that enhances the quality of governance and the plural participation of citizens. These types of theories accentuate the democratic side of the equation (as opposed to liberal individualism), and are more receptive and supportive to the value of collective action as a mechanism of human empowerment. A significant part of Feminist theories start from here, in that they demand the recognition of the collective specificity of women in male dominated societies. For example, they advocate the normative value of women rights as one form group rights.[23] It this, the transformation of democratic theory that resulted from Feminist activism is a source of inspiration for the ideas presented in this paper. But while group rights are a significant advance in earlier monist interpretations of democracy, they not fully suited to represent cultural minority communities.

In the argument about group rights, the value of culture is not recognised per se, but only insofar as those individuals who are members of a cultural group wish to exercise those rights. But even here, either culture has no bearing in political representation, or, the architecture of citizenship is designed for individuals that are culturally homologous.[24] Here minority members must 'fit' the architecture of citizenship. But even if the contemporary architecture

21 For an expansion of this argument, *see*: Ephraim Nimni, 'Nationalist multiculturalism in late imperial Austria as a critique of contemporary liberalism: The case of Bauer and Renner' (1999) 4(3) *Journal of Political Ideologies* 289–314.

22 Warren, *op. cit.*, 9.

23 Will Kymlicka, *Multicultural Citizenship* (Oxford University Press 1995) 34.

24 A minority of liberal theorists dissent from this view, *see* in particular Kymlicka, *op. cit.*, 1995 and Will Kymlicka and Christine Straehle, 'Cosmopolitanism, Nation-States, and

of citizenship has been in most cases, successfully transformed by the incorporation of Feminist demands, this might not suffice in the case of cultural minorities. This is because this limited pluralisation of citizenship still renders invisible citizens community insertion, something that becomes fatally problematic when – as in the case of indigenous peoples and disadvantaged territorial minorities – that very insertion is the source for the disadvantage in relation to the majority, and it is one expansive democratic theory wishes to remedy.[25] This can only be done by taking the argument one step further and instutionalise some form of collective rights.

While of course it will be absurd to institutionalise collective rights not wished by members of a community, individual will is not sufficient in creating forms of representation, and even less so in creating forms of collective minority protection. Collective rights cannot be adequately recognised without representatives or institutions that have the ability or legitimation to further the collectivity's goals.[26] While the idea of group rights allows for the abstract possibility of individual members of minorities to enjoy cultural rights, without some form of institutionalised representation (collective rights), those individuals are dangerously dependent on the good will of majorities. Consider the *Tyranny of the Majority*[27] when decisions are taken by a majority in a centralist -atomist system of governance (almost all liberal democracies), and these decisions are undesired by members of a minority group and in many cases, are seen by the minority as an active form of oppression. Here, the ensuing alienation can easily turn into distrust and hostility to the majority. In these circumstances, any resulting demands for assimilation cannot be considered fair, for these are the outcome of majority institutional coercion. It is not uncommon for securitized religious or ethnic groups to be penalized in this way by majorities through the liberal-democratic process. This can be done without infringing on the basic personal rights of the individual members. As Kymlicka & Straehle persuasively argue,[28] even if this abuse of power is considered an injustice, it can occur without violating individual civil and political rights, so long as individual members maintain the right to run for office, voice

Minority Nationalism: A Critical Review of Recent Literature' (April 1999) 7(1) *European Journal of Philosophy* 65–88.

25 In a provocative work, Leslie G. Carr calls this interpretation 'colour blind racism', *see*: Leslie G. Carr, *'Color-Blind' Racism* (Sage Publishers 1997).

26 Douglas Sanders, 'Collective Rights' (1991) 13(3) *Human Rights Quarterly* 369.

27 Alexis de Tocqueville, *Democracy in America* with an introduction by Joseph Epstein (Random House 2004) and John Stuart Mill (1998) *On Liberty and Other Essays* With a an introduction by John Gray (Oxford University Press 1998) 8.

28 Kymlicka and Straehle, *op. cit.*, 75.

their grievances, and indeed the right to vote. There is in this shallow, narrow and limited individual understanding of human rights, no obstacles to disempower minority communities fatally subjected to the tyranny of the majority. For this very reason, collective rights must guarantee the effective participation of minorities as specified in the OSCE Lund Recommendations,[29] so that vital interests of minorities cannot be overturned by majority decisions.

IV Do Collective Rights Essentialise Culture?

Collective cultural rights have been criticised from many quarters with the argument that they protect or essentialise some kind on unpalatable or reactionary behaviour, or, that the institutionalisation of these cultures in the form of collective rights 'fossilises' these cultures, turning them into conservative, static and unable to change. Very often these criticisms misunderstand the issue they are criticising, or have a superficial or inaccurate knowledge of these cultures. These criticisms tend to unfairly focus on immigrant minority communities and carry a more than fair dose of prejudice. These communities are seen as 'static', 'backward' unable to change, misogynist and bent upon oppressing women and unable to adapt to modernity.[30] In sharp contrast, these kinds of criticisms are rarely directed to the culture of titular nations, and that in itself is an important pointer of the unfair character of this approach.

Let's start from the discussion of dominant cultures. It is clear to most fair minded observers, that titular nation cultures, such as English, French, German, Swedish etc. These cultures cannot be defined as 'progressive', 'reactionary' 'misogynist', 'racist' and so on, even if there are interpretations of these cultures in the form of political ideologies that could well be understood in the manner above, or even if sometimes, the behaviour of the government of the titular nations, or, the dominant political forces within it could be understood in that way. For the sake of an example, if some could plausibly argue that the US Government committed crimes against humanity in recent wars, this accusation does not and cannot extend to the US culture and even less so, to any individual that is a US citizen or shares in the cultural mores of that nation.

29 *The Lund Recommendations on the Effective Participation of National Minorities in Public Life & Explanatory Note* (September 1999) Foundation on Inter-Ethnic Relations. <www.osce.org/documents/hcnm/1999/09/2698_en.pdf>.

30 A classical example is the debate around Susan Moller Okin's assertion that multiculturalism is bad for women. *See* Susan Moller Okin, Joshua Cohen, Matthew Howard, Martha C. Nussbaum, *Is Multiculturalism Bad for Women?* (Princeton University Press 1999).

Cultural values are not an explanation for what leaders or even sections of dominant communities do or do not do.

National and ethnic cultures are what Ernesto Laclau calls 'floating signifiers', they are not intrinsically associated with left, right center feminist or misogamist ideas, etc., even if significant groups that partake in those cultures can be identified as such. The cultures are arenas for struggle between contending forces that wish to hegemonise that particular community. When Fidel Castro said the '*the idiosyncrasy of the Cuban people will not allow Yankee imperialists to dominate our country*' was simply incorporating icons of Cuban nationalism into his ideological stance. Likewise when the Miami exiles said '*Cuba, the pearl of the Caribbean is now occupied by godless communists*' were doing the same from their ideological perspective. Cuban nationalism (or any nationalism for that matter) is neither intrinsically left or right, but an arena for struggle for hegemony between contesting ideologies. Ethnic and national culture are, as pointed before, important elements in the definition of our common humanity, but are equally floating signifiers, pitched at a high level of generality and amenable to be interpreted in different and contrasting ways. They are arenas for political struggle between antagonistic world views, each of which aims to monopolize the role of the 'true' defender or the 'true' interpreter of that culture in order to gain support and constitute itself as the dominant political force within that culture.

Why is it that same plural understanding is not afforded to minority cultures, particularly immigrant minority cultures? Discussions of this will takes away of our topic into a long discussion of racism and prejudice particularly in Europe. It is sufficient to say that minority cultures and minority religions are subjected to the same internal ideological battles and that like dominant cultures, minority cultures are equally pitched at a high level of generality and are the subject of internal contestation. Islam for example, is a very plural religion with contesting interpretations, and lively internal debates. But this is obscured in the West by a continuous accusation of fundamentalism, which paradoxically gives comfort and support to the fundamentalist forces the West wishes to neutralise.

The feminist writer Ayelet Shachar, expresses this same idea from a different direction:

> ... the components that constitute the nomos of a group at any given time never are as fixed or stable as they might appear. Over time, identity is negotiated, contested, transformed, defined, and redefined by group members through ongoing interactions both inside and outside the identity group. In this sense, nomoi groups are contingent, historical, and

> socially constructed entities, not the natural or fixed essences they often are thought to be. Identity groups constantly redefine their established traditions in relation to inside or outside challenges.[31]

The openness and plurality of minority cultures is crucially shaped by the attitude of the majority, to which they are vulnerable in a world of nation states, internal debate flourishes when the community is not under threat, and vice versa it decreases when the community is under threat by outsiders. This is a constant in minority communities, when under threat, they close ranks under a leadership that they might not all otherwise accept uncritically. To afford them collective rights and institutional representation is one of the best methods to secure a vibrant internal debate and to de-essentialise any attempt to fix or essentialise their identities.

V Are Human Rights Individual Rights?

Disadvantaged cultural minorities often seek more than the right of their individual members to equality and participation within the larger society. They require mechanisms that protect their culture from the tyranny of the majority, they seek either protection or autonomy as the means to ensure that their communities can survive and thrive in minority circumstances. In short, these minorities require some form of autonomy and/or community representation.[32] Here, many liberal critics vehemently disagree, for they see in granting communal or autonomous rights to minorities a grave transgression to a theory of rights that is exclusively oriented towards individuals[33] or as simply a violation of human rights as these are in their interpretation, entirely individual in nature and exclusively afforded to individuals.

These understandings of human rights are fallacious and some say, ethnocentric, in that they see human rights as granted to an 'ideal type' individual that is at best, little more than a transcendental abstraction. In this 'ideal type' the exemplary individual is often unconnected to real and existing human beings and at worst, a simple ethnocentric replication of the dominant individual type. Consider the 'veil of ignorance' and the 'original position',

31 Ayelet Shachar, 'On Citizenship and Multicultural Vulnerability' (2000) 28 *Political Theory* 72.

32 Sanders, *op. cit.*, 370

33 Jürgen Habermas, 'Struggles for Recognition in the Democratic Constitutional State' in Amy Gutmann (eds), *Multiculturalism, Examining the Politics of Recognition* (Princeton University Press 1974) 108–110.

concepts introduced by John Rawls in his book 'A Theory of Justice'.[34] This is a method of determining the cultural and political neutrality of policy based upon ignorance or 'benign neglect' of particular cultures, tastes, political position and inclinations of the individual within the social order of society. Here, for Rawls, fairness and human rights presumably require ignorance of everything except the transcendental and homologous human condition of the individual in question. An important Feminist critique of the 'veil of ignorance' doctrine persuasively argues that this theory fails because on its choice of an abstraction of human being in the exemplary image of a 'normal' member of the dominant group. This abstraction indeed invokes the characteristics of a WASP male member of the dominant majority. The consensus it creates is thus achieved by fiat[35] subsuming all into the above-mentioned male stereotype and ignoring differences. This important criticism equally applies to the discussion of the values of non-Christian minorities in secular democracies. The abstraction of the 'veil of ignorance' subsumes non-Christian communities into what they are not. As such is a mechanism of oppression, not emancipation, of its actually veiled female citizens. It also produces unwarranted and undesired generalisations. Do we all celebrate Christmas? If not, why we all get compulsory holidays in Christmas?

In a paradoxical way, these assertions on human rights are defined by Kinley[36] as a form '*Transcendental Fundamentalism*'. This is the idea based on the dubious claim that human rights are the fundamental, immutable and transcendent principles regardless of context and circumstance, an upon which our political, social and legal orders are based today. Kinley further argues that this kind of fallacious interpretation exhibits:

> ...a tendency towards human rights evangelicalism where human rights are touted as a panacea for many or all social, political, legal and economic ills. As such, human rights are considered to be beyond reproval or even critique. I refer to such a phenomenon as 'Reactionary Fundamentalism', and see the threat it poses to human rights as coming from the devitalisation of the body of human rights discourse and argument that is the inevitable consequence of all dogma that eschews the rigours of intellectual inquiry and challenge.[37]

34 John Rawls, *A Theory of Justice* (Oxford University Press 1999) 118.
35 Mari J. Matsuda, 'Liberal Jurisprudence and Abstracted Visions of Human Nature: A Feminist Critique of Rawls' Theory of Justice' (1986) 16 *New Mexico Law Review* 613–630.
36 David Kinley, 'Human Rights Fundamentalisms' (2007) 19 *Sydney Law Review* 545.
37 *Ibid.*, 547.

There is nothing odd with this claim, particularly when it challenges dogmatic assertions of human rights fundamentalism by using the very methodology bequeathed to us by the Philosophy of the Enlightenment (the rigours of intellectual enquiry and challenge). On a more concrete dimension, the practice becomes clear if we consider how one of the central tenants of the Philosophy of the Enlightenment, secularity and the value of reason, has been curiously reverted into a fundamentalist dogma by the European anti- Islamic crusaders of *laïcité.*

An inverted mirror image of this kind of transcendental human rights fundamentalism can be found in the caricatures of one of the most acerbic critics of the Philosophy of the Enlightenment, Joseph-Marie de Maistre, who defended hierarchical societies and a monarchical State. In his counter revolutionary 'Considerations on France' (1797) He wrote:

> The Constitution of 1795 like its predecessors was made for man. But there is no such thing as man in the world. In my lifetime I have seen Frenchmen, Italians, Russians, etc.; thanks to Montesquieu, I even know that one can be Persian. But as for man, I declare that I have never in my life met him; if he exists, he is unknown to me…[38]

In surprising and most perplexing turn of events, De Maistre finds support in an unexpected quarter. Hannah Arendt expresses her bitter disappointment on the value Human Rights following the genocide of European Jewry in words that are similar to those of De Maistre, but relying instead on another sharp Anglo critic of the Philosophy of the Enlightenment, Edmund Burke. She argues that World War Two events *offer an ironical, bitter, and belated confirmation of the famous arguments with which Edmund Burke opposed the French Revolution's Declaration of the Rights of Man.* Her claim is that the WW2 events 'amply justify' Burke's claim that human rights are an 'abstraction' and that it is much wiser to rely on inherited rights such as the rights of the Englishman *which one transmits to one's children like life itself,* rather than on the rights of 'man'<sic>. She then enigmatically supports Burke's idea that the rights we have spring from within the nation, so that no other concept is needed as a source of law.[39]

38 Joseph de Maistre, 'Considerations on France' in Richard A. Lebrun (eds), *Introduction by Isaiah Berlin Cambridge Texts in the History of Political Thought* (Cambridge University Press 1994) xxiii.

39 Arendt, *op. cit.*, 299.

So it appears that we are faced by a human rights dog's breakfast, a choice between two dangerous and unappealing conceptions of rights. One vision is egalitarian, but ethnocentric, and to a large extent, dogmatic Universalist. The other vision is ostensible pluralist, but inhumane, hierarchical undemocratic, with a propensity to inequality and hierarchical structures and images of human life of the sort that paradoxically (!) Arendt warned us about in other important works.

VI Human Rights and Popular Sovereignty

What escapes De Maistre, in criticising a 'non existing man' and likewise, Bourke and Arendt in the curious notion of rights by 'national inheritance', and, equally escapes Rawls and other dogmatic and monist transcendentalist defenders of human rights, who only see human rights as an abstract universal category, is that our common human characteristics, the point of departure for human rights, are *precisely constituted* through our insertion in time and space into a community. We are human *not in spite of cultural diversity, but because of cultural diversity*. Our common humanity derives from the irrevocably and specifically plural character of human existence. To paraphrase de Maistre, we are humans and worthy of universal human rights precisely because we are French, Italian, Russian and Persian, etc. To deny the importance and value of cultural diversity, and, our cultural insertion, denies the very notion of human rights, as this means denying an important constitutive element of human beings and of our common humanity. Recognition of difference is therefore a key part of the assertion of our common humanity, for human beings cannot be conceived outside their culturally and religiously diverse settings. Even cultural and postcolonial hybridity is constitutive. Universal human rights do not exist in abstraction but in a human world that is for all time culturally diverse. Without such diversity, the very notion of a common humanity is inconceivable. In the worst case scenario, and as a result of the two set of ideas criticised above, selective and tendentious understanding of human rights simply replicates selective attributes of the dominant culture. This is explicit in the reactionary thinking of Burke and De Maistre, as well as in the dogmatic universalism of Rawls. At the same time, this accusation is often and with some justification, held against Western powers and some Liberal Democracies. But the accusation of Western liberal hypocrisy does not undermine human rights, but on the contrary, it strengthens them, for we are able to critically analyse our own ethnocentric failings, which we can understand when we put to work one of the most subversive components of the Philosophy of the Enlightenment, that of rigorous intellectual enquiry and challenge.

This discussion above is crucially important for the discussion of national self-determination and popular sovereignty. The assertion of human rights as a foundational recognition of human plurality and cultural diversity is decisive to dismiss rigid models of popular sovereignty and national self-determination. The unrelenting understanding enshrined in both, liberal democratic theory and international law, that national self-determination is to be understood as the creation of separate territorial sovereignties (states) for aggrieved or deserving communities is insensitive to the reality that most states house diverse cultural communities. It is furthermore, skewed in favour of a small number of relative powerful national-territorial communities. More ominously, it is also informed by a narrow and perhaps ethnocentric interpretation of human rights in which see self-determination only the expression of the group will of atomised individuals whose cultural affiliation is rendered invisible. In this case, national self-determination has one 'fit all' meaning. In contrast, in a plural world, sovereign territorial self-determination must come to terms with the practical impossibility of generalising a common will without putting all communities in a democratic equal footing. For this reason, a discussion of human rights is necessary to show how monist understandings of national self-determination and popular sovereignty clash with a constitutive characteristic of humanity, its irrevocable cultural diversity.

If one of the most deserving human categories for self-determination, recognition and some form of sovereignty are indigenous peoples, the monist model of 'one fit all' is unsuitable or worse for the vast majority of indigenous and dispersed territorial minorities. They are gravely affected by the doctrine of indivisible sovereignty that originates from the centralist atomist conceptualisation of the nation state, and that leads to the inflexible paradigm presently understood in international law, that no right of self-determination can be recognised where it clashes with a world of sovereign states. This influential argument is unreceptive to the implementation of minority and territorially dispersed community rights and therefore unsuitable for indigenous communities.[40] In a partially dissenting voice, Will Kymlicka argues that autonomous self-government rights, which require collective rights and the delegation of legal powers to national minorities, should be awarded exclusively to groups of indigenous peoples and others who have been incorporated to settler states through conquest or colonialization.[41] It is now to these that we turn.

40 Catherine J. Iorns, 'Indigenous peoples and self determination: Challenging State Sovereignty' (Spring 1992) 24(2) *Case Western Reserve Journal of International Law* 199.

41 Kymlicka, *op. cit.*, 10–11.

VII Indigenous Peoples and Democratic Theory

The democratic normative basis of the model of National Self-Determination – the emancipation from alien rule – makes some territorial minorities and most indigenous peoples to be among those who most deserve this right. Yet, at the same time, because of their territorial configuration, these groups are unable to fulfil the requirements of national self-determination laid out in international law and the UN charter. With some few exceptions,[42] Indigenous peoples have been conquered, their territories occupied by settlers, and in many cases subjected to genocide by settler colonialism. In the majority of cases, they are now marginal minorities in their ancestral lands. The most recent tragedy is Palestine, which in a scandalous turn of events, the indigenous people of Palestine have been made the indirect victims of European racist genocides. In these circumstances, Palestinians, as well as other indigenous peoples have a unique normative claim for self-governance, cultural recognition and community rights.

For the reasons discussed earlier in this paper, the politics of national self-determination demanded and argued by indigenous peoples differs greatly from mainstream liberal and UN definitions of national self-determination and even more so, from the way self-determination is understood in international law. In many ways demands for self-determination of indigenous peoples test hitherto established notions of popular sovereignty in contemporary liberal democratic nation states, particularly those that have been built in colonial settler societies. As shown earlier, this problem does not only affect indigenous peoples; other scattered territorial minorities are also affected by the sovereign-territorial bias of mainstream understanding of self-determination, the Roma are a classical example.[43]

Out of necessity, these indigenous peoples and scattered communities have no choice but to radically redefine the forms of national self-determination, shifting toward models of non-territorial autonomy even when their ancestral nexus with the territory is strong. This is in many cases done by separating sovereignty into overlapping jurisdictions, and incorporating and being incorporated into forms of multi-level governance. This procedure in some way reminds the architecture of pre modern Empires, but also to some extent and important for us, of recent events in the European Union. Here the revised

42 Consider the case of Fiji as an exception.

43 Jarmila Lajčáková, 'Advancing Empowerment of the Roma in Slovakia through a Non-territorial National Autonomy' (2010) 9(2) *Ethnopolitics* 171. Ilona Klimova, *The Romani Voice in World Politics* (Ashgate 2015).

architecture of the EU and in particular the ongoing discussions about a tighter unity in a quasi-federal Europe could open interesting parallel opportunities. At a day to day level of politics, the idea of European politicians learning something from indigenous peoples elicits a broad smile for it will test their ethnocentrism to the limit. Nevertheless, forms of multi-level governance in the EU have been described as communal, when a particular community acquires jurisdiction over a particular domain. The strongest pressures for multilevel governance in the EU occur in de-facto multination states (Spain, Belgium, and UK among others) with politically active and regionally based national minorities and nationalist movements.[44] In most cases the desire for self-determination is coupled with a desire to integrate further into the EU, making their demands for independence to be significantly less than achieving nation state sovereignty. In the cases I am familiar with (Spain and the UK) there is an awareness of this in minority nationalists parties, but none of the main minority nationalist parties has engaged in a debate on the implications of this, particularly for the in some case large number of regional residents that do not belong to the regionally dominant national community.

Here there are, unsuspected but important parallel dimensions between the demands of stateless nations of the European Union and the demands of indigenous peoples, particularly in the way they frame their demands of national self-determination in conjunction with demands of multi-level governance. Such jurisdictions are defined by cultural boundaries for people whose residential areas intersect with others, with whom they share membership of other (multiple) jurisdictions. In the EU, the emerging idea is that the process of integration that results from the serious economic crisis is shifting the process of integration toward the idea of increased shared sovereignty and policy making shared across a growing number of spheres of influence that criss-crosses the existing nation state configuration. The direction in the integrated Europe is to move toward states that continuously loose, in a relentless process, authority over individuals and policies.[45] In more than one way, these trends appear to indicate a parallel path between indigenous demands for self-determination couched in a language that international jurists will find heterodox, and the pressures for European integration on the stateless nations of Europe, a pressure that has been thus far absorbed by minority nationalist

44 Liesbet Hooghe and Gary Marks, 'Unravelling the Central State, But How? Types of Multi-Level Governance' (2003) 87 Monograph 16 *Political Science Series* and Liesbet Hooghe, Gary Marks, and Carole Wilson, 'Does Left/Right Structure Party Positions on European Integration?' (2002) 35 *Comparative Political Studies* 965.

45 Liesbet Hooghe and Gary Marks, Multi-Level Governance and European Integration (Rowman & Littlefield Publishers 2001) 1–3.

movements. Nevertheless, we should accept that an admission of this parallelism will test Eurocentric sentiments to the limit.

Multi-level governance is more open to non-territorial arrangements and these are valuable options for dispersed minority communities. The best known examples are the Sami Parliaments in Scandinavian countries, as well as the different jurisdictions of the Plurinational State of Bolivia.[46]

Yet, notwithstanding the similarities with Consociationalism and national cultural autonomy, the new and imaginative way in which indigenous peoples operationalise the idea of national self-determination remains significantly under-theorised and little known outside the area of specialised studies of indigenous peoples. The practice of indigenous peoples, coupled with the challenges emerging in Europe as result of the demands for secession within the UK Spain and Belgium are pushing for solutions to the problems of representation of stateless nations that falls short of total sovereignty. These changes have the undeniable potential to transform the way we understand self-determination and popular sovereignty, and these changes are important and relevant to other types of communities affected by the rigidities of nation-state governance. Here indigenous groups are making a contribution to a paradigm shift in the way we understand democratic rights and this in time will help reshape democratic theory. The emerging models resemble in organization and characteristics the models for National Cultural Autonomy advocated around the turn of the twentieth century by Otto Bauer and Karl Renner, models designed to avoid the disintegration of the Austro-Hungarian monarchy, an implementing through a complex network of overlapping jurisdictions, maximum autonomy and maximum self-determination to minority communities while avoiding exclusive control over territory. This might be the right time to revisit these models and see if they can help to provide solution to the crisis in the EU, and indeed help theorize the innovative models for self-determination advanced by indigenous peoples. Much in the same way as nowadays the EU needs flexible models of self-governance and non-exclusive sovereignty to avoid the disintegration of the system, the Austrian late nineteen century socialists faced similar issues in the context of the Austro Hungarian dual monarchy. In light of the experience of indigenous peoples and the crisis in Europe, it might be wise to re-examine these old models, which highlight a crying need in 21st century

46 I have discussed this in some detail in Ephraim Nimni, *Indigenous Peoples and the Development of New Paradigms in the Theory and Practice of National Self Determination and Sovereignty*, European Consortium for Political Research Joint Sessions, University of St Gallen 12–17 April 2011.

Europe for the apparently contradictory demands for more self-governance and more integration.

VIII The United Nations and Indigenous Peoples

In 2007 The United Nations General Assembly, under the sustained pressure and lobbying from indigenous rights organizations, introduced a resolution that appears to address some of the demands of indigenous peoples. It does so, but only in a limited fashion. The resolution is both, an example of indigenous organisation and the innovations they developed, but at the same time, it is a clear example of the limitations imposed by international law on the UN resolutions on the vexed question of national self-determination. This is the United Nations Declaration on the Rights of Indigenous Peoples.[47] In part, this resolution differs in a significantly in its approach to earlier discussions on self-determination, For example, from the famous UN General Assembly declaration Granting the right of self-determination to Colonial Countries and Peoples of 1960.[48]

Consider the following differences: In the resolution of 2007, articles 3, 4 and 5 clearly state that indigenous peoples have the right to self-determination. Moreover, and in sharp distinction to the 1960 resolution, the right of self-determination is defined as encompassing rights to autonomy and self-governance in internal affairs while not mentioning sovereignty. Specifically, article 9 mentions the right of indigenous peoples to belong to an indigenous nation. In earlier UN discussions on Indigenous peoples, the special *rapporteur* on indigenous peoples, Rodolfo Stavenhagen, had on many occasions stated for the record that one of the areas that most clearly illustrates the vulnerable nature of indigenous peoples' human rights is the administration of justice and the failure to recognize customary indigenous law in governance and self-determination.[49]

In spite of all the above, article 46 of the 2007 Declaration of the Rights of Indigenous Peoples repeats verbatim the restrictions of the 6th article 6of the 1960 Declaration on the Self Determination of Colonial peoples, stating that: *Nothing in this Declaration may be interpreted as* (....) *authorizing or encouraging any action which would dismember or impair, totally or in part, the territorial*

47 UN General Assembly Resolution 61/295 on 13 September 2007.

48 UN General Assembly Resolution1514 (XV) 947th plenary meeting, 14 December 1960.

49 Rodolfo Stavenhagen, Special Rapporteur, General Assembly of the United Nations Document No A/59/258, 12 August 2004, Australian Indigenous Law Reporter, 17, 2005.

integrity or political unity of sovereign and independent States. Without doubt, the United Nations is primarily a society of states in 2007 as it was in 1960.

On this regard, no significant progress can be done in moving forward in a truly democratic fashion, without broadening the right of self-determination to include the needs of indigenous peoples and other territorially scattered minorities. For this to happen, the UN needs to discard the claim that states are the sole monopolisers of sovereignty. In this, the United Nations is not a union of nations but a union of sovereign states, with the intention of protecting the interests of the latter and not the former. In its equivocal and misleading use of terminology, the UN perpetuates the disadvantages of scattered minorities and stateless nations which are, as shown before, the vast majority of nations, including of course, indigenous peoples. This principle of only recognising the national right to self-determination as the creation of territorial states is not only equivocal but antidemocratic, because the majority of nations, including almost all indigenous nations, are stateless.

IX The Transformation of Democratic Theory – from the Nation State Demos to a Commowealth of Demoi

Since their development in the eighteen to the early twentieth century, democratic theories took for granted the insertion of political democracy within confines of the nation state. More often than not, they took this assertion at face value without explanation or justification.[50] Recently, and as a result of the newly recognised democratic shortcomings in the practice of democracy, important arguments and objections are beginning to emerge in the area of international political theory, questioning if the nation state can be the exclusive locus of democratic activity. In what I have described elsewhere as a Kuhnian Paradigm shift,[51] the emerging approaches are ambitiously addressing long neglected issues, such as whether it is possible to realize democracy beyond the skeleton of the nation state and in particular, if national self-determination should only mean the creation of separate states. Further

50 An interesting exception to this is the work of the Austrian socialists, Karl Renner and Otto Bauer, who developed the National Cultural Autonomy Model as a forerunner to contemporary consociationalism. *See* Nimni, 'Nationalist multiculturalism in late imperial', and Ephrain Nimni, *National Cultural Autonomy and its Contemporary Critics* (Routledge 2005).

51 Ephraim Nimni, 'Nationalism, Ethnicity and Self-Determination: A Paradigm Shift?' in Keith Breen and Shane O'Neill (eds), *After the Nation? Critical Reflections on Post-Nationalism* (Palgrave MacMillan 2010).

important questions emerging are what kind of democracy may exist outside the domain of the nation state, and how different might its foundations be, and what institutions and practices will reform or replace the regime of the contemporary nation-state.

Initially, contemporary advocates of cosmopolitanism began to challenge the insertion of democratic theory within the framework of the nation state. David Held for example, advocates in a number of important works, a model of cosmopolitan democracy that transcends the borders of the nation state, and that assumes the entrenchment of a cluster of rights and obligations enshrined within the constitutions of parliaments and assemblies, as well as various regional bodies such as the European Union, with a global parliament and an interconnected legal system.[52] The argument in Held's work is for broad conception pluralism within single fully inclusive demos.

While this approach can be commended for its departure from the domination of the nation state formation, it leaves intact the problem of community representation and the recognition of collective democratic subjects, the core of democratic demands of indigenous peoples and scattered minority communities. Taking the argument a step further, James Bohman[53] argues, that a form of radical plural democracy requires deeper transformations of democracy away from the morphology of the nation state. He further argues that the conditions exist for democratization beyond the limits of the nation-state, and that this expansion is not only possible, but necessary for the renewal of democratic theory. Taking the argument further, Bohman argues is that democracy must function *across* rather than simply *beyond* borders. The renewed democratic theory must not demolish cultural differences, as in the early republican model of the nation state, which was not only one of nation building, but simultaneously one of nation destroying.[54] This means that democracy must now become a democracy of the demoi, a plural and diverse conglomerate of democratic communities and constituencies. This is not only to change the institutional structure of the nation state , but also a change in the political subject that sustains the democratic formation, from a unified constituency to a plurality of diverse constituencies, from 'a people' to 'peoples'.[55] In other words, Bohman brings the debate about the expansion of the democracy to the

52 David Held, *Models of Democracy* (3rd edn, Polity Press 2006) 307–309.

53 James Bohman, 'From Demos to Demoi: Democracy across Borders' (2005) 18(3) *Ratio Juris* 297–298.

54 Walker Conor, 'Nation-Building or Nation-Destroying?' (1972) 24(3) *World Politics* 319–355.

55 James Bohman, *Democracy Across Borders: from Demos to Demoi* (The MIT Press 2007) 13.

recognition of the collective rights and collective personae of the constituent communities or demoi.

Bohman argument speaks to the needs and demands of indigenous peoples and territorial minorities, it that it eliminates the key stumbling block for the communitarian political participation of these communities: *territorial sovereignty as a condition for collective community participation.* This argument is crucially important for the emancipation of territorial minorities because it distinguishes this approach to democracy from cosmopolitan arguments that imagine a single institutional skeleton of authority, a kind of a global state. Even more so, its comprehensive understanding of democratic values is sharply different from those who link global democracy to what could be defined as a minimalist approach, a kind of compelling human rights legal apparatus existing above the nation-state, only limiting its sovereignty when it transgresses the agreed framework of human rights. This last approach is of no use for minority communities, for as argued earlier, majoritarian democracies can transgress the rights of cultural minorities without violating an individualist definition of democratic rights.

x Not Cosmopolitan, but Inter-national *Demoi*

To develop democracy beyond the borders of the nation state is important but it is not sufficient to overcome the pluralist deficit of the modern nation state. It is self-defeating to maintain the faulty configuration of the nation state, only to expand it to a gigantic world cosmopolitan constituency. Instead of perceiving democracy as *cosmopolitan* (*non-national and cultural*), democracy as the domain of single demos, democratic theory must break with this residue of the nation state and understand democracy not as a single body but as a plurality of constituent democracies. In this way, it becomes *inter-national and inter-cultural,* operating not beyond border but across borders, not negating but affirming the democratic value of the collective governance of nations and cultural communities, creating democratic models that incorporate self-determining constituent autonomous communities and recognising their right for effective collective representation.

Democracy must be organised in more than one unit in order to satisfy demands for recognition that result from the logic of pluralist democratic governance. In this, global democracy cannot be some analogical world of individuals enjoying equal rights which inevitably leads to misrecognition of minorities and the corresponding tyranny of the majority. Instead global democracy must be seen as a plurality of demos (demoi) within a federal arrangement instead of a state inspired conception of single demos.[56] In other words, democracy must be implemented in a *Commonwealth of Demoi*, understanding by that a highly interconnected world, where territories are shared between differing demoi and territorial polities cannot be the basis for exclusive sovereignties.

The growth of governance beyond nation states is perhaps one of the most important political developments of the last decades. In recent years these incipient transnational organizations have been challenged on normative grounds for their lack of democracy in the form of various democratic deficits.[57] This criticism is particularly strong in the case of the European Union, with the famous 'democratic deficit' being paraded by many, friends and enemies of European integration alike. This required a reconceptualization of the modalities of the European Union away from the analogies of the nation state, and the pioneering work of Francis Cheneval and in a different dimension, Kalypso Nicolaïdis is extremely helpful in this regard.

Cheneval[58] correctly argues that it is mistaken to analyze the European Union and its democratic deficit with democratic analogies from the nation state (He rather uses the term states people). He uses instead the term '*demoicracy*', a polity of multiple demoi as appropriate for the European Union. From here, any normative evaluation of democracy in the European Union must start from the premise that it is organisation with many demoi and not a nation state, in other words *a demoicracy*. This argument is important and constructive, for it is very helpful in establishing the foundational differences between the EU and nation states. It helps us move away from the morphology of the nation state, and since the democratic terminology associated with the nation state has become so common sensical and hegemonic, it is necessary, as Cheneval does, to create to neologisms to break out of this tight conceptual straitjacket. *Demoicracy* represents an intermediary level between nation-state and international politics. This is a key first step to move away from the morphology of the nation state while discussing democracy. Yet, the EU *demoicracy* cannot be composed exclusively by statespeople as its collective constituents,

56 Ferran Requejo, 'Value Pluralism and Multinational federalism' in Alain-G. Gagnon, Montserrat Guibernau, Francois Rocher (eds), *The Conditions of Diversity in Multinational Democracies* (l'Institut de recherche en politiques publiques-The Institute for Research on Public Policy (IRPP) 2004) 2.

57 Magdalena Bexell, Jonas Tallberg and Anders Uhlin, 'Democracy in Global Governance: The Promises and Pitfalls of Transnational Actors' (2010) 16 *Global Governance* 81–82.

58 Francis Cheneval and Frank Schimmelfennig, (2012) *The Case for Demoicracy in the European Union* <http://onlinelibrary.wiley.com/doi/10.1111/j.1468-5965.2012.02262.x/abstract> accessed 28 December 2012.

for as argued before, every European state, has ethnic and national minorities whose identity is different from the titular nation. Consider for example the Turkish permanent residents in Germany. They are culturally different from the titular nation of the Federal Republic of Germany, as explicitly defined in ethnic terms in the German constitution,[59] and in terms of their numbers, they are more than several titular nations of the European Union (Latvia, Estonia and Luxemburg among others). Consequently, in democratic terms, the case for their collective representation in the EU *demoicracy* is very compelling.

Nicolaïdis[60] follows a similar line of argument. She defines '*demoicracy*' as '*a Union of peoples, understood both as states and as citizens, who govern together but not as one*', and like Cheneval, she argues that the concept is best understood distinct from both "national and supranational versions of single demos polities". She further argues that the concept of 'demoicracy' can serve both as an analytical lens for the European Union and as a normative benchmark. Consequently, the normative discussion must follow different lines of argumentation from the ones utilised to evaluate democracy in nation states. Here also, the Union of states and citizens has not entirely escaped the morphology of the nation state. For that it is necessary to include as components of the community of demoi, intermediate categories, such as ethnic and national minorities, and dispersed communities that are culturally different from their respective titular nations in the context of the nation state.

The discussion on the European Union is refreshing and thought provoking, but it has to be considered an initial step, it is necessary to enlarge the characteristics of the participant demoi, to enhance democratic mechanisms of inter-national and inter-cultural representation.

A Commonwealth of Demoi holds the promise of expanding democracy through the incorporation of territorial and non-territorial representation of minority communities, something that the ideals of popular sovereignty and national self-determination have failed to do for the liberal democratic

59 The definition of a German in the Constitution of the Federal Republic of Germany is found in article 116 (1) Which states: *Deutscher im Sinne dieses Grundgesetzes ist vorbehaltlich anderweitiger gesetzlicher Regelung, wer die deutsche Staatsangehörigkeit besitzt oder als Flüchtling oder Vertriebener* ***deutscher Volkszugehörigkeit*** *oder als dessen Ehegatte oder Abkömmling in dem Gebiete des Deutschen Reiches nach dem Stande vom 31. Dezember 1937 Aufnahme gefunden hat.* (emphasis mine). This is one of the very few 'liberal democratic' constitutions that define a component of citizenship in ethnic terms (*deutscher Volkszugehörigkeit*), the other notable example is the basic law of the State of Israel. This is not a coincidence as both are constituted through the same central European organic definition of nation

60 Kalypso Nicolaidis, 'European Demoicracy and its crisis' (2012) *Journal of Common Market Studies* <http://onlinelibrary.wiley.com/doi/10.1111/jcms.12006/abstract> accessed 28 December 2012.

nation state model. In the meantime the democratic deficit of the nation state continues to hold up democratic values, forcing democrats into unpalatable contradictions.

> You can judge a society by the way it treats its minorities.
> MOHANDAS KARAMCHAND GANDHI

Bibliography

Arendt, Hannah, *The Origins of Totalitarianism* (Meridian Books 1962).

Australian Indigenous Law Reporter, 17, 2005.

Bauer, Otto, *The Question of Nationalities and Social Democracy* (Series ed Ephraim Nimni) (University of Minnesota Press 2000).

Bexell, Magdalena, Tallberg, Jonas and Anders Uhlin, 'Democracy in Global Governance: The Promises and Pitfalls of Transnational Actors' (2010) 16 *Global Governance* 81–101.

Bohman, James, 'From Demos to Demoi: Democracy across Borders' (2005) 18(3) *Ratio Juris* 293–314.

Bohman, James, *Democracy Across Borders: from Demos to Demoi* (The MIT Press 2007).

Brown, Michael E., *Ethnic Conflict and International Security* (Princeton University Press 1993).

Buchanan, Allen, *Justice, Legitimacy, and Self-Determination: Moral Foundations for International Law* (Oxford University Press 2004).

Carr, Leslie G., *'Color-Blind' Racism* (Sage Publishers 1997).

Cheneval, Francis and Frank Schimmelfennig, (2012) *The Case for Demoicracy in the European Union* <http://onlinelibrary.wiley.com/doi/10.1111/j.1468-5965.2012.02262.x/abstract> accessed 28 December 2012.

Conor, Walker, 'Nation-Building or Nation-Destroying?' (1972) 24(3) *World Politics* 319–355.

de Maistre, Joseph, 'Considerations on France' in Richard A. Lebrun (eds), *Introduction by Isaiah Berlin Cambridge Texts in the History of Political Thought* (Cambridge University Press 1994).

de Tocqueville, Alexis, *Democracy in America* with an introduction by Joseph Epstein (Random House 2004).

de Vieuzac, Bertrand Barère, *Rapport du Comité de salut public sur les idiomes* (*Report of the Committee of Public Health on Languages*) – 8 pluviôse an II: 27 January 1794 <http://www.tlfq.ulaval.ca/axl/francophonie/barere-rapport.htm> accessed 12 December 2012.

Govier, Trudy, *Social Trust and Human Communities* (McGill-Queen's University Press 1997).

Habermas, Jürgen, 'Struggles for Recognition in the Democratic Constitutional State' in Amy Gutmann (eds), *Multiculturalism, Examining the Politics of Recognition* (Princeton University Press 1974).

Held, David, *Models of Democracy* (3rd edn, Polity Press 2006).

Hooghe, Liesbet and Gary Marks, 'Unravelling the Central State, But How? Types of Multi-Level Governance' (2003) 87 Monograph 16 *Political Science Series* 233–243.

Hooghe, Liesbet and Gary Marks, Multi-Level Governance and European Integration (Rowman & Littlefield Publishers, Boulder 2001).

Hooghe, Liesbet, Marks, Gary and Carole Wilson, 'Does Left/Right Structure Party Positions on European Integration?' (2002) 35 *Comparative Political Studies* 965–989.

Iorns, Catherine J., 'Indigenous peoples and self determination: Challenging State Sovereignty' (Spring 1992) 24 (2) *Case Western Reserve Journal of International Law* 199–348.

Kedourie, Elie, *Nationalism* (Hutchinson 1960).

Kinley, David, 'Human Rights Fundamentalisms', inaugural professorial lecture, Department of Law, University of Sydney, (2007) 19 *Sydney Law Review* 545–575.

Klimova, Ilona, *The Romani Voice in World Politics* (Ashgate 2015).

Knudsen, Olav F., 'Post-Copenhagen Security Studies: Desecuritizing Securitization' (2001) 32 *Security Dialogue* 355–368.

Kymlicka, Will and Christine Straehle, 'Cosmopolitanism, Nation-States, and Minority Nationalism: A Critical Review of Recent Literature' (April 1999) 7(1) *European Journal of Philosophy* 65–88.

Kymlicka, Will, *Multicultural Citizenship* (Oxford University Press 1995).

Lajčáková, Jarmila, 'Advancing Empowerment of the Roma in Slovakia through a Non-territorial National Autonomy' (2010) 9(2) *Ethnopolitics* 171–196.

Mann, Michael, *The Dark Side of Democracy: Explaining Ethnic Cleansing* (Cambridge University Press 2005 and four reprints).

Matsuda, Mari J., 'Liberal Jurisprudence and Abstracted Visions of Human Nature: A Feminist Critique of Rawls' Theory of Justice' (1986) 16 *New Mexico Law Review* 613–630.

Mill, J. S, *Considerations of Representative Government* (1862) in H.B. Acton (eds) *Utilitarism, On Liberty and Considerations on Representative Government* (J.M. Dent & Sons 1976).

Mill, John Stuart, *On Liberty and Other Essays* With an introduction by John Gray (Oxford University Press 1998).

Moller Okin, Susan, Cohen, Joshua, Howard, Matthew and Martha C. Nussbaum, *Is Multiculturalism Bad for Women?* (Princeton University Press 1999).

Nicolaidis, Kalypso, 'European Demoicracy and its crisis' (2012) *Journal of Common Market Studies* <http://onlinelibrary.wiley.com/doi/10.1111/jcms.12006/abstract> accessed 28 December 2012.

Nimni, Ephraim, 'Nationalism, Ethnicity and Self-Determination: A Paradigm Shift?' in Keith Breen and Shane O'Neill (eds), *After the Nation? Critical Reflections on Post-Nationalism* (Palgrave MacMillan 2010).

Nimni, Ephraim, 'Nationalist multiculturalism in late imperial Austria as a critique of contemporary liberalism: The case of Bauer and Renner' (1999) 4(3) *Journal of Political Ideologies* 289–314.

Nimni, Ephraim, *Indigenous Peoples and the Development of New Paradigms in the Theory and Practice of National Self Determination and Sovereignty*, European Consortium for Political Research Joint Sessions, University of St Gallen 12–17 April 2011.

Nimni, Ephraim, *Marxism and Nationalism Theoretical Origins of a Political Crisis* (2nd edn, Pluto Press 1994).

Nimni, Ephraim, *National Cultural Autonomy and its Contemporary Critics* (Routledge 2005).

Rawls, John, *A Theory of Justice* (Oxford University Press 1999).

Requejo, Ferran, 'Value Pluralism and Multinational federalism' in Alain-G. Gagnon, Montserrat Guibernau, Francois Rocher (eds), *The Conditions of Diversity in Multinational Democracies* (l'Institut de recherche en politiques publiques-The Institute for Research on Public Policy (IRPP) 2004).

Sanders, Douglas, 'Collective Rights' (1991) 13(3) *Human Rights Quarterly* 368–386.

Shachar, Ayelet, 'On Citizenship and Multicultural Vulnerability' (2000) 28 *Political Theory* 64–89.

Stavenhagen, Rodolfo, Special Rapporteur, General Assembly of the United Nations Document No A/59/258, 12 August 2004.

Stratham, Paul, 'Understanding Anti-Asylum Rhetoric: Restrictive Politics or Racist Publics?' (August 2003) 74, Supplement s1 *The Political Quarterly* 163–177.

Sylvester, Douglas J, 'International Law as Sword or Shield–Early American Foreign Policy and the Law of Nations' (1999–2000) 32(1) *New York University Journal of International Law and Politics* 1–88.

The Lund Recommendations on the Effective Participation of National Minorities in Public Life & Explanatory Note (September 1999) Foundation on Inter-Ethnic Relations. <www.osce.org/documents/hcnm/1999/09/2698_en.pdf>.

UN General Assembly Resolution 61/295 on 13 September 2007.

UN General Assembly Resolution1514 (XV) 947th plenary meeting, 14 December 1960.

Warren, Mark, 'Democratic Theory and Self-Transformation' (1992) 86(1) *The American Political Science Review* 8–23.

Wittgenstein, Ludwig, *Philosophical Investigations* (John Wiley & Sons 2010).

Yiftachel, Oren, 'The Israeli Regime and the Question of Democracy' in C. Rubenberg (eds), *Encyclopedia of the Israeli-Palestinian Conflict* (Lynne Reinér Publishers 2011).

Yiftachel, Oren, *Ethnocracy Land and Identity Politics in Israel/Palestine*(Penn University Press, 2006).

CHAPTER 3

The Multiple Paths to Territorial Autonomy: Examples and Conceptual Underpinnings

Sia Spiliopoulou Åkermark

1 Introduction

There are different avenues and different theoretical and methodological choices in approaching territorial autonomy today. A purely legal approach would look at legal rules valid presently nationally or internationally and possibly pay some attention at the implementation of them. Focus would then be at interpretations and implementations in a constitutional system, under international agreements, the pronouncement of domestic and international judicial or monitoring organs. Such a study would look at how territorial autonomy is conceptualised in a particular moment of time and in a particular context, i.e. adjudication, dispute resolution, human rights monitoring, legislative processes etc.

However, it is argued in the present text that such a narrow approach is not adequate at a moment of time when challenges are piling up across Europe and globally and are directed against the idea of law itself, against democratic ideals of self-government and against the idea and practices of liberal civic societies, including human rights. We need a broader and more *longue durée* type of reflection. This is the effort in the present contribution. How did we end up having concepts and institutions of 'territorial autonomy' today? What are the legally reflected justificatory chains behind territorial autonomy?[1]

International law was institutionalised as a field of legal practice and as an academic discipline in the 19th century through imperial conferences where big powers met and decided on the norms to be applied in international affairs, as well as on the 'spheres of interest' of each of them. The fates of small countries and their inhabitants and of all new state creations that were emerging were marginally interesting for the powerholders of that time. Nor was

1 On my previous efforts to explore the layers of multiple justificatory grounds in law *see* Sia Spiliopoulou Åkermark, 'Shifts in the Multiple Justifications of Minority Protection' (2007/08) 7 *European Yearbook of Minority Issues* 5 and *Justifications of Minority Protection in International Law* (Kluwer Law 1997).

 DOI:10.1163/9789004405455_004

there any consistent concern for minority groups found in international legal thinking at the time.

The institutionalisation of international law took, however, place in tandem to the democratisation and constitutional processes across Europe during that long 19th century. These processes were unfolding against the background of the disintegration or, perhaps, the reconfiguration of empires, most notably the Austro-Hungarian, the Ottoman and later the Russian and even the French and British, resulting in multiple clashes such as the Napoleonic and the Crimean wars and societal revolutions across Europe and beyond.

In these painful constructions of new political systems and conceptions of citizenship and community in Europe as well as in colonial territories, problems of difference became even more pressing under the influence of romantic nationalism which exacerbated the emphasis on the coincidence of one nation for one state. This is also the time when territorial autonomy as a legal and political tool came to the forefront.

At the time when international law was constituted as an academic field, international law was understood as closely connected to the field of constitutional law, or what was then called 'state law' (Staatsrecht). An important theoretical step in this process was Robert von Mohl's launch of the theory of constitutional self-limitation of the state and of the primacy of law.[2] This move gave the preconditions needed for the construction of the idea of human rights, not simply as a natural law, or as a political or philosophical claim, but also as an element of implemented constitutional law as well as an international legal undertaking. The idea of constitutional self-limitation combined domestic democratic aspirations with the idea of independent international legal personality and state sovereignty. Consent and natural law were thus united in this formalistic legal doctrine. While this process was of course crucial for the development of modern European constitutions and, later on, for human rights undertakings, there were several other related experiments taking place all around Europe. Several European constitutions were adopted after the end of the Napoleonic era and it is remarkable that comparative analysis of such constitutional processes remains limited.[3]

The variety of situations addressed and of solutions invented in that period of the second part of the 19th century and until the internationalised

2 Robert von Mohl, *Die Polizeiwissenschaft Nach Den Grundsätzen Der Rechtstaates* (2nd edn, 1844).

3 Bo Stråth and Martti Koskeniemi, 'Between Restoration and Revolution, National Constitutions and Global Law: An Alternative View on the European Century 1815–1914', EReRe Research project description, <http://blogs.helsinki.fi/erere-project/files/2008/11/erere_project.pdf> accessed 07 September 2017.

institutionalisation that took place during the League of Nations era are reassessed in this contribution which draws upon examples from a broad conceptualisation of the idea of Europe and of territorial autonomy in the continent. Theoretically, this contribution poses the core and persistent question about the relationship between territorial autonomy, minority accommodation and diversity. It argues that territorial autonomy as an institution springs out of a multitude of 19th century experiences, ideologies and institutions linking it to both democratisation and self-government processes, the development of regional identities in parallel to the consolidation of the modern nation state, colonial projects and the disintegration of empires.

Following Flaubert's pronouncement, *l'histoire est toujours à refaire* (history is always open to reinterpretation) I try to locate the essential efforts behind theories and implementations of territorial autonomy since the 19th century, in ways combining the efforts already opened up by many scholars in recent decades. Such a view of history does not negate the role of accurate historical accounts and does not take a relativist approach to historical knowledge. On the contrary it broadens the claim for richer and multi-layered historical accounts which present the multiplicity and contingency of historical, political and legal events.

The oversimplified interpretation and conceptualisation of territorial autonomy only as a 'human right' or as the institutional form of singular and excluding cultural nationalism risks missing out on the richness of these long-term efforts and ideological, political and legal choices involved. While looking and searching ahead towards future potentials for multi-layered democratic governance in a globalised world, we must avoid nostalgia of the past which rests on mono-dimensional visions of this past.

The structure of the argument is as follows. After this introduction, two cases of territorial autonomy in the early 19th century are presented in Section 2, namely the Grand Duchy of Finland within the Russian empire and the short-lived Septinsular Republic in the Ionian Sea. Thereafter, follows a discussion of the Austrohungarian views son cultural autonomy of Karl Renner and Otto Bauer and as the other side of the same coin, the Italian theories of the risorgimento (revival) which argued for the unification of regions in the Apennine peninsula.

II Early 19th Century Constitutional Efforts of Autonomy in Europe

Several European constitutions were adopted after the end of the Napoleonic era and many included elements of territorial autonomy. Below we shall examine some of them. It is remarkable that comparative analysis of such constitutional processes remains limited.[4]

II.A *The Grand Duchy of Finland*

Democratisation and constitutionalism was by no means something taking place only in 'the West'; nor did it take place only at state-wide level. Of course, as all major social processes, it did not occur out of the blue. An early example of such constitutional and international innovation was the position that Finland was able to retain and expand within the Russian empire after the Peace Treaty of Fredrikshamn (1809). After 1809 Finland kept its position as an autonomous region, similarly to the position it held under the Swedish crown, and became a Grand Duchy under Tsar Alexander I. This autonomous Grand Duchy was ruled under the Swedish Constitution of 1772 and the Swedish 1789 Act on Associations and Security. Politicians and intellectuals from the eastern half of the Kingdom, as Finland was often referred to in the 18th century, had had a major impact in the constitutional order of Sweden. Among them Anders Chydenius and Peter Forsskål stand out for their contribution to the adoption of the first Freedom of the Press Act and the strong position established for the freedom of expression in the Kingdom of Sweden. In fact, those constitutional acts were kept in force in Finland until 1919 when the first constitution of the independent Republic of Finland was adopted.[5]

In the Grand Duchy of Finland under Russian rule, the four estates, i.e. nobles, freemen, priests and farmers were retained, with their freedoms and rights guaranteed by the Tsar already before the signing of the Peace Treaty in the Diet of Borgå in March 1809. Finland got its own Council of Government (*Regeringskonselj*). It was especially under the heading of and through the intense and convincing work of Gustaf Mauritz Armfelt that Finland was able to gain a special position between the East and the West. Armfelt, who was born in the territory we now call Finland, had been the favourite general and assistant under Swedish king Gustaf III. He left Sweden in the turbulent times after 1809 to serve under the Russian Tsar in 1811 and until his death in 1814.[6] Armfelt's anti-Napoleonic sentiment was a dominant force in this move.

The Finnish Council of Government was after 1816 renamed as Senate and functioned as the autonomous region's central administration as well as its

4 *Ibid.*

5 Heikki Ylikangas, 'Finlands administrativa ställning inom det ryska riket' (1995) 80(3) *Historisk Tidskrift För Finland* 289.

6 Stig Ramel, *Gustaf Mauritz Armfelt 1757–1814: dödsdömd kungagunstling i Sverige, ärad statsgrundare i Finland* (Atlantis 1997).

supreme court. For that purpose, the Council had two sections, one on 'economic matters' and one on 'legal matters', precursors of today's modern ministries. Armfelt pursued also the creation a Committee for Finnish Affairs in St Petersburg to communicate directly with the Tsar on matters pertaining to the autonomous region. The Committee was comprised of representatives from Finland itself and kept its position until the end of the Russian era of Finland in 1917. There was thus a centralisation in the management of the Finnish autonomous region.

After all, this autonomy was relative and curtailed by the fact that the Tsar never gathered the parliamentary assembly of the four estates into a regular *lantdag* (Diet) between 1809 and 1863.[7] As argued by Heikki Yllikangas, this meant in effect autonomy and continuity in relation to the era before 1809, but without any guarantees of permanence against the will of the Tsar. Importantly, however, feudalism was not introduced in Finland and peasants remained one of the four estates.

However, the emphasis on the relative autonomy of Finland as a Grand Duchy under the Russian Tsar after 1809 and the potential it offered was not something automatically understood or internalised. One of the crucial formulations of it came in 1839 when Israel Hwasser, who was at that time professor of medicine at Uppsala University, published his arguments in a pamphlet.[8] Hwasser had served as professor of medicine at Åbo university for more than ten years (1817–1829) and argued in his publication about the importance of the Borgå Diet and the 'emancipation' achieved by the Finnish 'nation' which should not be underestimated with reference to the weaker position of 'Swedishness' in Finland. Within few years Hwasser's views became accepted and used to pursue the claim for full independence for Finland.

In another corner of the old continent a different experiment of autonomy was being developed.

II.B *The Septinsular Republic in the Ionian Sea*

One of the most intricate and interesting autonomous regions in the early 19th century was that of the *Republic of the Seven United Islands* in the Ionian Sea (1800–1807). The so called *Septinsular Republic* (1800–1807, *Επτάνησος Πολιτεία*) was originally granted limited self-government under the cooperative rule of the Russian and Ottoman empires when they took over the islands having defeated Napoleonic France in the Ionian Sea. Already earlier, the Sultan had tolerated the relative freedom that the islands had retained throughout the

7 *Ibid.*, 291.

8 Israel Hwasser, *Om Borgå lantdag och Finlands ställning 1812* (Leffler & Sebell 1839).

Bysantine era. The *Septinsular Republic* of 1800 – 1807 was an institutional innovation of relative autonomy under the dual authority of the two empires. The islands adopted then their own oligarchic constitution in 1803.[9] It provided for the separation of powers with much emphasis on the importance of legislative activity and participatory rights. It established the balance and institutional platforms for cooperation and communication between the seven islands concerned. It protected its citizens against retroactive legislation and it established the inviolability of the private sphere, including home and property in ways which seem very progressive and modern still today.

French supremacy was restored in 1807 after Napoleonic victories between 1805–1807, including in Austerlitz, but the British fleet established its presence in the Ionian Sea successively from 1809 on. Also under British control, the islands kept a measure of self-government in what came to be known as the United States of the Ionian Islands (Ἡνωμένον Κράτος τῶν Ἰονίων Νήσων, 1815–1864) as a consequence of the Congress of Vienna.[10] Following the Treaty on the Ionian Islands signed in Paris (1815) and the Constitutional Chart of the islands (1817), the so-called Maitland Constitution, the islands were supervised by a Lord High Commissioner appointed by the Crown. However, they also had a bicameral legislature with a Legislative Assembly and a Senate and Greek as well as Italian where used as official languages.[11]

One of the key figures in the political and constitutional life of the Ionian Islands in the first decade of the 19th century was Ioannis Kapodistrias, who was to become later the first head of state of the independent Greek State. Ioannis Kapodistrias (1776–1831), was born in Corfu, then under Venetian rule, in a noble family with roots in the Istrian peninsula. Before taking up this position, however, Kapodistrias, served for several years as an ambassador of the Russian Tsar and later as Minister for Foreign Affairs, starting in 1809, i.e. the same year when Finland passed over to the Russian Empire following the Treaty of Fredrikshamn between Russia and Sweden.[12] During those years Kapodistrias could use the Ionian experiences also in Switzerland where he served as Russian ambassador in 1813–1814. He was highly involved in the negotiation

9 Constitution of the Septinsular Republic (1803) available in Greek and Italian, <www.modern-constitutions.de> accessed 19 December 2017.

10 Maria Paschalidi, *Constructing Ionian Identities: The Ionian Islands in British Official Discourses 1815–1864*, thesis, University College London, 2009. Available at <http://discovery.ucl.ac.uk/19415/1/19415.pdf> accessed 02 September 2017.

11 Constitutional Chart of the Ionian Islands (1817), Article VII.

12 Helene Koukkou, *Jean Capodistria, 1776–1831: Ministre des Affaires Étrangères de Russie (1815–1822), Premier Gouverneur de la Grèce libérée (1828–1831): visionnaire et précurseur d'une Europe unie* (Kauffmann 2003).

and drafting of legal instruments needed to create the Swiss Confederation and the adoption of the 1815 Federal Treaty (*Pacte fédéral*) which was combined with the constitutions of the cantons, balancing between the interests of the strong and wealthy on the one hand and the poorer parts of the confederation on the other. While from the Russian point of view this was a move to neutralise as well as to detach Switzerland from the Napoleonic danger, from the point of view of the Swiss cantons, this was a major constitutional deliberation and negotiation to achieve the relative political independence and societal freedom as well as the cooperation between them primarily in matters of security. Coordination was possible through the Diet, periodic meetings of the representatives of the cantons.[13] The logic of federalism and of delimited and asymmetrical territorial autonomy are thus interlinked historically and conceptually, even though the two institutions are today often treated as distinct.

The above discussed cases allow us to note the recognition and toleration of relative autonomy from the side of Great Powers who wanted to exercise a measure of control, but who had much more important and difficult things to attend to.

The structures of government allowed for some measure of legislative powers and political representation while languages were respected. Local dynamics and international processes are in constant interaction and are disentangled with difficulty, in particular since key figures such as Armfelt and Kapodistrias change sides, appear as local as well as international actors and transgress the conceptual divisions of east and west, north and south. Processes of democratic empowerment, through the introduction of representative legislatures, occur both at a European and at a very local level. What is also interesting in the Finnish case and that of the Septinsular Republic is the fact that they are both balancing between the democratic and freedom oriented ambitions on the one hand, and on the other hand the wish to retain identity characteristics of a linguistic, religious or cultural character and confirm thus the broad scope of such aspirations. Both were constantly dependent upon the priorities of great powers, but not devoid of own will and room of manoeuvre.

The Septinsular Republic was succeeded by the *United States of the Ionian Islands*, this time under British control, and the islands were eventually handed over as a gift to the slowly growing state of Greece in 1864. Sovereignty over the archipelago was transferred to Greece by Great Britain in conjunction to the

13 Hurst Hannum, *Autonomy, Sovereignty and Self-Determination: The Accommodation of Conflicting Rights* (University of Pennsylvania Press 1996) 352–355.

enthronement of Danish prince William of Schleswig-Holstein-Sonderburg-Glücksburg under the name King George I (and second monarch) of Greece.

We shall now turn to two other efforts taking place a little later, this time in the regions and states we now call Austria and Italy.

III Two Sides of the Same Coin? Thinking about the Nationality Question and Regions in 19th Century Autria and Italy

III.A *Austrohungarian Efforts*

Karl Renner and Otto Bauer introduced the idea of National Cultural Autonomy at the end of the 19th century as a response to the societal and political pressures upon the highly diverse and by the time shaky Habsburg empire.[14] This empire included a vast number of regional identities and languages such as Czechs, Slovaks, Poles, Ukrainians, Slovenes, Croats, Serbs, Bosnians, Romanians, Italians, Hungarians and of course Germans at a time when the principle of nationality and cultural sovereignty became forceful political claims. Renner and Bauer developed the principle of personality and of non-territorial cultural autonomy in order to surpass the problem of territoriality based on a notion of monolithic linguistic areas.[15] The principle of personality meant that individuals would be free to declare their 'nationality' and belong to a national community of their choice. So, Renner and Bauer tried to identify a moderate and liberal version of the idea of nationality in which 'nations' would be constituted through free association rather than by birth or through a singular linkage between 'territory' and 'nation'.

It has been noted that it is easy to criticise Renner and Bauer on the basis of historical arguments, such as the fact that their ideas were never really put in practice, or that their proposals were not well accepted before the First World War even within the Socialdemocratic Party in Austria in which they

14 Karl Renner (under the name Rudolf Springer), *Der Kampf der österreichischen Nationen um den Staat* [The Struggle of the Austrian Nations for the State] (Deuticke 1902); followed by *Das Selbstbestimmungsrecht der Nationen in besonderer Anwendung auf Österreich* (Deuticke 1918); Otto Bauer, *The Question of Nationalities and Social Democracy*. In Emphraim Nimni (eds) and Joseph O'Donnell (transl.) (University of Minnesota Press 2000) (originally published as *Die Nationalitätenfrage und die Sozialdemokratie*, Vienna 1907). For an analysis *see* Fredrik Lindström, *Empire and Identity: Biographies of Austrian identity in an Age of Imperial Dissolution* (Lund Univ. 2002).

15 Jan Erk, 'Non-Territorial Millets in Ottoman History', in Tove Malloy and Francesco Palermo (eds), *Minority Accommodation through Territorial and Non-Territorial Autonomy* (OUP 2015) 119, 125.

were operating, or finally that they themselves abandoned this project after 1918. Such criticism, however, obfuscates the fact that we do have several examples today where elements of their thinking is found in hybrid models combining territoriality and personality elements and involving some measure of individual choice, such as we find in Finland for the Swedish-speakers on the mainland or in South Tyrol as two very different solutions but both relying on an interplay between territory and language or cultural identity.[16] Indeed, the importance of this school is perhaps precisely in its early affirmation and effort for accommodation of the complexity of modern societies in need of composite and multi-layered solutions. In contrast to radical internationalism or Leninist/Stalinist ideas which both assumed the eventual irrelevance and disappearance of cultural and ethnic divisions, Renner and Bauer took them as spiritual, given and as long-lasting and tried to accommodate them in the constitutional order of the disintegrating Habsburg empire.

The core criticisms against cultural nationalism or non-territorial autonomy at a conceptual and normative level have been voiced by many authors and over a long period of time. They are directed towards three main concerns. Firstly, the Austrohungarian school rests upon the unity created on the basis of socialist class struggle and workers' solidarity, rather than on liberal ideas of the possibility of a civic polity. Secondly, the Austrohungarian school rests upon prepolitical and premordial characteristics such as language, ethnicity and nationhood and conceived diverse minority groups as constant spiritual entities rather than affirming the social and political dynamics shaping such identities and formations. Finally, this school is not able to avoid the territorial dimension, since law and institutionalised politics always have such a dimension through core concepts such as jurisdiction and effective control. All these possible critiques, however, do not diminish the importance of the intellectual and conceptual contribution they made in linking personal freedom and collective identity in constitutional frameworks.

III.B *Italian Risorgimento between Unity and Regional Diversity*

While considerable attention has been given by academia to the Austrohungarian experiences and theories pertaining to territorial autonomy, it is once more important to remember that this was not the only trajectory or ideology of the 19th century, as has been argued all through this paper. In contrast to the

16 Rainer Bauböck, 'Political Autonomy or Cultural Minority Rights? A Conceptual Critique of Renner's Model', *EIF Working Paper Series*, No. 1 <https://eif.univie.ac.at/downloads/workingpapers/wp1.pdf> accessed 14 December 2017.

disintegration processes of the Habsburg empire, seconded surely by the other great powers of the time who tried to achieve gains out of this development, the creation of the modern nation-state also involved integrating processes as those in the Apennine peninsula resulting in the nation-state of Italy. The unification of Italy, directed partly against the Austrohungarian empire, and the incremental creation of the modern nation-state of Italy lasted far longer than a century, culminating in the revolutions of 1848 and the adoption of the Constitution of that year following plebiscites across the various regions of the peninsula. It was completed as such through the unification of the states of the peninsula, the Kingdom of Two Sicilies and the Kingdom of Sardinia including Piedmont under King Victor Emmanuel of the House of Savoy in 1861. Until that time the various regions of the peninsula had been controlled by different foreign powers and great disparity characterised the identities and experiences of its regions.

Democratic nationalism went hand in hand with democratic internationalism in the *risorgimento* (revival) movement. One of its core thinkers, Giuseppe Mazzini, believed that 'the question of territory' should overcome 'the question of liberty'.[17] Simultaneously, the Italian development was however also a step towards an incremental and controversial secular understanding of the nation-state and of politics.[18] Rome came in fact to remain under the jurisdiction of the Pope until 1870 when it became part of the Kingdom of Italy. The development of ideas of democratic nationalism – internationalism was also an effort by the Risorgimento core figures Giuseppe Garibaldi and Count de Cavour to exit from the Napoleonic grip which had much experimented with the regions and people of Italy and to enter into the modern liberal economic, technological and societal progress resting upon a firm belief in constitutions, individualism and individual liberties and the co-existence of different interests and life styles in the same polity in spite of the use of force and the wars that had preceded it and had made possible these constitutional innovations.[19] However, after the unexpected death of Giuseppe Garibaldi attention to the

17 Stefano Recchia and Nadia Urbinati (eds), – *A Cosmopolitanism of Nations: Giuseppe Mazzini's writings on democracy, nation building, and international relations* (Princeton University Press 2009) 16. On the ideas of Mazzini *see* also Denis Mack Smith, *Mazzini* (Yale University Press 1994).

18 Sabina Donati, *A political history of national citizenship and identity in Italy, 1861–1950* (Stanford University Press 2013).

19 Enrico Dal Lago 'Lincoln, Cavour and National Unification. American Republicanism and Italian Liberal Nationalism in Comparative Perspective' (2013) 3(1) *Journal of the Civil War Era* 85.

regional multiplicity of Italy decreased, leading contemporary scholars to argue about a process of centralisation or even 'Piedmontisation'.[20]

In both the Austrohungarian effort as well as in the Italian revival and unification process the concept of autonomy is understood as political self-government and both aspired to combine liberal individualism with multilevel governance. The issue of the constitutional and institutional entrenchment of regions and of representation and participation became essential in all the cases discussed in the present paper. These efforts rest on the liberal ideals of freedom and of emancipation, either for the subordinated groups of the Habsburg empire, the bilingual Finnish population, the Ionian islands or of the unified Italian peninsula which had been controlled by various foreign powers over many centuries. In all these cases we find thus elements of moderate nationalism which tries to combine unity and diversity, perhaps not so different from today's efforts towards European integration.

The above discussed cases and their historical context boil down to two main conclusions. The first is that the idea of territorial autonomy is closely linked to the process of the creation of the nation-state, but only partly. Territorial autonomy is one of the alternatives adopted for the legal and institutional accommodation of reasonable diversity and moderate nationalism in that process. None of the examples of the Grand Duchy of Finland, the Septinsular Republic or the Italian unification and regional accommodation aimed at monoethnic, monolinguistic and excluding models of territorial autonomy. Such institutional accommodation was understood as being possible through constitutionally ruled parliamentary institutions and the separation of powers theory. The second conclusion is that it in all those cases visions of autonomy assumed the equality of individuals as well as the importance of rights for all citizens. These two elements which are created contingently in the 19th century and turn of the 20th century, constitute also the core difference from other similar efforts for instance the system of Ottoman millets, which was very much directed towards cultural toleration, but did not seem to imply individual equality or democratic, institutionalised participation of minority groups in the running and decision-making of the empire.[21]

20 Martin Clark, *The Italian Risorgimento* (2nd edn, Pearson/Longman 2009); Martin Collier, *Italian Unification 1820–71* (Heinemann/Harcourt 2003).

21 Jan Hendrik Willem, Verzijl, *International law in historical perspective. Vol. 2, International persons* (Sijthoff, Leyden 1969) 339–359. Verzijl discusses various forms of relative autonomy and limited international personality such as suzerainty and vassalage. The Ottoman empire offered several examples of suzerainty, vassalage and relative autonomy, as was the case for instance for the *Principality of Transylvania* which was occasionally under a de facto dual vassalage, that of the Sultan and that of the Habsburg dynasty and kept

However, these European experiences were not the only openings towards the window of autonomy and multi-layered governance in the disintegrating empires and newly consolidated nation-states. Below, I shall explore what I call the colonial path to territorial autonomy which offers a different narrative of the trajectories to what we today call 'territorial autonomy'.

IV The Colonial Path to Autonomy and the League of Nations

The colonial angle of the process towards the institutionalisation of territorial autonomy is reflected starkly in international legal arguments and documents from early 20th century. One such example is discussed here. In January 1919 the US Department of State published a study by W.W. Willoughby and C.G. Fennwick entitled *Types of Restricted Sovereignty and Colonial Autonomy*. The study did not draw a sharp distinction between restricted sovereignty and colonial autonomy. Westel Willoughby himself had practiced law and received a Ph.D. at John Hopkins university in 1881, before the department of political science had been established; in fact, he was to be the first professor of political science at that university. But he was also an authority in constitutional matters, after the publication of his first book on the Supreme Court.[22] Charles Fenwick at Brun Mawr College, dedicated his life to international law and published extensively on collective security and peace matters.[23] His most known work is though *Wardship in International Law* (1919) which was published by the US Government Printing Office, similarly to the previously mentioned study on restricted sovereignty. Wardship as a concept is associated to the idea of a guardian of the interests of minors, whereupon the guardian takes decisions regarding the property and person of an under aged.[24]

As we understand in the first pages of the 1919 Willoughby – Fenwick study on restricted sovereignty, the core interest for the authors was to exclude such cases of restricted sovereignty from the category of sovereign states who could then be members of the League of Nations and claim sovereign equality. In the introduction, the authors explain and outline the conception of state

negotiating its relative freedom both with Vienna and with Constantinople in the 16th and 17th centuries.

22 Westel Willoughby, *The Supreme Court of the United States: Its history and influence in our constitutional system* (1890).

23 *See* e.g. Charles G. Fenwick, 'Security and Understanding Lead Toward World Peace' (July 1, 1924) 114(1) *The ANNALS of the American Academy of Political and Social Science* 153–154.

24 Antony Anghie, *Imperialism, Sovereignty and the Making of International Law* (CUP 2004) e.g. 87–90 and 312.

sovereignty that should be followed by the US administration in the negotiations for a charter the League of Nations:

> A distinction must be made from the outset between sovereign and semi-sovereign States as technical terms of international law. Sovereign States consist of those States which exercise supreme authority over all persons and property within their borders and are *completely independent* of all control from without. Such restrictions upon their conduct as they are subject to exist in consequence of the general rules of international law and do not involve legal dependence upon another State or States. Semi-sovereign States are those which lack some of the attributes of a full Sovereign State, but which at the same time possess sufficient independence in the organization of their Government and in the control of their affairs to be able to claim *some degree of international personality*. Owing to the absence of a clear line of division between sovereign and semi-sovereign States, it is difficult at times to say to which group a particular State of restricted sovereignty belongs. The question is of importance because of the implications of *membership within the family of nations*. Sovereign States alone are members of the family of nations in the strict sense; they alone possess international personality to the fullest degree and are endowed with the rights and burdened with the duties arising from international law. But it must be observed that certain restrictions upon sovereignty, such as the act of neutralization, are not regarded as relegating the State to the class of semi-sovereign States which are excluded from the family of nations.[25]

On the other hand, argued these authors, certain States which possess full sovereignty, 'but whose civilization is regarded as backward in comparison with that of Europe, are *excluded from the family of nations* because it is believed that they have not reached that stage of political development at which it is possible for them adequately to fulfil the obligations which international law imposes upon the adult international person' (emphasis added).

While cases such as Albania, Australia, Belgium, Bosnia – Herzegovina, Bulgaria, Canada, Cracow, Crete, Cyprus, New Zealand, Rumania, Savoy, Serbia, Switzerland and Tibet were included in this study, we note that e.g. Finland and Greece were not. While it was possible to talk of 'vassal', 'suzerain', 'dependent', 'protected', 'guaranteed' or 'neutralised' *states*, including many present-day

25 W.W. Willoughby and Charles G. Fennwick, *Types of Restricted Sovereignty and Colonial Autonomy* (Government Printing Office 1919) 23. *Emphasis added.*

countries in Europe, colonially controlled territories were described as 'autonomous colonies and dependencies' and 'dominions'.

All varieties of dependency and autonomy are exemplified in the British possessions, argue the authors of the above-mentioned study from 1919. This includes e.g. self-governing dominions (mentioning e.g. Canada and Australia); colonies in which the executive power is vested in the governor acting along with a nominated or elected legislative assembly or council (e.g. Malta); colonies in which both the legislative and the executive power are vested in the governor alone (e.g. Gibraltar); British possessions, *sui generis* such as British India, the Channel Isles, the Isle of Man; as well as territories under the British Settlements acts of 1887.

What is of interest for our study is the structural understanding of the 'extent of autonomy' which is one of the recurring subtitles of the study. Here, the authors discuss the organization of government with an executive and a legislative authority as well as the powers of government, in particular as regards any restrictions imposed on such government. Issues of citizenship and control of migration, fiscal matters, trade and treaty making powers are the areas focused upon by the authors. Among the restrictions identified, are obligations pertaining to minorities. For instance, Bulgaria is described as a 'vassal state subject to the suzerainty of Turkey' and reference is made to the 1878 Treaty of Berlin where the rights and interests of Turkish, Romanian and Greek populations should be safeguarded.[26]

The study concludes with reference to the concept of 'independence' that 'it would appear that 'independence' as a technical term employed in treaties relating to such protected States does not mean full freedom of action as a positive attribute, but rather the absence of any such restrictions upon the protected State as would amount to an infringement of its international personality and take from it a certain theoretical legal competence to be the arbiter of its own destiny'.[27] This leaves open the question of the interpretation of what constitutes an infringement of international personality and when a state really can be considered to be an arbiter of its own destiny. For instance, Willoughby and Fennwick note with regard to the 1907 treaty between Great Britain, Germany, France and Russia concerning respect for the integrity of Norway – which had just proclaimed its independence after the break-up of the Union with Sweden in 1905 – and to protect that country against attacks from others: 'This agreement falls short of putting Norway in the position of a

26 *Ibid.*, 6.

27 *Ibid.*, 16.

neutralized State, but it at least assures Norway protection as an independent State'.[28]

Indeed, contemporary debates on 'failed states' do not seem so different from the debates that took place one hundred years ago. However, the authors of the 1919 study on restricted sovereignty locate also an important *conceptual link between freedom and statehood*, which incorporated considerations of minorities. They follow in this move the teachings and political thought of the democratising movements around Europe, such as those of the Italian Giuseppe Mazzini who has been mentioned above.

The creation of the modern state conception was to offer the institutional tool for sufficient liberty of its population and what Dieter Grimm has called a 'move beyond heteronomy'.[29] Such freedom however could not ignore the needs of minorities; this was an insight already before the First World War. States and their populations were to be at least to a sufficient extent independent arbiters of their own destinies.

If we today define democracy, in its widest sense, as the embodying of the ideal of self-government, then all those efforts of adapted solutions of layered sovereignty, and what we today call multilevel-government, become apparent as steps towards the realization of – or impediments to the realization of – such freedom to define our own destiny. The generalisation of this claim beyond national state borders and polities was a crucial break with earlier medieval and colonial traditions. This remains valid, even if it was never intended by many of those who proclaimed it as an operational political goal to be practiced and defended.

President Wilson's famous fourteen points pronounced in January 1918 in front of the US Congress never referred to a universal right of self-determination.[30] This was the time of particularity of responses and such responses were needed with regard to Italy whose frontiers should be effected along 'clearly recognizable lines of nationality', Austria-Hungary whose 'peoples' place among the nations 'we wish to see safeguarded and assured, and should be accorded the freest opportunity to autonomous development' and the Ottoman Empire which was a more complicated case in Wilsonian thinking. While the 'Turkish portions' should be assured a secure sovereignty, the

28 *Ibid.*, 7.

29 Dieter Grimm, *Sovereignty: The Origin and Future of a Political and Legal Concept* (Columbia University Press 2015).

30 Allen Lynch, 'Woodrow Wilson and the principle of "national self-determination": a reconsideration' (2002) 28(2) *Review of international studies* 419. The speech of Woodrow Wilson can be found here: <http://avalon.law.yale.edu/20th_century/wilson14.asp> accessed 12 September 2017.

'other nationalities' should be assured an undoubted security of life and an 'absolutely unmolested opportunity of autonomous development'. Particular solutions were to be found also for Russia, Poland, Rumania, Serbia, Montenegro and Belgium. Moreover, with regard to colonial territories a 'free, open-minded, and absolutely impartial adjustment of all colonial claims, based upon a strict observance of the principle that in determining all such questions of sovereignty the interests of the populations concerned must have equal weight with the equitable claims of the government whose title is to be determined'. Self-determination in this conceptualisation was not a part of the colonial issue, nor was there any mention of autonomy or self-government linked to 'colonial territories'. This position was then also reflected in the League of Nations mandates system.[31]

Article 22 of the League of Nations Charter provided in its two first paragraphs:

> To those colonies and territories which as a consequence of the late war have ceased to be under the sovereignty of the States which formerly governed them and which are inhabited by peoples not yet able to stand by themselves under the strenuous conditions of the modern world, there should be applied the principle that the well-being and development of such peoples form a sacred trust of civilisation and that securities for the performance of this trust should be embodied in this Covenant.
>
> The best method of giving practical effect to this principle is that the tutelage of such peoples should be entrusted to advanced nations who by reason of their resources, their experience or their geographical position can best undertake this responsibility, and who are willing to accept it, and that this tutelage should be exercised by them as Mandatories on behalf of the League.

There were then peoples 'not able to stand by themselves under the strenuous conditions of the modern world' who needed 'tutelage' by the 'advanced nations' who have 'resources', 'geographical position' and are willing to take care of the 'well-being and development' of the those in need of the 'sacred trust of civilisation'. Among the founding members of the League of Nations we find Greece, Poland, Rumania, The State of Serbia-Croatia-Slovenia and Czechoslovakia. Three Nordic countries, Denmark, Norway and Sweden were among the thirteen countries invited to accede to the Covenant, with Norway

---

31 Susan Pedersen, *The Guardians: The League of Nations and the Crisis of Empire* (OUP 2015) 3.

as an independent state only since the dissolution of the Union with Sweden in 1905; these were then not among the founding members. We find, however, neither Finland nor any other state in Eastern Europe and the Balkans among the countries invited to accede to the Covenant and thus become members of the League of Nations.

Otherwise Article 1(b) of the Covenant provided as regards membership:

> Any fully self-governing State, Dominion or Colony not named in the Annex may become a Member of the League if its admission is agreed to by two-thirds of the Assembly, provided that it shall give effective guarantees of its sincere intention to observe its international obligations, and shall accept such regulations as may be prescribed by the League in regard to its military, naval and air forces and armaments.

While then, on the one hand, the idea of self-determination and the autonomous development of nations and peoples were pronounced, there were instruments ready to use in order to impose prescriptions on core aspects of sovereignty for a great number of 'new' countries.

V The Heritage of Contingency and Complexity of the two Previous Centuries

We have been able to explore above how the idea of autonomy has been employed and conceptualised under various circumstances across Europe. Linked to claims for democratisation, participation, emancipation and the acceptance of regional and cultural diversity, it was sometimes seen as part of an individualistic liberal process towards progress and modernity, or as an element of socialist class struggle. For some of its proponents it was primarily directed towards the spiritual community of 'peoples' sharing the same culture, language or religion while for others it was mainly an instrument of government which allowed a reasonable and acceptable distance and proximity between the centre and peripheries.

During the first decades of the 20th century this meant selective minority protection in Southeast and Eastern Europe and the former Austrohungarian empire under the cultural paradigm, the mandate system for the 'undeveloped' far away and under the economic management paradigm, and, finally, a few limited cases of internationally as well as constitutionally entrenched territorial autonomy, most notably the Åland Islands, Upper Silesia and Memel.

Today there is a great number of territorial autonomies around the world functioning under very different conditions and historical experiences.[32] Conceptualising territorial autonomy exclusively as a human right, diminishes its importance and history as a tool of government which is as useful and meaningful as other expressions of power-sharing such as local autonomy, devolution, federalism as well as broader integrative projects such as European integration. Territorial autonomy shares though with human rights the ideal of freedom. While human rights strive mainly towards individual freedom as self-government through meaningful choices and through prohibiting violations by the state, so also territorial autonomy aspires providing the inhabitants of a territory meaningful possibilities to maintain their regional culture(s) and lifestyles as well as interact and participate in the government of the state in which they live. Human rights and territorial autonomy rest on the same ideal of a balance between autonomy and interaction in the perennial quest of fine-tuning the relation between individual and society.

At the normative level this prompts us to three conclusions. First, the cultural rights to language, religion and to express them through the formation of voluntary associations must be accepted as universal and be limited only when violating the rights of others. Both minorities and majorities, indigenous peoples and migrants, to mention but few possible categories, have equal right to their respective, contingent, fluid and multiple identities. This means further that, of course, human rights must be respected also in and by territorial autonomies, as well as states. The assessment of what is reasonable and appropriate is always contingent and open to evaluation and re-assessment, including through international monitoring and judicial organs, such as the European Court of Human Rights and the Advisory Committee on the Framework Convention for the Protection of Persons belonging to National Minorities.

Secondly, minority rights when implemented in good faith can be both far reaching, meaningful and sufficient for many such groups. There is considerable overlap between participatory requirements within minority rights and good governance within territorial autonomy. The importance of instruments

32 In addition to works already mentioned above *see* for instance Maria Ackrén, *Conditions for Different Autonomy Regimes in the World. A Fuzzy-Set Application* (Åbo Akademi University Press 2009); Yash Ghai & Sophia Woodman, *Practising Self-Government. A Comparative Study of Autonomous Regions* (CUP 2013); Levente Salat et al. (eds), *Autonomy Arrangements around the World* (Institutul pentru Studierea Problemelor, Minoritatilor Nationale 2014).

such as the Framework Convention for the Protection of National Minorities and other similar documents in the Council of Europe can therefore be expected to persist and perhaps even increase, even if short term political circumstances and waves of populist nationalism may question claims for multiculturalism and diversity.

Our inventory in the present text shows that regional and cultural difference and diversity claims and efforts have been put forward and resulted in important societal and political innovation in the past two centuries and in spite of the contrary efforts of applied socialism, fascism, jihadism, colonialism and all kinds of fundamentalist ideologies with racist undertones.

Finally, territorial autonomy is not a universal solution but offers one way of overcoming what has been called 'the contested nature of the larger polity's history and boundaries'.[33] It can only work if there is an absence of oppression and there are tools available for participation and inclusion in the larger polity in ways of reflexive recognition, respect and reciprocity. Human rights, territorial autonomy and democratic government aim, historically and conceptually, at promoting self-government and emancipation, i.e. freedom at an individual and collective level. All in all, territorial autonomy is, therefore, not simply about optimal institutional design, even though much of modern authorship seems to assume so. Territorial autonomy offers an intermediate way between the protection of singular group identities and the complexity, historical and sociological, and the demands on and duties of states. For all those reasons territorial autonomy remains a suitable tool at times of increased complexity, mobility and globalisation as has been the case in the past centuries.

Such thinking presupposes of course that freedom is indeed the prime ideal in our lives, societies and states. As a concept and as an ideal, freedom needs continuous reformulation and assessment. It constantly poses the question: what is it really to be free and self-governed? In what ways do we want and need to be self-governed and autonomous and in what ways are we prepared, and even happy, to be subjected to the decisions of others? What is the meaning of freedom at a time of globalisation, complexity and entanglement and of decrease in the relative importance of the nation-state? If, however, freedom and self-government are replaced by other ideals, such as for instance economic or military superiority or constant material expansion, then the above normative considerations may well be irrelevant.

33 Bauböck, *loc. cit.*

Bibliography

Ackrén, Maria, *Conditions for Different Autonomy Regimes in the World. A Fuzzy-Set Application* (Åbo Akademi University Press 2009).

Anghie, Antony, *Imperialism, Sovereignty and the Making of International Law* (CUP 2004).

Bauböck, Rainer, 'Political Autonomy or Cultural Minority Rights? A Conceptual Critique of Renner's Model', *EIF Working Paper Series*, No. 1 <https://eif.univie.ac.at/downloads/workingpapers/wp1.pdf> accessed 14 December 2017.

Bauer, Otto, *The Question of Nationalities and Social Democracy* in Ephraim Nimni (eds) and Joseph O'Donnell (transl.) (University of Minnesota Press 2000) (originally published as *Die Nationalitätenfrage und die Sozialdemokratie*, Vienna 1907).

Clark, Martin, *The Italian Risorgimento* (2nd edn, Pearson/Longman 2009).

Collier, Martin, *Italian Unification 1820–71* (Heinemann/Harcourt 2003).

Constitution of the Septinsular Republic (1803) available in Greek and Italian, <www.modern-constitutions.de> accessed 19 December 2017.

Constitutional Chart of the Ionian Islands (1817), Article VII.

Dal Lago, Enrico, 'Lincoln, Cavour and National Unification. American Republicanism and Italian Liberal Nationalism in Comparative Perspective', (2013) 3(1) *Journal of the Civil War Era* 85–113.

Donati, Sabina, *A political history of national citizenship and identity in Italy, 1861–1950* (Stanford University Press 2013).

Erk, Jan, 'Non-Territorial Millets in Ottoman History', in Tove Malloy and Francesco Palermo (eds), *Minority Accommodation through Territorial and Non-Territorial Autonomy* (OUP 2015).

Fenwick, Charles G., 'Security and Understanding Lead Toward World Peace' (July 1, 1924) 114(1) *The ANNALS of the American Academy of Political and Social Science* 153–154.

Ghai, Yash and Sophia Woodman, *Practising Self-Government. A Comparative Study of Autonomous Regions* (CUP 2013).

Grimm, Dieter, *Sovereignty: The Origin and Future of a Political and Legal Concept* (Columbia University Press 2015).

Hannum, Hurst, *Autonomy, Sovereignty and Self-Determination: The Accommodation of Conflicting Rights* (University of Pennsylvania Press 1996).

Hwasser, Israel, *Om Borgå lantdag och Finlands ställning 1812* (Leffler & Sebell 1839).

Koukkou, Helene, *Jean Capodistria, 1776–1831: Ministre des Affaires Étrangères de Russie (1815–1822), Premier Gouverneur de la Grèce libérée (1828–1831): visionnaire et précurseur d'une Europe unie* (Kauffmann 2003).

Lindström, Fredrik, *Empire and Identity: Biographies of Austrian identity in an Age of Imperial Dissolution* (Lund Univ. 2002).

Lynch, Allen, 'Woodrow Wilson and the principle of "national self-determination": a reconsideration' (2002) 28(2) *Review of international studies* 419–436.

Mack Smith, Denis, *Mazzini* (Yale University Press 1994).

Recchia, Stefano and Urbinati, Nadia (eds), *A Cosmopolitanism of Nations: Giuseppe Mazzini's writings on democracy, nation building, and international relations* (Princeton University Press 2009).

Paschalidi, Maria, *Constructing Ionian Identities: The Ionian Islands in British Official Discourses 1815–1864*, thesis, University College London, 2009. Available at <http://discovery.ucl.ac.uk/19415/1/19415.pdf> accessed 02 September 2017.

Pedersen, Susan, *The Guardians: The League of Nations and the Crisis of Empire* (Oxford 2015).

Ramel, Stig, *Gustaf Mauritz Armfelt 1757–1814: dödsdömd kungagunstling i Sverige, ärad statsgrundare i Finland* (Atlantis 1997).

Renner, Karl (under the name Rudolf Springer), *Der Kampf der österreichischen Nationen um den Staat* [The Struggle of the Austrian Nations for the State] (Deuticke 1902).

Renner, Karl, *Das Selbstbestimmungsrecht der Nationen in besonderer Anwendung auf Österreich* (Deuticke 1918).

Salat, Levente et al. (eds), *Autonomy Arrangements around the World* (Institutul pentru Studierea Problemelor, Minoritatilor Nationale 2014).

Spiliopoulou Åkermark, Sia, 'Shifts in the Multiple Justifications of Minority Protection' (2007/08) 7 *European Yearbook of Minority Issues* 5–18.

Spiliopoulou Åkermark, Sia, *Justifications of Minority Protection in International Law* (Kluwer Law 1997).

Stråth, Bo and Martti Koskeniemi, 'Between Restoration and Revolution, National Constitutions and Global Law: An Alternative View on the European Century 1815–1914', EReRe Research project description, <http://blogs.helsinki.fi/erere-project/files/2008/11/erere_project.pdf> accessed 07 September 2017.

Verzijl, Jan Hendrik Willem, *International law in historical perspective. Vol. 2, International persons* (Sijthoff, Leyden 1969).

von Mohl, Robert, *Die Polizeiwissenschaft Nach Den Grundsätzen Der Rechtstaates* (2nd edn, 1844).

Willoughby, Westel, *The Supreme Court of the United States: Its history and influence in our constitutional system* (Baltimore 1890).

Willoughby, Westel and Charles G. Fennwick, *Types of Restricted Sovereignty and Colonial Autonomy* (Government Printing Office 1919).

Wilson, Woodrow, 'President Woodrow Wilson's Fourteen Points' <http://avalon.law.yale.edu/20th_century/wilson14.asp> accessed 12 September 2017.

Ylikangas, Heikki, 'Finlands administrativa ställning inom det ryska riket' (1995) 80(3) *Historisk Tidskrift För Finland* 289–303.

CHAPTER 4

Distribution of Legislative Powers in a Sub-state Context – a Comparison of Double Enumerations in Federal and Autonomy Settings

Markku Suksi

1 Introduction

There exist various kinds of sub-state entities that are based on the idea of self-government in the sense that the population of the area participates, primarily by means of electing regional decision-making bodies, in the exercise of law-making powers for the territorial entity. Primarily, such arrangements include constituent states in federations, such as Canada,[1] or autonomies in states that in principle are unitary, such as Denmark and Finland.

In a regular federation, the distribution of legislative powers between the federation and the states is normally arranged so that the federal legislature has enumerated powers, while the states are in the possession of so-called residual powers, perhaps as a reminder of their original sovereignty as states before being incorporated into the federation.[2] For a typical autonomy arrangement embedded in a unitary state, the situation is often the reverse: the parliament of the country functions on the basis of residual powers, while the autonomy arrangement has enumerated powers, granted to the autonomous entity either under the constitution of the country or by delegation under ordinary legislation of that country.

1 The author wishes to thank Director John Packer and the Human Rights Research and Education Centre at the University of Ottawa for hosting me during October-November and thus facilitating my research. This work was supported by the Pool of Professors (via Svenska Kulturfonden) in Finland under Grant Decision of 13 June 2013 and the Finnish Society of Sciences and Letters under Grant Decisions of 29 April 2015 and 24 August 2015.

2 In principle (although some variations of the theme exist), this seems to be so, for instance, in the United States, Australia, Switzerland, Germany (with a list of concurring powers), and Austria, supported by a supremacy clause or a principle of federal preemption. The distribution of powers in Belgium seems to be a further variation of this theme, and in Switzerland, too, the cantons are in the possession of an original sovereignty and residuality in legislative powers, although the Swiss constitution actually lands in an enumeration of both the federal and the cantonal powers, subject to the provision that federal law takes precedence over cantonal law.

 | DOI:10.1163/9789004405455_005

Amongst the 100 or so countries in the world that are either federally organized or that contain an autonomy arrangement, there exist a number of states where the distribution of legislative powers is organized in an atypical manner so as to warrant a study of these constitutional arrangements as a separate contingent:[3] constitutional systems that organize the distribution of legislative powers in a sub-state setting along two lists of enumerations, one for the national level and another for the sub-state level, are likely to feature interesting similarities and differences

Canada is an unusual federation in relation to its federal units, the provinces, just as Denmark and Finland are unusual unitary states in relation to those self-governing or autonomous entities that are part of their constitutional set-up (in this article, the Faroe Islands and the Åland Islands, respectively).[4] In Canada, the legislative powers of both the federal level and the provinces are enumerated in lists of law-making powers that in principle are meant to be exclusive in relation to each other. In fact, Canada has sometimes been characterised as a quasi-federal.[5] In Denmark, the position of the Faroe Islands (and Greenland) in relation to Denmark proper is often characterized in terms of a commonwealth, while in Finland, the Åland Islands has a *sui generis* status typical of a host of other autonomous territories in the world. In a manner similar to Canada, in Denmark and Finland, the legislative powers of not only the legislative assemblies of the autonomies but also the national parliaments are enumerated. The focus of this article is therefore on the issue of double enumeration of legislative powers, because the distribution of powers in

---

3 Other examples that could be mentioned are the relationship between mainland China, on the one hand, and Hong Kong and Macau, on the other, as well as the relationship between France and New Caledonia. In India, both the Union and the states exercise their legislative powers on the basis of their respective exclusive enumerations of legislative competences and both orders of government on the basis of a listing of concurring powers, but the federation or the centre nonetheless seems to be in the possession of the residual powers. This feature makes India at least an untypical federation. It could be argued that the Indian distribution of powers should also be dealt with in this analysis, but for reasons of space, India will be excluded here, although might be analysed at some further point of time in another piece of research.

4 The distribution of legislative powers between the Danish Parliament and the Legislative Assembly of Greenland is organized in a manner that comes close to the solution concerning the Faroe Islands, but does not entail any enumeration of powers for the Danish Parliament and allows the Greenlandic legislature to transfer by its own decisions law-making powers from Denmark to Greenland for the purposes of legislating for Greenland. In fact, in the Self-Government Act concerning Greenland 2009, the Danish Parliament went so far as to make possible the transfer of all legislative areas to Greenland and the declaration of independence by Greenland.

5 *See* K.C. Wheare, *Federal Government*, (OUP, 4th edn, 1964) 19. *See* also Gregory J. Inwood, *Understanding Canadian Federalism – an Introduction to Theory and Practice* (Pearson 2013) 108, 264–267.

federal settings and also for more regular autonomy arrangements has already been dealt with in other pieces of research.[6] The aim is here to draw attention to double enumeration as one strategy of determining how legislative powers could be delineated in a sub-state setting. Until now, this method of distribution of powers has not been subjected to much systematic analysis.

The research questions in this article relate to the phenomenon of divided sovereignty, which poses a more general legal-theoretical problem: how and where can law be made and under which conditions? More specifically on the issue of double enumeration of legislative powers, how is it possible to split up the legal order in two material spheres that are exclusive in relation to each other so that each legislator knows, at least by and large, its own area of competence? As a consequence of law-making in two separate fields of competence, the issue is the following: how are possible competence problems adjudicated?

This article examines the topic of distribution of legislative powers from the perspective of constitutional law and uses the method of comparative law to provide replies to the research questions. It is hoped that the article could provide some reference points for different countries when constitutional changes involving sub-state matters are contemplated and that the article could contribute to debates concerning sub-state solutions by shedding light on how sovereignty can be divided internally within a state.

II A Framework for Various Sub-state Situations

From the point of view of self-government as a combination of participation through elections and exercise of law-making powers, various kinds of sub-state entities can be identified. On one dimension, there is a distinction between territorial autonomies and federal entities, while on another dimension, there is a distinction between legislative powers proper and mere exercise of governmental powers in the form of administrative self-government of a regional nature (*see* below, figure 1).

As indicated above, in a classical federation law-making powers are enumerated for the federation, while the residual powers belong to the constituent states. At the same time, there is some form of institutional representation for the states at the federal level, while the populations of the several states

6 On distribution of powers in federal settings, *see*, e.g., Ronald L. Watts, *Comparing Federal Systems* (McGill-Queen's University Press 2008) and George Anderson, *Federalism: an Introduction* (OUP 2008). On distribution of powers in autonomy settings, *see*, e.g., Thomas Benedikter, *The World's Working Regional Autonomies: an Introduction and Comparative Analysis* (Anthem Press 2007) and Markku Suksi, *Sub-State Governance through Territorial Autonomy* (Springer-Verlag 2011).

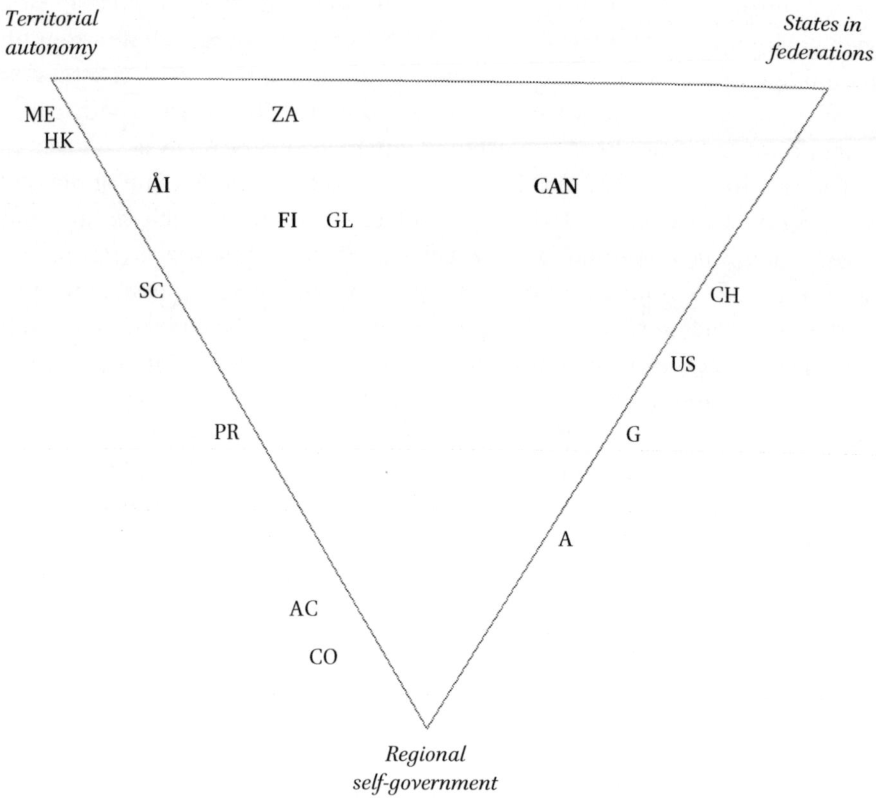

FIGURE 1 Comparison between territorial autonomy, states in federations and regional self-government. Please note that the positions of the different sub-state entities in the figure are approximate and of a work-in-progress nature. The abbreviations stand for the following: ME = Memel Territory; ZA = Zanzibar; HK = Hong Kong; ÅI = Åland Islands; CAN = Canada; FI = Faroe Islands; GL = Greenland; SC = Scotland; PR = Puerto Rico; AC = Aceh; CO = Corsica; CH = Switzerland; US = United States; G = Germany; A = Austria.

participate in the exercise of federal powers by means of regular elections. This set-up is practiced in, *inter alia*, Switzerland, Germany and Austria, and the European Union may also be said to conform to this idea of organization, although the EU is not normally referred to as a federation but as a union of states. What is typical for federations (and also for the EU) is the principle of federal supremacy, that is, federal pre-emption of the legislative powers of the constituent states in the event their legislative decisions are in conflict with the federal legislation. The principle of federal supremacy tends towards a piecemeal enlargement of the powers of the federal law-maker, because a constant re-definition of the competence line is taking place.

An autonomy arrangement is in many ways a mirror image of a federal arrangement. The legislative powers are residual for the national level, while they are enumerated for the autonomous entity. There is no institutional representation at the national level, but regular elections create an avenue for the population of the autonomous entity to participate in national decision-making. In addition, it appears to be a feature of a significant number of autonomy arrangements that there is an absence of the supremacy doctrine. This means that in principle, the legislative body of the central government is not competent to enact law within the sphere of competence of the sub-state legislature, although the central government might want to push its legislative powers in an illegitimate and unconstitutional manner into the area of the autonomy powers.

Apart from typical federal and autonomy situations, a number of mixed cases exist, such as Canada with respect to its provinces, Denmark with respect to the Faroe Islands (and in a similar manner with respect to Greenland, although Greenland will not be dealt with here) and Finland with respect to the Åland Islands. As concerns representation, there is no actual institutional representation of these entities in the national legislatures, but there is a senate in Canada that features appointed persons drawn from the various provinces, while the Faroe Islands and the Åland Islands have designated seats in the unicameral parliaments of the two countries. However, what makes all of these cases particular is that the legislative powers of both the national level and the sub-state level are enumerated, leading to exclusive law-making powers in both enumerations. At the same time, a defining feature emerges that unites these jurisdictions, namely the absence of a general supremacy doctrine or national preemption. This means that the central government and the lawmaker of the entire country is normally not going to interfere in the exercise of the law-making competences in the sub-state entities and that therefore, these sub-state entities are very autonomous in the exercise of their respective spheres of competence.

III Sub-state Arrangements with Double Enumerations

In the Constitution of Canada 1867,[7] the principal enumeration of competences for the two law-making spheres is established in Section 91 on the powers of the Parliament and Section 92 on the exclusive powers of the provincial legislatures. With certain additions from other provisions in the Constitution,

7 For the Constitution Act 1867, *see* <http://laws-lois.justice.gc.ca/eng/Const//index.html #docCont> accessed 4 January 2018.

such as the treaty powers, the matters such as regulation of trade and commerce, unemployment insurance, naturalization and aliens and criminal law are assigned to the federal level on the basis of Section 91 of the Canadian Constitution. With certain additions from other provisions in the Constitution, the matters such as direct taxation for provincial purposes, local government, property and civil rights in the province, administration of justice in the province and penalties for violation of provincial law are assigned to the provincial level on the basis of Section 92 of the Canadian Constitution.

Interestingly, the enumerations of the powers of the federation and of the provinces are defined as exclusive in the opening paragraphs to the two Sections, although there is an indication of some residuality attached to the federal powers in the opening paragraph of Section 91 by means of the grant to the federation of powers to make laws for the entire country for the peace, order and good government (hereinafter: p.o.g.g.) in relation to all matters not coming within the classes of subjects assigned exclusively to the legislatures of the provinces. This partial and – as we shall see – limited residuality for the federal law-maker is yet another indication of the unusual construction of the Canadian federalism when compared with other federations, because normally, one would expect to find residuality in federations at the sub-state level. The double enumeration in Canada also indicates that the federation is in control of a greater part of so-called public law at the same time as the federal law-maker is in charge of certain important facets of so-called private law, while the provinces are competent in both public and in particular private law and in matters of a merely local or private nature in the province. The characteristics of this double enumeration are at least in part explained by the fact that the legal order of Quebec is of a French provenance. Because the two enumerations are already 150 years old and have remained largely unamended, there exist pressures on the constitutional interpretation to accommodate the double enumeration to the conditions of today.

The set-up is somewhat similar concerning structure of the double enumeration for the Åland Islands, although it is not directly established by provisions in the Constitution of Finland 2000. Section 75(2) of the Constitution makes reference to the fact that the Åland Islands have legislative powers, but Section 75 and Section 120, in particular, are based on the idea that there is a separate piece of law that establishes the modalities of the self-government or autonomy of the Åland Islands. The recognition of the principle that two legislators exist within the Finnish constitutional order is followed up in the Self-Government Act of Åland 1991,[8] which establishes two lists of legislative powers, one for the

8 For a translation into English of the Self-Government Act 1991, *see* <http://www.finlex.fi/fi/laki/kaannokset/1991/en19911144.pdf> accessed 4 January 2018.

national parliament in Section 27 and another for the Legislative Assembly of the Åland Islands in Section 18. Hence the double enumeration is not found in the Constitution, as in Canada, but in an Act of a constitutional nature that in some countries would be understood as an organic law.

Under Sections 27 and 29 of the Self-Government Act, the issues such as freedom of association, freedom of movement, general criminal law, abortion, telecommunications and social insurance are under the legislative competence of the Parliament of Finland also in respect of the territory of the Åland Islands. According to Section 18, the Legislative Assembly of the Åland Islands shall have legislative powers in the territory of Åland in respect of issues such as local government law and elections, firefighting and rescue service, education, social welfare, health and environment.

The starting point with the two enumerations in relation to the Åland Islands is to establish, once and for all, the distribution of legislative powers for the jurisdiction of Åland so that in some matters, the Parliament of Finland is competent to legislate for the Åland Islands, meaning that Åland is not exempted from the application of the national law in these fields of law, while in some other matters, the Legislative Assembly of the Åland Islands is competent to legislate for the Åland Islands, meaning that the jurisdiction of Åland is exempted from the application of national law in those fields of law, where the legislator of the Åland may enact law or may refrain from enacting law (in which case national law shall not gain applicability so as to fill the normative vacuum). This constitutional arrangement is established in the Self-Government Act 1991, which in itself is not, however, part of the formal Constitution, although it certainly is of a constitutional nature, for instance, because it can only be amended in the same order as the Constitution and by the consent of the Legislative Assembly of Åland.[9]

Generally speaking (but with certain exceptions), the Parliament of Finland is in charge of the so-called private law for the purposes of the Åland Islands

9 Currently, the Government of Finland is considering a committee proposal to enact a new self-government act for the Åland Islands, where the principle of double enumeration would be formally changed so that in principle, the Parliament of Finland would keep enumerated powers, while the Legislative Assembly of the Åland Islands would have residual powers. However, in practice, double enumeration would result from the fact that the current lists of enumeration would constitute the starting point for transfer of competence decisions by which the Legislative Assembly of the Åland Islands would determine, in individual pieces of legislation, that a certain competence is transferred from the Parliament of Finland to the Legislative Assembly of the Åland Islands. The proposal is modelled against the background of the distribution of competence system of the Faroe Islands. A smaller portion of the powers of the Parliament of Finland can already now be transferred, under Section 29, from the Parliament of Finland to the Legislative Assembly of the Åland Islands, but the legislative decision is then passed by the Parliament of Finland. *See* Suksi (n 6) 303 f.

and of the general criminal law, while the Legislative Assembly is in charge of the so-called public law for the purposes of the Åland Islands, including such criminal law that introduces sanctions within the fields of competence of the Åland Islands. Because most of the Ålandic powers are in the sphere of public law (with some exceptions for private law), they clearly imply the need and the existence of relatively broad administrative decision-making machinery in individual cases of implementation of the acts of Åland. In fact, the public sector of the Åland Islands appears, proportionally speaking, to be greater than that of mainland Finland, partly because of this public law orientation.

For Faroe Islands, no provisions on the distribution of legislative powers exist in the Constitution of Denmark 1953, which is curious because the autonomy arrangement was instituted as early as 1948 by ordinary legislation and it could have been taken into account and recognized when the Constitution of Denmark was enacted in 1953 by means of inserting explicit provisions on the autonomy of the Faroe Islands.[10] Perhaps the arrangement is today best described as one based on customary constitutional law or a constitutional convention. At any rate, the legislative powers of the Faroe Islands, first identified in the Home Rule Act 1948,[11] are today supplemented by the provisions in the Act on the Transfer of Legislative Powers 2005 (hereinafter: the Takeover Act),[12] both of which are pieces of ordinary law enacted by means of simple majority in the Danish Parliament. The latter act amends the former by making it possible for the Faroese legislative assembly to transfer, by its own legislative decisions, legislative powers from the Danish Parliament and add them to those powers that the Legislative Assembly of the Faroe Islands already has either on the basis of explicit reference in the 1948 Act or on the basis of earlier transfer decisions. This means that an enumeration of legislative powers of the Faroe Islands is emerging in a piecemeal manner, but is of a more fragmentary nature than any explicit listing in a constitution or comparable act: the various separate transfer decisions can, taken together, be understood as such an enumeration. At the same time, the situation is exceptional in that the sub-state

10 However, four provisions in the Danish Constitution mention the Faroe Islands (sections 28, 32, 42, 86), but they deal with the representation of the Faroe Islands in the Danish Parliament and with the organization of the national referendum in the Faroe Islands and with the voting age in local government elections.

11 Lov nr. 137 af 23. Marts 1948 om Færøernes Hjemmestyre, or the so-called Home Rule Act 1948, available in translation into English at <http://stm.dk/_p_13089.html> accessed 4 January 2018.

12 Lov nr. 578 af 24. Juni 2005 om de færøske myndigheders overtagelse af sager og sagsområder, or the so-called Takeover Act 2005, available in translation into English at <http://stm.dk/_p_13089.html> accessed 4 January 2018.

entity can take over by its own decision legislative powers from the national law-maker. There is, however, a limit to this take-over, because Section 1(2) of the 2005 Act prohibits the transfer of a small number of enumerated matters, leaving the following ones in the hands of the Danish Parliament: the Constitution; citizenship; the Supreme Court; foreign-, security- and defence policy; and currency and fiscal policy.

With these limitations by means of the listed matters, an enumeration is established also for the national law-maker, mainly in the core areas of public law.[13] The powers that can be transferred after negotiations between the governments of Denmark and the Faroe Islands include matters such as industrial property rights, air traffic, passport, criminal law and aliens affairs (several of the matters have since been transferred). In addition to these, enumerations of matters can be found in the 2005 Takeover Act and in the 1948 Home Rule Act that place powers with the Parliament of Denmark and that can be transferred without negotiations on the basis of legislative decisions of the Legislative Assembly of the Faroe Islands. Apparently in order to establish which competences that still remain with the Danish Parliament, the Legislative Assembly of the Faroe Islands enacted on 10 May 2006 a particular Faroese Act in which all those 24 competences were listed that had not as of that point of time been transferred from the Danish Parliament to the Faroese Legislative Assembly but that could be transferred (and which, as a consequence, are not featured in the enumeration of matters that according to Section 1(2) of the 2005 Takeover Act belong to the Danish Parliament).[14] The matters still held by the Parliament in 2006 that can be later transferred without negotiations to the Legislative Assembly included matters such as emergency services, general retirement pension, health, hospitals and lighthouses (several of the matters have since been transferred).

Because individual matters are transferred from the Danish Parliament on the basis of separate legislative decisions of the Legislative Assembly of the Faroe Islands, it is possible to say that an ever increasing list of competence, fragmented in nature because it manifests itself in separate legislative enactments, is being created in the Faroe Islands. Hence in principle, both

13 Concerning Greenland, where takeover can be complete so as to lead to independence, because no list of matters exist where transfer from the national parliament to the Faroe Islands is prohibited.

14 Løgtingslóg nr. 41 frá 10. mai 2006 um ræði á málum og málsøkjum, sum seinast broytt við løgtingslóg nr. 55 frá 26. mai 2011, at <http://www.logir.fo/Logtingslog/41-fra-10-05-2006-um-raedi-a-malum-og-malsokjum-sum-seinast-broytt-vid-logtingslog> accessed 4 January 2018.

law-makers are operating on the basis of an enumeration, although current practice could display characteristics that deviate from this general proposition.

IV Management of Double Enumerations

As established above, the federal parliament of Canada has,[15] according to Section 91 of the Constitution, legislative powers both in the field of public law (including criminal law) and private law, and the federation also exercises treaty powers, while the provincial legislatures have law-making powers in similar spheres, except that the provinces do not have treaty powers. Only a minimum of amendments have introduced new matters into the above scheme of distribution of legislative powers, which means that over time, a need has emerged to develop the relationship between the legislative powers of the federation and the provinces by means of interpretation. Initially, the Judicial Committee of the Privy Council in Britain was the body that interpreted the competence line, but since 1949, the Supreme Court of Canada is in charge of this dimension of constitutional interpretation.

From the outset, the starting point has been, on the basis of the chapeaus to Sections 91 and 92, that the legislative powers of the federation and the provinces are exclusive in relation to each other. For a good part of the time the Constitution has operated, the ideology concerning the two spheres of competence was based on the idea of watertight compartments, which means that there was little or no interaction between the two spheres of competence. During the past several decades, however, the understanding of cooperative federalism has been gaining ground and constitutes today the main approach to how law-making powers are exercised in Canada. Cooperative federalism is often driven by the federal government with financial incentives created for the provinces, but provinces have also developed horizontal mechanisms of cooperation.

Even within the paradigm of cooperative federalism, the spheres of competence established in Sections 91 and 92 are highly relevant for law-making activities in Canada, when both the federal and the provincial legislators feel the need to act in the modern society with changing legislative objectives. As a consequence, the Supreme Court of Canada has developed a testing sequence for breach of the competence line that is, at least in principle, applicable in relation to both federal and provincial legislation. The first step of the testing sequence is the so-called pith and substance test, which deals with the validity

15 This section is based on Markku Suksi, *Double Enumeration of Legislative Powers in a Sub-State Context – A Comparison between Canada, Denmark and Finland* (Springer-Verlag, 2018) pp. 43–77.

of the impugned legislation. If the law is not faulted on this basis, the second step could be the so-called interjurisdictional immunity test, which deals with the applicability of the impugned law. In case the law is not declared inapplicable on this basis, a third step could follow, the so-called paramountcy test, which deals with the operability of the impugned law.

The analytical framework applied to a piece of law, whether federal or provincial, when inconsistency with the distribution of legislative powers in Sections 91 and 92 is claimed, starts with a so-called "pith and substance" text, which tries to extract the dominant feature, the main thrust or the true nature and character of the law, after which the court assigns the legislation to a federal or a provincial head of power. This is done for detecting whether the impugned legislation aims at a subject matter outside the jurisdiction of the legislative body enacting it.[16] The aim of this test is actually not to enforce exclusivity, because it instead creates tolerance for the co-existence of laws of the two orders of government in the same field, that is, recognizes the possibility of overlap *intra vires* between federal and provincial laws as long as the enactment of the one legislator does not enter the essence of law-making powers of the other legislator.[17] However, if such an intrusion into the essential character of the powers of the other law-maker is found, there is a successful validity attack at hand and the review will result in the legislation in question being declared of no force or effect, that is, the impugned law is invalid (*ultra vires*).[18] Invalidity is in such a case *ex tunc*, that is, from the moment of entering into

16 Peter W. Hogg, *Constitutional Law of Canada* (Thomson & Carswell, 5th edn suppl, Vols 1 & 2, 2014) ss. 15.4 – 15.5(a).

17 As the Supreme Court said in the *Reference re Securities Act*, [2011] S.C.J. No. 66, 2011 SCC 66, [2011] 3 S.C.R. 837 (S.C.C.), "the Canadian constitutional law has long recognized that the same subject or 'matter' may possess both federal and provincial aspects. This means that a federal law may govern a matter from one perspective and a provincial law from another. The federal law pursues an objective that in pith and substance falls within Parliament's jurisdiction, while the provincial law pursues a different objective that falls within provincial jurisdiction (*Canadian Western Bank v Alberta*, [2007] S.C.J. No. 22, 2007 SCC 22). This concept, known as the double aspect doctrine, allows for the *concurrent application* of both federal and provincial legislation, but it does not create *concurrent jurisdiction* over a matter (in the way, for example, s. 95 of the Constitution Act, 1867 does for agriculture and immigration)".

18 In the *Reference re Securities Act, ibidem*, the Supreme Court found that the pith and substance of the draft Act was outside of the federal power in Section 91(2), "the regulation of trade and commerce" and entered the provincial legislative powers established in Section 92(13, 16) on "property and civil rights" and on "matters of a merely local or private nature", namely the regulation of contracts, property and professions. In *Canadian Western Bank v Alberta*, [2007] S.C.J. No. 22, 2007 SCC 22, application of provincial insurance legislation under Section 92(13) to banks created under Section 91(15) by federal legislation was found constitutionally valid in the "pith and substance" test, without any need to engage interjurisdictional immunity or paramountcy.

force. If only a part of a law is challenged, the provision of the act may be saved under the so-called ancillary doctrine or necessary incidental doctrine, but that requires that the statute considered as a whole must be valid.[19] It is also possible to use this test in relation to draft laws in situations where they are referred to the Court for advisory opinion. This doctrine of "pith and substance" facilitates cohabitation of two legislators, but it has sometimes been held that the "pith and substance" test seems to be somewhat tilted in favour the validity of federal law over provincial law.

The second part of the analytical framework is the "interjurisdictional immunity" test, which asks whether law, having been found to be constitutionally valid, is inapplicable to particular persons, places or things by virtue of those subjects being within the exclusive jurisdiction of the other level of government.[20] In practice, interinstitutional immunity provides for a limited degree of immunity mainly for federal undertakings from laws enacted by the provinces and thus deals with the application of the law. After the *Canadian Western Bank* and *Lafarge* judgments, the scope of this doctrine is narrower than it used to be, because it is not enough that the impugned law affects undertakings regulated by the other order of law, but actually impairs their activities.[21] A successful applicability attack results in the legislation being left intact as drafted, but the law is "read down" so as to be inapplicable in the context in question. This test has mainly been used to protect federal acts, rarely provincial acts, in a manner which produces some lack of reciprocity, but this doctrine was limited by the Supreme Court in a number of relatively recent cases.[22]

---

19 *See* Hogg (n 16) s. 15.6, 15.9(c). For the ancillary powers test, *see General Motors of Canada v City National Leasing*, [1989] S.C.J. No. 28. The application of the ancillary powers doctrine could be seen as favouring the federal parliament's powers, but in the case of *Quebec (Attorney General) v. Lacombe*, 2010 SCC 38, [2010] 2 S.C.R. 453, it is clarified that the doctrine can also be applied for the benefit of the provinces.

20 *See* Hogg (n 16) s. 15.8(c), s. 15.9.

21 *British Columbia v Lafarge* [2007] S.C.J. No. 23, 2007 SCC 23. *See Quebec (Attorney General) v Canadian Owners and Pilots Association*, 2010 SCC 39, [2010] 2 S.C.R. 536, in which a divided court (7–2) found that provincial law on protection of agricultural land that had the effect of preventing aerodromes, enacted under Section 92(13, 16) of "property and civil rights" and "matters of a merely local or private nature" as well as Section 95 on "agriculture" and thus valid, violated the federal general power in the area of aeronautics enacted on the basis of the chapeau of Section 91 "to make laws for the peace, order, and good government of Canada". The paramountcy doctrine did not apply, because there was not found any operational conflict or frustration of federal purpose.

22 As concluded in Hogg (n 16) s. 15.8(f), "[t]he doctrine of interjurisdictional immunity ought to be reciprocal, protecting provincial subjects from incursions by *federal* laws", with examples provided. *See* also the cases of *Reference re Assisted Human Reproduction*

The third part of the analytical framework is the "paramountcy" doctrine, that is, whether a provincial law, found to be both valid and applicable, is inconsistent with valid federal law and therefore inoperative under the doctrine of paramountcy. The doctrine of paramountcy can be viewed as an exception to the "pith and substance" doctrine, because it provides for the priority of federal law in cases where there is, in individual application situations, a direct conflict between federal and provincial law that affects the operability of provincial law.[23] In the case of *Canadian Western Bank*, the Supreme Court summarized the doctrine by holding that conflict can manifest itself in two ways, in a narrow "impossibility of dual compliance" when it is not possible to comply with both laws at the same time, and in a broader "frustration of federal purpose" when the operation of a provincial law would frustrate the purpose of federal law.[24] However, the "standard for invalidating provincial legislation on the basis of frustration of federal purpose is high",[25] which means that the paramountcy doctrine is not the same as a general doctrine of federal preemption or precedence. A successful operability attack results in provincial legislation being declared inoperative for as long as the conflict in question continues to exist.[26] In areas where the paramountcy doctrine can be applied, the federal Parliament is therefore ultimately supreme and the provincial legislatures are subordinate.[27]

Although far-reaching exclusivity, to the point of amounting to an idea of "watertight compartments" of an earlier Canadian type, exists between the

Act and *Canada (Attorney General) v PHS Community Services Society* for arguments that interjurisdictional immunity should also apply to provinces, not only to the federation.

23 As concluded in the case of *Marine Services International Ltd v Ryan Estate*, [2013] S.C.J. No. 44, 2013 SCC 44 (S.C.C.) "federal paramountcy applies where there is an inconsistency between a valid federal legislative enactment and a valid provincial legislative enactment, but not between a common law rule and a valid provincial law".

24 *Canadian Western Bank v Alberta*, [2007] S.C.J. No. 22, 2007 SCC 22. For an analysis of the paramountcy doctrine, rich in case materials, *see* Hogg (n 16) ch. 16.

25 *Marine Services International Ltd v Ryan Estate*, [2013] S.C.J. No. 44, 2013 SCC 44 (S.C.C.).

26 As stated in Hogg (n 16) s. 16.6, the paramountcy doctrine "will affect the operation of the provincial law only so long as the inconsistent federal law is in force. If the federal law is repealed, the provincial law will automatically 'revive' (come back into operation) without any reenactment by the provincial Legislature".

27 *See British Columbia v Lafarge* [2007] S.C.J. No. 23, 2007 SCC 23, in which the Supreme Court did not find the interjurisdictional immunity test applicable, but decided the case on grounds of federal paramountcy, because there was the federal Marine Act enacted on the basis of Section 91(10) and a provincial land use by-law enacted on the basis of Section 92(8, 13, 16) simultaneously in force, both incapable of simultaneous enforcement so as to create an operational conflict because a judge could not have given effect to both the federal law and the municipal law, and therefore, federal law set aside provincial law.

legislative competences of the Parliament of Finland and the Åland Islands, some pith and substance and even ancillary powers thinking is from time to time visible in the opinions of the Supreme Court concerning the competence of the Åland Islands. In an Opinion concerning the Ålandic Act on the Amendment of the Ålandic Act on the Application in the Åland Islands of the Parliament's Enactments concerning Alcohol,[28] the Supreme Court noted that already early drafting documents to the Ålandic Act had made the point that the obligation for the holder of a license to serve alcohol to offer a receipt when alcohol is sold belongs to the legislative competence of the Parliament of Finland, while the Ålandic Act itself would be applied within the Ålandic jurisdiction. For reasons such as fight against corruption, tax control, accounting, and consumer protection, the proposal of the Government of the Åland Islands to the Legislative Assembly goes on to hold, on the basis of Section 27(42) and the principles underlying the Self-Government Act, that lawmaking competence is on the Parliament. However, the Supreme Court held that there is no reason to focus on smaller terminological differences and that handing over a bill, receipt and other certificate can be connected with the same act of verifying that payment of a purchase has taken place.

Neither the fact that the Parliament of Finland was going to receive a legislative proposal that would introduce an overlapping rule, nor the fact that both the government of Finland and of the Åland Islands are of the opinion that general rules on handing over a receipt is within the legislative competence of the Parliament were relevant factors for the determination of whether or not the Åland Islands have legislative competence in the matter. Instead, the Supreme Court thought that as long as no general duty to hand over a receipt has existed, it has been natural to derive such a duty from the area of law within which this duty has been introduced. As a consequence, it is natural to refer the limited duty to hand over a receipt on the occasion of serving alcoholic beverages to the same area of law as the actual sale. Therefore, a business operator who has a license to serve alcoholic beverages can also be placed under a duty to hand over a receipt for such sales. The fact that this duty serves several objectives of control does not diminish its proximity to the license to serve alcoholic beverages. It seems that in this case, the Supreme Court was thinking that the introduction of a duty to hand over a receipt in the Ålandic Act on the sale of alcoholic beverages was an ancillary provision to Section 18(13) (licenses for the sale of alcoholic beverages) and therefore within the competence of the Legislative Assembly of the Åland Islands.

28 Opinion of the Supreme Court, 6 June 2013 (Dnr OH 2013/86).

A consequence of simultaneous application of the Ålandic Act and the draft act in mainland Finland, once adopted, would be that there would, in the Åland Islands, exist a double sanctions system (criminal law in the Åland Islands and administrative law sanctions according to the legislation enacted by the Parliament) for an act that only means that no receipt has been handed over in the process of selling and serving alcoholic beverages. The Supreme Court was of the opinion that this was not a circumstance that affected the distribution of legislative competence and that, if such a situation would occur, the rule of *ne bis in idem* would become applicable.

In spite of the fact that the Ålandic and the mainland Finnish legislative competences are exclusive in relation to each other, it is not prohibited for the Legislative Assembly to take in provisions from Finnish law. In fact, under Section 19(3) of the Self-Government Act, it is possible, for the purposes of achieving uniformity and clarity of an act of Åland, to include provisions in acts of Åland on matters relating to the legislative powers of the Parliament, provided that in their substance, they coincide with the corresponding provisions of an act of Parliament. The inclusion of such provisions in an act of Åland shall, however, not alter the separation of the legislative powers of the Legislative Assembly and the Parliament of Finland.

Such inclusion of provisions from laws enacted by the Parliament of Finland in the acts of Åland results in the enactment of acts of a mixed nature in the Åland Islands. This "mixity" is a result of the fact that the exercise of legislative powers in the Åland Islands does not always produce clear-cut regulation of legal relationships within the Ålandic sphere of competence only, but spills over to the other side of the competence line. The consequence is that a part of the provisions that should be included in the act of Åland with a view to preserving the regulatory logic of the enactment might not belong to the legislative competence of the Legislative Assembly. Therefore, Section 19(3) makes it possible to enact coherent and systematically structured acts of Åland by using in the act of Åland such norms that belong to the legislative competence of the Parliament of Finland and that materially coincide with the corresponding norms in an act enacted by the Parliament of Finland. The possibility to enact mixed legislation tries to ensure that an act of Åland is informative in relation to all those persons to whom the act is applied. The incorporation of provisions from acts enacted by the Parliament of Finland into acts of Åland does not, however, change the legislative competence between the two lawmakers in any way. If a deviation from the competence has taken place, then the Legislative Assembly has made an incursion into the legislative competence of the Parliament of Finland. A deviation in the choice of words only does not constitute a breach of competence unless it at the same time involves a material deviation from competence.

The consequence of Section 19(3) of the Self-Government Act is that an act of Åland can contain provisions that originally have been enacted within the competence of the Parliament of Finland. In such a situation, the provision originally enacted by the Parliament of Finland continues to be applicable in the Åland Islands on the basis of the legislative competence of the Parliament of Finland. The further consequences of this become apparent if the Parliament of Finland amends the original provision, because then the provision amended by the Parliament of Finland applies in the Åland Islands as amended, but the Ålandic mixed act would continue to feature the original wording in its unamended form. At such a point, the good aim of producing an informative act of Åland is, of course, countered. In order to satisfy the need of an individual or a business enterprise to always receive correct information about the contents of legal provisions, acts of Åland of a mixed nature should be automatically amended if the Parliament of Finland amends provisions that have been incorporated into acts of Åland.

As concerns the quantity of "mixity" in an act of Åland, it has sometimes been suggested that the proportion of provisions stemming from an act enacted by the Parliament of Finland should not exceed 50 percent. There is no such rule in the Self-Government Act, and the interpretations of the Supreme Court do not indicate that such a rule of proportion would be imposed in practice. However, there exist some opinions of the Supreme Court that indicate that Ålandic enactments that consist entirely or mainly of provisions that belong to the legislative competence of the Parliament of Finland cannot be passed by the Legislative Assembly.[29]

It is also important to take note of the fact that the Legislative Assembly may, within its legislative competence, enact so-called acts of reference (Swedish: *blankettlag*), which means that an act enacted by the Parliament of Finland is made applicable in the Åland Islands within the legislative competence of Åland by means of an act of Åland. The situation is in this respect different from the acts of a mixed nature, because the acts of reference are enacted within the competence of Åland. This method of enactment is often used to legislate on technical standards, such as foodstuffs, product safety, chemicals and motor vehicles.[30] By choosing to enact an act of reference, the Legislative

29 *See*, e.g., the following Opinions of the Supreme Court: 5 April 1963, 19 June 1979.

30 *See* also Sören Silverström, 'Implementation of EU legislation in the Åland Islands' in Sia Spiliopoulou Åkermark (ed), *Constitutions, Autonomies and the EU* (Åland Islands Peace Institute 2008) 45, who makes the point that the implementation of technical EU

Assembly has decided to apply the same provisions as in mainland Finland, and in such a situation, it is beneficial if the normative situation in the Åland Islands can follow the development of the provisions in mainland Finland. Typically, an act of Åland of this sort makes reference to the act or acts enacted by the Parliament of Finland by mentioning the name and number of the act or acts and declares that future amendments made by the Parliament of Finland to the act or acts will also apply in the Åland Islands.

The method of act of reference has also often been used in the implementation of EU law, because the short implementation period prescribed by an EU directive may leave such a narrow time-frame that the law-drafting mechanism of the Åland Islands does not have the time to react. In such situations, the Government and the Legislative Assembly of the Åland Islands may choose to enact the act of Åland according to the wording it received in the Parliament of Finland, which leads to certain savings in time and resources. The capacity to draft laws in such quantities as required by changes in the formal legal environment (the EU, international treaties) and by changes in society is, after all, limited in the Åland Islands.[31] Therefore, from time to time, acts of reference are used in a manner which incorporates by Ålandic legislative decision the contents of an act passed by the Parliament of Finland.

Sometimes, acts of reference are enacted by the Legislative Assembly so that they not only make reference to an act passed by the Parliament of Finland, but also contain one or a couple of material provisions, such as an exception of some sort to the contents of the referenced act of the Parliament of Finland. In such cases, the act of reference actually becomes of a mixed nature, too, albeit of a different kind than the above-mentioned acts of a mixed nature. The use of acts of reference may thus from time to time lead to normative situations which are not easy to understand for the individual or even the public authorities and courts that implement such acts of reference.[32]

directives may cause the Legislative Assembly to choose such a legislative strategy that directives are implemented by way of referring to the relevant state implementing legislation. "However, there are also many directives requiring Ålandic legislation which are not simple copies of State legislation".

31 As pointed out in Silverström (n 30) 45, only eight civil servants are responsible for the drafting of legislation in the Government of the Åland Islands, which is very little in comparison with any Member State, although the volume of EU norms relevant for the Åland Islands is almost at the same level as the volume of EU norms relevant for a Member State.

32 One example of such a legislative technique could be the Åland Act on the Application on the Åland Islands of some Acts on Re-Districting of Municipalities 1997. According to this Act of Åland, the Act on Re-Districting of Municipalities 1997 of mainland Finland shall be applied in the Åland Islands, but with exceptions specified in the Act of Åland.

In Section 32 of the Self-Government Act, a particular normative procedure is established that normally should not affect the formal distribution of powers but that distributes administrative tasks between the Åland Islands and state authorities. The procedure uses so-called consent decrees, issued by the President of Finland after the Åland Delegation has given an opinion on the draft. The purpose of consent decrees is to make possible transfers of duties belonging to the state administration to administrative agencies of the Åland Islands or duties of an agency of Åland to the state administration. Such transfer may be agreed upon by the Government of the Åland Islands and the Government of Finland, and the transfer may be arranged for a certain period of time or until further notice. If notice is given on an existing agreement by either of the two parties, the relevant consent decree shall be amended or repealed as soon as possible and in any case within one year from the date of the notice. Unless the decree is amended or repealed within the said time, the agreement shall be deemed to have been terminated one year after the notice. This means that it is the agreement between the parties that controls the validity of the decree. The mechanism of consent decrees has, however, some normative implications for the legislative powers of the Legislative Assembly, because under sub-section 2 of the provision, an act of Åland which is contrary to a consent decree shall not apply to the extent the act of Åland is contrary to the consent decree while the decree is in force. Here the principles of the hierarchy of norms are, at least to some extent, turned upside down, but in practice, the Åland Islands can always terminate such an agreement which has resulted in such application of a consent decree that raises competence problems.

Consent decrees are prepared jointly by the executive organs of the Åland Islands and mainland Finland, and they deal typically with such public functions that in one way or another leave the inhabitants of the Åland Islands without public services in certain matters that belong either to the legislative competence of the Legislative Assembly or the Parliament of Finland. Examples of matters where consent decrees exist are tasks related to the production of the list of voters for elections of the Legislative Assembly and municipal boards in the Åland Islands by the population registry authorities of the state of Finland and the emergency transportation of persons for medical reasons on vessels belonging to the Coast Guard. In these cases, organs of the Finnish

---

The exceptions mentioned in the particular Act of Åland transfer those functions that in mainland Finland were held by the Ministry of the Interior, the provincial government and the Council of State to the Government of the Åland Islands. In addition, this Act of Åland prescribes that costs that are caused by the implementation of the legislation on the re-districting of municipalities in the Åland Islands are payable out of the means of the budget of the Åland Islands instead of being paid from the state budget.

state administration have agreed to take care of functions which otherwise are the responsibility of the Åland Islands.[33] Hence there exists a certain measure of inter-governmental cooperation with the autonomy arrangement, made visible also in several other respects in the Self-Government Act 1991 by means of references to consultation and cooperation between the Governments of Finland and the Åland Islands. Although the competence line is strict, the practical management of issues requires cooperation.

The adjudication committee, created under Section 6(2) of the Home Rule Act 1948 to deal with competence disputes between Denmark and the Faroe Islands, has never been called to resolve any dispute concerning competence. Therefore, it is possible to say that this committee is not a body that would actively perform any dispute resolution function and as a consequence of that, there does not exist any interpretations that would amount to practice which could give rise to characterisations of the dispute resolution in the same way as concerning Canada in relation to the provinces or Finland in relation to the Åland Islands. However, it can be presumed that competence issues have arisen between the two entities, Denmark proper and the Faroe Islands, and that the competence issues have been solved through political negotiations between the governmental bodies of Denmark and the Faroe Islands. Given the ease at which the Faroe Islands can take over legislative competence from the Parliament of Denmark, one practical possibility from the Faroese side to respond to competence problems, at least after 2005, would be to transfer the contentious matter from the Parliament to the Legislative Assembly of the Faroe Islands according to the procedures of the Takeover Act 2005, that is, either with or without negotiations.

After 2006 and the enactment of the above-mentioned Faroese law listing the competences that still remain with the Parliament of Denmark, several competences have been taken over by the Faroe Islands, such as criminal law; media matters; emergency services; the established church and religious communities that deviate from the established church; matters that concern company law, economic associations and foundations as well as annual accounts (book-keeping); holidays; measures and weights; meteorology; copyright; property; criminal law; and pilotage. As a consequence, competences still held by the Danish Parliament are function as legal counsel; health; function as medical doctor; function as midwife; hospitals; care of disabled. Because of the principle that money follows legislative competence, it appears as if the

33 Åland Decree on the Taking Care of some Tasks that Relate to Elections to the Legislative Assembly and to Municipal Elections as well as to Advisory Municipal Referendums in the Åland Islands 1999 and Åland Decree of the President of the Republic concerning the Tasks of the Border Guards in the Åland Islands 2004.

expensive competences were still held by the Danish Parliament, and subsidies are paid to the Faroe Islands for taking care of (parts of) those competences in the Faroe Islands on behalf of the Danish government. In those areas of competences that have not been transferred from Denmark to the Faroe Islands, there exist some partly delegated law-making powers that the Parliament of Denmark has delegated to the Faroe Islands.

In spite of the fact that the double enumeration strategy for distribution of legislative powers purports to establish two clear-cut spheres of legislative competence, one for the national level and another for the sub-state level, the constitutional regulation of the interaction of the two spheres of legislation contains certain safety valves for such unusual situations where the regular distribution of competence is difficult to apply. Thus, when the existing material enumerations of competences are not able to provide all the answers, management of "unusual situations" is required. In such instances, the Constitution of Canada contains the possibility for the federation to legislate for the peace, order and good government (p.o.g.g.) on the basis of the chapeau of Section 91 of the Constitution, while for the Åland Islands, the two orders of governments can rely on their respective extension clauses (Section 18(27) for Åland and Section 27(42) for Finland) implementing underlying principles of legislative competence in the Self-Government Act. However, none of these clauses in Canada or Finland establish any general doctrine of precedence of national law, but allow for limited adjustments in a circumscribed manner. For the Faroe Islands, the easy assumption of competence by the Legislative Assembly can, in such situations and as an extension, probably be viewed as a presumption of competence in the Faroe Islands.

V Concluding Remarks

Our review of exclusive enumerations of law-making powers in a context of duality of legislative competences in three countries, Canada, Denmark and Finland, reveals the existence of a group of countries where the distribution of legislative competences is not arranged in a manner typical for a classical federation or for a regular autonomy arrangement. The emergence of double enumeration is a result from negotiations between the state and the sub-state levels, but in principle, such negotiation is an on-going feature of only Denmark and the Faroe Islands, while negotiations precede the creation of the constitutional provisions in Canada and Finland. In terms of rigidity and flexibility, the Finnish arrangement with respect to the Åland Islands appears to be the most rigid one, and in comparison, the Canadian arrangement with respect to the provinces is only marginally less rigid, while flexibility characterizes the Danish arrangement with respect to the Faroe Islands.

The point with the double enumerations in all three countries is to create exclusive legislative competences where the two orders of government would always know when and at which instances they are competent to enact legislation. In Finland, the distribution of competences is purportedly established as a very strict one, almost as if the two spheres of legislative competences existed in watertight compartments, if an early Canadian characterization of double enumeration is allowed in a Finnish context. In Canada, the 150 year long practice with a double enumeration that has survived almost unamended has led, through interpretations of the Supreme Court, to a cohabitation of competences, while in Denmark, the model has recently been changed into a dynamic re-distribution of competences, where the sub-state entity is in a position to determine which of the competences the sub-state entity should hold, save for a short list of reserved competences for the national parliament. Therefore, the method used for the distribution of legislative powers ranged from amendment in Finland through judicial interpretation in Canada to political decision (by the sub-state entity) in Denmark. A general feature of the three systems of double enumeration is that they lack any general supremacy clause or preemption doctrine. However, the three constitutional orders have varying techniques for reacting to "unexpected" competence issues not resolved on the basis of a reading of the double enumerations. In Finland, each list of enumeration is supplemented by an extension clause for implementing underlying principles of each list, while in Canada, there is some limited paramountcy as a last resort, coupled with a limited p.o.g.g. power that may give some leverage to the federal level, but without disturbing the general order of double enumeration. In Denmark, however, the resolution of "unexpected" situations is somewhat confusing, but the flexible political decision-making by the legislature of the Faroe Islands could probably function as an instance of final resort.

The manner in which the normative competence control is fashioned may range between symmetrical and asymmetrical. Competence control is symmetrical in Canada, where the enactments of both the federal legislature as well as the provincial legislatures can become objects of competence control. In Finland, competence control is asymmetrical, because there is a systematic control of competence only of the enactments of the Legislative Assembly of the Åland Islands, not of the Parliament of Finland. In Denmark, the system is perhaps somewhat unclear, but it appears that the competence control would be asymmetrical in a manner similar to the Finnish one, although the system of competence control as established on the basis of the 1948 Home Rule Act has not been used even once. The above account also suggests that normative competence control can be either systematic or unsystematic. In Canada, the competence control is unsystematic for the reason that all legislative enactments at the federal level and provincial level do not undergo competence control, but only those legislative enactments that are brought to the judicial system by way of individual applications. In Finland, the situation is the opposite as concerns the legislation enacted by the Legislative Assembly of the Åland Islands, because all pieces of law enacted by the Legislative Assembly undergo a competence examination by the Åland Delegation, and if a problem is detected or indicated, the matter is dealt with by the Supreme Court of Finland, pending the possible exercise of (partial) veto by the President of Finland. In Denmark, competence control has in practice been non-existent, but would appear to be unsystematic, because not all legislation would be examined as to breach of competence, but only such pieces of law of the Faroe Islands where breach of competence is indicated (which has not happened so far, at least formally within the established system of competence control).

Bibliography

Anderson, George, *Federalism: an Introduction* (OUP 2008).

Benedikter, Thomas, *The World's Working Regional Autonomies: an Introduction and Comparative Analysis* (Anthem Press 2007).

Hogg, Peter W., *Constitutional Law of Canada* (Thomson & Carswell, 5th edn suppl, Vols. 1 & 2, 2014).

Inwood, Gregory J., *Understanding Canadian Federalism – an Introduction to Theory and Practice* (Pearson 2013).

Silverström, Sören, "Implementation of EU legislation in the Åland Islands" in Sia Spiliopoulou Åkermark (ed), *Constitutions, Autonomies and the EU* (Åland Islands Peace Institute 2008).

Suksi, Markku, *Double Enumeration of Legislative Powers in a Sub-State Context – A Comparison between Canada, Denmark and Finland* (Springer-Verlag 2018).

Suksi, Markku, *Sub-State Governance through Territorial Autonomy* (Springer-Verlag 2011).

Watts, Ronald L. *Comparing Federal Systems* (McGill-Queen's University Press 2008).

Wheare, K.C., *Federal Government*, (OUP, 4th edn, 1964).

Canadian Supreme Court Cases

Reference re Securities Act, [2011] S.C.J. No. 66, 2011 SCC 66, [2011] 3 S.C.R. 837 (S.C.C.)

Canadian Western Bank v Alberta, [2007] S.C.J. No. 22, 2007 SCC 22.

General Motors of Canada v City National Leasing, [1989] S.C.J. No. 28.

Quebec (Attorney General) v. Lacombe, 2010 SCC 38, [2010] 2 S.C.R. 453

British Columbia v Lafarge [2007] S.C.J. No. 23, 2007 SCC 23.

Quebec (Attorney General) v Canadian Owners and Pilots Association, 2010 SCC 39, [2010] 2 S.C.R. 536.

Canadian Western Bank v Alberta, [2007] S.C.J. No. 22, 2007 SCC 22.

Marine Services International Ltd v Ryan Estate, [2013] S.C.J. No. 44, 2013 SCC 44.

Reference re Assisted Human Reproduciton Act and Canada Attorney General v PHS Community Services Society, 2011 SCC 44, [2011] 3 S.C.R. 134.

British Columbia v Lafarge, [2007] S.C.J. No. 23, 2007 SCC 23.

Supreme Court of Finland: Opinion, 6 June 2013 (Dnr OH 2013/86).

Websites for Legal Materials

<http://laws-lois.justice.gc.ca/eng/Const//index.html#docCont> accessed 4 January 2018 for "Canadian Constitutional Act of 1867".

<http://www.finlex.fi/fi/laki/kaannokset/1991/en19911144.pdf> accessed 4 January 2018 for "Åland Self-Government Act of 1991".

<http://stm.dk/_p_13089.html> accessed 4 January 2018 for "Lov nr. 578 af 24. Juni 2005 om de færøske myndigheders overtagelse af sager og sagsområder, or the so-called Takeover Act 2005" and "Lov nr. 137 af 23. Marts 1948 om Færøernes Hjemmestyre, or the so-called Home Rule Act 1948".

<http://www.logir.fo/Logtingslog/41-fra-10-05-2006-um-raedi-a-malum-og-mal sokjum-sum-seinast-broytt-vid-logtingslog> accessed 4 January 2018 for "Løgtingslóg nr. 41 frá 10. mai 2006 um ræði á málum og málsøkjum, sum seinast broytt við løgtingslóg nr. 55 frá 26. mai 2011".

<https://www.regeringen.ax/sites/www.regeringen.ax/files/law/code/hela.pdf> accessed 4 January 2018 for "Åland Decree on the Taking Care of some Tasks that Relate to Elections to the Legislative Assembly and to Municipal Elections as well as to Advisory Municipal Referendums in the Åland Islands 1999 (SoÅ 1999:24)" and "Decree of the President of the Republic concerning the Tasks of the Border Guards in the Åland Islands 2004 (SoÅ 2004:21; SoF 420:2004)".

CHAPTER 5

Autonomous Communities and Environmental Law: The Basque Case

Daniele Conversi and Xabier Ezeizabarrena

1 Introduction

Nationalism and environmentalism have proved to be historically at odds with each other. The traditional emphasis on territory, land and soil, the rhetorical celebration of landscape and natural beauty and, at least in some countries, the idealisation of peasants as prototypes of national purity, have been contrasted and contradicted by megaprojects informed by patriotic grandeur and competitive state-building. The latter have often contributed to the destruction of both the environment and the rural economy. Characteristically, the centralising state has opened up national folklore museums while encouraging urbanisation and accepting rural displacement, thus contributing to the destruction of traditional lifestyles. Concurrently, modern states have created national parks and nature reserves, while contemplating the consequences of their accelerated development plans and unrestrained abuse of the environment. Finally, when war comes, nationalism provides additional fuel to state builders engaged in sweeping infrastructure building and war machine expansion to annihilate both the environment and the human species.

In recent years, however, a new wave of evidence seems to suggest that at least some regional governments run by nationalist parties have been, and are still, more effective in tackling the environmental crisis of our time, enacting more vigorous eco-friendly legislation than their respective central governments. The key question here is: Do regional governments controlled by sub-state nationalist parties have a better record in implementing robust environmental policies and effective sustainable development than their central governments?

This chapter explores the case of the Basque Autonomous Community (BAC) in Spain, with occasional reference to the broader national territory envisioned by Basque nationalists (thus including Navarre) and other meso-level institutions such as the provinces and municipalities. Our analysis illustrates how at least some regions administered by sub-state nationalist parties (SSNPs) have a better record of environmental protection than their respective central states.

 | DOI:10.1163/9789004405455_006

Ever since the approval of the 1978 Constitution, and the regional autonomy statutes that followed, Spain has been divided into 17 autonomous communities, resulting in a largely asymmetric distribution of power; that is, with some communities having more autonomy than others. The BAC and Navarre are autonomous communities that currently (2019) enjoy the highest level of autonomy in Spain, including the unique capacity to levy their own taxes through the *conciertos económicos* (economic agreements) and the *fueros* (local charters). It is within this framework that we aim to uncover the development of environmental legislation at the regional level, particularly compared to the central government, and the contemporary challenges it is intended to tackle.

II Basque Autonomy and the Environment

Since 1978, the protection of the environment in Spain and the Basque Country was directly assumed by means of Article 45 of the Constitution. This was accompanied by a complex distribution of duties between the Spanish and Basque governments through Articles 148 and 149 and the 1979 Basque Statute of Autonomy. Later on, as Spain became a member state of the EC (later EU), European bodies enacted the main environmental policies, mostly through directives and regulations.

Focussing on the implementation of EU environmental law in Spain, we need to begin in September 1997. While negotiating the Treaty of Amsterdam (signed in October 1997), the Spanish government avoided signing an annex statement proposed by Germany, Austria and Belgium that would have incorporated the participation of sub-state entities within EU institutions. The political and legal consequences for environmental policies are thus substantial in European decentralised structures, among which the enforcement of the principle of subsidiarity should prevail. Subsidiarity remains a key principle of this multi-level framework for exercising environmental competencies, either at the EU- or the state-level, or sharing them among these and sub-national entities such as the Basque Country.[1]

1 *See* Daniele Conversi, 'Between the Hammer of Globalization and the Anvil of Nationalism: Is Europe's Complex Diversity under Threat?' (2014) 14(1) *Ethnicities* 25–49; John Loughlin, 'The Regional Question, Subsidiarity and the Future of Europe', in Stephen Weatherill and Ulf Bernitz (eds), *The Role of Regions and Sub-National Actors in Europe* (Hart 2005); *Whose Europe?: National Models and the Constitution of the European Union*, Kalypso Nicolaidis and Stephen Weatherill (eds), (OUP 2003); Joxerramon Bengoetxea, 'The Participation of

Spain is not, however, a signatory of the above-mentioned statement to foster regional or sub-national participation within the EU. This could have been avoided earlier on by including at least one representative of each of Spain's autonomous communities as part of the state delegation negotiating the treaty – considering that EU bodies enact most of the environmental legislation in the regions. This contrasts with Germany, Austria and Belgium, where regional or *Länder* delegates can take part in various EU bodies.[2] The Spanish state, however, seems determined to avoid sub-national participation in the EU Council of Ministers.[3] As most environmental legislation is the result of direct or indirect implementation of EU law, Basque institutions have faced substantial difficulties in developing effective environmental policies in recent years.

On the other hand, the Basque parliament has enacted positive practical legislation to foster more sustainable activities, including a General Law for the Protection of the Environment (*Ley 3/1998, General de Protección del Medio Ambiente del País Vasco*) as a general framework for environmental protection. This relies upon a rights and duties based approach which was considered to be trend-setting in Spain in the late 1990s, as compared with the requirements of Article 45 of the Spanish Constitution that entailed a formal legislative development for each environmental policy.

Thus, the Basque Provinces and Navarre lack direct representation within the EU when dealing with environmental issues. As for their 'locus standi' before the European Court of Justice, they can only act through the indirect route available for legal persons, because sub-state bodies do not have the necessary direct legitimacy. In this sense, the field for effective political action at the European level has been reduced by the lack of political will of recent Spanish governments, in particular the neo-conservative Popular Party (PP).

Infra-State Entities in European Union Affairs in Spain: the Basque Case', in Stephen Weatherill and Ulf Bernitz (eds), *The Role of Regions and Sub-National Actors in Europe* (Hart 2005).

2 Enrique Lucas Murillo de la Cueva, 'Comunidades Autónomas y políticas europea', Civitas-Ivap, Madrid, (*Comunidades Autónomas y política europea* (Civitas IVAP-Civitas 2000) 143 also adds the most recent case of the United Kingdom.

3 A. Mangas Martín also refers to this question; see Araceli Mangas Martín, 'La participación directa de las Comunidades Autónomas en la actuación comunitaria: fase preparatoria', in Pablo Pérez Tremps (ed), *La participación europea y la acción exterior de las Comunidades Autónomas* (Institut d´Estudis Autonómics 1999).

II.A *Politics: Locality and the Global Fight against Climate Change*

Climate change has increasingly been recognised as the greatest threat to humankind and to the very existence of life on earth.[4] The threat is so all-pervasive that the very lives of our children and grandchildren will necessarily need to be drastically different from ours. After the modest 1997 Kyoto protocol, the 2015 Paris Agreement set the basis for a first comprehensive and unanimous, although belated, effort to coordinate the coming transition. Yet, it is now clearer than ever that there exists no global matrix capable of finding solutions to a problem that is so eminently complex and universal.[5]

The fight against climate change can only be successful if policies can be coordinated throughout all levels of governance and can range comprehensively from individual or personal lifestyle choices to global governance, from destabilising current patterns of mass consumption to the circular economy, from the transition to renewable energies to the search for either a *steady state economy*,[6] or *degrowth*.[7] In all these areas, sub-state governments are called

4 Zimmerer Jr (ed), *Climate Change and Genocide: Environmental Violence in the 21st Century*. (Routledge 2015); Levene M and Conversi D., 'Subsistence Societies, Globalisation, Climate Change and Genocide: Discourses of Vulnerability and Resilience' (2014) 18(3) *The International Journal of Human Rights* 281–297.

5 Luis Moreno and Daniele Conversi, 'Cambio climático y modelo de bienestar en la era del antropoceno', in Germán Jaraíz Arroyo (ed), *Bienestar Social y Politicas Publicas. Retos para Pactar el Futuro* (Los Libros de la Catarata 2018).

6 As above, economic research on the possibilities and promise of a *steady state economy* has been developing swiftly. Daniel W. O'Neill, 'Measuring Progress in the Degrowth Transition to a Steady State Economy' (2012) 84 *Ecological Economics* 221–231; Hubert Buch-Hansen, 'Capitalist Diversity and Degrowth Trajectories to Steady-State Economies' (2014) 106 *op. cit.* 167–173; Frederik Berend Blauwhof, 'Overcoming Accumulation: Is a Capitalist Steady-State Economy Possible?' (2012) 84 *op. cit.* 254–261.

7 There is a rapidly expanding literature on *degrowth:* Leandro Vergara-Camus, 'Capitalism, Democracy, and the Degrowth Horizon' (2017) *Capitalism Nature Socialism* 1–17; Damir Tokic, 'The Economic and Financial Dimensions of Degrowth' (2012) 84 *Ecological Economics* 49–56; Onofrio Romano, 'How to Rebuild Democracy, Re-Thinking Degrowth' (2012) 44(6) *Futures* 582–589; Barbara Muraca, 'Towards a Fair Degrowth-Society: Justice and the Right to a "Good Life" Beyond Growth' (2012) 44(6) *op. cit.* 535–545; Kent A. Klitgaard and Lisi Krall, 'Ecological Economics, Degrowth, and Institutional Change' (2012) 84 *Ecological Economics* 84, 247–253; Ernest Garcia, 'Degrowth, the Past, the Future, and the Human Nature' (2012) 44(6) *Futures* 546–552; Marco Deriu, 'Democracies with a Future: Degrowth and the Democratic Tradition' (2012) 44(6) *op. cit.* 553–561; Claudio Cattaneo et al., 'Degrowth Futures and Democracy' (2012) 44(6) *op. cit.* 515–523; Sébastien Boillat, Julien-François Gerber, and Fernando R. Funes-Monzote, 'What Economic Democracy for Degrowth? Some Comments on the Contribution of Socialist Models and Cuban Agroecology' (2012) 44(6) *op. cit.* 600–607; Carlos Taibo, *Decrecimiento, Crisis, Capitalismo*, Colección de estudios internacionales, no. 5 (Servicio Editorial de la Universidad del Paìs Vasco – Euskal Herriko Unibertsitateko Argitalpen Zerbitzua 2010).

upon to put into practice a wide range of policy measures, from expanding public transport infrastructure to limiting the use of private cars, from tackling many types of pollution to allowing citizens space for the development of urban farming.[8]

In respect of climate change, efforts at the sub-state level elsewhere include the trend-setting 'Climate Change Strategy' in Wales and Scotland and a law recently approved by the Catalan Parliament, *Ley 16/2017, del cambio climático*.[9] In the BAC, a proposal pending since 2012 has not yet materialised in the Basque parliament. Besides these efforts, there remain gaps between environmental law and its enforcement throughout Spain.

The Basque government approved a 'General Basque Strategy on Climate Change 2050', in preparation for 'the decisive event', the 2015 United Nations Climate Change Conference (COP 21) held in Paris from 30 November to 12 December 2015.[10] The planning effort focused mainly on the requirements issued during recent decades at the UN and EU levels.

II.B *Basque Autonomy and the Environment: A Legal Panorama*

One of the areas commonly addressed when discussing climate change mitigation is the so-called *circular* or *regenerative economy* promoted by the EU with the goal of minimising emissions, and energy waste. In the Basque Country, a 'Plan for Prevention and Waste Management' was approved in 2015,[11] even though the main obligations fall upon the *Juntas Generales* (provincial

8 Luis Moreno and Daniele Conversi, 'Modelo social y límites al crecimiento en el antropoceno' (2017) 12 *Eunomía. Revista en Cultura de la Legalidad* 310–314; Moreno and Conversi, 'Cambio climático y modelo de bienestar en la era del antropoceno'.

9 Elin Royles and Nicola McEwen, 'Empowered for Action? Capacities and Constraints in Sub-State Government Climate Action in Scotland and Wales' (2015) 24(6) *Environmental Politics* 1034–54; Diario Oficial de la Generalitat de Catalunya No. 7426, 3-8-2017.

10 EuskoJaurlaritza, *Climate change strategy of the Basque Country to 2050/Stratégie du Pays Basque sur le changement climatique à l'horizon 2050* (Eusko Jaurlaritzaren Argitalpen Zerbitzu Nagusia/Servicio Central de Publicaciones del Gobierno Vasco 2015). Estrategia de Cambio Climático 2050 del País Vasco, <http://www.ingurumena.ejgv.euskadi.eus/contenidos/informacion/klima_2050/en_def/adjuntos/KLIMA2050_en.pdf>.

11 EuskoJaurlaritza, *Plan de Prevención y gestión de residuos de la Comunidad Autónoma del País Vasco: hacia una economía circular (2020)* (Eusko Jaurlaritzaren Argitalpen Zerbitzu Nagusia/Servicio Central de Publicaciones del Gobierno Vasco 2015), <http://www.euskadi.eus/informacion/plan-de-prevencion-y-gestion-de-residuos-2020/web01-s2ing/es/>.

parliaments), the *Diputaciones Forales* (provincial governments) and the town councils.[12]

The Basque Parliament has approved two important environmental measures in the last five years. The first concerns 'fracking', the practice of injecting, under high pressure, 'millions of water, dangerous chemicals, and sand deep into the earth, fracturing hard rock to release oil and gas for shale gas development.'[13] The Basque regulation of fracking was enshrined in Act 6/2015 (additional protection measures), but different criteria were adopted by the regional parliament and the regional government. Attempts at regulating fracking clashed with ongoing exploratory practices in some Basque regions, mainly in Araba (Alava). The law avoids adopting a general ban on fracking, while tending to establish specific measures to regulate it locally,[14] with restrictive measures for soil protection – forbidding the use of the technique in specific protected areas and encouraging the requirement of strategic environmental assessments for any 'fracking' project. Thus, although far from comprehensive, this regulation is a step forward in comparison to the pro-fracking policies adopted by the PP-led central government. Both the PP-led governments and the Constitutional Court considered fracking to be an area linked to the economic and energy spheres, thereby within the exclusive competence of the central government. The PP government has remained notoriously aligned with the US *'frackopoly'* industry, just as this has become increasingly contested by a global anti-fracking movement,[15] resulting in policy gaps with those communities that advocate sustainability.[16] In many countries where shale gas development has been considered, permit applications have proliferated from the private sector to use enormous amounts of public water for hydraulic fracturing even in areas where water is a scarcely available resource. Despite its negative effects on both the environment and human health, the rapid growth

12 *Plan de Prevención y gestión de residuos de la Comunidad Autónoma del País Vasco: hacia una economía circular* (2015), <http://www.euskadi.eus/informacion/plan-de-prevencion-y-gestion-de-residuos-2020/web01-s2ing/es/>.

13 Wenonah Hauter, *Frackopoly: The Battle for the Future of Energy and the Environment* (The New Press 2016). 'Ley 6/2015, de 30 de junio, de medidas adicionales de protección medioambiental para la extracción de hidrocarburos no convencionales y la fractura hidráulica o "fracking"'. Boletín Oficial del País Vasco, 9-7-2015, <https://www.boe.es/buscar/doc.php?id=BOE-A-2015-8274>.

14 Fernando López Ramón, *Observatorio de polÌticas ambientales: 2016* (CIEMAT 2016).

15 Hauter, *op. cit. See* also: <https://www.youtube.com/watch?v=BeGmMhflJ4E> accessed 2 February 2019.

16 Qingmin Meng, 'Fracking Equity: A Spatial Justice Analysis Prototype' (2018) 70 *Land Use Policy* (no. Supplement C) 10–15.

of fracking is linked to an overall lack of international ecological directives. This lack of global environmental regulation is notoriously the flip-side of the *deregulation* championed by neo-liberals. It is precisely for this reason that citizens have taken up autonomous initiatives concerning 'environmental monitoring'.[17] Yet, research on the consequences of fracking often lacks a comprehensive approach capable of integrating environmental concerns with economic and energy considerations.

The second measure is Act 4/2015 for the prevention of soil pollution – particularly relevant for the general restoration and management of former industrial zones.[18] This Act is significant considering the post-industrial nature of many areas like Bilbao and its environs, as it focuses on the obligation of companies to restore neglected areas or abandoned industrial structures in collaboration with local public administrations.

In environmental law, one of the main administrative tools is the 'environmental impact assessment'.[19] Here, the responsibility for efficient law enforcement applies similarly to the Basque Country and to Spain, as both parliaments are entitled to make laws in this area. In both Spain and the Basque Country, conflicts of interest are rife, as the administrative level responsible for issuing the Environmental Impact Declaration (EID) is typically the respective environmental ministry or department – members of the same government which formally promotes the environmental project being assessed.[20] Conflicts of interest thus emerge nearly every time a project with a potentially negative environmental impact is considered.[21] This suggests that economic criteria are

---

17 Jennifer Gabrys, 'Citizen Sensing, Air Pollution and Fracking: From "Caring About your Air" to Speculative Practices of Evidencing Harm' (2017) 65(2) *The Sociological Review* (suppl) 172–192.

18 'Ley 4/2015, para la prevención y corrección de la contaminación del suelo'. Boletín Oficial del País Vasco de 2-7-2015.

19 *See* 'Ley 21/2013, de Evaluación Ambiental' and 'Ley 3/1998, General de Protección del Medio Ambiente del País Vasco' EuskoJaurlaritza, *Ley 3/1998, de 27 de febrero, general de protección del medio ambiente del País Vasco/3/1998 legea, otsailaren 27koa, Euskal Herriko ingurugiroa babesteko lege orokorra* (Departamento de Medio Ambiente y Acción Territorial [Separata de: B.O.P.V. No. 59, viernes 27 de marzo de 1998].

20 Eventually, some environmental criteria were introduced under the jurisdiction. *See*, for example, the recent Judgment of the Spanish Supreme Court: Sentencia del Tribunal Supremo 1298/2017, 18-7-2017 on Environmental Impact Assessment for a project developed in Madrid.

21 At the same time, in none of the aforementioned governments is the environmental ministry or department the one with real political weight.

still accorded absolute priority over environmental criteria in both public and private projects.[22]

The common cause of this environmental conundrum is linked to the failure to comply with the EU's principle of integrating environmental protection within general policies. This principle is clearly spelled out in Articles 4.2(e) and 11 of the Functioning Treaty of the EU, establishing the requirement for integration of environmental protection in all public policies. Of course, the 2008–2016 economic recession and the goodwill of incumbent governments have also been important factors impacting on a broader assessment of existing environmental measures, both worldwide and at the domestic level.

II.C *Food Sovereignty*

Amongst the range of options available to sub-state governments, a key area is the possibility of implementing practices of food sovereignty (FS) at regional and local levels. As a well-tested empowerment dynamic, FS can be defined as 'the right of peoples to define their own food and agriculture; to protect and regulate domestic agricultural production and trade in order to achieve sustainable development objectives; to determine the extent to which they want to be self reliant; to restrict the dumping of products in their markets; and to provide local fisheries-based communities the priority in managing the use of and the rights to aquatic resources'.[23]

Are regional governments run by sub-state nationalist parties more likely to implement FS practices? Again, the answer is not straightforward. On the one hand, the very existence of an FS social movement, along with left-wing nationalist parties in some regions, is likely to put pressure on incumbent regional governments, irrespective of their political colour. For instance, calls to 'food sovereignty' tend to unite civil society organisations in the pursuit of a national food policy agenda, as occurred in Canada.[24] In the Basque case, the 'patriotic left' coalition EH Bildu and *Podemos Euskadi* have included FS in their political programmes and electoral platforms, but other parties have so far failed to respond to the challenge and incorporate it in their programmes.

22 Xabier Ezeizabarrena, *El principio constitucional de participación ante la evaluación de impacto ambiental de las grandes infraestructuras* (Instituto Vasco de Administración Pública 2006).

23 Statement on peoples' food sovereignty, *Peoples Food Sovereignty Network 2002*, Patel 2009 cited in Raj Patel, 'Food Sovereignty' (2009) 36(3) *The Journal of Peasant Studies* 663–706.

24 Sarah J. Martin and Peter Andrée, 'Putting Food Sovereignty to Work: Civil Society Governmentalities and Canada's People's Food Policy Project (2008–2011)' (2017) 13(4) *Journal of Civil Society* 374–391.

On the other hand, FS per se is hardly implementable top down without the full participation of grassroots movements. Even in countries where FS is constitutionally enshrined, like in Ecuador or Bolivia, its principles cannot be simply implemented from above. Moreover, state governments often directly deal with international corporations, including the fossil fuels industry, bypassing popular consultations and the very right of local communities to be informed. In the words of Raj Patel, 'the modern food system has been architected by a handful of privileged people. Food sovereignty insists that this is illegitimate, because the design of our social system is not the privilege of the few, but the right of all. By summoning this language, food sovereignty … offers a way of fencing off particular entitlements, by setting up systems of duty and obligation'.[25]

It is in this respect that local communities, including stateless nations and indigenous peoples, seem to offer new channels of participation. A growing global trend among producers and consumers pushes towards the implementation of local food policies at the regional level irrespective of state policies – like the Declaration of Nyéléni (27 February 2007) held at the Forum for Food Sovereignty in Sélingué, Mali, and signed by about 500 delegates representing over 80 countries. This type of declaration of intent can be enforced more easily at a local rather than at a state level. Even though the number of states which have adopted FS in their constitutions has increased in the global South,[26] the regional level of interest resonates also, indeed prevalently, amongst indigenous peoples, as with the People's Food Policy Project (PFPP) in Canada.[27]

Broader 'food security' debates are also moving nearer to a FS agenda through issues of delimitation of scale, with demands that people be allowed to participate fully in key decisions about the distribution of goods – with an extended awareness of and concern about the need to defend consumers against the import of unhealthy 'junk' foods.[28] Notions of food security thus relate to justice claims among stateless nations, including economic, sociocultural and political dimensions of justice. The debate on food practice is intimately related to the broader debate about regional sustainability. The latter is, in turn, strictly related to debates on the social model adopted at either the

25 Patel *op.cit.*

26 Daniele Conversi, 'Sovereignty in a Changing World: From Westphalia to Food Sovereignty' (2016) 13(4) *Globalizations* 484–498.

27 Martin and Andrée, *op. cit.*

28 Ana Moragues-Faus, 'Problematising Justice Definitions in Public Food Security Debates: Towards Global and Participative Food Justices' (2017) 84 *Geoforum* 95–106.

regional or the state level. This directly affects the current scenario of impending climate change meltdown.[29]

II.D *Current Limitations*

The decentralised structure of the Spanish legal system consists of a mixture of federal and unitary powers divided among the 17 autonomous communities.[30] Both BAC's and Navarre's autonomous governments have a number of important legislative environmental powers.[31] Yet norms and rules may overlap due to the cession of Spanish sovereignty since Spain became a member of the European Community – and, later, the EU. During this process, Spain's autonomous communities have often been taken aback by the measures adopted by subsequent central governments, particularly under mono-coloured PP cabinets. The latters' weak and corporate-friendly environmental policies have prioritised a short-termist approach based solely on economic growth criteria.

The widespread use of the notion of sustainability did provide an initial common framework for action in policy making. The watershed Brundtland Commission report defined 'sustainable development' as 'the ability to make development sustainable to ensure that it meets the needs of the present without compromising the ability of future generations to meet their own needs'.[32] Since this modest definition was adopted globally in the 1980s, it has increasingly become an out-dated tool, incapable of addressing the vastly complex and vital challenges emerging, with global climate and ecological cataclysm rapidly looming.

However, even on this limited scale, it is critical to assess sustainable development's relationship with political autonomy. In general, sustainable development cannot be achieved by agencies acting randomly and autonomously; rather, a strenuous concerted effort is needed to reach action across all sectors. The role of Basque institutions should thus be contextualised within the broader development and enforcement of EU law, which currently remains the main

29 Moreno and Conversi, 'Cambio climático y modelo de bienestar en la era del antropoceno'.

30 Luis Moreno, *The Federalization of Spain* (F. Cass 2001). Daniele Conversi, 'Autonomous Communities and the Ethnic Settlement in Spain' in Ghai Y (ed), *Autonomy and Ethnicity. Negotiating Competing Claims in Multi-Ethnic States* (Cambridge University Press 2000).

31 See, for example, Article 148 of the Spanish Constitution together with the Statute of the Basque AC and the Statute of Navarre (LORAFNA, or Ley Orgánica de Reintegración y Amejoramiento del Régimen Foral de Navarra; or '*Amejoramiento del Fuero*', Organic Law on Reintegration and Improvement of the Regional Regime of Navarre, also *Fuero Improvement*).

32 Gro Harlem Brundtland, *Our Common Future* (OUP 1987). Also known as: *The Brundtland report* (World Commission on Environment and Development 1987) 5 , 11 and 16.

source of environmental law and nature protection in Europe.[33] Like other sub-state bodies, Basque and Navarrese institutions face legal and institutional challenges the moment they participate in the EU decision-making process.[34]

The EU has gradually been assuming more competencies in environmental policy, thus influencing the legislative itinerary and executive powers of Spain's autonomous communities.[35] Yet the margins of legal manoeuvre in all of the 17 autonomous communities have been considerably reduced in recent years.[36]

It may be irrelevant to know which entity is responsible for the implementation of EU law as long as it is properly enforced. In cases of non-compliance, insufficient compliance or incorrect implementation, EU law would consider the member state directly responsible, regardless of its respective domestic regulations. But, while many environmental policies lie within the competencies of the autonomous communities, the basic laws enforced by the state often reinterpret the constitutional system in favour, not merely of the central government, but of the ruling party with its majoritarian political agenda and predisposition.[37]

During the last decade, it has become harder to distinguish Basque environmental policies from those directly implemented by the state and the EU, since all policies tend to be enforced within a context of 'shared sovereignty'.[38]

III Pioneers of Sustainable Governance? The Environmental Record of Nationally Based Autonomous Regions

Because the impact of climate change is primarily felt at the local and regional level, sub-state governments are becoming key actors, often possessing the competencies to implement policy actions needed for both adaptation and

33 José Manuel Castells Arteche, 'Europa-Euskal Herria' (1999).

34 Gurutz Jáuregui, 'La actividad internacional de la Comunidad Autónoma del País Vasco. La implicación europea', (1999) 36 *Euskonews & Media*, <http://www.euskonews.com/0036zbk/frgaia.htm>.

35 The shared 'foral' root of the Basque Country and Navarre are clearly stated in the First Additional Clause of the Constitution, as well as in its developed legal approaches afterwards. Article 2.1 of the 1979 Basque Statute states: 'Álava, Guipúzcoa and Vizcaya, as well as Navarra, have the right to form part of the Autonomous Community of the Basque Country'.

36 Murillo de la Cueva, *Comunidades Autónomas y política europea* 60–61 and 63–65.

37 Daniele Conversi, 'Majoritarian Democracy and Globalization Versus Ethnic Diversity?' (2012) 19(4) *Democratization* 789–811.

38 The enforcement of international law is a distinct issue worth separate analysis per se.

mitigation.[39] Sustainable development can be identified as an 'outside-in' policy, that is, one that finds its way into the domestic policy agenda as a consequence of international pressures.[40] Global decision-making can have specific differential effects on more centralised policies than consociatonal, federal or con-federal polities; it can spur intergovernmental co-operation between central and sub-national levels of government.

It has in fact been argued that sub-national governments in federal countries acted as pioneers of sustainable development. However, others have contested this claim, suggesting it consists of little more than 'symbolic politics, devoid of political significance and not moving beyond cosmetic, rhetorical engagement'.[41]

III.A *Nationalism and Ecologism*

Parallels and connections can be made between the discourses of nationalism and those of environmentalism. However, this relationship is fraught with contradictions. While environmentalism can 'appeal to land and emotions, to soil and soul and thus to latent nationalist sentiment', nationalism has historically not reciprocated, but rather 'scavenged environmental discourses' to enhance its legitimacy and broaden its electoral base.[42] If we apply the classical distinction between *ethnic* and *civic* nationalism,[43] civic values and goals are fully assumable within those of contemporary environmentalism, while the goals of ethnic nationalism are ultimately 'incompatible with those of Green political actors'.[44]

To cite an example of the thorny relationship between nationalism and environmentalism, an alliance was established in 1991 between the Green Party of England and Wales and the main Welsh nationalist political party, *Plaid Cymru* (Party of Wales), with a social-democratic orientation and a pro-independence agenda. This resulted in the election of Cynog Dafis as MP for Ceredigion and

39 Ibon Galarraga, Gonzalez-Eguino Mikel and Markandya Anil, 'The Role of Regional Governments in Climate Change Policy' (2011) 21(3) *EET Environmental Policy and Governance* 164–182.

40 Karoline Van den Brande, 'Intergovernmental Co-operation for International Decision making in Federal States: The Case of Sustainable Development in Belgium' (2012) 22(4) *Regional & Federal Studies* 407–433.

41 Sander Happaerts, 'Sustainable development in Quebec and Flanders: Institutionalizing symbolic politics?' (2012) 55(4) *Canadian Public Administration* 553–573.

42 P. Hamilton, 'The Greening of Nationalism: Nationalising Nature in Europe' (2002) 11(2) *Environmental Politics* 27–48.

43 Anthony D. Smith, *Nationalism and Modernism: A Critical Survey of Recent Theories of Nations and Nationalism* (Routledge 1998), 125–127 and 210–212.

44 Hamilton, *op. cit.*

Pembroke North in the 1992 general election, By 1995 the relationship had become strained and the alliance ended.[45] But the alliance remained at the European level, where Plaid joined Cornwall's *Mebyon Kernow*, the Scottish National Party and several other regionalist, autonomist and pro-independence parties within the European Free Alliance (EFA).[46] This alliance has for many years suggested the possibility of a situational cooperation, variable by locality, region, state and the EU, favouring a shared understanding and common interests between European environmentalism and sub-state nationalism. The election of Cynog Dafis as MP for Ceredigion and Pembroke North was a historic event both for Welsh nationalism and the Green Party. However, the subsequent, acrimonious break-up of the alliance suggests that relationships between environmentalism and nationalism are situationally contingent.[47]

Other historical cases also cast doubt on the shifting nature of these alliances. The experience of the former Soviet Union seems to indicate that, once independence has been achieved, some former stateless nations have been quick to join the ranks of mega-polluters and environmental offenders. A study of pre-1990 eco-nationalist movements in the Baltic republics, Russia and Ukraine shows that anti-nuclear activism was instantly dropped once independence had been gained, as attention became entirely focussed on consolidating the newly achieved institution of statehood.[48]

Therefore, there is no guarantee that 'stateless nations' as aspiring 'nation-states' can be permanent allies in environmental transitional policies, just as indigenous peoples are not unavoidably 'eco-warriors'. Yet, at the same time, the overall record is one of increasing cooperation and collaboration, including participation in 'inter-subnational' networks, as the next section explains.

45 Carwyn Fowler and Rhys Jones, 'Can Environmentalism and Nationalism be Reconciled? The Plaid Cymru/Green Party Alliance, 1991–95' (2006) 16(3) *Regional & Federal Studies* 315–331.

46 All were represented in the European Parliament within the broader *Greens–European Free Alliance* (Greens/EFA), which includes the European Green Party formed by the major national Green parties.

47 Fowler and Jones, 'Can Environmentalism and Nationalism be Reconciled? The Plaid Cymru/Green Party Alliance, 1991–95'.

48 Jane I. Dawson, *Eco-nationalism: Anti-Nuclear Activism and National Identity in Russia, Lithuania, and Ukraine* (Duke University Press 1996); *see* also Tove H. Malloy, 'Minority Environmentalism and Eco-nationalism in the Baltics: Green Citizenship in the making?' (2009) 40(3) *Journal of Baltic Studies* 375–395.

IV The Network of Regional Governments for Sustainable Development (nrg4SD)

The publication of the Brundtland Report inspired governments to bring sustainable development into public policy.[49] This also affected local administrations and autonomous regions. Sub-state institutions in stateless nations have played an increasingly active role in the search for 'sustainability transitions',[50] gradually exerting more agency in multilateral decision-making. Since sub-state entities are often unrecognised players in multilateral institutions, 'they use several extra-state mechanisms to gain representation'.[51]

A lack of representation and operative space led to the foundation in 2002 of the Network of Regional Governments for Sustainable Development (nrg4SD), to address the United Nations (UN) and other multilateral organisations. Launched at the World Summit on Sustainable Development (WSSD) or 'Earth Summit 2002' in Johannesburg, South Africa, nrg4SD convened ten years after the first Rio de Janeiro Earth Summit in 1992.[52] This was followed by the Saint-Malo Declaration in October 2008 which set the foundations for the network.[53] nrg4SD works simultaneously as an extra-state route to multilateral decision-making and to encourage bilateral co-operation between regions through knowhow transfer. The network provides a relevant example of international activity dedicated to environmental protection at the international level by means of bilateral or multilateral international agreements signed and developed by various sub-state level governments concerned about global environmental problems.[54]

49 Brundtland, *op. cit.*

50 Sander Happaerts, Karoline Van den Brande and Hans Bruyninckx, 'Governance for Sustainable Development at the Inter-subnational Level: The Case of the Network of Regional Governments for Sustainable Development (nrg4SD)', (2010) 20(1) *Regional & Federal Studies* 127–149; Hans Bruyninckx, Sander Happaerts and Karoline van den Brande (eds), *Sustainable Development and Subnational Governments: Policy-Making and Multi-Level Interactions* (Palgrave Macmillan 2012); Ibon Galarraga, Mikel Gonzalez-Eguino and Anil Markandya, 'The Role of Regional Governments in Climate Change Policy' (2011) 21(3) *Environmental Policy and Governance* 164–182.

51 Happaerts, Van den Brande and Bruyninckx, *op. cit.*

52 *See* <http://www.nrg4sd.org>. The BAC is a member, *see* <http://www.nrg4sd.org/basque-country-spain/>.

53 Not to be confused with the previous Saint-Malo Declaration signed in 1998 by the British Prime Minister Tony Blair and the French President Jacques Chirac in response to the Kosovo conflict. *See* <http://www.bcn.cat/climatechange/en/saint-malo.html>.

54 Bruyninckx, Happaerts and van den Brande (eds), *op. cit.*; Sander Happaerts, Karoline Van den Brande and Hans Bruyninckx, 'Subnational Governments in Transnational

During one of the side events of the WSSD Preparatory Committee (PrepCom) meetings held in Bali in 2001, a number of sub-state governments expressed concerns that there was no institution representing their general views. Indeed, some of the UN activities in the run up to the Johannesburg Earth Summit were focused on the city and town level, rather than at the sub-state government level. There was a long, informal discussion that included a number of sub-state government representatives who were present in Bali.[55] About six weeks before the WSSD, the representatives decided to formally establish the nrg4SD.[56] Wales took the lead in consolidating the network.[57] Yet, regions such as Flanders, the Basque Country and North Rhine-Westphalia retained 'diverging views on nrg4SD and its functioning'.[58] Due to these differences, the Network went through a period of stagnation, becoming

Networks for Sustainable Development' (2011) 11(4) *International Environmental Agreements: Politics, Law and Economics* 321–339; Happaerts, Van den Brande and Bruyninckx, 'Governance for Sustainable Development at the Inter-subnational Level: The Case of the Network of Regional Governments for Sustainable Development (nrg4SD)'; Andrea Collins et al., 'Assessing the Environmental Consequences of Major Sporting Events: The 2003/04 FA Cup Final' (2007) 44(3) *Urban Studies* 457–476; Bruyninckx, Happaerts and van den Brande, *op. cit.*; Francesca Dickson, 'The Internationalisation of Regions: Paradiplomacy or Multi-level Governance?' (2014) 8(10) *Geography Compass* 689–700; Fernando Rei, Kamyla Borges Cunha and Natalia Vera Pérez, 'La paradiplomacia medioambiental global y el papel de las comunidades autónomas españolas' (2013) 53(2) *Foro Internacional* 337–362; Sander Happaerts, 'Are you Talking to us? How Subnational Governments Respond to Global Sustainable Development Governance' (2012) 22(2) *Environmental Policy and Governance* 127–142.

55 These included Flanders; *see* Karoline Van den Brande, Sander Happaerts and Hans Bruyninckx, 'Multi-Level Interactions in a Sustainable Development Context: Different Routes for Flanders to Decision-Making in the UN Commission on Sustainable Development' (2011) 21(1) *op. cit.* 70–82; Luc Bas, 'Flemish Activity and Perspective at the EU and the UN' (2008) 3 *Revista Internacional de los Estudios Vascos* (*RIEV*) 151–164; Catalonia, the Basque Country – Galarraga, Gonzalez-Eguino and Markandya, 'The Role of Regional Governments in Climate Change Policy'; Wales – Elin Royles, 'A "Responsibility" to Act Globally: Investigating the Welsh Assembly Government's Engagement in nrg4SD', in Hans Bruyninckx, Sander Happaerts and Karoline Van den Brande (eds), *Sustainable Development and Subnational Governments: Policy-Making and Multi-Level Interactions* (Palgrave Macmillan UK 2012); Western Australia and Quebec – Happaerts, 'Sustainable development in Quebec and Flanders: Institutionalizing symbolic politics?'.

56 <http://www.nrg4sd.org>.

57 Paul Williams, 'The Governance of Sustainable Development in Wales' (2006) 11(3) *Local Environment* 253–267.

58 Happaerts, Van den Brande and Bruyninckx, 'Governance for Sustainable Development at the Inter-subnational Level: The Case of the Network of Regional Governments for Sustainable Development (nrg4SD)', *op. cit.*

the target of criticism because of its relative ineffectiveness, as merely adding another bureaucratic layer unable to tackle global problems.

The Network's first declaration highlighted, among its key political aims, the necessity to include the sub-state level within the United Nations framework. According to the Gauteng Declaration, signed in Johannesburg by representatives of 22 regional governments (RGs) in August 2002, 'The defining feature of the emerging group of governments participating in the new RG network for sustainable development is that they govern territories that are the largest and first level of political subdivision within individual nation states represented at the United Nations.'[59]

A proposal on the creation of a Sustainable Development Knowledge Platform was the outcome of the Rio+20 Summit in 2012, regulated by UN General Assembly Resolution 67/290 (2013) which, among other matters, defines its purpose as providing political leadership, guidance and recommendations for sustainable development.[60]

Other initiatives followed, both inside and outside Europe, such as the 'Declaration of Local and Subnational Leaders of Africa' released at the Climate Change Conference in Agadir, Morocco (11–13 September 2017) on the heels of the Paris Agreement.[61] These are often described, sometimes critically, as examples of a more limited, less global, *Territorial Approach to Climate Change* (TACC), following the Saint-Malo Declaration.[62]

It seems, therefore, that sub-state governments are concerned about sustainable development and include it within their political agendas. There are a number of factors that can explain the relative success of these new policies: the close relationship between sub-state governments and their respective

59 The Gauteng Declaration – <http://www.nrg4sd.org/wp-content/uploads/2015/06/gauteng-en.pdf>. These Regional Governments may include a variegated rainbow-like array of distinctive entities such as regions, provinces, states, prefectures, autonomous communities, communes, departments, districts, divisions, emirates, federations, governorates *kilil*, nations, *oblastey*, *welayatlar* and zones.

60 <http://www.un.org/ga/search/view_doc.asp?symbol=A/RES/66/288&referer=/english/&Lang=E>.

61 'Declaration of Local and Subnational Leaders of Africa Fighting against Climate Change in Africa Together', <http://www.climate-chance.org/dev.climate-chance.org/wordpress/wp-content/uploads/2017/09/Déclaration-des-élus-locaux-et-régionaux-dAfrique-ENG.pdf>.

62 *See* 'Territorial Approach to Climate Change (TACC)', <http://www.adaptation-undp.org/territorial-approach-climate-change-tacc>.

societies, the perspective and approach of these governments regarding environmental protection and the more proactive role of the United Nations Commission for Sustainable Development (CSD) concerning the new Network.

There is growing concern in Basque politics regarding the environment, and there may be some positive approaches, even in the international arena. The next section explores the Basque role in providing a potential model to tackle current environmental challenges.[63]

V Can Stateless Nations and Autonomous Regions Provide a Model for Contemporary Environmental Challenges? The Basque Case

The Spanish parliament and government have tended to define most Spanish environmental law as 'basic'. This means that environmental law enacted by the Spanish parliament cannot be amended or developed by Basque representative institutions. This is in line with Article 149.1.23 of the Constitution on the territorial organisation of the state, which also enshrines the autonomous communities' entitlement 'to establish additional protection standards'. Thus, misuse of this definition may limit the Basque parliament's room for manoeuvre in relation to legislation on environmental protection, or even to enact new laws with more binding levels of protection.

A legal structure with powers and duties at the Basque and Navarrese government and parliament levels is balanced by competencies attributed to the historical territories (Araba, Bizkaia and Gipuzkoa) and, at the municipal level, with town planning and local environmental policies with regard to waste management and public transport. In respect of the latter, the Basque parliament has recently enacted general legislation on the regulation of local institutions.[64]

The Basque legal framework inspired the creation of an efficient 'Basque economic sphere', with a notable industrial presence (particularly in Bizkaia

63 For more general opinions by Basque authors, *see* Demetrio Loperena Rota, *Desarrollo sostenible y globalización* (Thomson-Aranzadi 2003); Itziar Eizagirre and Amaia Lizarralde, *Garapen iraunkorra: garatzeko bizi ala bizitzeko garatu* (Alberdania 2005); Xabier Ezeizabarrena, *Río+20 (1992–2012): el reto del desarrollo sostenible* (Universidad de Deusto [Cuadernos Deusto de Derechos Humanos, 70], 2013).

64 'Ley 2/2016, de Instituciones locales de Euskadi'. Boletín Oficial del País Vasco No. 70, 14-4-2016, <https://www.euskadi.eus/y22-bopv/es/bopv2/datos/2016/04/1601544a.shtml>.

and Gipuzkoa) in a proactive economy, with the highest rate of GDP and the lowest rate of unemployment in Spain.[65]

Therefore, in the Basque context, the principle 'Think globally, act locally' can be seen as an all-encompassing approach to enforcing international environmental covenants and agreements, adapting them to the regional reality of every Basque territory, and aspiring to improve the protection standards already recognised in Spanish legislation.

With regard to the enforcement of Basque environmental policies, the tasks and goals are summarised in the IV Main Environmental Programme 2015–2020, produced by the Basque government's Department of the Environment, Territorial Planning and Housing (*Departamento de Medio Ambiente, Planificación Territorial y Vivienda*).[66] This document contains the main environmental objectives of the BAC together with the funding programme. It is an ambitious programme that needs to be coordinated with other crucial tasks – above all, a sturdier climate change strategy. The two main Basque instruments of environmental law might thus need to be amended: the General Law on Environmental Protection[67] and the Statute of Autonomy.[68]

Moreover, it may be more difficult to link environmental protection with the establishment of nationalist mono-coloured governments (from 1980 to 1986 the Basque National Party, PNV, ruled without any other party). However, the 'Foral' *Diputaciones* (provincial governments) and most of the local authorities are governed by coalition governments led by the PNV, with the support of other parties, mostly the Socialist Party (PSE).[69] In general, Basque environmental protection is enforced with tools similar to those used at the state

65 In 2017, the unemployment rate in the Basque country was 12 per cent compared with 22 per cent in Spain; 8.8 per cent in the case of Gipuzkoa with the lowest rate across the whole of Spain. <http://en.eustat.eus/elementos/ele0008400/ti_Almost_half_the_population_of_the_Basque_Country_was_in_work_in_2010/not0008486_i.html>.

66 IV Programa Marco Ambiental del País Vasco 2015–2020, <http://www.ingurumena.ejgv.euskadi.eus/informacion/programa-marco-ambiental-2020/r49-5832/es/>.

67 Ley 3/1998, General de Protección del Medio Ambiente del País Vasco.

68 The latter was sternly resisted by the Spanish state and most other autonomous communities. The project for a new statute encompasses a system of relations with Spain and the EU that includes key challenges in relation to sustainable development. The basis for drafting a new Statute of Autonomy is *Ley Orgánica 3/1979, del Estatuto de Autonomía para el País Vasco* (Organic Law 3/1979 of the Statute of Autonomy for the Basque Country). Such a new statute could in principle clarify the position of Basque institutions in relation to the EU and Spain, establishing new goals concerning sustainable development after 40 years of democracy.

69 The Basque government is currently a coalition between the PNV (Basque National Party) and the PSOE-PSE (Socialist Party). The same coalition has operated in the three provinces of Araba, Gipuzkoa and Bizkaia together with the capital cities of Vitoria, Donostia

level. Important international efforts taken by the Basque government include participation in the UN Commission for Sustainable Development and in the constitution of the nrg4SD, whereas domestic efforts still require a higher degree of political will.

Environmental protection is a complex task identifiable as 'horizontal' and, therefore, directly connected with sectional economic interests, social disputes and territorial solidarity. Because concern about environmental issues is growing, these often tend to become incorporated into the usual face-saving green marketing policies, sometimes identified as 'greenwash'.[70] Public debate still remains entrenched and fossilised around the opposition between the two pillars of classic short-termism: economy vs. ecology. Public policies need to overcome this dichotomy and prove the economic benefits of ecological investments within long-term environmental analysis and protection of natural resources. The common *eco-* suffix can provide the basis for a shared understanding between proponents of sustainable policy agendas.

VI Conclusion

While this chapter cannot offer a systematic and comprehensive international comparison, it can help to confirm some emerging trends, particularly in Europe. Here, several regional governments often associated with 'sub-state nations' have implemented a variety of relatively advanced policies in relation to sustainable development, the circular economy, environmental protection, cleaner production and the fight against climate change. We have explored the case of the Basque Country, with occasional references to other cases.

However, two major stumbling blocks lie ahead. First, these steps are often the hostages of parties and policies shaped by less collaborative central governments intent on appeasing big capital and large multinational corporations. The PP-dominated Spanish government (2012–2018), in particular, has long enjoyed a mediocre reputation in terms of environmental protection. According to the (rather triumphalist) *Environmental Performance Index* (EPI), Spain performed worse than many European countries in terms of various variables in the 2014 ranking.[71]

---

and Bilbao since 2015. The situation in Navarre is more complex with a coalition government formed by four groups: *Geroa Bai, EH Bildu, Podemos Navarre* and a far-left coalition.

70 Guy Pearse, *Greenwash: Big Brands and Carbon Scams* (Schwartz Publishing 2012); Eveline Lubbers (ed), *Battling Big Business: Countering Greenwash, Infiltration, and Other Forms of Corporate Bullying* (Common Courage Press 2002).

71 For Spain's EPI ranking, *see* <http://archive.epi.yale.edu/epi/country-profile/spain>.

Spain has particularly loose regulation concerning soil use with a traditional stress on cementification and an over-reliance on the building sector, a legacy of decades of *desarollismo* (developmentalism) initiated under the Franco dictatorship. These economic, political and ideological obstacles also impinge on the capacity of local and regional autonomous governments to enact and act on more advanced environmental policies. This, in turn, is related to economic performance. Economic recession in Spain has been closely associated with a failed, yet persisting, model of economic and urban growth heavily based on the building industry.[72] The Spanish crisis was shaped by the negative interaction between globalising forces and Spain's specific path-dependent structures of economic incentives, internal regulations, corporate corruption in the building sector and other policies at the root of the housing bubble.[73]

The second problem is that none of these instruments and policies are sufficient to tackle the impending environmental catastrophe caused by a spiralling accumulation of factors such as climate change and overconsumption. The possibility of public policy shaping a 'degrowth' agenda or a 'steady state economy' is still not contemplated in official circles, where investment in infrastructure, regardless of sustainability, remains a priority – even though the latter may often appear not to be informed by sustainable development goals.

In the Basque case, some important initiatives have been tempered by a central government dominated, until recently, by a neoconservative party (the PP) in the thrall of state-wide and international corporate power.[74] Sturdier initiatives often come from even lower levels of the multilevel perspective. For instance, the above-mentioned practice of *food sovereignty* has become an important component of local struggles.[75] In general, the sluggishness of these steps can hardly match the urgency of the challenge posed by impending climate devastation, which requires unprecedented coordination and cooperation across every single level of local, regional, national, state-wide, European and global actors.

72 Marisol García, 'The Breakdown of the Spanish Urban Growth Model: Social and Territorial Effects of the Global Crisis' (2010) 34(4) *International Journal of Urban and Regional Research* 967–980.

73 An important aspect is the peculiar way *modernity* has been experienced throughout Spain since the years of *desarrolismo*. *See ibid. See* also Daniele Conversi, 'Modernity, Globalization and Nationalism: The Age of Frenzied Boundary-Building', in J. Jackon and L. Molokotos-Liederman (eds), *Nationalism, Ethnicity and Boundaries: Conceptualising and Understanding Identity through Boundary Approaches* (Routledge 2014).

74 Led nowadays by the Socialist Party (PSOE) thanks to the impeachment approved recently in the Spanish Parliament.

75 Conversi, 'Sovereignty in a Changing World: From Westphalia to Food Sovereignty'.

Overall, the Basque case, along with a few other cases, shows an example of how local and regional governments led by sub-state nationalist parties (SSNPs) are, or could be, able to articulate environmental policies more effectively than the respective central governments run by state-wide parties – or independently from them, if allowed. This lesson can easily be extrapolated from our assessment of the Basque case, but there is a broader argument for 'national sustainabilities' encompassing other stateless nations to which this chapter is linked.[76] Although we cannot provide a broader explanation for these contrasting records, we can assume that autonomous regions run by regional nationalist parties are more dependent than central governments on long-term investments, while offering a better record of transparency, reliability and political legitimacy. Further studies are needed to explore the reasons and motives behind the healthier environmental record of sub-state nationalist parties.

Bibliography

Bas, Luc, 'Flemish Activity and Perspective at the Eu and the Un', (2008) 3 *Revista Internacional de los Estudios Vascos* (RIEV) 151–164.

Bengoetxea, Joxerramon, 'The Participation of Infra-State Entities in European Union Affairs in Spain: The Basque Case,' in Stephen Weatherill and Ulf Bernitz (eds), *The Role of Regions and Sub-National Actors in Europe* (Hart 2005) 47–66.

Blauwhof, Frederik Berend, 'Overcoming Accumulation: Is a Capitalist Steady-State Economy Possible?', (2012) 84 *Ecological Economics* 254–261.

Boillat, Sébastien, Julien-François Gerber and Fernando R. Funes-Monzote, 'What Economic Democracy for Degrowth? Some Comments on the Contribution of Socialist Models and Cuban Agroecology', (2012) 44(6) *Futures* 600–607.

Brundtland, Gro Harlem, *Our Common Future* (OUP 1987). Also known as: *The Brundtland Report* (World Commission on Environment and Development 1987).

Bruyninckx, Hans, Sander Happaerts and Karoline van den Brande (eds), *Sustainable Development and Subnational Governments: Policy-Making and Multi-Level Interactions*, (Palgrave Macmillan 2012).

Buch-Hansen, Hubert, 'Capitalist Diversity and De-Growth Trajectories to Steady-State Economies', (2014) 106 *Ecological Economics* 167–173.

Castells Arteche, José Manuel, 'Europa-Euskal Herria', (1999).

Cattaneo, Claudio, Giacomo D'Alisa, Giorgos Kallis and Christos Zografos, 'Degrowth Futures and Democracy', (2012) 44(6) *Futures* 515–523.

76 Jones R and Ross A., 'National Sustainabilities' (2016) 51 *Political Geography* 53–62.

Collins, Andrea, Andrew Flynn, Max Munday and Annette Roberts, 'Assessing the Environmental Consequences of Major Sporting Events: The 2003/04 FA Cup Final', (2007) 44(3) *Urban Studies* 457–476.

Conversi, Daniele, 'Majoritarian Democracy and Globalization Versus Ethnic Diversity?', (2012) 19(4) *Democratization* 789–811.

Conversi, Daniele, 'Between the Hammer of Globalization and the Anvil of Nationalism: Is Europe's Complex Diversity under Threat?', (2014) 14(1) *Ethnicities* 25–49.

Conversi, Daniele, 'Sovereignty in a Changing World: From Westphalia to Food Sovereignty', (2016) 13(4) *Globalizations* 484–498.

D'Alisa, Giacomo, Federico Demaria and Giorgios Kallis (eds), *Degrowth: A Vocabulary for a New Era* (Routledge 2014).

Dawson, Jane I., *Eco-Nationalism: Anti-Nuclear Activism and National Identity in Russia, Lithuania, and Ukraine* (Duke University Press 1996).

Deriu, Marco, 'Democracies with a Future: Degrowth and the Democratic Tradition', (2012) 44(6) *Futures* 553–561.

Dickson, Francesca, 'The Internationalisation of Regions: Paradiplomacy or Multi-Level Governance?', (2014) 8(10) *Geography Compass* 689–700.

Eizagirre, Itziar and Amaia Lizarralde, *Garapen Iraunkorra : Garatzeko Bizi Ala Bizitzeko Garatu* (Irun 2005).

Eusko Jaurlaritza, *Climate Change Strategy of the Basque Country to 2050/StratéGie Du Pays Basque Sur Le Changement Climatique à L'horizon 2050* (Vitoria-Gasteiz: Eusko Jaurlaritzaren Argitalpen Zerbitzu Nagusia/Servicio Central de Publicaciones del Gobierno Vasco 2015).

Eusko Jaurlaritza, *Ley 3/1998, De 27 De Febrero, General De ProteccióN Del Medio Ambiente Del PaíS Vasco/3/1998 Legea, Otsailaren 27koa, Euskal Herriko Ingurugiroa Babesteko Lege Orokorra* (Departamento de Medio Ambiente y Acción Territorial [Separata de: B.O.P.V. No. 59, viernes 27 de marzo de 1998]).

Eusko Jaurlaritza, *Plan De Prevención Y Gestión De Residuos De La Comunidad Autónoma Del País Vasco: Hacia Una Economía Circular (2020)* (Eusko Jaurlaritzaren Argitalpen Zerbitzu Nagusia/Servicio Central de Publicaciones del Gobierno Vasco 2015).

Ezeizabarrena, Xabier, *El principio constitucional de participación ante la evaluación de impacto ambiental de las grandes infraestructuras* (Instituto Vasco de Administración Pública 2006).

Ezeizabarrena, Xabier, *Río+20 (1992–2012): El reto del desarrollo Sostenible*. Bilbao: Universidad de Deusto (Cuadernos de Derechos Humanos, 70) (2013).

Fowler, Carwyn and Rhys Jones, 'Can Environmentalism and Nationalism Be Reconciled? The Plaid Cymru/Green Party Alliance, 1991–95', (2006) 16(3) *Regional & Federal Studies* 315–331.

Gabrys, Jennifer, 'Citizen Sensing, Air Pollution and Fracking: From "Caring About Your Air" to Speculative Practices of Evidencing Harm', (2017) 65(2) *The Sociological Review* 172–192.

Galarraga, Ibon, Mikel Gonzalez-Eguino and Anil Markandya, 'The Role of Regional Governments in Climate Change Policy', (2011) 21(3) *Environmental Policy and Governance* 164–182.

Garcia, Ernest, 'Degrowth, the Past, the Future, and the Human Nature', (2012) 44(6) *Futures* 546–552.

García, Marisol, 'The Breakdown of the Spanish Urban Growth Model: Social and Territorial Effects of the Global Crisis', (2010) 34(4) *International Journal of Urban and Regional Research* 967–980.

Hamilton, P, 'The Greening of Nationalism: Nationalising Nature in Europe', (2002) 11(2) *Environmental Politics* 27–48.

Happaerts, Sander, 'Are You Talking to Us? How Subnational Governments Respond to Global Sustainable Development Governance', (2012) 22(2) *Environmental Policy and Governance* 127–142.

Happaerts, Sander, 'Sustainable Development in Quebec and Flanders: Institutionalizing Symbolic Politics?', (2012) 55(4) *Canadian Public Administration* 553–573.

Happaerts, Sander, Karoline Van den Brande and Hans Bruyninckx, 'Governance for Sustainable Development at the Inter-Subnational Level: The Case of the Network of Regional Governments for Sustainable Development (Nrg4sd)', (2010) 20(1) *Regional & Federal Studies* 127–149.

Happaerts, Sander, Karoline Van den Brande and Hans Bruyninckx, 'Subnational Governments in Transnational Networks for Sustainable Development', (2011) 11(4) *International Environmental Agreements: Politics, Law and Economics* 321–339.

Hauter, Wenonah, *Frackopoly: The Battle for the Future of Energy and the Environment* (The New Press 2016).

Jáuregui, Gurutz, 'La Actividad Internacional De La Comunidad Autónoma Del País Vasco. La Implicación Europea', (1999) 36 *Euskonews & Media*. <http://www.euskonews.com/0036zbk/frgaia.htm>.

Klitgaard, Kent A and Lisi Krall, 'Ecological Economics, Degrowth, and Institutional Change', (2012) 84 *Ecological Economics* 247–253.

Krämer, Ludwig (ed), *European Environmental Law. A Comparative Perspective* (Routledge 2003).

Loperena Rota, Demetrio, *Desarrollo Sostenible y Globalización* (Thomson-Aranzadi, 2003).

López Ramón, Fernando (ed), *Observatorio De Polìticas Ambientales: 2010* (Thomson Reuters-Aranzadi: Centro de Publicaciones, Ministerio de Medio Ambiente y Medio Rural y Marino 2010).

López Ramón, Fernando, *Observatorio De Polìticas Ambientales: 2016* (CIEMAT 2016).

Loughlin, John, 'The Regional Question, Subsidiarity and the Future of Europe', in Stephen Weatherill and Ulf Bernitz (ed), *The Role of Regions and Sub-National Actors in Europe* (Hart 2005) 157–170.

Lubbers, Eveline (ed), *Battling Big Business: Countering Greenwash, Infiltration, and Other Forms of Corporate Bullying* (Common Courage Press 2002).

Malloy, Tove H, 'Minority Environmentalism and Eco-Nationalism in the Baltics: Green Citizenship in the Making?', (2009) 40(3) *Journal of Baltic Studies* 375–395.

Martin, Sarah J and Peter Andrée, 'Putting Food Sovereignty to Work: Civil Society Governmentalities and Canada's People's Food Policy Project (2008–2011)', (2017) 13(4) *Journal of Civil Society* 374–391.

Meng, Qingmin, 'Fracking Equity: A Spatial Justice Analysis Prototype', (2018) 70 *Land Use Policy* Supplement C 10–15.

Moragues-Faus, Ana, 'Problematising Justice Definitions in Public Food Security Debates: Towards Global and Participative Food Justices', (2017) 84 *Geoforum* 95–106.

Moreno, Luis, *The Federalization of Spain*, The Cass Series in Regional and Federal Studies (F. Cass 2001).

Moreno, Luis and Daniele Conversi, 'Modelo Social Y LíMites Al Crecimiento En El Antropoceno', (2017) 12 *Eunomía. Revista en Cultura de la Legalidad* 310–314.

Moreno, Luis and Daniele Conversi, 'Cambio Climático Y Modelo De Bienestar En La Era Del Antropoceno,' in Germán Jaraíz Arroyo (ed), *Bienestar Social Y Politicas Publicas. Retos Para Pactar El Futuro* (Los Libros de la Catarata 2018).

Muraca, Barbara, 'Towards a Fair Degrowth-Society: Justice and the Right to a "Good Life" Beyond Growth', (2012) 44(6) *Futures* 535–545.

Murillo de la Cueva, Enrique Lucas, *Comunidades Autónomas y política europea* (Civitas IVAP-Civitas 2000).

Nicolaidis, Kalypso and Stephen Weatherill (eds), *Whose Europe?: National Models and the Constitution of the European Union* (OUP 2003).

O'Neill, Daniel W, 'Measuring Progress in the Degrowth Transition to a Steady State Economy', (2012) 84 *Ecological Economics* 221–231.

Patel, Raj, 'Food Sovereignty', (2009) 36(3) *The Journal of Peasant Studies* 663–706.

Pearse, Guy, *Greenwash: Big Brands and Carbon Scams* (Schwartz Publishing 2012).

Pérez Tremps, Pablo (ed), *La participación europea y la acción exterior de las Comunidades Autónomas,* (Institut d'Estudis Autonòmics 1999).

Rei, Fernando, Kamyla Borges Cunha and Natalia Vera Pérez, 'La Paradiplomacia Medioambiental Global Y El Papel De Las Comunidades Autónomas Españolas', (2013) 53(2) *Foro Internacional* 337–362.

Romano, Onofrio, 'How to Rebuild Democracy, Re-Thinking Degrowth', (2012) 44(6) *Futures* 582–589.

Royles, Elin, 'A "Responsibility" to Act Globally: Investigating the Welsh Assembly Government's Engagement in Nrg4SD,' in Hans Bruyninckx, Sander Happaerts and Karoline Van den Brande (eds), *Sustainable Development and Subnational Governments: Policy-Making and Multi-Level Interactions* (Palgrave Macmillan UK 2012) 160–179.

Royles, Elin and Nicola McEwen, 'Empowered for Action? Capacities and Constraints in Sub-State Government Climate Action in Scotland and Wales', (2015) 24(6) *Environmental Politics* 1034–1054.

Smith, Anthony D, *Nationalism and Modernism: A Critical Survey of Recent Theories of Nations and Nationalism* (Routledge 1998).

Taibo, Carlos, *Decrecimiento, Crisis, Capitalismo*, Colección De Estudios Internacionales, No. 5 (Servicio Editorial de la Universidad del Paìs Vasco – Euskal Herriko Unibertsitateko Argitalpen Zerbitzua 2010).

Tokic, Damir, 'The Economic and Financial Dimensions of Degrowth', (2012) 84 *Ecological Economics* 49–56.

Van den Brande, Karoline, 'Intergovernmental Co-operation for International Decision Making in Federal States: The Case of Sustainable Development in Belgium', (2012) 22(4) *Regional & Federal Studies* 407–433.

Van den Brande, Karoline, Sander Happaerts and Hans Bruyninckx, 'Multi-Level Interactions in a Sustainable Development Context: Different Routes for Flanders to Decision-Making in the UN Commission on Sustainable Development', (2011) 21(1) *Environmental Policy and Governance* 70–82.

Vergara-Camus, Leandro, 'Capitalism, Democracy, and the Degrowth Horizon', *Capitalism Nature Socialism* (2017), 1–17. doi: 10.1080/10455752.2017.1344868.

Williams, Paul, 'The Governance of Sustainable Development in Wales', (2006) 11(3) *Local Environment* 253–267.

PART 2

European and Middle Eastern Perspectives

CHAPTER 6

Territorial Autonomy and Minority Self-Government in Spain: Catalonia and the Basque Country

Eduardo J. Ruiz Vieytez

I Introduction

This paper intends to evaluate the use of territorial autonomy as a constitutional instrument to accommodate minority nations within the Spanish political system. Spain is generally perceived as one of the most decentralized countries in Europe, as well as a successful model in the treatment of and provision for its minorities. However, this external perception of the Spanish political system turns out to be highly questionable when we study its functions from an internal perspective. This article argues that the real debate in the Spanish constitutional system is not about autonomy, but about the recognition of the multinational character of the country and the political asymmetry that it implies. My main thesis is that the political reality of Spain is markedly asymmetric. However, this is not reflected in constitutional law.

The paper is structured in four main parts. Firstly, I will briefly refer to the debate on the multinational character of the Spanish kingdom. The second part, will describe the constitutional framework dealing with territorial diversity and its evolution in the first 20 years since it came into force in 1978 after the Franco dictatorship. In the third section, I will analyse the tensions raised by the evolution of this very system in the last 20 years. I will then point out some of the basic differences that occur in the specific situations of Catalonia and the Basque Countries and draw some conclusions.

II Spain as a Multinational Country

From a constitutional perspective, modern Spain is a classic example of a complex state. In constitutional terms, it does not define itself as a federal state, and it shows theoretical characteristics of a unitary state while also possessing significant scope for complete political decentralization. At the same time, Spain is one of the most diverse societies in Europe.

 | DOI:10.1163/9789004405455_007

If we measure diversity in linguistic parameters, Spain has one of the highest percentages of population with a different mother tongue to the majority language (circa 20%). However, the multinational nature of the society is the subject of fierce debate and the way in which certain minority communities, particularly Catalonia and the Basque Country, are accommodated is a permanent source of friction. National unity and challenges to Spanish national identity, mainly from Catalonia and the Basque Country, probably constitutes the most debated issue on the Spanish political agenda.

Following the 1978 Constitution, present-day Spain is made up of seventeen Autonomous Communities and two Autonomous Cities (Ceuta and Melilla). However, from an analysis of voting patterns in each region, it emerges that after over forty years of democracy and free elections Catalan and Basque societies (the latter including part of Navarre) regard themselves as different nations, while the rest of Spain clearly identifies itself with the idea of Spain as one nation. When it comes to Spanish society as a whole, Spain is seen as a nation by the majority of its citizens, while only 18% regard it as a multinational State.[1] Therefore, there is in Spain a significantly asymmetric and uneven multinational reality that has not been constitutionally recognized. In this sense, the definition given by Linz at the start of the transition to democracy still rings true: 'Spain today is a state for all Spaniards, a nation-state for a large part of the Spanish population, and only a state but not their nation for important minorities'.[2]

This identitarian asymmetry generates relationships of permanent distrust that in turn lead to constitutional development in asymmetric terms. This issue has been part of the Spanish political debate since the emergence of Basque and Catalan nationalism in the late 19th century. As the Spanish state was shaped and consolidated, it came up against several rival national projects and this confrontation has not yet been resolved.[3] On the one hand, the national construction process has been unable to completely integrate its peripheral national realities into the concept of Spain as a nation. On the other hand, these peripheral national projects have not been strong enough to impose a multinational articulation of the state on the central viewpoint.[4]

1 Francisco Llera, 'Spain: Identity Boundaries and Political Reconstruction' (2009) 15(3/4) *Nationalism and Ethnic Politics* 312.

2 Juan Linz, 'Politics in a Multi-Lingual Society with a Dominant World Language: The Case of Spain' in Savard, Jean-Guy, and Wigneault, Richard (eds) *Les États Multilingues: Problèmes et Solutions* (Presses de l'Université Laval 1975) 423.

3 Michael Keating and Alex Wilson, 'Renegotiating the State of Autonomies: Statute Reform and Multi-level Politics in Spain' (2009) 32(3) *West European Politics* 537.

4 Ferran Requejo, *Multinational federalism and value pluralism: the Spanish case* (Routledge 2005) 89.

Thus, although the Spanish state includes at least two territories where national feelings are repeatedly expressed by the local majority (Catalonia and the Basque Country), the constitutional order has not formally recognised them and the model steers a path between the contradictory intentions of accommodating and concealing this diversity at the same time. Territorial autonomy was developed as an instrument to try to find a level of accommodation to this diversity, but it also created new identities and permanent comparisons between the degree of self-government the different autonomous communities were allowed.

III Territorial Autonomy as an Instrument for Constitutional Accommodation: 1977–1997

The political transition after the military regime of Francisco Franco (1939–1975) paved the way for a new constitution. Although the territorial model of the state is not specified in the 1978 constitution, the system is based on the unbreakable unity of the Spanish nation and at the same time it permits the creation of autonomous communities. Article 2 of the constitution states:

> The Constitution is based on the indissoluble unity of the Spanish nation, the common and indivisible motherland of all Spaniards; it recognizes the right to autonomy of the nationalities and regions of which it is composed, and solidarity amongst them.[5]

Therefore, the Constitution of 1978 is categorical in establishing national unity and opposes the assumption of a plurinational state. According to the constitution, the various nationalities are only a part of the Spanish nation. In parallel, Article 3 acknowledges linguistic diversity. According to this article, in Spain, Castilian Spanish has an official status in any part of the state, while other languages can share this official status in their respective autonomous communities. This constitutional configuration does not help the majority group to acknowledge that the minority languages spoken in the state are a common heritage, since their recognition is limited to specific autonomous communities. However, it is a step forward in comparison with the political tradition of denying cultural diversity in the Spanish kingdom.

5 Article 2 reads in the original Spanish version: 'La Constitución se fundamenta en la indisoluble unidad de la Nación española, patria común e indivisible de todos los españoles, y reconoce y garantiza el derecho a la autonomía de las nacionalidades y regiones que la integran y la solidaridad entre todas ellas'.

Within this constitutional framework, the right to autonomy of all nationalities and regions became a central point of the Spanish political agenda. The basic justification for an extensive decentralization is ambiguous, since it stems both from reasons of accommodating diversity and the search for greater administrative efficiency. In any case, the constitution avoids using concrete definitional terms such as 'federal', 'confederal' or 'unitary'. One of the reasons for this is that the development of the Spanish territorial model had not been totally settled by 1978. Also, the term 'nationalities' was deliberately used in an ambiguous manner in order to facilitate political consensus including left-wing and Catalan forces. The accepted wording for the territorial model is 'autonomies state' or 'autonomic state', a neologism in comparative law.

Since the Constitution did not define the system in unequivocal terms nor did it map Spain's nationalities and regions, the territorial model of Spain was shaped through institutional evolution and political agreements. The autonomic map and the access to political self-government for the territory as a whole (except for Ceuta and Melilla) were decided at an initial stage, in the first 'autonomic agreements' of the main two Spanish parties, in 1981. Later, through new political agreements concluded in 1992, again between the two main central parties, the resulting map equated to the degree of autonomy for the 17 Autonomous Communities, except for the specificities resulting from Basque historic rights.

From a comparative constitutional law perspective, some voices defend the autonomic state as being in some way comparable to the federal models in place in Germany, Belgium or Austria.[6] However, others deny such a thesis,[7] maintaining that the current Spanish model is more like a regional state, with Italy as the closest example.[8] Finally, some authors prefer to underline

6 Among others, Eliseo Aja, *El Estado autonómico. Federalismo y hechos diferenciales* (Alianza 2003). Others with a more cautious approach tend to say that Spain is a decentralized state very close to the federal systems: Pablo Pérez, Tremps *Derecho Constitucional, vol. II. Los poderes del Estado. La organización territorial del Estado* (5th edn, Tirant lo blanch 2002) 298.

7 For example, Agustín Ruiz Robledo, 'Veinticinco años de estado autonómico' (2003–2004) 58–59 *Revista de Derecho Político* 727; Luis Pomed Sánchez, 'Situación actual y perspectivas de futuro del Estado Autonómico' (1999) 1 *El Ebro* 62; López Mira, 'Veinticinco años de Estado autonómico: una mala solución organizativa para un problema político' (2003–2004) 58–59 *Revista de Derecho Político* 747; Enrique Alvarez Conde, *Curso de Derecho Constitucional, vol. II. Los órganos constitucionales. El Estado autonómico* (3rd edn, Tecnos 2000) 365; Miguel Angel Aparicio Perez (eds) *Temas de Derecho constitucional (I)* (Cedec 1998) 252.

8 Pedro Bon, 'La Constitución española en el marco del constitucionalismo contemporáneo" (2003) 69 *Revista Española de Derecho Constitucional* 23.

the original features of the system.[9] The fact that all the autonomous communities enjoy ample political self-government argues in favour of the federal character of the autonomic state. However, even recognizing the high level of self-government in the Spanish autonomous communities, the so-called autonomic state cannot be understood as an authentic federal state for a number of reasons. On the one hand, and apart from the lack of a federal definition, the autonomous communities are not constituent parts of the state, since they did not exist prior to the constitution and they needed a subsequent autonomy act to be established. On the other hand, the constitution categorically insists in articles 1(2) and 2 that there is a unique and exclusive source of sovereignty. The process of decentralization from a unitary political power is too explicit in the constitution to be understood as the evolution of a federal system. At the same time, the dominance of the central institutions over the regional ones does not fit perfectly with a federal theory.

Thus, the model developed in Spain responds to a unitary state with strong political decentralization and tends to the symmetry of the autonomous powers.[10] In this regard, the Spanish model drifts away from the traditional unitary state model and also from those that are partially decentralized like the United Kingdom, Denmark or Finland. At the same time, the Spanish model differs from the classical federal state models, like the United States and Switzerland, although slightly less than other European federal states like Austria or Russia. The theoretical model closest to the current Spanish model is probably the one of the Italian Republic. Nevertheless, Italy differs from Spain by guaranteeing the asymmetry of the different regions in the constitution itself.[11]

The tension between symmetry and asymmetry in Spain has been present since the approval of the constitution and the first stages of autonomies' evolution. Nevertheless, in the Spanish regions there are many important dynamics of social and political mobilization that are the result of emulation and envy,[12] so that in the 'non-historic' ACs (those different from Basque Country,

9 Giovanni Poggeschi, *Le nazioni linguistiche della Spagna autonómica: Universalitá de la lingua castigliana e vitalità delle lingue regionali* (Cedam 2002); Antonio Reposo, *Profili dello Stato autonomico. Federalismo e regionalismo* (Giappichelli 2000).

10 *See* Eduardo Ruiz Vieytez, 'Federalism, Subnational Constitutional Arrangements and the Protection of Minorities in Spain' in Allan Tarr, Robert Williams and Joseph Marko (eds) *Federalism, Subnational Constitutions and Minorities Rights* (Praeger 2004) 133–153.

11 Some authors maintain that the Spanish model tends to be permanently open and the symmetry would be one of its typical elements: Antonio Torres del Moral, *Principios de Derecho Constitucional* (4th edn, Universidad Complutense 1998) 718. But, as Pomed says, the presence of differential facts does not federalize the system: Sánchez, *op. cit.*, 63.

12 Luis Moreno, *La federalización de España. Poder político y territorio* (2nd edn, siglo XXI 2008) 117.

Catalonia and Galicia) being different from other communities in asymmetrical terms is commonly perceived as a privilege rather than a means of accommodating diversity. Thus, three particular moments show evidence of these difficulties. First, the debate about the granting to Andalusia of autonomy by means of Article 143 (ordinary procedure) or 151 (aggravated procedure), became a symbol of emulation and of the comparative effect triggered by the first autonomous communities (the Basque Country and Catalonia). Second, the proposed Transitory Provision 3 concerning the Galician Statute[13] project, which was designed to limit the autonomous capacities of the future Galician community (and probably of all upcoming communities), thus providing a way to consolidate the asymmetry between Catalonia and the Basque Country on the one hand, and the rest of the regions. Third, the approval of an Organic Law (partially deemed unconstitutional in 1983) to harmonise the autonomy process, that would apply *a posteriori* to the Basque and Catalan communities. In the three cases, the result was to favour equalisation and opposing asymmetry.

In addition, the Constitutional Court adopted a leading role in defining the borders between state and regional competences in most issues. The doctrine of the court generated further distrust in the Basque Country and in Catalonia regarding its moderating role, reducing its political legitimacy in the eyes of the Basque and Catalan minorities. As a consequence, at the end of the 90s, Spain had not yet found a stable legal formula on the territorial structure of the state.[14]

IV New Tensions, Divergences and Asymmetries: 1997–2017

IV.A *Reform of Autonomy in Catalonia and the Basque Country*

Once the first stages of the development of the autonomic states were over, a degree of calm presided over political relations in Spain during what remained of the 80s and 90s. However, the new millennium saw the reappearance of new

13 Transitory Disposition 3 of the Statute of Galicia project stated the following: 'With regard to those competences that deal with those matters which, in accordance with the Constitution and in this Statute are also the object of state competences, the demarcation of these will depend on the decisions of the Parliament by law. Until said demarcation does occur and, subject to what the same stipulates, the Joint Committee may determine the faculties that correspond to the Autonomous Community with regard to specific matters of interest to the same and without detriment to that laid down in Article 87.2 of the Constitution'.

14 Javier Pérez Royo, 'Una asignatura pendiente: la reforma de la Constitución' (2003) 69 *Revista Española de Derecho Constitucional* 227.

tensions related to territorial organisation; the only one of the main constitutional debates that had not been definitively settled or defined when the constitution was adopted.[15]

By the late 90s, the system of autonomies had evolved towards a fairly symmetrical political decentralization, with significant powers in executive domains, but more restricted when it came to the legislative capacity of the autonomous communities. Yet, tensions between the political and identity aspirations of the majority sectors in Catalonia and the Basque Country on the one hand, and the majority of the state and the rest of the communities on the other, happened to be recurrent. The relation between majority and minority representative political parties was basically dependent upon the existence of parliamentary majorities or the need of central parties to get the parliamentary support of Catalan or Basque parties in exchange for additional competences for their communities. This political landscape reinforced the traditional distrust between both sides. The tension severely increased when the so-called historic communities expressed their will to amend their respective statutes. In this sense, the Basque and Catalan experiences were significantly different.

In the Basque case, 1998 marked a breaking off of political relations between the two political blocks, pro-sovereignty and unionist. After a general ceasefire proclaimed by the armed group ETA, the Basque parties gathered around the idea of self-determination as an instrument to achieve both a peaceful solution (Northern Ireland was the reference in that period) and a new political status for a new generation. However, the process of 1998–99 and the later attempt known colloquially as the 'Ibarretxe Plan' after the Basque president promoting it, both failed. The idea of establishing a new framework for the relationship between Spain and the Basque Country based on free association by reforming the Basque Statute was supported by pro-sovereignty groups, but it entered into a head-on collision with the major Spanish parties. Opposition by central parties and institutions was absolute throughout the process and no sincere political dialogue took place regarding a renovation of the autonomy. As a consequence, the Basque Act of Autonomy or Statute remains unchanged to date since its approval in 1979. Even after the new political scenario deriving from the ending of violence by ETA in 2011, there has not been any significant evolution. The pro-sovereignty majorities in the Basque parliament keep bringing demands for self-determination or a new status with greater autonomy to

15 The other major questions when the constitution was drafted were the democratisation of the State, the option of a parliamentary monarchy model and the declaration of the non-denominational nature of the State.

the political agenda under the idea of the 'right to decide'. Spanish political parties and public opinion remain fiercely opposed to such a debate.

The Catalan attempt to amend the Statute on Autonomy was a quite different process. This was put forward in 2003 in a much more favourable context, characterized by better political relations between the different Catalan political parties. However, the process for the reform of the Catalan Statute generated tension within the Spanish Socialist Party (PSOE) itself and in its relations with the Catalan Socialist Party (PSC), its sister party in Catalonia. The process also distanced the positions of the Popular Party (PP) from the rest of the Catalan parties.

Differently from what had happened with the 'Ibarretxe Plan', the reform of the Statute of Catalonia was followed with attention in the rest of Spain, mainly with an attitude of distrust. This is due to the fact that in the 'non-historical' autonomies, which lack their own national project, the differentiation of other communities in asymmetric terms is seen as privilege instead of a tool to accommodate diversity. In part as a consequence of this, other autonomous communities beyond the Basque Country and Catalonia started parallel processes of reforming their statutes. Notably, this was the case for Valencia, Catalonia's neighbouring region, whose new statute was passed before the Catalan new statute was approved. Similarly, a new statute was also approved for the region of Andalusia.[16]

The two parallel processes of reform in Valencia and Andalusia are evidence of the other communities' aspirations to equal the level of competences of the historical communities, thus preventing them from becoming a special case. In other words, there has been a clear aim towards reducing the asymmetry of the country and reaffirming that Catalonia or the Basque Country are a part of Spain.[17] Thus, in the case of the reform of the Andalusian Statute, the process was started without a significant social demand for it, and once the Catalan process had already been initiated. Besides that, the new proposal for Andalusia copied many of the articles in the new Catalan statute that, surprisingly, did not cause the same effect in the two regions. The conservative Popular Party opposed the new Statute of Catalonia, while being in favour of the Andalusian reform, even holding different positions for clauses that were exactly the same in both texts. Some sectors of the Spanish Socialist Party also showed a significant distrust towards the new Catalan Statute, while displaying their

16 Art. 151 is the article through which regional statutes were envisioned for the Basque Country, Catalonia and Galicia.

17 Moreno, *op. cit.*, 123–124.

full support for the Andalusian one. As for the Valencian case, this dynamic of promoting symmetry between regions in order to neutralise the historical nationalities was expressed in legal terms in the so-called 'Camps Clause',[18] which was introduced into the Statute of Valencia as Additional provision 2.[19] The new Statute for Valencia was approved just before the Catalan Statute in 2006. Additional Provision 2 is a tangible demonstration of the opposition to any kind of asymmetry that some communities (namely Catalonia or the Basque Country) may achieve in the future. This clause states that whatever new competences are obtained by any other autonomous community, they must be considered as incorporated by Valencia as well. As a matter of fact, the final wording of the clause has little immediate effect, but it holds significant political meaning. It is an expression of distrust and opposition to possible future advances in self-government of the historical communities, in a kind of preventive comparative grievance, to claim a general and permanent application of symmetry to the whole country.

Apart from these processes, it is noteworthy that several communities have since reformed their statutes to expressly brand themselves as historical nationalities or to refer to specific identities or historical rights, always with an eye on emulating the two most conflictive communities. This dynamic of unrelenting persecution between historical communities and other autonomies, or between asymmetry and symmetry, brings with it considerable constitutional fatigue, not only at the state majority level, but also in the minority nations that could have been accommodated through territorial autonomy. Today, the majority positions in both the Basque Country and Catalonia are oriented to the defence of the so-called 'right to decide'.

18 Camps was the president of the region at that time.

19 Additional Provision 2 of the Statute of the Valencian Community (Organic Law 1/2006, April 10th, concerning the Reform of Organic Law 5/1982, July 1st, of the Statute of Autonomy of the Community of Valencia) states the following: '1. Any modification of State legislation that, of a general nature and national applicability, implies an increase in the competences of the Autonomous communities shall be applicable to the Community of Valencia, with its competences being considered to have increased on the same terms. 2. The Community of Valencia shall ensure that the level of self-government established in the present Statute is updated on equal terms with the other Autonomous Communities. 3. To this end, any increase in the competences of the Autonomous Communities that is not taken into account by the present Statute, or that has not been attributed, transferred or delegated to the Community of Valencia previously, shall require the legitimate institutions of self-government to promote the corresponding initiatives to ensure said updating'.

IV.B *The Debate on the Right to Decide*

The expression 'right to decide', as currently used in the Basque and Catalan contexts, means the ability of a specific territorially defined collective to freely determine its internal and external political status and the way in which it delivers its political, economic, social and cultural development. Its content is thus wholly indistinguishable from that of the right to self-determination, or from a political notion of sovereignty. The main question that emerges around it is who is entitled to exercise that right. In other words, whether the citizens of the Basque Country or Catalonia are entitled, as distinct societies, to exercise this right of decision separately from the population of the Spanish state as a whole.

If the right to decide means the right of a people to be consulted about the political status of a territory and that the result of such consultation be respected,[20] then it fully corresponds to the right to self-determination. In this sense, some authors consider the right to decide to be a product deriving from an evolution or transformation of the right to self-determination within the context of representative democracies.[21] The right to decide would have to face all debates and unsolved theoretical problems around the right to self-determination. In particular, the points about the existence of a different people and about the meaning of internal self-determination would be the most relevant ones in the Spanish context.

However, in the last few years there have been some attempts to build a new different right to decide, particularly in the context of Catalonia. Ridao maintains that the right to decide does not equal self-determination, but it is rather an independent right which was recognised by the Spanish Constitutional Court in its ruling 42/2014.[22] According to this interpretation, the right

---

20 Tornos distinguishes between three possible meanings of the right to decide: a) as a right to self-determination and *ius secessionis*; b) as a right to call a part of the electoral body for a consultation; c) as an aspiration on the part of the Catalan people to be consulted: Joaquín Tornos, 'El derecho a decidir no existe pero el Gobierno debería convocar la consulta' in Eduard Sagarra (coord.) *¿Existe el derecho a decidir? Preguntas y respuestas sobre el proceso abierto en Cataluña* (Tibidabo ediciones 2014) 316–320.

21 Jaume López, 'Del dret a l'autodeterminació al dret a decidir. Un possible canvi de paradigma en la reivindicació dels drets de les nacions sense estat' (Centre UNESCO de Catalunya 2011) 4, <http://focir.cat/ca/llibres/del-dret-lautodeterminacio-al-dret-decidir-un-possible-canvi-de-paradigma-en-la-reivindicacio-dels-drets-de-les-nacions-sense-estat/>.

22 The ruling states that 'Respect for references to the «right to decide» is subject to a constitutional interpretation, as this is not proclaimed independently or directly linked to the first principle governing the declaration of sovereignty of the Catalan people. Rather, references are included in the initial part of the Declaration (in direct relation to initiation

to decide constitutes a legitimate political aspiration in accordance with freedom of expression and participation in the political sphere.[23] The judgement of the Constitutional Court opposing Resolution 5/X issued by the Catalan Parliament[24] expressly cites self-determination in order to deny such a right to the Catalan citizens. However, the same judgement recognises the right to decide as a legitimate political aspiration.[25] The collective decision by the Catalan people about their political future via a consultative referendum would therefore be fully constitutional, as the Constitution does not impose unity, can be reformed, and as the exercising of this right goes neither against the democratic principle nor against basic rights.[26] However, the Constitutional Court simply reiterates that the aspiration of a sovereign Catalonia is legitimate, provided that it is included in the legal system via the constitutional reform mechanisms envisaged in it.[27]

of a «process») and in different principles in the Declaration (second, third, seventh and ninth, second paragraph). As we shall see, these principles are suitable for the Constitution and provide an outlet for the interpretation that the «right on the part of Catalan citizens to decide» is not proclaimed as the manifestation of a right to self-determination that is unrecognised by the Constitution, or as an attribution of unrecognised sovereignty within it. Rather, it is viewed as a political aspiration which can only be attained via a process that is in accordance with constitutional legality in terms of the principles of «democratic legitimacy», «pluralism», and «legality», expressly proclaimed in the Declaration and closely linked to the «right to decide»' (*Fundamento Jurídico* 3).

23 Joan Ridao, 'El derecho de Cataluña a decidir su futuro político colectivo. Las vías para su probable ejercicio' in Eduard Sagarra (coord.) *¿Existe el derecho a decidir? Preguntas y respuestas sobre el proceso abierto en Cataluña* (Tibidabo ediciones 2014) 38.

24 Resolució 5/X del Parlament de Catalunya, per la qual s'aprova la Declaració de sobirania i del dret a decidir del poble de Catalunya (Declaration of Sovereignty and the right of the Catalan people to decide), adopted by the Catalan Parliament on 23rd January 2013 by 85 votes in favour, 41 against and 2 abstentions.

25 Ridao, *op. cit.* , 40.

26 Joan Ridao, 'La juridificación del derecho a decidir en España. La STC 42/2014 y el derecho a aspirar a un proceso de cambio político del orden constitucional' (2014) 91 *Revista de Derecho Político* 108.

27 In the case of the 2008 Law governing Consultation about the Basque Country, the Constitutional Court pointed out in its ruling 103/2008 dated 11th September (*Fundamento Jurídico* 4) that: 'The relevant Law presumes the existence of a subject – "the Basque people" – the holder of a "right to decide" that may be exercised [Section 1 b) of the Law being contested], equivalent to the holder of sovereignty, the Spanish people, and capable of negotiating the terms of a new relationship with the State set up by the Spanish Nation between the latter and one of the Autonomous Communities in which it is organised. However, identification of an institutional subject equipped with such qualities and competences is impossible without prior reform of the Constitution in force'.

Even those who defend the right to decide as a separate right recognise that its legal basis is still very precarious.[28] This weakness is also clear, as the debate has hardly taken place outside the Spanish context. Speaking from a legal-positive standpoint, there is at present no right to decide that legally addresses the claim for consultation about a pro-independence option.[29] In the best case, it could be considered a political principle that is not yet recognised as a legal right by either international law or constitutional law.[30] As a matter of fact, both the subject and contents of the so-called right to decide fully coincide with those of the right to self-determination, whose interpretation in different contexts is the real legal and political controversy. A case in point is that when the Government of Catalonia accelerated the preparation of a unilateral referendum for October 2017, the references to the right to decide disappeared in the justification of the process, and the official language shifted again towards the classical right to self-determination. In any case, the ongoing debate remains unsolved, since there is a clash of political aspirations between a unique sovereignty for the whole of Spain and the possibility for minority nations such as the Basque Country or Catalonia of having their own sovereignty and ability to determine their own political status, as evidenced by the declaration of a new Catalan Republic by the Parliament of Catalonia on 27 October 2017, and the subsequent suspension of autonomy by the Spanish senate.

IV.C *Economy Crisis and the Catalan Challenge*

From 2008, a deep and lasting economic crisis has severely affected Spain. According to surveys carried out by the Sociological Research Centre, the number of Spaniards in favour of 'a state with autonomous communities like that at present' started to decrease and those supporting the explicit option 'for a

28 Joan Ridao, 'El procés de «juridificació» internacional del dret de secessió. De l'autodeterminació externa al «dret a decidir» en base als principis democràtic i d'efectivitat' *Fòrum sobre el dret a decidir. Dret comparat i context internacional* (Institut d'Estudis Autonòmics 2014) 87.

29 Xabier Pons, 'El denominado derecho a decidir y el Derecho Internacional' in Eduard Sagarra (coord.) *¿Existe el derecho a decidir? Preguntas y respuestas sobre el proceso abierto en Cataluña* (Tibidabo ediciones 2014) 75; Xabier Pons, 'Legalidad internacional y derecho a decidir' (2014), 27 *Revista Electrónica de Estudios Internacionales* 84.

30 Enric Fossas, 'Interpretar la política. Comentario a la STC 42/2014, de 25 de marzo, sobre la Declaración de soberanía y el derecho a decidir del pueblo de Cataluña' (2014) 101 *Revista Española de Derecho Constitucional* 289; Josep Maria Vilajosana Rubio, 'Principi democràtic i justificació constitucional del dret de decidir' (2014) 19 *Revista d'estudis autonòmics i federals* 178–210.

centralised state' then started to grow.[31] The economic crisis certainly accelerated this process and by the summer of 2012 the Spanish citizens who favoured a (more) centralised state outnumbered those who favoured the current territorial model, and undoubtedly those supporting increased self-government for the historical communities and recognition of their right to secession.[32] Obviously, these figures are totally different in the regions of the Basque Country and Catalonia.

In addition, the economic crisis underlined the differences between Spanish regions and the competition for scarce resources. A special mention has to be made of the water resources in certain catchment areas. Also, the distribution of debts and benefits among the different autonomous communities has been disputed and financial balances challenged.[33]

The result of all these processes is a kind of constitutional fatigue in respect to the accommodation of the territories of Catalonia and of the Basque Country. This fatigue is coupled with constant political deadlock, and the consequences of the economic crisis. All this has provoked large segments of society, especially young people, to become depoliticized, or to support new political parties. In addition, the past years have seen an increase in the pro-independence feelings of the historical nationalities, particularly in Catalonia, up to the point that in 2012 the option in favour of independence enjoyed the support of an absolute majority of Catalan society for the first time.[34]

The fact that in Spain political issues connected with sovereignty, territoriality, symbols and language are addressed very passionately, does not help in finding constructive solutions. Territorial debates are too frequently understood through a win-lose lens and as matters of collective honour, thereby leading political forces to adopt extreme positions and to emphasize the victory-defeat interpretation. Spanish public opinion with regard to the demands for self-government made in Catalonia and the Basque Country is characterised by permanent distrust, as they are perceived as substantially non-loyal

31 Mireia Grau, 'Self-government reforms and public support for Spain's territorial model: changes and stability (1992–2010)' (2011) 13 *Revista d'Estudis Autonòmics i Federals* 194.

32 Centro de Investigaciones Sociológicas, *Barómetro de Julio, Estudio n° 2951* (July 2012) 15. <www.cis.es>.

33 Christopher. Connolly, 'Independence in Europe: Secession, Sovereignty, and the European Union' (2013) 24 *Dutch Journal of Comparative & International Law* 58–59. David Roca, 'Vers la fin de l'État des autonomies en Espagne' (2007) 72 *Revue Française de Droit Constitutionnel* 879–881.

34 *Baròmetre d'Opinió Política* (2a onada 2012). <http://www.ceo.gencat.cat/ceop/AppJava/pages>.

projects. At the same time, the pro-sovereignty (majority) sectors of both communities have grown in the last few years, particularly in Catalonia, where positions in favour of full independence have dramatically increased after the debacle of the reform of the Statute. At the end of the day, political dynamics have turned into a permanent contest between supporters and detractors of the asymmetry of the state. The majority of the population in both the Basque and Catalan societies are calling for asymmetrical special treatment, so that they can be accommodated once and for all within the State model, while the rest of the Spanish population, on the other hand, is asking for all communities to be treated equally in such a way that it helps blur or obscure the unfinished nature of their national project.[35] Spanish society is not prepared to accept particular nor special situations that are viewed as privileges.

In this respect, the role played by the constitution and by the legal order more broadly is also controversial. The 1978 Constitution has become an almost sacred document, while at the same time reinforcing the myth of its consensual nature, something that does not correspond to reality in the territorial case. To add fuel to the fire, the Spanish Constitutional Court, although having the power of arbitration, has not made much effort to earn itself significant legitimacy in the eyes of the Basque Country and Catalonia in the context of the relationships between the autonomous communities and the state. In Spanish political culture, legitimacy tends be conflated with legality. When faced with proposals that could affect the constitutional order (such as, for instance, those involved in the reform of the 2004 Basque Statute or the calling of a referendum in the Basque Country in 2008), the Spanish Constitutional Court responds on the basis of positive legality. It has also refused to consider Catalonia as a nation, it has questioned the language policies of Catalonia and has denied any possibility of unilateral referenda or consultations on the political status of the Basque Country or Catalonia.[36] In practice, the Constitutional Court is not seen any longer as a neutral referee from the perspective of Basque and Catalan political parties.

35 Michael Keating, 'Rethinking sovereignty. Independence-lite, devolutionmax and national accommodation' (2012) 16 *Revista d'estudis autonòmics i federals* 25.

36 This is especially the case with Constitutional Court judgements no 247/2007, December 12th 2007 (concerning the Region of Valencia Statute of Autonomy, no 103/2008), September 11th 2008 (concerning the Basque Country consultation law), no 31/2010, June 28th 2010 (concerning the Catalonia Statute of Autonomy). *See* Silvia Acierno and Julio Baquero Cruz, 'The order of the Spanish Constitutional Court on the proposal to convert the Basque Country into a freely associated community: keeping hands off constitutional politics' (2005) 3(4) *International Journal of Constitutional Law* 687–695; Joan Costa-Font and Ramon Tremosa-Balcells, 'Support for State opting out and stateless national identity in the Basque Country' (2008) 37(6) *Journal of Socio-Economics* 2464–2477.

IV.D *Regulating the Right to Decide as a New Instrument for Accommodation*

Within this complex context, Connolly criticises Spain's inflexibility in contrast to the accommodating strategies pursued by the British and Canadian authorities.[37] Other scholars have already put forward the idea that sovereigntist processes can be regulated, either at the international or constitutional level. This would mark a major step towards democratising the processes of self-determination.[38] In multicultural states, there are no obvious or direct solutions to political differences. The most necessary principle is that of defining legitimate, democratic and acceptable procedures for the populations who are affected by them.[39]

Thus, the regulation of sovereigntist processes would be an instrument to ensure stability in situations of tension, by providing a feasible framework of possibilities for all the possible options. A more detailed proposal has already been put forward in a different work.[40] The main idea is that of incorporating this option into the autonomy framework of all Spanish communities, without differences or privileges. In this way some of the nationalities could develop the corresponding decisional processes, while the rest would have the obligation to respect the outcome of the process and to facilitate mutual understanding and a deep participatory debate. The introduction of such a competence or regulation within the constitutional framework would in itself act as an instrument of accommodation for significant pro-independence sectors in both Catalonia and the Basque Country.

V Catalonia and the Basque Country: Two Different Minority Nations

For many years, we have considered Basque society to be extremely fragmented, in terms of both culture and identity, and one in which the citizens have no shared basic points of reference (the very name of the country, language, map, basic symbols...are still disputed). Some of the political projects proposed by

37 Connolly, *op. cit.*, 102.

38 Daniel Weinstock, 'Constitutionalizing the Right to Secede' (2001) 9(2) *Journal of Political Philosophy* 182–203; Susana Mancini, 'Rethinking the boundaries of democratic secession: Liberalism, nationalism, and the right of minorities to self-determination' (2009) 6(3–4) *International Journal of Constitutional Law* 553–584.

39 Thomas Fleiner, 'The Current Situation of Federalism in Switzerland' (2009) 9 *Revista d' Estudis Autonomics i Federals* 68.

40 Eduardo Ruiz Vieytez, 'Minority Nations and Self-determination. A Proposal for the Regulation of Sovereignty Processes' (2016) 23(3) *International Journal on Minority and Group Rights* 402–421.

the main parties of the Basque Country are antagonistic and contradictory. Thus, socio-political fragmentation has been traditionally perceived as much higher in the Basque Country than in Catalonia. However, the process of the last few years in Catalonia has also brought Catalan society to a significant political fragmentation. Today, we can say that in both countries, as far as sovereignty is concerned, the different political projects are fairly contradictory.

Despite the similar fragmentation outlined above, profound structural differences remain between the Basque Country's and Catalonia's political realities and national projects. Both minorities stand out for being richer than the average in the Spanish kingdom but the basis of the development models are rooted in different historical, economic, political and cultural factors.[41] The origin of Basque nationalism was based on pro-independence and anti-capitalist feelings, partly due to the frustration of the pre-industrial Basque elites, with the impact of the industrialisation of the economy and the centralisation of the State. Conversely, Catalan nationalism arose from the frustration of the Catalan bourgeoisie's attempts to influence Spanish politics in favour of their interests as well as from the rejection of the cultural homogenisation of the State. Not least important is the fact that Basque nationalism came into being after the abolition of its chartered regime, a more traumatic and faster process, accompanied by a considerable socio-economic transformation with its resulting immigration from other regions of Spain that created a new, non-native proletariat. On the contrary, in Catalonia the development process was more progressive.

The Basque and Catalan countries show other important differences. The Basque Country makes up scarcely 5% of the Spanish population, while Catalonia makes up a significant 18%. Catalan nationalism has historically shown a strong desire to influence the configuration of the Spanish state and to 'Catalanise' Spain. This willingness to influence the Spanish political debate was apparent at the time of the Second Republic, but also in the constitutional consensus of 1978 and the collaborationist spirit of Catalan nationalism in the eighties and nineties. Conversely, Basque nationalism has since its inception been less interested in the configuration of the Spanish State. Its proposals were, at most, to create a bilateral pact, between Spain and the Basque Country as two fully sovereign entities on an equal basis of coexistence. This also explains its greater ideological separation and its lesser involvement in the

41 Juan Díez Medrano *Naciones divididas. Clase, política y nacionalismo en el País Vasco y Cataluña* (Centro de Investigaciones Sociológicas 1999).

governability of Spain. In addition, Basque society has traditionally been more conflictive and radical and Catalan society more homogenous and integrated. However, in recent years, with the pro-independence process in Catalonia, this pattern seems to be shifting.

An additional and legally relevant difference between the Basque and Catalan minorities is the role played by the so-called historic rights, recognised by the Spanish constitution through additional provision 1. During the negotiations leading to the Spanish constitution, the main Basque party, PNV,[42] rather than advocating for a right to self-determination, asked for the recognition and restoration of the historic rights derived from the Basque 'chartered' system (*regimen foral*)[43] and a bilateral pact with the Crown. This is the origin of additional provision 1 of the constitution, and also of the additional provision of the Basque Statute which makes a somewhat vague reference to not waiving the historic rights of the Basque people. In the Basque case, these historic rights are an important line of symbolic argument, since they belong exclusively to the Basque territories, thereby justifying their special and thus asymmetric treatment and legitimizing such treatment in the eyes of the rest of the state population. Even if this did not fully correspond to the so-called right to decide, it could serve as grounds for legitimizing a special asymmetrical statute, as a kind of agreed sovereignty.[44] At the same time, this political solution does not exist in the case of Catalonia. In addition, in *Euskadi*, by comparison with the rest of the Spanish state, and unlike in Catalonia, the constitutional framework has less legitimacy, given the significantly lower support it received in the referendum held on 6 December 1978 on the adoption of the constitution.[45]

---

42 PNV stands for *Partido Nacionalista Vasco* to be translated as Basque National(ist) Party. The word 'nationalist' must not be understood in an ethnic or exclusivist way. Today, the PNV is the biggest party of the Basque Country, it defends the right of self-determination and can be considered as a centre-wing party. Following elections in 2016, it leads the Governments of the Basque Autonomous Community and its three provinces.

43 This expression refers to the traditional system of public and private law that was present in each of the four Basque territories (Biscay, Gipuzkoa, Alava and Navarre) until the nineteenth century, including specific institutions like parliaments, governments, judicial authorities, police forces and treasuries. This chartered system was finally abolished in 1876 through a Spanish law that was explicitly abrogated by the 1978 Constitution.

44 Xabier Ezeizabarrena, *Derecho de libre determinación y derecho a decidir: nueva soberanía y derechos humanos en el siglo XXI* (Universidad de Deusto 2017).

45 There was a much higher abstention rate in the Basque Country than the Spanish average and the support obtained by the Constitution as just 30% of the electorate compared to a 60% average in the whole country.

VI Conclusions

From a historical perspective, the 1978 Spanish Constitution was a significant step forward in recognising the right to autonomy of nationalities and regions. Territorial autonomy has given minority nations significant powers and advances in cultural, identity, economic or social policies that they had never enjoyed in the contemporary period.

However, the substantial asymmetry that characterises Spanish society with regard to national identity is hardly reflected by today's constitutional order. Only the Basque Country enjoys a financial independence that gives this nation a more accommodated position within the current system. There is a significant resistance by broad sectors of Spanish society to recognising the existence of peripheral or minority nations such as the Basque Country and Catalonia. This ongoing conflict about a bilateral or multilateral accommodation for these two communities, or between asymmetry and symmetry, has resulted in considerable political fatigue. And, in the case of Catalonia, to a direct confrontation through the celebration of a not-permitted referendum on 1 October 2017 and a declaration of independence by its parliament on 27 October 2017.

The initial construction of the state of autonomies as an open model was the result of a lack of consensus on the territorial model that was being defined. The constitutional evolution of the state of autonomies has clarified it, but it has not resolved the problem. This situation presents a difficult future for the national cohesion of the state in the medium and long term.

Today there seems to be very little chance of achieving a broad-based agreement in the Basque Country on updating self-government within the current legal framework. The current social and political conditions are very different to those of 1979 when the statute was negotiated. As for the Catalan conflict, it seems that the severe political clash will be difficult to overcome. In this difficult context, territorial autonomy has not provided a satisfactory solution to the accommodation of these two nations within the Spanish system. Possibly, this is not due to the autonomy system in itself, but to the reluctance of the state to recognize its plurinational nature and to incorporate a proper regulation of the pro-sovereignty processes, as has been done by other European countries. These two significant measures could transform the current system of autonomy into a valid and stable model of constitutional integration.

Bibliography

Acierno, Silvia and Julio Baquero Cruz, 'The order of the Spanish Constitutional Court on the proposal to convert the Basque Country into a freely associated community:

keeping hands off constitutional politics' (2005) 3(4) *International Journal of Constitutional Law* 687–695.

Additional Provision 2 of the Statute of the Valencian Community (Organic Law 1/2006, April 10th, concerning the Reform of Organic Law 5/1982, July 1st, of the Statute of Autonomy of the Community of Valencia),<https://www.global-regulation.com/translation/spain/1446607/law-1-2006%252c-of-10-april%252c-reform-of-the-organic-law-5-1982-of-1-july%252c-statute-of-autonomy-of-the-valencian-community.html>.

Aja, Eliseo, *El Estado autonómico. Federalismo y hechos diferenciales* (Alianza 2003).

Baròmetre d'Opinió Política (2a onada 2012). <http://www.ceo.gencat.cat/ceop/AppJava/pages>.

Barómetro de Julio, Estudio n° 2951 (Centro de Investigaciones Sociológicas July 2012) <www.cis.es>.

Bon, Pedro, 'La Constitución española en el marco del constitucionalismo contemporáneo' (2003) 69 *Revista Española de Derecho Constitucional* 13–67.

Connolly, Christopher, 'Independence in Europe: Secession, Sovereignty, and the European Union' (2013) 24 *Dutch Journal of Comparative & International Law* 51–105.

Costa-Font, Joan and Ramon Tremosa-Balcells, 'Support for State opting out and stateless national identity in the Basque Country' (2008) 37(6) *Journal of Socio-Economics* 2464–2477.

del Moral, Antonio Torres, *Principios de Derecho Constitucional* (4th edn, Universidad Complutense 1998).

Enrique Alvarez Conde, *Curso de Derecho Constitucional, vol. II. Los órganos constitucionales. El Estado autonómico* (3rd edn, Tecnos 2000).

Ezeizabarrena, Xabier, *Derecho de libre determinación y derecho a decidir: nueva soberanía y derechos humanos en el siglo XXI* (Universidad de Deusto, 2017).

Fleiner, Thomas, 'The Current Situation of Federalism in Switzerland' (2009) 9 *Revista d' Estudis Autonomics i Federals* 51–90.

Fossas, Enric, 'Interpretar la política. Comentario a la STC 42/2014, de 25 de marzo, sobre la Declaración de soberanía y el derecho a decidir del pueblo de Cataluña' (2014) 101 *Revista Española de Derecho Constitucional* 273–300.

Grau, Mireia, 'Self-government reforms and public support for Spain's territorial model: changes and stability (1992–2010)' (2011) 13 *Revista d'Estudis Autonòmics i Federals* 186–214.

Keating, Michael and Alex Wilson, 'Renegotiating the State of Autonomies: Statute Reform and Multi-level Politics in Spain' (2009) 32(3) *West European Politics* 536–558.

Keating, Michael, 'Rethinking sovereignty. Independence-lite, devolutionmax and national accommodation' (2012) 16 *Revista d'estudis autonòmics i federals* 9–29.

Linz, Juan, 'Politics in a Multi-Lingual Society with a Dominant World Language: The Case of Spain' in Savard, Jean-Guy, and Wigneault, Richard (eds.) *Les États Multilingues: Problèmes et Solutions* (Presses de l'Université Laval 1975) 367–444.

Llera, Francisco, 'Spain: Identity Boundaries and Political Reconstruction' (2009) 15 (3/4) *Nationalism and Ethnic Politics* 305–335.

López, Jaume, 'Del dret a l'autodeterminació al dret a decidir. Un possible canvi de paradigma en la reivindicació dels drets de les nacions sense estat' (Centre UNESCO de Catalunya 2011), <http://focir.cat/ca/llibres/del-dret-lautodeterminacio-al-dret-decidir-un-possible-canvi-de-paradigma-en-la-reivindicacio-dels-drets-de-les-nacions-sense-estat/>.

Mancini, Susana, 'Rethinking the boundaries of democratic secession: Liberalism, nationalism, and the right of minorities to self-determination' (2009) 6 (3–4) *International Journal of Constitutional Law* 553–584.

Medrano, Juan Díez, *Naciones divididas. Clase, política y nacionalismo en el País Vasco y Cataluña* (Centro de Investigaciones Sociológicas 1999).

Miguel Angel Aparicio Perez (eds) *Temas de Derecho constitucional (I)* (Cedec 1998).

Mira, López, 'Veinticinco años de Estado autonómico: una mala solución organizativa para un problema político' (2003–2004) 58–59 *Revista de Derecho Político* 737–748.

Moreno, Luis, *La federalización de España. Poder político y territorio* (2nd edn, 2008).

Pérez, Pablo, Tremps *Derecho Constitucional, vol. II. Los poderes del Estado. La organización territorial del Estado* (5th edn, Tirant lo blanch 2002).

Poggeschi, Giovanni, *Le nazioni linguistiche della Spagna autonómica: Universalitá de la lingua castigliana e vitalità delle lingue regionali* (Cedam 2002).

Pons, Xabier, 'El denominado derecho a decidir y el Derecho Internacional' in Eduard Sagarra (coord.) *¿Existe el derecho a decidir? Preguntas y respuestas sobre el proceso abierto en Cataluña* (Tibidabo ediciones 2014) 71–112.

Pons, Xabier, 'Legalidad internacional y derecho a decidir' (2014), 27 *Revista Electrónica de Estudios Internacionales* 26–87.

Reposo, Antonio, *Profili dello Stato autonomico. Federalismo e regionalismo* (Giappichelli 2000).

Requejo, Ferran, *Multinational federalism and value pluralism: the Spanish case*(Routledge 2005).

Resolució 5/X del Parlament de Catalunya, per la qual s'aprova la Declaració de sobirania i del dret a decidir del poble de Catalunya (Declaration of Sovereignty and the right of the Catalan people to decide) (2013), <https://www.parlament.cat/document/intrade/7176>.

Ridao, Joan 'El procés de «juridificació» internacional del dret de secessió. De l'autodeterminació externa al «dret a decidir» en base als principis democràtic i d'efectivitat' *Fòrum sobre el dret a decidir. Dret comparat i context internacional* (Institut d'Estudis Autonòmics 2014).

Ridao, Joan, 'El derecho de Cataluña a decidir su futuro político colectivo. Las vías para su probable ejercicio' in Eduard Sagarra (coord.) *¿Existe el derecho a decidir? Preguntas y respuestas sobre el proceso abierto en Cataluña* (Tibidabo ediciones 2014).

Ridao, Joan, 'La juridificación del derecho a decidir en España. La STC 42/2014 y el derecho a aspirar a un proceso de cambio político del orden constitucional' (2014) 91 *Revista de Derecho Político* 93–135.

Robledo, Agustín Ruiz, 'Veinticinco años de estado autonómico' (2003–2004) 58–59 *Revista de Derecho Político* 707–735.

Roca, David, 'Vers la fin de l'État des autonomies en Espagne' (2007) 72 *Revue Française de Droit Constitutionnel* 861–892.

Royo, Javier Pérez, 'Una asignatura pendiente: la reforma de la Constitución' (2003) 69 *Revista Española de Derecho Constitucional* 215–235.

Rubio, Josep Maria Vilajosana, 'Principi democràtic i justificació constitucional del dret de decidir' (2014) 19 *Revista d'estudis autonòmics i federals* 178–210.

Sánchez, Luis Pomed, 'Situación actual y perspectivas de futuro del Estado Autonómico' (1999) 1 *El Ebro* 55–70.

The Constitutional Court ruling no 31/2010, June 28th 2010 (concerning the Catalonia Statute of Autonomy), <https://www.tribunalconstitucional.es/ResolucionesTraducidas/31-2010,%20of%20June%2028.pdf>.

The Constitutional Court ruling 103/2008 dated 11th September (*Fundamento Jurídico* 4), <https://www.tribunalconstitucional.es/ResolucionesTraducidas/103-2008,%20of%20September%2011.pdf>.

Tornos, Joaquín, 'El derecho a decidir no existe pero el Gobierno debería convocar la consulta' in Eduard Sagarra (coord.) *¿Existe el derecho a decidir? Preguntas y respuestas sobre el proceso abierto en Cataluña* (Tibidabo ediciones 2014) 316–320.

Vieytez, Eduardo Ruiz, 'Federalism, Subnational Constitutional Arrangements and the Protection of Minorities in Spain' in Allan Tarr, Robert Williams and Joseph Marko (eds) *Federalism, Subnational Constitutions and Minorities Rights* (Praeger 2004) 133–153.

Vieytez, Eduardo Ruiz, 'Minority Nations and Self-determination. A Proposal for the Regulation of Sovereignty Processes' (2016) 23(3) *International Journal on Minority and Group Rights* 402–421.

Weinstock, Daniel, 'Constitutionalizing the Right to Secede' (2001) 9(2) *Journal of Political Philosophy* 182–203.

CHAPTER 7

Territorial and Cultural Self-Governance in Italy: Strengths and Challenges of South Tyrol's Autonomy

*Andrea Carlà and Sergiu Constantin**

1 Introduction

Scholars and practitioners from all over the world generally agree that South Tyrol is an illustrative example of successful ethnic[1] conflict resolution and minority protection through territorial and cultural self-governance. Sometimes this autonomous Italian province is presented as a 'model' of diversity governance for various other cases of societies divided along ethno-cultural lines across the world.[2]

A large part of the rich academic literature dealing with the case of South Tyrol has a historical and legal-institutional focus.[3] Some scholars have examined the specific South Tyrolean context from the perspective of conflict

* During the collaborative writing of the chapter, parts II and III were written by Sergiu Constantin, part IV by Andrea Carlà and parts I and V by both.

1 Please note that in the Italian constitutional tradition, the concept of nation is 'understood as *demos* and not as *ethnos*', therefore 'legally speaking, in Italy there are no ethnic but only linguistic minorities'. *See* Francesco Palermo, 'Asymmetric, "Quasi-Federal" Regionalism and the Protection of Minorities: The Case of Italy', in Alan Tarr, Robert Williams, Joseph Marko (eds), *Federalism, Sub-National Constitutions, and Minority Rights* (Praeger Publishers 2004), 114.

2 Roland Benedikter, 'Overcoming Ethnic Division in Iraq: A Practical Model from Europe' *The National Interest*, (11 February 2004); 'Il Dalai Lama a Bolzano: "Modello Alto Adige per il Tibet"' *Alto Adige* (10 April 2013) <http://www.altoadige.it/cronaca/bolzano/il-dalai-lama-a-bolzano-modello-alto-adige-per-il-tibet-1.352699> accessed 8 November 2018; Roland Benedikter, 'East Ukraine's four perspectives. A solution According to the south Tyrol Model', (2015) 37 *Ethnopolitics Papers*.

3 Jens Woelk, Francesco Palermo, Joseph Marko (Eds.), *Tolerance through Law* (Martinus Nijhoff Publishers 2008); Elisabeth Alber and Carolin Zwilling, 'South Tyrol' (Online Compendium Autonomy Arrangements in the World, January 2016) <world-autonomies.info> accessed 8 November 2018. For historical accounts, *see* for example Rolf Steininger, *South Tyrol. A Minority Conflict of the Twentieth Century* (Transaction Publishers 2003); Georg Grote, *The South Tyrol Question, 1866–2010: From National Rage to Regional State* (Peter Lang 2012).

 | DOI:10.1163/9789004405455_008

settlement theory.[4] However, few studies have explored the impact of South Tyrol's autonomy arrangements on inter-group relations.[5]

Building on this literature, this chapter focusses on the strengths and challenges of South Tyrol's autonomy arrangements and has a twofold objective. First, it provides a thorough analysis of South Tyrolean institutions and mechanisms of self-governance and minority protection, showing how their interplay has sparked various dynamics that appease the ethnic tensions in the region. Second, the chapter examines the so-called 'climate of cohabitation' that exists among the three language groups after more than forty years of territorial and cultural self-governance. We rely on public surveys and empirical studies and discuss recent attempts to reform some of the main pillars of the autonomy system. South Tyrol's autonomy statute was designed to ensure the protection of the Italian, German and Ladin[6] language groups and to guarantee their peaceful cohabitation. However, South Tyrolean society has changed in the last decades and nowadays the autonomous province faces new challenges at regional, national and European levels.

The chapter is divided into five sections. While the next part provides a brief historical overview, the third section presents in detail the specific institutional mechanisms put in place by the current autonomy framework. The fourth part analyses the impact of these arrangements on the climate of cohabitation in the province. In the conclusion, we discuss to what extent South Tyrol can actually be seen as a model for solving ethnic tensions in other divided societies. Although often suggested, the idea of copying and reproducing the entire set of South Tyrol's mechanisms and institutions in a different political, cultural and socio-economic context, most probably has very limited chances of success. However, South Tyrol provides key lessons for a better understanding of minorities' needs and inter-group dynamics that should be addressed, as well as of institutional mechanisms that could appease ethnic tensions.

---

4 Stefan Wolff, *Disputed Territories: the Transnational Dynamic of Ethnic Conflict Settlement* (Berghahn Books 2003); Filippo Andreatta and Emanuele Castelli (eds), *Solutions and Failures in Identity-based Conflicts* (FBK Press 2015).

5 Andrea Carlà, 'Living Apart in the Same Room: Analysis of the Management of Linguistic Diversity in Bolzano' (2007) 6(2) *Ethnopolitics* 285; Günther Pallaver, 'South Tyrol's changing political system: from dissociative on the road to associative conflict resolution' (2014) 42(3) Nationalities Papers 376.

6 Ladins, the descendants of the Romanized local Raetian population live in the southeastern alpine valleys of the Dolomites Mountains, located in the Italian provinces of South Tyrol, Trento and Belluno. Ladin is a Rhaeto-Romance language.

II Historical Background

For centuries, the House of Habsburg ruled the alpine area that today covers the Italian autonomous region of Trentino-South Tyrol. This territory became part of Italy after the defeat of the Austro-Hungarian Empire in the First World War. While Trentino was more populous and overwhelmingly Italian, South Tyrol had a large majority German-speaking population, which opposed the annexation and claimed the right to self-determination.

In the 1920s, the fascist regime of Mussolini came to power and started to target Italy's linguistic minorities with various repressive policies aiming at their forced and fast assimilation. In South Tyrol, the persecution included measures such as closing down German-language schools, associations and newspapers, imposing an Italian monolingual administration, as well as Italianization of place names and even personal names. In addition, Mussolini's regime offered incentives to Italian workers from other parts of the country to move to South Tyrol with the aim of changing the demographic structure of the province.[7] In 1939 Mussolini and Hitler agreed to solve the South Tyrolean question through the so–called 'Option' given to the German-speaking population of the province. According to this arrangement, German speakers had to choose between remaining in Italy (and accepting assimilation) or moving to the German Reich (and preserving, thus, their linguistic and cultural identity). The majority of German speakers decided to emigrate but the outbreak of the war hindered the full implementation of the Nazi-Fascist plan. Most of those who left returned after the war.[8]

At the end of the Second World War, the newly established South Tyrolean People's Party (*Südtiroler Volkspartei* - SVP) collected more than 150,000 signatures in favour of self-determination. In September 1946, Austrian foreign minister Karl Gruber and Italian prime minister Alcide De Gasperi signed an agreement that *inter alia* guaranteed the German-speaking population of South Tyrol equality of rights with the Italian-speaking inhabitants, education in the mother tongue, proportional representation in civil service as well as legislative and executive autonomy.[9] The Gruber–De Gasperi agreement acknowledged Austria's protective function vis-à-vis the German-speaking

---

7 The percentage of Italians living in South Tyrol rose from around 3% of the population in 1910, to approximately 35% in 1943. *See* Carlá (n 5) 313.

8 Emma Lantschner, 'History of the South Tyrol Conflict and its Settlement' in Jens Woelk, Francesco Palermo, Joseph Marko (eds), *Tolerance through Law. Self-Governance and Group Rights in South Tyrol* (Martinus Nijhoff Publisher 2008) 6–9.

9 It is worth noting that the Gruber–De Gasperi agreement contained no provision regarding the rights of Ladin language group.

population of South Tyrol. Moreover, it was included as an annex in the Paris Peace Treaty (1947) which confirmed the existing Italian-Austrian border.[10]

The Italian Constitution of 1948 established the special autonomous region[11] of Trentino–South Tyrol comprising two provinces: Trento and South Tyrol. While the former had a larger population out of which more than 90% spoke Italian as their mother tongue, the latter had more than 60% German-speaking residents.[12] At the level of the region Trentino–South Tyrol, 71.5% of the residents belonged to the Italian language group.[13] Thus, the representation of the German-speaking population in the regional legislative body was limited and the German speakers were unable to influence the decision-making process because they were outvoted. On paper, South Tyrol had autonomy as part of the autonomous region Trentino–South Tyrol, but in reality, the self-governing powers of the province of South Tyrol were rather limited. Italy considered the Gruber–De Gasperi agreement to have been implemented and ignored the increasing dissatisfaction of the German-speaking population of the province. The situation escalated and, in less than a decade, the tensions erupted into violence. A series of bomb attacks targeted industrial areas, historical monuments and security forces.[14] The Italian government's crackdown led to mass arrests and allegations of inhuman treatment by law enforcement institutions.

In 1960, Austria made use of its protective function as kin-state and brought the South Tyrol question before the United Nations.[15] One year later, the Italian government established the so-called 'Commission of 19' with the mandate to propose solutions for the conflict.[16] Based on this commission's report, the Italian government prepared a so-called 'Package' of 137 measures that required

10 The anchoring of South Tyrolean autonomy in international law is highly relevant because Italy could not claim later that what happens in South Tyrol is an internal matter. The Italian government had to fulfil its obligations under international law.

11 Since 1948, Italy has had 20 regions and an asymmetric territorial-administrative system. Five out of the 20 regions have a special autonomous regime; that is, they have autonomy statutes of constitutional rank, significant legislative and administrative competences and a bilateral relationship with the central government. The five special regions are Trentino–South Tyrol, Aosta Valley, Friuli–Venezia Giulia, Sicily and Sardinia.

12 Carlà (n 5) 313.

13 Lantschner (n 9) 10.

14 As Steininger points out, the individuals who carried out these attacks have been called 'freedom fighters, idealists, patriots, South Tyrolean activists, bomb throwers, terrorists, or all of these'. *See* Steininger (n 3) 5.

15 The UN General Assembly issued two resolutions on South Tyrol, recommending all parties involved to negotiate a solution to the conflict. *See* UNGA Res 1497 (31 October 1960) and UNGA Res 1661 (28 November 1961).

16 The 'Commission of 19' was composed of 11 Italian speakers, seven German speakers and one Ladin speaker. The Italian members were representing not only the central

a comprehensive reform of the First Autonomy Statute of 1948. The core element of the Package was the significant transfer of legislative and administrative powers from the regional to the provincial level. At the end of 1969, the SVP and the Italian and Austrian parliaments approved the Package. There are two issues worth noting here. First, there was a heated debate within the SVP over whether to accept or reject the compromise. Only 52.8% of the SVP delegates voted in favour of the Package. Thus, the SVP gave up the unrealistic goal of external self-determination and opted for internal self-determination through a genuine autonomy for South Tyrol.[17] Second, neither the regional nor the provincial legislative bodies had a say with regard to the Package and there was no direct consultation of the local population via referendum.[18]

In 1972, the Second Autonomy Statute (ASt) established a system of consociational democracy based on the principle of power-sharing, which takes into consideration the needs and expectations of the German, Italian and Ladin language groups. Moreover, most of the legislative and administrative powers were transferred from the region Trentino-South Tyrol to the two provinces of South Tyrol and Trento.[19] In 1992, Austria and Italy formally acknowledged the settlement of the conflict before the United Nations.

In the last decade, increasing societal changes and challenges have triggered a lively debate in South Tyrol over the need to update the ASt of 1972. It is submitted that a reform is necessary in order to properly address current issues and challenges at the regional,[20] national,[21] and European levels.[22] Acknowledging that a purely top-down process of legal amendment without the

---

government but also the governments and parliaments of the region Trentino-South Tyrol and the province of South Tyrol respectively.

17 Elisabeth Alber and Carolin Zwilling, 'Continuity and change in South Tyrol's governance' in Levente Salat, Sergiu Constantin, Alexander Osipov, István Gergő Székely (eds), *Autonomy Arrangements around the World: A Collection of Well and Lesser Known Cases* (Romanian Institute for Research on National Minorities 2014) 38.

18 Sergiu Constantin, 'South Tyrol: Conflict Resolution and Self-Governance' in M. Sanjaume-Calvet and D. Turp (eds), *The Emergence of a Democratic Right of Self-Determination in Europe* (Maurits Coppieters Center 2016) 204.

19 The 1972 Statute of Autonomy relegated the region Trentino–South Tyrol to the role of an administrative-territorial 'roof' over Trento and South Tyrol, which became the only two special autonomous provinces of Italy. *See* Sergiu Constantin and Elisabeth Alber, 'Autonomy and Minority Representation in South Tyrol' in László Komáromi and Zoltán T. Pállinger (eds), *Good Governance - Enhancing Representation* (Pázmány Press 2016) 113.

20 E.g. education policies, the role of the region and the role of municipalities.

21 E.g. financial autonomy and the future of regions having special statutes within Italy's constitutional reform.

22 E.g. cross-border cooperation and effects of Europeanization on governance and South Tyrol as part of the Alpine macro-region.

participation of the citizenry would be controversial, South Tyrol's provincial parliament established in April 2015 a consultative participatory process called the 'Convention for the Revision of the Autonomy Statute' (hereinafter Autonomy Convention).[23] A similar consultation mechanism was established in the autonomous province of Trento.[24] These parallel processes aim to reform the ASt with the help of the region's population through deliberative democracy mechanisms. The ASt is a constitutional law so it can only be amended by the Italian parliament through the procedure for amending the Italian Constitution. According to Article 103 ASt, the parliament of the region Trentino-South Tyrol has the right to initiate amendments of the ASt, following the proposals put forward by the parliaments of the autonomous provinces of South Tyrol and Trento. Because the ASt concerns the entire Trentino-South Tyrol region, the two autonomous provinces South Tyrol and Trento will have to coordinate the outcomes of their consultation processes in the regional parliament. As Woelk points out, the two provinces need 'to formalize the approval of a draft autonomy statute for the autonomous region [Trentino-South Tyrol] in order to send the draft to the Italian parliament'.[25]

In January 2016, the Autonomy Convention began with nine 'Open Space' public discussion events organized across South Tyrol. Nearly 2,000 people participated in 258 working groups and exchanged ideas and proposals on various topics such as self-determination, the transfer of further competences from the central to the provincial level, monolingual and multilingual school systems, the Austrian-Italian Euroregion 'Tyrol–South Tyrol–Trentino' and social issues.[26] During the period of the 'Open Space' events, 1,829 people registered as potential members of the consultative body called the 'Forum of 100'. Its members were selected by means of a stratified random sampling method, which took the 2011 census data on language, age, and gender proportions into account. The 'Forum of 100' met regularly and gave input to the main working

23 South Tyrol's Provincial Law no. 3/2015, establishing a consultative participatory process called the 'Convention for the Revision of the Autonomy Statute'.

24 Trento's Provincial Law no. 1/2016 establishing a consultative process called *Consulta*. The 25 members of the *Consulta* represent institutions as well as different sectors of the civil society.

25 Jens Woelk, 'Participatory Process Started to Reform the Autonomy Statute of Trentino-South Tyrol' (National Observatory on Language Rights Blog, 15 October 2016) <http://odl.openum.ca/participatory-process-started-to-reform-the-autonomy-statute-of-trentino-south-tyrol/> accessed 8 November 2018.

26 A summary of the Open Space discussion events and the minutes of each single working group, moderated and self-organized by the participants themselves, is available online (in German, Italian and Ladin) at <http://www.konvent.bz.it./> accessed 8 November 2018.

body called the 'Convention of 33'.[27] At the end of a one-year process, in September 2017, the Convention of 33 presented its reform proposals to the provincial parliament, which may or may not take them into consideration when drafting the revised ASt.

III South Tyrol's Legal-institutional Design: Self-Governance, Power Sharing and Minority Protection

The ASt established several specific mechanisms and institutions, which ensure, at the same time, a certain degree of separation and 'forced' cooperation among language groups and between the state and the province. This section examines the three main pillars of South Tyrol's autonomy system: first, the joint commission that plays an essential role in the continuous development of the autonomous system; second, the main elements of South Tyrol's consociational democracy; third, the financial arrangements between the state and the autonomous province.

III.A *Implementation of the Autonomy Statute through Joint Commissions*

The executive measures implementing the ASt are regulated through enactment decrees, following the consultation of a joint commission made up of six members, of whom three represent the state and three the autonomous province.[28] Until recently, an essential feature of this so-called Commission of Six[29] was the double parity between actors involved. Not only the commission had an equal number of members representing the state and the autonomous province, but also the Italian and German language groups had an equal

27 The 'Convention of 33' consisted of five legal experts nominated by the provincial parliament, 12 persons nominated by the provincial parliament representing both the political majority and minority, eight members of the 'Forum of 100', four persons representing the Council of the municipalities, two representing the trade associations and two persons representing the trade unions.

28 Article 107(2) ASt.

29 Technically, the Commission of Six is a sub-commission of the so-called Commission of Twelve that deals with the implementation of the autonomy statute at the level of the entire region of Trentino–South Tyrol. However, today this Commission of Twelve plays a limited role because most competences belong to the two provinces (Trento and South Tyrol) and not to the region. According to Art. 107 (1) ASt, in the Commission of Twelve both the state and the region have six representatives. The members representing the region are appointed as follows: two by the regional parliament, two by the provincial parliament of South Tyrol and two by the provincial parliament of Trento. Finally, three of the members of the Commission of Twelve must belong to the German language group.

number of representatives. The rule was that one of the members representing the state must belong to the German language group, and one of South Tyrol's representatives must be an Italian speaker.[30] The ASt did not guarantee the Ladin language group's representation in the joint commission. When this mechanism was established, the main concern was to ensure a symmetrical balance between the state and the province, on the one hand, and between the two largest language groups in South Tyrol, on the other.[31] However, in 2014, the state appointed a Ladin member for the first time. This was a *de facto* and not *de jure* representation of the Ladin language group in the joint commission. At the end of 2017, the ASt was amended with the aim of strengthening the protection of the Ladin minority.[32] According to this new regulation, one of the members of the Commission of Six representing the state must belong to the German or Ladin language group and one of those representing the province must belong to the Italian language group. Moreover, the majority of the representatives of either the German or Italian language group in the provincial parliament may renounce the right to nominate their own member in the joint commission in favour of a Ladin speaker.[33] Currently, the three state-appointed members of the Commission of Six belong to the Italian, German and Ladin language groups respectively. Out of the three province-appointed members, two are German speakers and one is Italian speaker.

The design and composition of the joint commission aim to encourage confidence building and collaboration between all actors involved: state and province on the one hand, and language groups on the other. The significant differences among these actors in terms of size, territory and population are irrelevant within this joint commission where they all have the same weight. In case of divergent opinions, the only way out of a deadlock is through negotiation and compromise. The state, the province and the language groups are 'forced' to cooperate in the Commission of Six in order to find a solution that is acceptable to all. The joint commission drafts the texts of the enactment decrees and submits them to the Italian government for assessment and, in the end, approval. Once approved, an enactment decree enters into force,

30 The logic behind this arrangement is that German speakers are a minority in Italy and Italian speakers are a minority in South Tyrol.

31 The SVP sees itself as a collective party of German and Ladin South Tyroleans of all social classes. Therefore, those members of the Commission of Six representing the German language group and the province defended, in principle, also the interests of the Ladin language group.

32 Constitutional Law no. 1/2017 regarding amendments to the special statute for Trentino-South Tyrol on the protection of the Ladin linguistic minority.

33 Article 9 (1) (b) of the Constitutional Law no. 1/2017.

bypassing the Italian parliament. A law adopted by the national legislative body cannot amend or repeal such an enactment decree implementing the ASt. This can be done only through a subsequent enactment decree adopted through the same procedure. It is particularly remarkable that six appointed individuals make regulations that prevail over the laws adopted by the democratically elected Italian parliament. These enactment decrees enjoy an exceptional status within the Italian legal system. They occupy a special position in the hierarchy of norms: below the constitutional norms but above the ordinary laws of the parliament. The special status of the enactment decrees derives from the necessity of upholding the principle of parity with regard to state-province and majority-minority relations in the process of implementation of the ASt. The Italian parliament has almost 1,000 MPs and only a handful of deputies and senators represent South Tyrol. This special mechanism designed to guarantee minority representation and influence in the decision-making process with respect to the implementation of the ASt would be meaningless if the Italian parliament could amend or repeal the hard-negotiated enactment decrees drafted by the Commission of Six. The principle of parity trumps the principle of democratic legitimacy.[34]

Finally, it is worth noting the transformation of the Commission of Six regarding two essential aspects. Firstly, it was designed as a consultative body but became the main decision-making institution with respect to the implementation of the ASt. Secondly, it was established as a temporary body but functions even today, more than forty years after the ASt entered into force.[35] In fact, the work of the Commission of Six guarantees the further development of South Tyrol's autonomy. Without this joint commission, the autonomy system would be 'frozen', as the existing enactment decrees can only be amended or repealed by another enactment decree.

III.B *South Tyrol's Consociational Democracy*

South Tyrol's legal-institutional design fits into the general framework of consociational theory.[36] The four main elements of this complex system are the

34 Francesco Palermo, 'Implementation and Amendment of the Autonomy Statute' in Jens Woelk, Francesco Palermo, Joseph Marko (eds), *Tolerance through Law. Self-Governance and Group Rights in South Tyrol* (Martinus Nijhoff Publisher 2008) 148.

35 According to Art. 108 ASt, most of the enactment decrees containing the executive measures of the autonomy statute should have been issued within two years after its entry into force in 1972.

36 Consociationalism is at the heart of academic and political debate in many divided societies. According to the consociational theory, in such contexts four basic elements are required for engineering a democratic and stable political system: (1) grand coalition

following: proportionality principle, power sharing, special veto mechanism, and cultural autonomy and language rights.

III.B.1 Proportionality Principle

In South Tyrol, all language groups must have representation in legislative and executive bodies, and access to public jobs and resources, according to the principle of proportionality. The ASt established a quota system based on the numerical strength of the Italian, German and Ladin language groups. South Tyrol's residents self-declare their *belonging* or *affiliation*[37] to one of the three groups. The size of a language group is the sum of all the declarations of belonging and affiliation to the respective group.[38]

There are two types of declaration of belonging/affiliation: while the first is anonymous, the second contains personal data of the individual who submitted it. The anonymous declarations go to the Provincial Statistical Institute (ASTAT), which calculates the numerical strength of the three language groups. Only Italian citizens who reside in South Tyrol can submit these anonymous declarations, every ten years, during the national census. The declaration with personal data enables the individual who submitted it to exercise certain rights in South Tyrol (e.g. to work in public service and to apply for social housing).[39]

government between parties representing all groups; (2) cultural autonomy; (3) proportionality principle for voting system and civil service; (4) right of veto. *See* Arend Lijphart, *Democracy in Plural Societies: A Comparative Exploration* (Yale University Press 1977).

37 Is there a difference between a declaration of *belonging* and one of *affiliation*? The answer is yes and no. A concrete example may explain better this paradox. According to the 2011 census, the German language group consisted of 314,604 persons. Out of this total number, 310,360 were persons who submitted a declaration of *belonging* to the German language group and 4,244 were persons who submitted a declaration of *affiliation* to this group. Thus, there is no difference between the two types of declaration from the statistics point of view. However, the two types of declaration are different from a symbolic perspective. Some individuals, for whatever reason, might not want to declare their belonging to a specific language group. For instance, bilingual persons born in mixed families might not feel comfortable to choose one language group over the other. Therefore, they may declares their *affiliation* (instead of *belonging*) to one of the language groups. For statistical data mentioned above, *see* ASTAT, *South Tyrol in figures* (Autonomous Province of South Tyrol 2015) 15.

38 According to the 2011 census, 69.41% of South Tyrol's population belong to German language group, 26.06 % to the Italian language group and 4.53% to the Ladin language group. *See* ASTAT (n 37).

39 In other words, individuals who do not submit a declaration of belonging (or affiliation) to a language group cannot apply for public jobs and social housing. Allocation of public jobs and social houses is proportional to the size of the language groups. The quotas create a segmental competition meaning that for jobs allocated to Italian language group, for instance, only candidates who have declarations of belonging (or affiliation) to the

South Tyrol's residents, including foreigners,[40] can submit such a declaration to the Bolzano/Bozen Court, which stores them in sealed envelopes in order to protect the personal data. A person who has made such a declaration has the right to withdraw or change it, under several conditions that aim to prevent eventual attempts to abuse the system (e.g. individuals switching from one language group to another for reasons of expediency). A person may change his/her declaration five years after the date of submission but the new declaration only enters into effect after two years. Individuals may withdraw their declarations at any time but a person who does so can submit a new declaration only three years after the date of withdrawal and this new declaration shall take effect two years after he/she submits it to the Bolzano/Bozen Court.

III.B.2 Power Sharing

The parliament of South Tyrol consists of 35 members elected for a mandate of five years through direct and universal suffrage based on an open list proportional representation voting system.[41] All candidates must make public their declaration of belonging/affiliation to one of the three language groups in order to establish, after elections, how many seats each group gained in the legislative body. Voters can indicate up to four preferences for candidates selected from the party list for which they vote. It is possible, thus, that some candidates placed at the lower end of the party lists win mandates, while others from the top of the list are not elected. The ASt guarantees the representation of the Ladin language group in the provincial parliament. If no Ladin candidate gains enough votes to win a seat through the regular procedure, one parliamentary mandate is assigned to the Ladin candidate most voted for from any party list.

Italian language group will compete. These candidates cannot apply for jobs allocated to German or Ladin language groups. All public bodies functioning in South Tyrol apply the quota system based on the size of language groups at provincial and municipal level. To take an example, in Bolzano/Bozen, the capital of the province, municipal and provincial administration function in parallel. As the Italian language group in Bolzano/Bozen amounts to 73.8% of the city's population, a similar percentage of civil servants working for the municipal administration have declared belonging/ affiliation to the Italian language group. As the German language group represents 69.41% of the provincial population, a proportional share of civil servants working for the provincial administration in Bolzano/Bozen have declared belonging/affiliation to the German language group. However, all civil servants must be bilingual (*see* sub-section 3.2.4). For statistical data mentioned above, *see* ASTAT (n 37) 16.

40 EU citizens as well as citizens of non-EU states who have long-term resident permit or refugee status. *See* Article 20/ter (7/bis) of Italian President's Decree no. 752/1976.

41 Article 47 (3) ASt and South Tyrol's Provincial Law no. 5/2013 on the election of provincial parliament in 2013 and the composition of provincial government.

This Ladin candidate takes the seat of a colleague from his/her party list. More precisely the Ladin will replace his/her colleague who, based on the number of votes received, would have been the last elected candidate from the respective party list. The provincial parliament elects its rotating presidency from among its members; a German speaker for the first half of the mandate and an Italian speaker for the second half. A Ladin member of the parliament may become president of the legislature, if either the German or the Italian language group accepts leaving this position to the Ladin group for the respective half of the mandate of the rotating presidency.[42] The two vice-presidents of the parliament must belong to different language groups.

Italian citizens can only vote in South Tyrol's provincial elections after four years of permanent residence in the province.[43] The restriction is justified by the need to prevent potential attempts to influence the election results by means of demographic changes, i.e a sudden increase in the number of Italian-speaking residents who move to South Tyrol in the pre-election period. The 2013 provincial electoral law allows voting by correspondence, under several conditions, and requires a gender quota in the lists of candidates; that is, at least one third of the candidates from each party list must be women.[44]

The composition of South Tyrol's government reflects the numerical strength of the language groups as represented in the provincial parliament.[45] The Ladin language group may be represented in the government by derogation from the proportional principle.[46] The government is composed of a maximum of nine members and gender proportional representation is ensured.[47] The head of the government is also the president of the autonomous province of South Tyrol. He/she is *de facto* not *de jure* a member of the German language group[48] and has three vice-presidents. The first two belong to the German and

42 Article 48c ASt.

43 Article 25 ASt.

44 Articles 5 and 8 of South Tyrol's Provincial Law no. 5/2013 on the election of provincial parliament in 2013 and the composition of provincial government.

45 Article 50 ASt.

46 South Tyrol's government has maximum nine members and if only one out of the 35 members of the parliament is Ladin, a rigid application of proportionality principle would mean no representation of Ladin speakers in the provincial government.

47 Article 2(3) of South Tyrol's Provincial Law no. 5/2013 on the election of provincial parliament in 2013 and the composition of provincial government.

48 The head of the government is *de facto* not *de jure* a member of the German-speaking group. The provincial parliament, which elects the president, always has a majority of German speakers therefore the head of the government (and president of the province) is a member of the German-speaking group. In theory, he/she could also be an Italian or Ladin speaker if the majority of parliament's members would vote for him/her.

Italian language groups respectively. The third vice-president is Ladin, when one of the members of the government belongs to this language group.[49]

In municipalities where a language group has at least two councilors in the local council, the respective language group has the right of representation in municipal government. Local public administration must ensure the proportional representation of language groups in the composition of their organs, based on the numerical strength of the language groups as determined by the declarations of belonging/affiliation.[50]

III.B.3 Special Veto Mechanism

The ASt grants language groups a specific mechanism to defend their vital interests in the provincial parliament. The majority of parliament's members belonging to a language group may trigger a so-called 'alarm-bell' procedure[51] if they deem a draft law prejudicial to the equality of rights between citizens belonging to different language groups, or to the cultural characteristics of the groups themselves. In this scenario, they request that each language group votes separately on the contested draft law. If their request for separate voting is not accepted, or if the parliament adopts the draft law after the separate voting despite the opposition of two thirds of its members belonging to the language group that had requested separate voting, the majority of the respective language group's members may challenge the contested law before the Constitutional Court.[52] This procedure is not the equivalent of an absolute veto right because the representatives of a language group cannot block the approval of a controversial regulation. The law enters into force but the Court may strike it down eventually as unconstitutional. The ASt lays down similar rules regarding

49 Article 3 (1) (a) (2) of the Constitutional Law no 1/2017.

50 Articles 61 ASt.

51 Article 56 ASt.

52 For a better understanding of this mechanism, let us consider a hypothetical example. Out of the 35 members of the provincial parliament, 25 are German speakers, nine are Italian speakers and one is a Ladin speaker. Seven Italian speakers argue that a draft law on the parliament's agenda is prejudicial to the rights of the Italian language group. They request that language groups vote separately on the contested draft law. The German-speaking members of the parliament vote first and the result is the following: 20 votes for the draft law and five against it. Then comes the vote of the Italian-speaking members of the parliament: two votes for the draft law and seven against it. Finally, the Ladin representative votes in favour of the draft law. Summing up the votes of all 35 members of the parliament, the draft law is approved with 23 votes in favour and 12 against. However, more than two thirds of the Italian-speaking members of the parliament – that is, seven out of nine – voted against the draft law. Therefore, the majority of the Italian language group in the parliament – that is, at least five Italian members – can challenge the law before the Constitutional Court.

administrative documents that are prejudicial to a language group. Members of the provincial parliament and municipal councils may challenge such acts before the regional Court of Administrative Justice.[53]

III.B.4 Cultural Autonomy and Language Rights

The three language groups enjoy a strong autonomy in terms of protection and promotion of their cultural identity. The German and Italian language groups enjoy monolingual education in their mother tongues from kindergarten to secondary school level. Teachers must be native speakers of the language of instruction. The teaching of the second language (i.e. German in Italian-language schools and Italian in German-language schools) is compulsory.[54] In the Ladin valleys, the Ladin language is used in the kindergartens. Ladin schools are bilingual in the sense that half of the subjects are taught in German and the other half in Italian. In addition, Ladin pupils study their mother tongue as a separate subject.[55]

Parents have the right to choose in which school they enroll their children. However, the school administration can refuse the enrolment of a pupil who does not have a sufficient knowledge of the language of instruction. In such case, parents have the right to challenge the school's decision before the administrative court.[56]

The self-governance principle informs the structure and administration of education and culture in the province. Each language group has its own education as well as cultural department within the provincial administration. The allocation of funds in the field of culture follows the proportionality principle.[57]

In South Tyrol, Italian and German languages have equal status.[58] All public offices function in both languages. The only exceptions are the monolingual Italian military and the trilingual public administration of the Ladin valleys. All public servants must be bilingual (or trilingual in the Ladin valleys). Persons applying for public offices must submit certificates which prove their language skills.[59] Citizens' relations with public authorities are governed by the

53 Article 92 ASt.
54 Article 19 (1) ASt.
55 Article 19 (2) ASt.
56 Article 19 (3) ASt.
57 Art. 15(2) ASt.
58 Article 99 ASt.
59 Until a few years ago, the only language certificate accepted by South Tyrol's authorities was the so-called *patentino*, a document issued by the provincial authorities after an examination organized exclusively in the province. However, this system was challenged

rule of separate use of languages. This means that public authorities (including the police) must use the language employed by the petitioner or, in the case of documents issued on the initiative of a public authority, the assumed language of the recipient. The joint use of Italian and German languages is requested for documents for public use, documents issued to an individual but intended for public use and documents intended for more than one office.[60] Moreover, all provincial and regional laws and regulations are published in both languages.[61] Ladins can use their mother tongue in oral and written communications with the public authorities of the Ladin valleys.[62]

Criminal and civil proceedings are conducted in the language(s) chosen by the defendants and parties.[63] A criminal trial can be monolingual or bilingual (Italian-German), if the co-defendants choose different languages, or if the party joining the prosecution as a plaintiff opts for the other language. A defense lawyer can always use a language different from that of the trial. The language of the trial can be changed at all stages of jurisdiction.[64] The territorial scope of application of these specific norms on the language use in criminal proceedings is restricted to the region Trentino-South Tyrol.[65]

Ladin speakers may use their mother tongue in civil proceedings in front of the Justice of the Peace with jurisdiction over the Ladin valleys.

---

before the European Court of Justice in the case *Angonese v. Cassa di Risparmio di Bolzano SpA*, Judgement of 6 June 2000, C-281/98, EU:C:2000:296. The Court held that requiring job applicants to prove their language knowledge exclusively by means of *patentino* certificate constitutes a form of indirect discrimination and breaches EU law. Therefore, the system had to be amended. Currently, besides the *patentino*, the provincial authorities also accept certificates issued by several well-known institutions such as the *Goethe-Institut* and *Istituto Dante Alighieri*.

60 Article 100(4) ASt.

61 Article 57 ASt.

62 However, provincial authorities located outside Ladin valleys, which are dealing with Ladin related issues (e.g. the office for Ladin culture in Bolzano/Bozen) must reply in Ladin or attach a Ladin translation to written replies drafted in German or Italian. *See* Günther Rautz, 'A "Minority within a Minority": The Special Status of the Ladin Valleys' in Jens Woelk, Francesco Palermo, Joseph Marko (eds), *Tolerance through Law. Self-Governance and Group Rights in South Tyrol* (Martinus Nijhoff Publisher 2008) 283–284.

63 It is worth noting that the rules providing residents of South Tyrol with extensive language rights in the judicial system have to be applied to all EU citizens as held by the European Court of Justice in cases *Bickel and Franz* (Judgment of 24 November 1998, C-274/96, EU:C:1998:563) and *Grauel Rüffer v Pokorná* (Judgement of 27 March 2014, C-322/13, EU:C:2014:189). The Court held that a restrictive interpretation of the Italian law only granting the right to have criminal/civil proceedings conducted in German to German-speaking Italian citizens who are residents of South Tyrol would infringe the principle of non-discrimination on the grounds of nationality.

64 Article 15 of Italian President's Decree no. 574/1988.

65 Italian Constitutional Court, Judgment no. 213 of 19 June 1998.

The autonomous province of South Tyrol has exclusive legislative power regarding place names.[66] All geographical indications must be bilingual (or trilingual in the Ladin valleys). Unofficially, German and Ladin place names are widely used across the province. However, even today, only the Italian place names are official[67] because of the continuous political deadlock[68] around this issue, which has historical reasons. During the fascist period, a key component of the forced Italianization was the replacement of all German place names with thousands of invented or adapted Italian geographical indications. On the one hand, many German speakers see these Italian place names as symbols of fascist oppression and want them removed. On the other hand, Italian speakers point out that, according to the ASt, the two languages have equal status and all place names must be officially bilingual. So far, the political elites representing the two main language groups have been unable to reach agreement on a settlement of this issue.

III.C *South Tyrol's Financial Arrangements*

The ASt contains several detailed regulations regarding South Tyrol's finances.[69] Most taxation powers belong to the state.[70] However, the central government allocates 90% of taxes collected in South Tyrol[71] to the province, which enjoys full autonomy of expenditure. The state cannot change this financial arrangement without first agreeing with the province. In November 2009, South Tyrol and the central government signed the Milan agreement. It confirmed South Tyrol's 90% share of taxes but the province agreed to take over some new competences from the state without additional financial resources for their exercise. In October 2014, provincial and central authorities complemented the Milan agreement by signing in Rome a so-called Guarantee agreement fixing South Tyrol's contribution to the restructuring of the Italian

66 Article 8, ASt.

67 The only official German name is Südtirol (South Tyrol), because it is mentioned in Article 116 of the Italian Constitution, which lists Trentino-South Tyrol among the five special autonomous regions.

68 For details, *see* Section 4.

69 Articles 69–86, ASt.

70 According to Articles 72–73 ASt, South Tyrol may impose certain levies and taxes in matters that fall under its competences. Regional taxation regards *inter alia* taxes on tourism, motor vehicles and productive activities and an additional tax rate on the income tax. *See* Thomas Benedikter, 'South Tyrol's Financial System' in Jens Woelk, Francesco Palermo, Joseph Marko (eds), *Tolerance through Law. Self-Governance and Group Rights in South Tyrol* (Martinus Nijhoff Publisher 2008) 110.

71 Articles 70, 71 and 75, ASt.

public debt. These developments occurred in the context of South Tyrol's opposition to centrally imposed financial restrictions by the state government following the 2008 global financial crisis and the subsequent fiscal austerity measures. It is worth noting that the Constitutional Court 'played a crucial role in defining the scope (and procedures) regarding [South Tyrol's] financial autonomy regime'.[72]

IV The Impact of Autonomy Arrangements on South Tyrolean Society

As shown above, the ASt created a 'complex power-sharing system' through which the German and the Ladin language groups enjoy one of the most advanced minority protection regimes.[73] This system combines several elements that have sparked different dynamics, whose interplay has contributed to appeasing ethnic tensions in the province. In particular, the transfer of powers from the regional to the provincial level has relativized the majority-minority relations, as the German-speaking population is the majority at provincial level whereas the Italian-speaking population is the majority in the region Trentino-South Tyrol and in Bolzano/Bozen, the capital of South Tyrol. At the same time, the application of proportionality principles in legislative and executive political bodies and in public offices has guaranteed to all the language groups access to power and participation in the decision-making process. Furthermore, institutional mechanisms, such as the Commissions of Six, have provided the language groups with institutional equality and encouraged exchange of information and communication between state and provincial authorities. As pointed out by de Villiers, the special status granted to South Tyrol within the Italian territorial-administrative system, gave this autonomous province a feeling of uniqueness that curtailed secessionist demands.[74] The combination of individual and collective rights highlights the importance of the language groups and collective identities but avoids the worst aspects of communitarianism

72 Moreover, '[p]articularly after the reform of the Italian Constitution in 2001, the Court has evolved into a "platform for conflict management" (…) solving all State-region conflicts'. *See* Elisabeth Alber and Carolin Zwilling (n 17) 43.

73 Stefan Wolff, 'Complex Power Sharing as Conflict Resolution: South Tyrol in Comparative Perspective' in Jens Woelk, Francesco Palermo, Joseph Marko and the European Academy Bozen/Bolzano (eds), *Tolerance through Law. Self-Governance and Group Rights in South Tyrol* (Martinus Nijhoff Publisher 2008).

74 Bertus de Villiers, 'Power-sharing Options in Complex Societies – Possible Lessons from South Tyrol for Young Democracies on Ways to Protect Ethnic Minorities at a Regional Level' (2017) 16(1) *JEMIE* 9.

where individuals become invisible within their community. The South Tyrol system is characterized by a mix of segregationist and integrationist elements, most represented in the combination of territorial and cultural self-governance, which preserves the different linguistic identities, fostering at the same time intergroup interactions. Last, but not least, South Tyrolean autonomy and its minority protection rules allows for a certain degree of flexibility which has permitted various changes and amendments in order to adapt the system to emerging needs and challenges.

In line with consociational theory, the ASt encouraged the collaboration of language groups' elites and the development of mutual trust. This process of social learning has spilled over into the society at large.[75] As pointed out by Larin and Röggla, several structural conditions contributed to this positive development.[76] First, South Tyrol is a small territory with a small population,[77] where the German and Ladin-speaking communities are territorially concentrated. Second, besides the linguistic cleavage, there are crosscutting cleavages and all the language groups share a common Catholic tradition, which facilitated cooperation between the political elites.[78] Third, the conflict in South Tyrol has not reached a high level of violence.

Besides these conditions, according to de Villiers, the success of South Tyrolean autonomy has been facilitated by a combination of factors.[79] Particularly relevant has been the role played by Austria as kin state and protector of the German-speaking population, which derives from the Gruber-De Gasperi agreement. Moreover, the international context with the development of the European Union supported the conflict settlement. Some scholars highlight political agency and the presence of outstanding political leaders, such

75 Joseph Marko, 'Is there a South Tyrolean "Model" of Conflict Resolution to be Exported?' in Jens Woelk, Francesco Palermo, Joseph Marko (eds), *Tolerance through Law. Self-Governance and Group Rights in South Tyrol* (Martinus Nijhoff Publisher 2008).

76 Stephen J. Larin and Marc Röggla, 'Participatory consociationalism? No, but South Tyrol's Autonomy Convention is evidence that power-sharing can transform conflicts' IPSA colloquium Democratization and Constitutional Design in Divided Societies (23–27 June 2017).

77 South Tyrol's territory covers 7,400 km² and it has around half a million inhabitants. For details, *see* ASTAT (n 37).

78 The SVP and the *Democrazia Cristiana*, SVP's Italian-speaking coalition partner until early 1990s, shared a commitment to Christian values as well as anti-communism. *See* Larin and Röggla (n 76); Max Haller, 'South Tyrol – an economic or political success story?' in Christoph von Hartungen, Hans Heiss, Günther Pallaver, Carlo Romeo and Martha Verdorfer (eds), *Demokratie und Erinnerung: Südtirol – Österreich – Italien* (Studien-Verl 2006).

79 de Villiers (n 74) 8–9.

as Silvius Magnago, the former SVP chairman who fostered a successful and peaceful solution in the 1970s and 1980s, the key years in the development of the autonomous institutions.[80] Time has played an important role as well. The process to implement the ASt took more than twenty years. This slow implementation might have allowed the South Tyrolean population to get accustomed to the autonomy framework, favouring the process through which the language groups have learned to trust each other and cooperate.

It also necessary to consider economic factors. On the one hand, since the late 1980s South Tyrol has entered a post-industrial phase, in which heavy industries, traditionally controlled by the Italian language group, are not any longer the core of economic development, whereas tourism and agriculture, historically in the hands of the German and Ladin language groups, are among the driving sectors of the South Tyrolean economy. On the other hand, in the past decades South Tyrol has experienced remarkable economic growth, both absolutely and in comparison with the rest of Italy. In March 2017, Eurostat announced that South Tyrol's per capita GDP reached 42,400 euro, which means that it is the richest among the Italian regions and provinces and number 21 in the ranking of EU regions.[81] According to Wolff, economic prosperity makes 'sufficient resources available and prevents ethnic competition in economic terms'.[82] At the same time, as pointed out by Haller, the appeasing of ethnic tensions might have allowed such economic prosperity.[83]

The ASt has fostered peaceful cohabitation, providing a feeling of protection among the language groups, in particular the German-speaking population. South Tyrolean institutional arrangements have desecuritized the relationship between the language groups and between the German-speaking population and the Italian state.[84] Having been guaranteed political control and its existence as a cultural community, the German-speaking population has accepted, so far, being a minority within Italy. As a result, today, most of the population has accepted living in a multilingual society and South Tyrol is characterized by a positive and peaceful climate of cohabitation. Several elements point in this direction. Most recently, controversial Fascist monuments, which in the

80 Haller (n 78).

81 'Dati Eurostat, Alto Adige al vertice in Italia per PIL pro capite' (South Tyrol's provincial administration, 30 March 2017) <www.provincia.bz.it/news/it/news.asp?news_action=4&news_article_id=583982> accessed 8 November 2018.

82 Wolff (n 4) 149.

83 Haller (n 78).

84 Andrea Carlà, 'Societal Security in South Tyrol: A Model to Deal with Ethnic Conflicts'. (2013) 12 *European Yearbook on Minority Issues* 56.

past many German speakers wanted destroyed, have been transformed in the locus of common collective memory. For example, in Bolzano/Bozen the Victory monument built during the Fascist period and closed for decades, has been re-opened as a museum which presents the impact of Fascist and Nazi dictatorships on South Tyrolean society.[85]

The peaceful climate of cohabitation clearly emerges in surveys. According to a 2014 survey, only 7% of the population sees cohabitation as a problem; according to 30.9%, cohabitation is less problematic than it was in the past, and 35% see it as an enrichment. Furthermore, a large segment of South Tyrol's population defines cohabitation as good (41.2%) or satisfactory (41.4%). Around a quarter of the population have seen improvements in recent years and have positive expectations for the future.[86] The success of the South Tyrol system in overcoming ethnic tensions is most clearly illustrated by attitudes toward multilingualism and cultural diversity, which today are seen as advantages rather than problems. The percentage of people who think that the presence of more language groups in South Tyrol is an enrichment or could be an enrichment under some conditions increased from 58.6% in 1991 to 77.9% in 2014.[87] Furthermore, 72.6% of the population think that knowing one or more language is a personal enrichment and 45.7% see it as an advantage. Finally, a great majority of the population considers knowledge of a second language important for good cohabitation in particular, and important or quite important in general.[88]

Beyond these successful developments, however, South Tyrol and its system of minority protection present also some problematic aspects. Indeed, some of the South Tyrolean institutional arrangements are based on a rigid separation between the language groups and have institutionally entrenched the linguistic divisions within the South Tyrol's population in many aspects of social and political life – what Marko calls the 'ethnic "Midas effect"'.[89] Each group has its own organizations (such as political parties, trade unions,

85 This is a remarkable development, considering that still in 2002 the Italian speaking population rejected the decision of the Bolzano city government to change the name of the square where the monument is located from *Piazza della Vittoria* (Victory Square) to *Piazza della Pace* (Peace Square). In a referendum, 62% of the inhabitants of Bolzano/Bozen voted for keeping the old name.

86 ASTAT, *Südtiroler Sprachbarometer/Barometro linguistico dell'Alto Adige 2014* (Provincia Autonoma di Bolzano-Alto Adige 2015) 171, 173, 178.

87 ASTAT, *Südtiroler Sprachbarometer/Barometro linguistico dell'Alto Adige 2004* (Provincia Autonoma di Bolzano-Alto Adige 2006) 190, 193; ASTAT (n 86), 181.

88 ASTAT (n 86) 180–181, 184.

89 Marko (n 75) 386.

youth and sport associations, and mass media).[90] Thereby, contacts between language groups are still limited to a certain extent, also because most of the Italian-speaking population is concentrated in the urban areas, especially in Bolzano/Bozen.

Furthermore, some of the most important mechanisms of the ASt do not take into consideration the new demographic reality of South Tyrolean society, which has witnessed great transformations since 1972. For instance, the legal-institutional framework is blind vis-à-vis individuals coming from mixed families, i.e. parents belonging to different language groups. Furthermore, since the mid-1990s, South Tyrolean society has become more diverse and complex due to the arrival of many foreigners. Migrants are a growing presence in South Tyrol, representing 9.1% of the province's population in 2017.[91] This increasing diversity represents a challenge for the ASt, which was designed to accommodate the needs and expectations of the three official language groups.[92]

A linguistic cleavage remains within South Tyrolean society, especially in the area of politics, which is characterized by two linguistically distinct sub-areas.[93] The South Tyrolean party system is traditionally characterized by the division between German and Italian-speaking parties. Nevertheless, there are some signs that some political dynamics might start to change. The German-speaking population has voted mainly for the SVP. However, the past decades

---

90 *See* Günther Pallaver, 'South Tyrol's Consociational Democracy: Between Political Claim and Social Reality', in Jens Woelk, Francesco Palermo, Joseph Marko and the European Academy Bozen/Bolzano, *Tolerance through Law. Self-Governance and Group Rights in South Tyrol* (Martinus Nijhoff Publisher 2008) 311–312. However, there are a small number of 'mixed' cultural and academic institutions, such as the Eurac Research and the Free University of Bolzano/Bozen, and cooperation between the cultural departments of the language groups is increasing. The Eurac Research is a trilingual (Italian, German, English) research center established in 1992, which pursues *inter alia* basic and applied research in the field of minority protection and the governance of cultural diversity (see <www.eurac.edu/> accessed 8 November 2018). The Free University of Bolzano/Bozen is a trilingual (Italian, German, English) institution established in 1997 (*see* <www.unibz.it/> accessed 8 November 2018).

91 Centro Studi e Ricerche IDOS, *Dossier Statistico Immigrazione 2018* (IDOS Edizioni 2018) 434.

92 Andrea Carlà, 'Land of welcome, land of fear: explaining approaches to "new" diversity in Catalonia and South Tyrol' (2017) *Journal of Ethnic and Migration Studies* <http://www.tandfonline.com/doi/full/10.1080/1369183X.2017.1352465> accessed 8 November 2018.

93 Matthias Scantamburlo and Günther Pallaver, 'The 2013 South Tyrolean Election: The End of SVP Hegemony', (2014) 24(4) *Regional and Federal Studies* 493, 495.

have witnessed the rise of nationalist right wing German-speaking parties,[94] which have on their political agenda the secession of South Tyrol. In the 2013 provincial election these parties received more than 25% of the votes, though in the last 2018 election they experienced a significant setback, getting 12%. Although people do not vote for these parties exclusively for their secessionist goal, their electoral results might reflect a certain level of dissatisfaction within the German language group regarding the autonomous arrangement. On the other side of the linguistic spectrum, a large part of the Italian language group has historically tended to vote for Italian nationalist right-wing parties, though more recently these parties seem to have lost appeal. In the 2018 provincial election many Italian speakers opted instead for the League (*Lega*), an Italian right-wing populist party which got more than 11% of the votes. It should be noted that there are interethnic parties as well, which have performed well in the past years, in particular the Green Party (Verdi-Grüne-Verc) and the newly founded Team Köllensperger, which received more than 6% and 15% of the votes respectively in the last provincial election.

The linguistic cleavage in the political system reflects the fact that the institutional separation has perpetuated an understanding of linguistic identities as mutually exclusive. Although today a common territorial sense of belonging is slowly emerging, 80.7% of the German-speaking population identify with the term '*Südtiroler*' ('South Tyrolean' in German language), whereas the majority of the Italian language group (59%) identifies as 'Italian', and 18.7% chooses '*Altoatesino*' (an Italian term for 'South Tyrolean').[95] The South Tyrolean population is characterized by a different sense of identities among the language groups, which still feel that, to a certain extent, they are in competition with each other and express grievances. Part of the South Tyrolean population, especially Italian speakers, think that their language group is disadvantaged in various sectors of public life. Almost 70% of the Italian speaking population feel always or sometimes at a disadvantage in the labor market, and between 50% and 60% in public administration, politics and society, and communication.[96] Since the 1990s, politicians, journalists and scholars use the expression *disagio degli italiani* ('uneasiness of Italians') to indicate the discomfort expressed by the Italian language group in South Tyrol.[97]

94 i.e. the Freedomites (*Die Freiheitlichen*) and the South Tyrolean Freedom (*Südtiroler Freiheit*).

95 ASTAT (n 86) 170.

96 ASTAT (n 86) 185–186, 189.

97 For a comprehensive analysis of the '*disagio*' *see* Andrea Carlà, 'South Tyrol: an autonomy for all?' PSA 66th Annual International Conference (21–23 March 2016); and the special

Specific problems derive from the system of separate and monolingual schools vis-à-vis its impact on bilingualism and social interaction among the language groups. On the one hand, it is undeniably true that progress has been made in the last decades regarding second language (Italian or German) learning. Today, most South Tyroleans have a basic knowledge of the other main language of the territory and half of the population speaks the second language rather well. However, part of South Tyrol's population, especially Italian speakers, still struggle with the second language. Half of the Italian speakers are not able to have conversations in German and 20% of the German speakers can hardly speak Italian.[98] To address this problem, many residents, especially members of the Italian language group, would like to supplement the existing system with the option of bilingual schools or classes. However, the political leadership of the German language group opposes this idea fearing that bilingual schools would become an instrument of assimilation. Separate schools hinder to a certain extent the social interaction among groups. According to a 2014 survey, two-thirds of the population mainly have friends within their own language group.[99]

Whereas South Tyrolean autonomous arrangements have brought without any doubt peaceful cohabitation, South Tyrol is still characterized by underlying tensions among the language groups, which at times come to the fore of public debate. Examples are the recent attempts to amend language policies and the ongoing process of ASt reform. In the past few years South Tyrol has witnessed lively discussions regarding the issue of place names. In 2012, the provincial parliament enacted a law that allows the use of only the German language for minor place names, like mountaintops.[100] However, the Italian government challenged the provincial law before the Constitutional Court, arguing that it violated the principle of bilingualism established in the ASt. As of this writing, the decision is still pending, but at times, villages and the German-speaking alpine club (*Alpenverein Südtirol*) have taken the initiative to use only German place names on their (public) signs displayed on mountain

focus on "*Il disagio degli Italiani in Alto Adige*" in Günther Pallaver (ed), 13 *Politika* (Edition raetia 2013).

98 ASTAT (n 86). A recent study presented in 2017 has shown that knowledge of the other language among South Tyrolean high school students has worsened in the past seven years, especially within the German-speaking group. *See* Chiara Vettori, Andrea Abel (Eds.), *KOLIPSI II. Gli studenti altoatesini e la seconda lingua: indagine linguistica e psicosociale* (Eurac Research 2017).

99 ASTAT (n 86) 148–150. However, in the last decade, the level of inter-group friendship witnessed a great improvement.

100 South Tyrol's Provincial Law no. 15/2012 regarding the establishment of the provincial repertoire of place names and the provincial cartographic council.

paths. Such actions have been followed by protests from most of the Italian-speaking population and its political and cultural elites. Recently, there have been attempts to find a political compromise within the Commission of Six. In February 2017, the joint commission discussed a new proposal that would allow derogations from the principle of bilingualism in some cases and delegate decision-making power to a commission composed of German and Italian-speaking experts. However, the agreement failed when one of the Italian-speaking members of the Commission of Six, acting on concerns expressed by the Italian-speaking population, opposed the proposal because it did not explicitly state that all place names are bilingual until decided otherwise.

Problems emerged also during the ongoing participatory process known as the Autonomy Convention presented in the previous section. Contrary to the expectation of its proponents, who thought that the local population would come together to support a shared new vision of South Tyrol, the work of the Autonomy Convention has been characterized by a number of disputes along linguistic lines.[101] German-speaking right wing parties have mobilized their supporters and they have managed to hijack to a certain extent the work agenda. They insisted, for example, on including among the main points of discussion the right to self-determination of the South Tyrolean population. While the Italian speakers had a limited participation in the work of the Autonomy Convention,[102] those who participated presented proposals to modify some of the basic principles of the ASt, like the introduction of bilingual schools, which was opposed by many of the German-speaking representatives. At the end, the 'Convention of 33' instead of presenting one document agreed among its members, submitted a final report that includes most of the claims of German-speaking right wing forces, whereas Italian-speaking representatives have presented four separate reports with their own proposals. It remains to be seen whether the provincial parliament will find a compromise.

V Conclusions

South Tyrol's system of territorial and cultural self-governance provides groups and individuals with a complex set of specific institutions and mechanisms

101 However, as Larin and Röggla (n 76) argue, the Autonomy Convention is also an expression of the capacity of South Tyrolean institutions to foster peaceful cohabitation as the discussions during the process did not end up in violence and mass protests due to the improved relationship among the language groups.

102 For a discussion of the possible reasons why the Italian-speaking population did not participate much in the work of the Convention *see* Andrea Carlà, 'Convenzione, italiani cercansi', *Alto Adige* (27 February 2016).

that aim to ensure their effective equality. The joint exercise of power, proportionality principle, cultural autonomy, and mechanisms to defend each group's interests established a system of consociational democracy in the province.

South Tyrol provides key lessons for a better understanding of minorities' needs and inter-group dynamics that should be addressed, as well as of institutional mechanisms that could appease ethnic tensions. First, the South Tyrolean case is relevant because it shows that institutional arrangements, such as power sharing and autonomy, can resolve ethnic conflicts, though which arrangements and what success depend on the specific history and circumstances of each case.[103] Second, the main challenge of successful institutions to appease divided societies is to spark different dynamics and find the correct interplay and equilibrium among them. The South Tyrol system works through a fine balance between the separation and preservation of the language groups and their identity, the forced cooperation of the groups, and, though with some limits, a certain degree of interaction and integration among the groups. Third, as the South Tyrol case shows, minority protection arrangements should not be conceived as fixed static solutions but rather as dynamic mechanisms that need to adapt constantly to changing circumstances and new societal realities.[104] South Tyrol is an example of such a flexible system of self-governance and minority protection, which has been continually corrected, changed and updated and is still evolving.

As correctly pointed out by Alcock, South Tyrolean autonomous arrangements are the 'envy' of other minorities around the world, which dream of enjoying a similar system of minority protection.[105] However, one may reasonably ask whether South Tyrol can be a model for other divided societies. Although often suggested, the idea of copying and reproducing the entire set of South Tyrol's mechanisms and institutions in a different political, cultural and socio-economic context, most probably has very limited chances of success. As emerged from this chapter, South Tyrol's system of minority protection and self-government is a complex unique tailor-made answer to various challenges faced by this culturally diverse territory. Its success derives from specific conditions and factors that have existed in South Tyrol. Furthermore, whereas South Tyrol is clearly a successful case of institutional design for a divided society, which has brought peace and appeased the ethnic conflict, the territorial and cultural self-governance system has also some weaknesses and certain

103 de Villiers (n 74).

104 Antony Alcock, 'The South Tyrol autonomy: A short introduction', (2001) <http://www.provincia.bz.it/news/it/pubblicazioni.asp?publ_page=2> accessed 8 November 2018, 18.

105 Alcock (n 104) 1.

problems and tensions among the language groups remain. Ethnic politics still play a salient role in South Tyrol. While certain principles and mechanisms that work well in South Tyrol could function in other cases of divided societies, it is not feasible to simply reproduce the whole complex South Tyrolean arrangement in other political, cultural and socio-economic contexts. Such action might actually risk reproducing the negative outcomes of the South Tyrolean system of diversity governance rather than its successes.

To conclude, rather than look at South Tyrol as a model to export to other divided societies, it might be more useful to see the province as a locus of inspiration. South Tyrol, with its history of success in dealing with ethnic conflicts and its expertise accumulated in the field, could be a neutral space, where the academic community as well as political leaders and representatives of civil society could meet to discuss how to solve ethnic conflicts and find appropriate legal-institutional solutions for divided societies.[106]

Bibliography

Alber, Elisabeth and Carolin Zwilling, 'Continuity and change in South Tyrol's governance' in Levente Salat, Sergiu Constantin, Alexander Osipov, István Gergő Székely (eds), *Autonomy Arrangements around the World: A Collection of Well and Lesser Known Cases* (Romanian Institute for Research on National Minorities 2014).

Alber, Elisabeth and Carolin Zwilling, 'South Tyrol' (Online Compendium Autonomy Arrangements in the World, January 2016) <http://www.world-autonomies.info> (accessed 15 December 2017).

Andreatta, Filippo and Emanuele Castelli (eds), *Solutions and Failures in Identity-based Conflicts* (FBK Press 2015).

Alcock, Antony, 'The South Tyrol autonomy: A short introduction,' (2001) <http://www.provincia.bz.it/news/it/pubblicazioni.asp?publ_page=2> (accessed 8 November 2018).

ASTAT, *Südtiroler Sprachbarometer/Barometro linguistico dell'Alto Adige 2004* (Provincia Autonoma di Bolzano-Alto Adige 2006).

ASTAT, *Südtiroler Sprachbarometer/Barometro linguistico dell'Alto Adige 2014* (Provincia Autonoma di Bolzano-Alto Adige 2015).

106 It is worth noting that the Institute for Minority Rights of Eurac Research has launched a project entitled 'Dialogue and conflict resolution', which is supported by the South Tyrolean government. The project aims to facilitate knowledge transfer within the global scientific community and to foster the role of South Tyrol as an inspiring place for individuals and institutions working on minority issues, divided societies and conflict resolution. For details, *see* <http://www.eurac.edu/imr> accessed 8 November 2018.

ASTAT, *South Tyrol in figures* (Autonomous Province of South Tyrol 2015).

ASTAT, 'Popolazione straniera residente 2015', (2016) 30 *Astatinfo*.

Benedikter, Thomas, 'South Tyrol's Financial System' in in Jens Woelk, Francesco Palermo, Joseph Marko (eds), *Tolerance through Law. Self-Governance and Group Rights in South Tyrol* (Martinus Nijhoff Publisher 2008).

Benedikter, Roland, 'Overcoming Ethnic Division in Iraq: A Practical Model from Europe' *The National Interest*, (11 February 2004).

Benedikter, Roland, 'East Ukraine's four perspectives. A solution According to the south Tyrol Model' (2015) 37 *Ethnopolitics Papers*.

Carlà, Andrea, 'Living Apart in the Same Room: Analysis of the Management of Linguistic Diversity in Bolzano' (2007) 6(2) *Ethnopolitics*.

Carlà, Andrea, 'Societal Security in South Tyrol: A Model to Deal with Ethnic Conflicts' (2013) 12 *European Yearbook on Minority Issues*.

Carlà, Andrea, 'South Tyrol: an autonomy for all?' *PSA 66th Annual International Conference* (21–23 March 2016).

Carlà, Andrea, 'Convenzione, italiani cercansi', *Alto Adige* (27 February 2016).

Carlà, Andrea, 'Land of welcome, land of fear: explaining approaches to "new" diversity in Catalonia and South Tyrol' (2017) *Journal of Ethnic and Migration Studies*. <http://www.tandfonline.com/doi/full/10.1080/1369183X.2017.1352465> (accessed 15 December 2017).

Constantin, Sergiu, 'South Tyrol: Conflict Resolution and Self-Governance' in M. Sanjaume-Calvet and D. Turp (eds), *The Emergence of a Democratic Right of Self-Determination in Europe* (Maurits Coppieters Center 2016).

Constantin, Sergiu and Elisabeth Alber, 'Autonomy and Minority Representation in South Tyrol' in László Komáromi and Zoltán T. Pállinger (eds), *Good Governance - Enhancing Representation* (Pázmány Press 2016).

Grote, Georg, *The South Tyrol Question, 1866–2010: From National Rage to Regional State* (Peter Lang 2012).

Haller, Max, 'South Tyrol – an economic or political success story?' in Christoph von Hartungen, Hans Heiss, Günther Pallaver, Carlo Romeo and Martha Verdorfer (eds), *Demokratie und Erinnerung: Südtirol – Österreich – Italien* (Studien-Verl 2006).

Larin, Stephen J. and Marc Röggla, 'Participatory consociationalism? No, but South Tyrol's Autonomy Convention is evidence that power-sharing can transform conflicts' *IPSA colloquium Democratization and Constitutional Design in Divided Societies* (23-27 June 2017).

Lantschner, Emma, 'History of the South Tyrol Conflict and its Settlement' in Jens Woelk, Francesco Palermo, Joseph Marko (eds), *Tolerance through Law. Self-Governance and Group Rights in South Tyrol* (Martinus Nijhoff Publisher 2008).

Lijphart, Arend, *Democracy in Plural Societies: A Comparative Exploration* (Yale University Press 1977).

Marko, Joseph, 'Is there a South Tyrolean "Model" of Conflict Resolution to be Exported?' in Jens Woelk, Francesco Palermo, Joseph Marko (eds), *Tolerance through Law. Self-Governance and Group Rights in South Tyrol* (Martinus Nijhoff Publisher 2008).

Palermo, Francesco, 'Asymmetric, "Quasi-Federal" Regionalism and the Protection of Minorities: The Case of Italy', in Alan Tarr, Robert Williams, Joseph Marko (eds), *Federalism, Sub-National Constitutions, and Minority Rights* (Praeger Publishers 2004).

Palermo, Francesco, 'Implementation and Amendment of the Autonomy Statute' in Jens Woelk, Francesco Palermo, Joseph Marko (eds), *Tolerance through Law. Self-Governance and Group Rights in South Tyrol* (Martinus Nijhoff Publisher 2008).

Pallaver, Günther, 'South Tyrol's Consociational Democracy: Between Political Claim and Social Reality,' in Jens Woelk, Francesco Palermo, Joseph Marko and the European Academy Bozen/Bolzano, *Tolerance through Law. Self-Governance and Group Rights in South Tyrol* (Martinus Nijhoff Publisher 2008).

Pallaver, Günther (ed), *Politika 13* (Edition raetia 2013).

Pallaver, Günther, 'South Tyrol's changing political system: from dissociative on the road to associative conflict resolution' (2014) 42(3) *Nationalities Papers*.

Rautz, Günther, 'A "Minority within a Minority": The Special Status of the Ladin Valleys' in Jens Woelk, Francesco Palermo, Joseph Marko (eds), *Tolerance through Law. Self-Governance and Group Rights in South Tyrol* (Martinus Nijhoff Publisher 2008).

Scantamburlo, Matthias and Günther Pallaver, 'The 2013 South Tyrolean Election: The End of SVP Hegemony,' (2014) 24(4) *Regional and Federal Studies*.

Steininger, Rolf, *South Tyrol. A Minority Conflict of the Twentieth Century* (Transaction Publishers 2003).

United Nations, UNGA Res 1497 (31 October 1960) and UNGA Res 1661 (28 November 1961).

Vettori, Chiara, Andrea Abel (eds.), *KOLIPSI II. Gli studenti altoatesini e la seconda lingua: indagine linguistica e psicosociale* (Eurac Research 2017).

Villiers, de Bertus, 'Power-sharing Options in Complex Societies – Possible Lessons from South Tyrol for Young Democracies on Ways to Protect Ethnic Minorities at a Regional Level' (2017) 16(1) *JEMIE*.

Woelk, Jens, Francesco Palermo, Joseph Marko (eds), *Tolerance through Law. Self-Governance and Group Rights in South Tyrol* (Martinus Nijhoff Publishers 2008).

Woelk, Jens, 'Participatory Process Started to Reform the Autonomy Statute of Trentino-South Tyrol' (National Observatory on Language Rights Blog, 15 October 2016) <http://odl.openum.ca/participatory-process-started-to-reform-the-autonomy-statute-of-trentino-south-tyrol/> (accessed 15 December 2017).

Wolff, Stefan, *Disputed Territories: the Transnational Dynamic of Ethnic Conflict Settlement* (Berghahn Books 2003).

Wolff, Stefan, 'Complex Power Sharing as Conflict Resolution: South Tyrol in Comparative Perspective' in Jens Woelk, Francesco Palermo, Joseph Marko and the European

Academy Bozen/Bolzano (eds), *Tolerance through Law. Self-Governance and Group Rights in South Tyrol* (Martinus Nijhoff Publisher 2008).

Domestic Legislation

Constitutional Law no. 1/2017 regarding amendments to the special statute for Trentino-South Tyrol on the protection of the Ladin linguistic minority.

Italian President's Decree no. 752/1976.

Italian President's Decree no. 574/1988.

South Tyrol's Autonomy Statute of 1972.

South Tyrol's Provincial Law no. 5/2013 on the election of provincial parliament in 2013 and the composition of provincial government.

South Tyrol's Provincial Law no. 3/2015, establishing a consultative participatory process called the 'Convention for the Revision of the Autonomy Statute'.

Trento's Provincial Law no. 1/2016 establishing a consultative process called *Consulta.*

Case Law

European Court of Justice, Judgement of 6 June 2000, *Angonese v. Cassa di Risparmio di Bolzano SpAI*, C-281/98, EU:C:2000:296.

European Court of Justice, Judgment of 24 November 1998, *Bickel and Franz*, C-274/96, EU:C:1998:563.

European Court of Justice, Judgement of 27 March 2014 *Grauel Rüffer v Pokorná*, C-322/13, EU:C:2014:189.

Italian Constitutional Court, Judgment no. 213 of 19 June 1998.

CHAPTER 8

Self-Determination, Federalism and Autonomy in the Middle East

Thomas Schmidinger

1 Introduction

Middle Eastern states have tended to be extremely centralized after their independence from the European powers that 'managed' the states after the end of the Ottoman Empire. However, prior to the administrative centralization of the Ottoman Empire in the 19th century many kinds of autonomies existed in the areas controlled by the Ottoman Empire. The currently centralized Middle Eastern state resulted from applying the attractive ideologies of the modern state, (anti-)colonialism and nationalism. These new states felt threatened by autonomy for ethnic or religious groups as well as all kinds of federalism. Real autonomy for ethnic minorities only occurred whenever these centralized states were destabilized and weak as in Syria and Iraq. This essay considers the historical and contemporary concepts and realities of autonomies and federalisms in the Middle East and the difficulties to establish federalist structures that are also accepted by central governments. The examples of the Democratic Federation of Northern Syria – Rojava and the Kurdistan Region of Iraq provide insights on these issues. Additional the special cases of Palestine and the United Arab Emirates (UAE) are discussed.

Federalism as a form of state that combines a general national government with various kinds of regional governments exists in many states in Europe, Asia, the Americas and Australia. Examples of federal states include Russia, the United States of America, Canada, Germany, Austria, Switzerland, India, Australia, Brazil, Argentina, Nigeria or Ethiopia. However, states in the Middle East and North Africa rarely have federal structures. The only stable classic federal state in the whole region is the United Arab Emirates, a federation of seven emirates. All other forms of federalism, autonomy or self-determination within an existing state resulted from very specific historic developments and – at least from the perspective of some of its actors – as first steps towards independence from the central state. This article considers the historic development towards highly centralized states in the region and compares two forms of autonomy and federalism, namely the two Kurdish entities in Iraq and Syria.

 | DOI:10.1163/9789004405455_009

Role models for European federal states were the ancient Greek unions of city-states such as the Achaean League, or the Swiss Confederation[1] or the Union of Utrecht in the 16th century.[2] Classic examples for modern federal states include the United States of America or the Federal Republic of Germany. However, more centralistic states sometimes allow a special status of autonomy for national, linguistic and ethnic minorities such as Italy's South Tirol and the Valle d'Aosta.

The different forms of federalism now existing around the world have different degrees of self-determination and self-perception. Federalism concerns different fields of policies, including gender and feminist policies.[3] However, the different forms of federalism do not only differ in the extent of the autonomy of various sub-entities, but also in the policy areas where they have varying levels of self-determination.

II From Pre-modern Empires to Centralized States

Pre-modern empires, like the Ottoman Empire, were not centralized states. The pre-modern empires had centers surrounded by vassal states and tribal chiefdoms with different dependencies and doubtful loyalties.

The Ottoman Empire's center of power, the Sublime Porte, had regional entities that recognized religious minorities with certain degrees of autonomy and self-determination if they stayed loyal towards the Sultanate. According to traditional Islamic law, members of the religions of the book – mainly Jews and Christians, but the status was also at least party extended towards other monotheists (Karaites, Samaritans, Mandeans and even Zoroastrians) – could preserve their religion and a certain degree of autonomy with the status of Dhimmī, a kind of ward of Islam. In the Ottoman Empire this system led to the creation of three different millets for the Jews, the Armenian Christians and the Orthodox Christians. Other churches, like the Old Church of the East (Nestorians) did not have such a formalized status, but were nevertheless considered part of the Ahl al-Dhimma, the protected religions. The autonomy of these millets was not geographical but personal. Every member of the

1 Ernst Deuerlein, *Föderalismus. Die historischen und philosophischen Grundlagen des föderativen Prinzips* (Paul List Verlag 1972) 14.

2 J.C. Bootman, *The Union of Utrecht: its Genesis and Consequences* in J.C. Boogman and G.N. Van der Plaat, (eds), *Federalism. History and Current Significance of a Form of Government* (Martinus Nijhoff 1980) 5–35.

3 Melissa Haussmann, Marian Sawer, Jill Vickers (eds), *Federalism, Feminism and Multilevel Governance* (Ashgate 2010).

Armenian Church was a member of the Armenian millet and every Jew was a member of the Jewish millet.

However, geographic forms of autonomy also existed. Until the middle of the 19th century, semi-autonomous principalities and chiefdoms were dominant in the Kurdish parts of the Ottoman Empire, but also in the Persian Empire. On the Ottoman side, the relationship between these principalities and the Sublime Porte was reorganized in the 15th century by Sultan Selim's minister İdris-i Bitlisî, who was himself a Kurdish prince from Bitlis (Kurdish: Bedlis).[4]

Until the 18th century, a belt of Kurdish principalities on both sides of the border between the Ottoman and Persian Empires provided a malleable buffer zone that shrewdly shifted help from one empire to the other when conflicts arose. However, when these empires modernized in the 19th century, the predominant ideology was centralized control and an end to semi-autonomous principalities and chiefdoms on the periphery of the Middle East's largest empires. This centralization was connected with the crisis of the Ottoman Empire in the west, where the Sublime Porte lost much of its European territories with the treaties of Passarowitz (1718), Belgrade (1739), Küçük Kaynarca (1774), Bucharest (1812), the second Serbian uprising and the creation of the Principality of Serbia in 1815/17 and the creation of the Greek state in 1829. After a century of decline in Europe, the Porte considered all forms of loose and decentralized territorial control as a threat to the empire's integrity. This supports the Kurdish scholar Özlem Galip's claims that the centralization reforms of the 19th century simply sought 'to ensure control over the eastern part of the empire after losses in the Balkans and the independence of Greece, but the fact that they were seen as threatening arrangements led to the series of Kurdish revolts'.[5]

Revolts of Kurdish tribal leaders against centralization attempts enabled the Sublime Port to finally demolish all autonomous principalities in the east. In 1835, the central government took over the principality of Soran and in 1878 integrated it into the newly established Vilâyet Mosul. The Emirate of Badinan that covered present day Dohuk governorate in Iraq, lost its autonomy in 1843. Although the last Emir of Botan, Bedirxan Beg originally offered his help to the Ottomans 'against rebellious local leaders'[6] he later on led an anti-Ottoman uprising in 1847 that ended the emirate that his ancestors had ruled since the 15th century from the present-day town of Cizre. When massacring the Christian

4 Gérard Caliand, *The Kurdish Tragedy* (Zed Books 1994) 24.

5 Özlem Belçim Galip, *Imagining Kurdistan. Identity, Culture and Society* (I.B. Tauris 2015) 46.

6 Barbara Henning, *Narratives of the History of the Ottoman-Kurdish Bedirhani Family in Imperial and Post-Imperial Contexts. Continuities and Changes* (University of Bamberg Press 2018) 96.

Assyrians and the Yazidis of the region and fighting the Ottomans, Bedirxan Beg had an ally: Nurallah Beg, the last Emir of the Emirate of Hakkâri, who also lost his chiefdom. Also in 1847 the principality of Bitlis lost its autonomy. And finally, the last ruler of Bâbân left Suleymania in 1850.[7]

A similar development of state centralization happened in the Persian Empire. Mukriyan and the Kurdish chiefdoms in Khorasan lost their autonomy in the middle of the 19th century. In 1867, the principality of Ardalan was transformed into an ordinary province of the Persian Empire and became simply the province of Kurdistan.[8]

However, the decline of the Kurdish vassal states did not immediately lead to a centralized state. Some regions had a power vacuum that led to a retribalization of vast areas, such as the former Emirate of Botan after Bedirxan Beg was exiled.[9] The Sublime Porte never completely controlled some regions such as Dêrsim. Parallel to the centralization of the Ottoman Empire, the Tanzimat reforms also changed the old millet system. However, until 1869, the Ottoman Empire did not recognize the concept of citizens; finally, the constitution of 1876 acknowledged that 'all Ottomans, equal in the eyes of the law, enjoy the same rights and obligations regardless of ethnicity or religion, althrough Islam remained the religion of the state'.[10]

Finally, both the Persian Empire and the Ottoman Empire left the 19th century as much more centralized states then they had been 100 years earlier. Moreover, with the losses of most of its European provinces, the Ottoman state leaders considered all kinds of regional autonomies and kind of autonomies as a threat for the unity of the remaining empire. The centralism of the late 19th century was a reaction to the decline of the empire.

III Unitary States against Imperialism

After World War I, the new nation states finally created from the remnants of the Ottoman Empire became highly centralized nation states. Although the last functionaries of the Ottoman Empire signed the treaty of Sèvres that

7 Gökhan Çetinsaya, *The Ottoman Administration of Iraq, 1890–1908* (Routledge 2006) 75.

8 Sabri Ateş, *Ottoman-Iranian Borderlands. Making a Boundary. 1843–1914* (Cambridge University Press 2013) 37.

9 Joost Jongerden, 'Elite Encounters of a Violent Kind: Milli İbrahim Paşa, Ziya Gökalp and Political Struggle in Diyarbekir at the Turn of the 20th Century' in Joost Jongerden and Jelle Verheij (eds), *Sozial Relations in Ottoman Diayarbekir, 1870–1915* (Brill 2012) 60.

10 Feroz Ahmad, *The Young Turks and the Ottoman Nationalities. Armenians, Greeks, Albanians, Jews and Arabs, 1908–1918* (The University of Utah Press 2014) 5.

intended an autonomous region for the Kurds, the new Turkish Republic was created as a unitary state. Moreover, with the historic memories of the decline of the Ottoman Empire and the support for Kurdish autonomy by the victorious nations of World War I, the new leadership of Mustafa Kemal considered all kinds of federalism or autonomy a threat to the new republic. Thus, 'the cornerstones of what was to become the Kemalist State doctrine were the principals of a unitary state of a strict division of state and religion, which was much more far-reaching than in western European democracies'.[11]

Federalist attempts in Syria were mainly initiated by the French colonial power. After World War I, Syria was not governed as a central state, but divided into different ethno-religious defined sub-states: Mandatory Syria – including present day Lebanon and the Turkish province of Hatay – was divided into the État de Damas, the État d'Alep, the predominantly Christian État de Grand Liban (the later Lebanon), the État des Alaouites for the Alawites and the Djébel Druze for the Druze. Although the Sanjak of Alexandretta became a part of the État d'Alep in 1923, it had a special autonomous status within this state. In 1922, the French rulers of Syria created a Syrian Federation governed through a Federal Council that included the État de Damas, the État d'Alep and the État des Alaouites. In 1924, this Syrian Federation was replaced by the State of Syria, that excluded the State of the Alawites but included the State of Damascus and Aleppo. After 1924, the region was made up by the State of Syria, the state of the Alawites, the Jebel Druze and the Lebanon. Even after the anti-French uprising 1925–1927, these territories remained separated from Syria and only in 1936, due to continual nationalist and financial pressure, the Druze and Alawite States were incorporated into the Syrian state.[12] However, they were removed again in 1936 and reincorporated in 1942.[13] Attempts to claim an autonomy for the Kurds or specifically for the Kobanê Region in the 1920s[14] failed as well as attempts for an autonomy of the Jezira Region for the local Christian and Kurdish population.[15]

11 Joerg Baudner, 'The domestic effects of Turkey's EU accession negotiations: a missed opportunity for Europe?' in Cengiz Fırat and Lars Hoffmann (eds), *Turkey and the European Union. Facing new challenges and opportunities* (Routledge 2014) 180.

12 Emma Lundgren Jörum, *Beyond Syria's Borders. A History of Territorial Disputes in the Middle East* (I.B.Tauris 2014) 20.

13 Philip Shukry Khoury, *Syria and the French Mandate. The Politics of Arab Nationalism, 1920–1945* (Princeton University Press 1987) 59.

14 Jordi Tejel, *Syria's Kurds. History, politics and society* (Routledge 2009) 27.

15 Thomas Schmidinger, *Krieg und Revolution in Syrisch-Kurdistan. Analysen und Stimmen aus Rojava* (Mandelbaum Verlag 2017) 61.

Although France did not create the sectarian divisions in Syrian politics, it helped to articulate them. Thus, for Syrian and Arab nationalists, an important political goal became all of Syria within a unitary state. Lebanon was considered a part of Greater Syria by all Syrian regimes until the Syrian state recognized the independence of Lebanon in 2008.

From a Syrian nationalist perspective, this division of the Syrian state into sub-states was a colonial attempt to divide and rule. All kinds of federalism were thus suspected as steps towards separatism.

Anti-imperialism and Arab unity also meant rejecting any kind of federalism. Turkey had a similar process; like the Arab nationalists in Syria, Mustafa Kemal understood himself as an anti-imperialist. His struggle to unify Turkey was part of his struggle for independence. Turkish and Arab nationalists – may they be 'left wing' anti-imperialists or right-wingers – saw every attempt to federalize their states as an imperialist strategy to divide and rule. All kinds of Arab nationalists and Turkish Kemalists sought to build a unitary state.

IV Cultural Autonomy?

Although Iraq became independent from British rule much earlier than Syria from France and although Iraq was never divided by Britain into different sub-states, the rulers of Iraq considered as separatist all attempts for any kind of autonomy for the Kurds or the Assyrians. Thus, after the Iraq's independence in 1932, the new state's first massacre was committed in 1933 against Assyrians whose own national inspirations threatened the unity of Iraq. In the so-called Semele massacre, hundreds of Assyrians were killed. Iraqi soldiers under the command of the Kurdish officer Baqr Sidqi destroyed 64 Assyrian villages.[16]

Kurdish struggles for autonomy in independent Iraq were always – in part, even rightly so – considered as separatist struggles. However, the Baathist Arabic-nationalist regime seriously negotiated with Mullah Mustafa Barzani, the leader of the Kurdish uprising about a Kurdish autonomy. Already in March 1970, the regime announced a negotiated plan for a Kurdish autonomy that allowed the Barzanis 'to maintain up to 15,000 peshmerga ("those who face death") forces, and envisioned full participation by the Kurds in Iraq's political

16 Thomas Shairzid, 'Von Semele bis zur Anfal-Kampagne. Verfolgung und Widerstand der Assyrerinnen und Assyrer' in Mary Kreutzer and Thomas Schmidinger (eds), *Irak. Von der Republik der Angst zur bürgerlichen Demokratie* (*Ça ira 2004*) 206.

institutions after a four-year period, but came up short in definitively resolving all aspects of the legal status of Iraqi Kurdistan'.[17]

However, the regime's settlement with Barzani did not work. The regime's increasing totalitarianism did not allow a final settlement of the open questions between Barzani and the regime. From a position of strength, the regime finally unilaterally established an autonomous region for the Kurds in 1974.[18] This step was not negotiated with the Kurdish leader Mullah Mustafa Barzani and was considered as a move to appease and split the Kurdish movement. However, even the most radical Pan-Arabists of Iraq admitted that they did not manage to govern Iraq as a unitary state and that autonomy for the Kurds – even though only on paper – was necessary to rule Iraqi territory.

On March 11, 1974, the Iraqi government promulgated Act 33 which established a formal autonomy for the three Kurdish provinces Dohuk, Erbil and Suleymania (without Kirkuk). According to Article 1 of Act 33 'the region of Kurdistan shall enjoy autonomy and shall be regarded as a single administrative unit "within the legal, political and economic unity of Iraq". The autonomous region extends only over those areas with a majority of Kurdish population, based on a 1957 census. Article 2 provides that Arabic and Kurdish are the official languages in the region, and that both languages shall be taught in schools; Arabic is a required subject beginning in the fourth primary grade'.[19]

In reality, the 'autonomy' for the Kurds inside the Iraqi state under Baathist rule, was never a political autonomy. Barzanis Democratic Party of Kurdistan (Partiya Demokrata Kurdistanê, PDK) split and only a minor wing of the party under Mullah Mustafa Barzanis oldest son Ubaydullah Barzani and the party Hashim and Aziz Aqrawi[20] cooperated with the regime, while Mullah Mustafa went into exile in 1975. The Kurds later called the autonomy of 1974, the 'cultural autonomy' because the new leaders of the Neo-PDK under Hashim and Aziz Aqrawi and Ubaydullah Barzani never had a political autonomy. Their party and their administration of Kurdistan willingly implemented Baathist policies decided in Bagdad. However, they managed to implement some cultural

17 Rex J. Zedalis, *Oil and Gas in the Disputed Kurdish Territories. Jurisprudence, regional minorities, and natural resources in a federal system* (Routledge 2012) 13.

18 Andrea Fischer-Tahir, 'Widerstand und genozidale Verfolgung in Kurdistan (1968–2003). Akteure, Möglichkeiten und Grenzen, Perspektiven' in Mary Kreutzer and Thomas Schmidinger (eds), *Irak. Von der Republik der Angst zur bürgerlichen Demokratie* (*Ça ira, 2004*) 165.

19 Hurst Hannum, *Autonomy, Sovereignty, and Self-Determination. The Accommodation of Conflicting Rights* (University of Pennsylvania Press 1996) 192.

20 David Mc Dowall, *A Modern History of the Kurds* (I.B.Tauris 2004) 37.

and linguistic rights for the Kurds. Even during the worst years of the Anfal operations in 1988–1989, school education in the Kurdish cities was bilingual and Kurdish was used as an official language in the territory of the autonomy. However, this was not a political autonomy until the uprising in 1991 led to a completely different kind of autonomy.

V Two Special Cases: Palestine and the UAE

The Palestinian Territories gained a far-reaching autonomy after the Oslo Peace Process in the 1990s, but it cannot be considered as a classic example of federalism and political autonomy. The Palestinian National Authority is rather a state in its making in an occupied territory. Until 2018, Palestine has been recognized as an independent state by 136 states, including Russia, China, India, Brazil and most African, Asian and Latin American states. The Palestinian National Authority did not seek some kind of federalism or autonomy inside Israel, but an independent Palestinian state.

Thus, the only stable federal state in the larger Middle Eastern region, the United Arab Emirates (UAE), was created out of seven Emirates, all ruled as absolute monarchies: Abu Dhabi, Ajman, Dubai, Fujairah, Ras al-Khaimah, Sharjah and Umm al-Quwain. From the beginning, these seven Emirates did not have an equal status. Two emirates, Dubai and Abu Dhabi, had a kind of veto right as 'decisions by the Supreme Council of Rulers were to be taken by majority vote, but both Abu Dhabi and Dubai had to be part of the majority'.[21] Because of its strong dependence on oil revenues, the UAE's international and regional policy is dominated by Saudi Arabia. Traditionally, the Emir of Abu Dhabi also serves as the president of the federal state. In fact, the federalism of the UAE is based on Saudi Arabia's regional dominance and the personal relationship between the absolutist monarchs of the seven Emirates.

The UAE are a very special case because they are the world's only federal system of absolutist monarchies. This unique case is the result of a very specific political economy of oil revenues and a society predominantly made up of non-citizens who have no chance for political representation and who hardly have any chance for political organizing.

Therefore, Palestine and the UAE cannot be compared with any other forms of federalism in the world.

---

21 Ibrahim El Abed, 'The Historical Background and Constitutional Basis to the Federation' in Ibrahim Al Abed and Peter Hellyer (eds), *United Arab Emirates. A new perspective* (Trident Press 2001) 132.

VI Establishment of Autonomous Regions for the Kurds in Iraq and Syria

Substantial changes happened in two states that were weakened by internal and external conflicts: Iraq and Syria. The decline of these states allowed certain actors, above all the Kurds, to establish autonomous regions without the consent of the central states. In Iraq, this de facto autonomous state became de jure after a regime change. In Syria, this has not yet happened.

The present Kurdistan region of Iraq did not result from the 'autonomy' established by the Baath regime in the 1970s, but resulted from the Kurdish uprising after the Second Gulf War in 1991 and the western powers' reaction to Iraq's suppression of the uprising and the subsequent mass flight of civilians.

The creation of the safe haven for the Kurds was legally based on UN-Resolution 688 and implemented by the 'Operation Provide Comfort' by the USA, UK and France.[22] Under the protection of these forces, Kurdish peshmerga could take over most Kurdish inhabited territories of Iraq. However, they could not take over Kirkuk, Sinjar and the southern Kurdish regions such as Khanaqin or Mandali.

This article does not attempt to recount the complete history of this self-governed region. However, despite the election of a parliament and the erection of formal governmental structures, the region was de facto governed directly by political parties and their militias. Before 1991, political parties and their armed formations already played a crucial role in resisting the Baathist regime.[23] After 1991, they became the nucleus of the new administration. However, the historic conflict between the two biggest players, the Patriotic Union of Kurdistan (*Yekêtiy Nîştimaniy Kurdistan*, YNK, PUK) and the Democratic Party of Kurdistan (*Partiya Demokrata Kurdistanê*, PDK) led to a failure to establish a common political structure for the Kurdish parastate in Iraq. In fact, the two main parties split the territory and fought a civil war – or as the Kurds call it 'fratricide' (Birakujî) between 1994 and 1998, when the Washington Agreement led the path to a ceasefire between the two parties.[24]

However, the territory was still split between two administrations and until 2003 smaller regions around Halabja were also controlled by different Islamist fractions. Two governments resided in Erbil (PDK) and Suleymania (YNK) and

22 Azad O. Saluh, *Freies Kurdistan. Die Selbstverwaltete Region Kurdistans. Hintergründe, Entwicklungen und Perspektiven* (Verlag Dr. Köster 2005) 84.

23 Andrea Fischer-Tahir, *Wir gaben viele Märtyrer: Widerstand und kollektive Identitätsbildung in Irakisch-Kurdistan* (Unrast Verlag 2003).

24 Sheri Laizer, *Martyrs, Traitors and Patriots. Kurdistan after the Gulf war* (Zed Books 1996) 58ff.

two different autonomous regions existed until 2006, when the Kurdistan Regional Government Unification Agreement between YNK and PDK agreed that the two administrations should be unified. The agreement also noted that 'a new post of Vice President of the Region will be established by amendment to the Law of the Presidency of the Region. The Vice President will be from the PUK and will also serve as the Deputy Commander-in-Chief of the peshmerga forces of the Kurdistan Region'.[25] While the YNK received the Ministers of Interior, Justice, Education, Health, Social Affairs, Religious Affairs, Water Resources, Transportation, Reconstruction, Planning, and Human Rights, the PDK received the Ministers of Finance, Peshmerga Affairs, Higher Education, Agriculture, Martyrs, Culture, Electricity, Natural Resources, Municipalities, Sports and Youth, and Minister of Region for the affairs of areas outside the Region. Until the next election, the speaker of the parliament should have been from the YNK, the Prime Minister from the PDK. In all governorates of the Kurdistan Region, the PDK and YNK established a joint committee to resolve problems.

Thus, the unity of the KRG was based on an agreement of both parties to share power and influence. Other parties played a minor role; these parties included the Kurdistan Islamic Union (*Yekgirtuy Islamî Kurdistan*), the Kurdistan Islamic Group (*Komelî Îslamî le Kurdistan*), the Kurdistan Islamic Movement (*Bizûtinewey Îslamî le Kurdistan*), the Communist Party of Kurdistan (*Partiya Komunîstî Kurdistan*), the 2009 founded Listi Gorran and some other minor groups also holding seats in parliament. Although Listi Gorran is the largest opposition party since the elections in 2009 and won more seats than the YNK in 2013, the KRG is still dominated by the PDK and the YNK, as they are the only parties who have their own armed peshmerga units and thus still control the territory they had before the unification of the KRG in 2006.

With the overthrow of Saddam Hussein in 2003, the Kurds could not only take over additional territory, but they also received a legal recognition for their autonomy. Starting with the Transitional Administrative Law of 2004, the new Iraqi constitution of 2005 finally recognized the Kurdistan Region (KRI) and the Kurdistan Regional Government (KRG) as a federal region with a variety of competences and powers: 'The constitution enshrined the role of the peshmerga while also blocking the deployment of Iraqi Security Forces (ISF) without the prior permission of the Kurdistan parliament; it gave the KRG control over future oil fields, while also specifying the sharing of responsibility for

25 *Kurdistan Regional Government Agreement*, January 21, 2006 <http://cabinet.gov.krd/a/d.aspx?r=24&l=12&a=8891&smap&s=010000>.

the operations of existing oil fields, which meant that Kirkuk would be shared if it were to be integrated in the KRI in the future'.[26]

Article 140 of the new constitution guaranteed a solution for the disputed territories, including Kirkuk that should be resolved before the end of 2007.

Although the post-2003 Iraqi governments did not question Kurdistan's autonomy, the Kurdish autonomous region's borders were never fixed. Article 140 of the Iraqi constitution was never implemented and the 'disputed territories' of 2003 are still disputed territories in 2018. While the power structure on the ground changed twice, the legal uncertainty did not change. After the Kurdish-controlled territory expanded in 2003, the Kurds gained further positions in 2014, when the Iraqi Army withdraw and left disputed territories like Kirkuk to the defense of the Kurdish peshmerga.[27] The KRG used that opportunity to create facts on the ground. The struggle against the so-called 'Islamic state' (ISIS) also inspired enormous popularity for the Kurds in Europe and the US and led to an extensive foreign military support for the peshmerga. 'In addition to the direct supply of weapons, training, and military equipment to the peshmerga, what tipped the balance back to the Kurds in the fight against ISIS was the decision by the US and its key allies to conduct a series of airstrikes across northern Iraq'.[28]

However, this expansion of the Kurdish-controlled territory was accompanied by a crisis of legitimacy for the KRG, due to the dissolution of its parliament and the arbitrary extension of the term of office of KRG-president Masoud Barzani.[29] Tensions with the Iraqi central state increased over the future administration of the disputed territories and the use of oil revenues. Already in October 2014, the Iraqi state cut the budget for the Kurdistan region[30] with severe economic and social consequences for the Kurds. Civil servants did

26 Gareth Stansfield, 'The Kurdish Experience in Post-Saddam Iraq' in Gareth Stansfield and Mohammed Shareef (eds), *The Kurdish Question Revisited* (Hurst & Company 2017) 360.

27 Christoph Osztovics, 'Bedrohung von Außen, interne Spannungen und Parteirivalitäten in Kurdistan – Irak' in Ferdinand Hennerbichler, Christoph Osztovics, Maria Anna Six-Hohenbalken and Thomas Schmidinger (eds), *Wiener Jahrbuch für Kurdische Studien 2015, Band 3. 100 Jahre Völkermord an ArmenierInnen und die KurdInnen* (Caesarpress 2015) 251.

28 Benjamin Isakhan, 'The Iraqi Kurdish Response to the "Islamic State". Political Leverage in Times of Crisis' in Gareth Stansfield and Mohammed Shareef (eds), *The Kurdish Question Revisited* (Hurst & Company 2017) 444.

29 Christoph Osztovics, 'Systemkrisen in Irakisch-Kurdistan' in Katharina Brizić, Agnes Grond, Christoph Osztovics, Maria Six-Hohenbalken and Thomas Schmidinger (eds), *Wiener Jahrbuch für Kurdische Studien 2016, Band 4. Şingal 2014: Der Angriff des „Islamischen Staates", der Genozid an den Êzîdî und die Folgen* (Caesarpress 2016) 176.

30 Ofra Bengio, 'The "Other Iraq" after Mosul: What Future for the Kurdish Region?' in Andrea Plebani (ed), *After Mosul Re-Inventing Iraq* (Ledizioni 2017) 78.

not receive salaries for months. The economy of the region, already suffering the consequences of the war against ISIS, virtually collapsed.

The unilateral referendum about the independence of Kurdistan, held on September 25, 2017[31] finally led to the loss of all the disputed territories the KRG had taken over in 2014. Iraqi troops and People's Mobilization Units occupied Kirkuk on October 16, 2017 while most of the peshmerga left the city without fighting. The following day, the peshmerga left Sinjar and other disputed territories and Iraqi army and loyal militias controlled the territories. Until early 2018, the Kurdistan region still suffers under an extensive blockade by the government in Baghdad.

Although the KRG lost much of its competences and territory following the referendum of September 25, all relevant political parties in Baghdad in principle accept the autonomy of Kurdistan. at least within the three governorates Dohuk, Erbil and Suleymania. A decision of Iraq's Federal Supreme Court, published on January 9, 2018, defines even territories outside the three governorates as 'disputed territories' that were already under Kurdish control in 1991.[32] However, the fundamental fact of a Kurdish autonomy is still not in dispute.

Similar to Iraq's Kurdistan Region, Rojava or the Democratic Federation of Northern Syria also resulted from a unilateral move of Syrian Kurds. Thus, the territory controlled by the Syrian Democratic Forces is more a para-state than an autonomous region within Syria.

In July 2012, People's Protection Units (*Yekîneyên Parastina Gel*, YPG), which had been established by units of fighters of Kurdistan Worker's Party (*Partiya Karkerên Kurdistanê*, PKK), took over positions, weapons and ammunition of the Syrian army, which only continued to maintain its presence in the largest Kurdish city, al-Qamishli (Kurdish: Qamişlo). Besides the YPG, an all-female army, the Women's Protection Units (*Yekîneyên Parastina Jin*, YPJ) was also set up. Although it is still disputed to what degree the Syrian regime and the YPG cooperated in this shift of power, cooperation clearly occurred but the regime never officially recognized any kind of autonomy for the Kurds.[33]

When the YPG/YPJ acquired Kurdish regions in the summer of 2012, this raised questions regarding the civil administration of the Kurdish regions. The sharp rivalry between various Kurdish parties became a problem. In 1957,

31 Christoph Osztovics, 'Aktuell – Irak' in Katharina Brizić, Agnes Grond, Christoph Osztovics, Maria Six-Hohenbalken and Thomas Schmidinger (eds.), *Wiener Jahrbuch für Kurdische Studien 2017, Band 5. Sprache – Migration – Zusammenhalt: Kurdisch und seine Diaspora* (Praesens Verlag 2017) 251.

32 *Iraqi Federal Court decision*, 113/2017.

33 Schmidinger, *Krieg und Revolution in Syrisch-Kurdistan. Analysen und Stimmen aus Rojava*, 120.

when the Kurdish parties first began their underground organization, they fragmented very rapidly and became victims of the repressive regimes. In the 1980s, the Syrian regime supported the Kurdistan Workers Party (PKK) against Turkey. The price for this support was to stay away from any political interference within Syria. Only after the exile of the PKK party leader Abdullah Öcalan and his abduction from Kenya by the Turkish state, the old PKK supporters become active in Syria and founded, in 2003, the Democratic Union Party (*Partiya Yekitîya Demokrat*, PYD), which would start to play a decisive political role in Rojava in 2012. They were opposed by the Kurdish National Council in Syria (*Encûmena Niştimanî ya Kurdî li Sûriyeyê*, ENKS), a concentration of almost all other parties, which shared a different understanding of the management of the acquired new territory and had support from Kurdistan's Regional Government in Iraq. While the PYD successfully partnered with representatives of ethnic and religious minorities so that groups such as the Christian Syriac Union Party became part of the political system, the new Kurdish rulers have still not managed to integrate relevant Kurdish parties of the Kurdish National Council ENKS into Rojava's political system.

After protracted and failed negotiations between the rival Kurdish party blocks, the PYD and its People's Councils in West Kurdistan proclaimed three autonomous cantons in January 2014, Efrîn, Kobanê und Cizîrê. This region has a kind of constitution, a 'Social Contract' with a very progressive perspective on human rights, gender equality and minority rights.[34] With the rise of jihadist groups of Jabhat a-Nusra, but above all the so-called 'Islamic State' (IS) the cantons became increasingly involved in combats with these jihadist militias. The canton of Kobanê suffered the most: after a first failed large attack by ISIS in the summer of 2014, it was overrun by jihadist fighters in the autumn of 2014 and was only liberated after many losses.[35]

Eventually, the Syrian Democratic Forces (*Hêzên Sûriya Demokratîk*, SDF) emerged from this alliance on October 10, 2015. The SDF, despite being dominated by the YPG and YPJ, also comprises military councils of Arabs, Syriac-Assyrians and Turkmens. In 2017 they took over a vast territory in the Euphrates Valley, including ar-Raqqa, the 'capital city' of the self-proclaimed 'Islamic State'.[36] In early 2018, the SDF controlled most of the territory northeast of

34 Bawar Bammarny, 'The Legal Status of the Kurds in Iraq and Syria' in Rainer Grote and Tilmann J. Röder (eds), *Constitutionalism, Human Rights, and Islam after the Arab Spring* (OUP 2016) 492.

35 Thomas Schmidinger, *Rojava* (Mandelbaum Verlag 2016).

36 Thomas Schmidinger, 'Militärische Expansion mit US-Unterstützung. Aktuelle Entwicklungen in Syrisch-Kurdistan' in Katharina Brizić, Agnes Grond, Christoph Osztovics, Maria Six-Hohenbalken and Thomas Schmidinger (eds), *Wiener Jahrbuch für Kurdische*

Euphrates river, the region of Efrîn and the Kurdish quarter of Aleppo. This means that the SDF controls more than 20% of the Syrian territory. More than half of this territory is not inhabited by Kurds, but mainly by Arabs.

This was reflected by a change of the name of the territory. The cantons declared autonomous in 2014 founded a federation on March 17, 2016 and called their parastate Democratic Federation of Rojava – Northern Syria (*Federaliya Demokratîk a Rojava – Bakurê Sûriyê*). In December 2016, this name was changed into Democratic Federation of Northern Syria (*Federaliya Demokratîk a Bakûrê Sûriyê*). The co-president Hediya Yousef declared this was an act to include the Arab and other non-Kurdish citizens into the newly formed entity.[37]

In early 2018 Turkish occupation of Efrîn destroyed one of the three founding members of the federation and led to a mass exodus of civilians from the region. As a result of the loss of the most western part of the Federation and the conquest of Arab territories from the so called 'Islamic State' the remaining federation changed its name to 'Autonomous Administration of North and East Syria' (*Rêveberiya Xweser a Bakur û Rojhilatê Sûriyeyê*) in December 2018. Although the Autonomous Administration and its Syrian Democratic Forces gained a lot of international reputation when it finally won the war against the 'Islamic State' in March 2019, the Autonomous Administration of North and East Syria has not been recognized by the Syrian regime. From a Syrian legal perspective, it is not yet an autonomous region, but the Kurdistan Region of Iraq also began that way and became legalized only 12 years after its start in 1991.

VII Conclusion: Two Kurdish Autonomous Regions – Two Forms of Autonomy

Although the Kurdistan Region of Iraq and the Democratic Federation of Northern Syria are both entities dominated by Kurdish political parties, they differ greatly in their structure and their relationship with the state. While the KRG in Iraq mainly wants to become an independent nation-state, the Democratic Federation of Northern Syria refers in its social contract to a 'democratic federal system […] in the Western Kurdistan, Beth Nahrin, and Syria, which ensures the participation of all individuals and groups on an equal footing in the discussion and decision, implementation, and taking into account the

Studien 2017, Band 5. Sprache – Migration – Zusammenhalt: Kurdisch und seine Diaspora (Praesens Verlag 2017) 238.

37 Interview with Hediya Yousef, December 7 2017.

different ethnicities and religions according to the characteristics of each organized group on the basis of co-existence and brotherhood of peoples, and equality of all peoples in rights and duties, and the foundation on a geographical concept and the decentralization of political and administrative within a unified Syria, and respect for human rights charters and the preservation of civil peace and global'.

Already in the preamble, it states that 'Syria's Kurds, Arabs, Assyrians, Turkmen and Armenians, Chechens, Circassians, Muslims and Christians and Yezidis and various others are aware that the nation-state, which has brought the problems […] and tragedies of our people'.[38]

While the political system in the Kurdistan region of Iraq is a parliamentarian democracy with a strong president, the system of the Democratic Federation of Northern Syria is a kind of council democracy that transfers political decisions on local and regional levels according to principles of subsidiarity and especially the theory of 'democratic autonomy' of Abdullah Öcalan, based on eco-libertarians such as Murray Bookchin or Janet Biel.[39]

However, besides these theoretical differences, both entities are strongly dominated by rival Kurdish political parties: The PDK of the Barzani family in Iraqi Kurdistan and the PYD, as sister party of Öcalans PKK in Syria. Behind these different parties have different ideologies with different concepts of economic development: The conservative post-feudal PDK of Barzani sees economic development predominantly in a neoliberal economy based on oil revenues, while the PYD still discusses different concepts of socialism or at least some kind of a social welfare state.

Notwithstanding their commitments towards different forms of democracy, both entities suffer extreme shortcomings when realizing democracy. The two Kurdish entities in Syria and Iraq have a relationship shaped by rivalry and conflict rather than by cooperation. The Kurdish-Kurdish border between 2012 and 2017 was closed most of the time for most of the people.[40] In both entities, opposition activists can become victims of oppression. There are political prisoners and the security apparatus is extremely influential both in the Kurdistan Region of Iraq and the Democratic Federation of Northern Syria.

These shortcomings and rivalries are not surprising at all, if we consider the circumstances these entities were established. Both Kurdish regions resulted

38 Preamble of the Social Contract of the Democratic Federation of Northern Syria.

39 Michael Knapp, Anja Flach and Ercan Ayboga (eds), *Revolution in Rojava. Democratic Autonomy and Women's Liberation in Syrian Kurdistan* (Pluto Press 2018).

40 Thomas Schmidinger, 'Kurdistan: Die Rückkehr der Kurden in die Machtpolitik des Mittleren Ostens' in Horst Schreiber, Monika Jarosch, Lisa Gensluckner, Martin Haselwanter and Elisabeth Hussl (eds), *Gaismair-Jahrbuch 2016. Zwischentöne* (StudienVerlag 2015) 80.

from weak or even failed states that enabled Kurdish parties to establish their own power structures. Such an environment strengthens military logic and authoritarianism and not the development of civil and democratic structures.

However, both entities are still autonomous regions in formation. Their future development still depends on the development of Iraq, Syria and the whole region. It is hard to imagine that stabile and democratic autonomous regions could be established in the long run without a democratization and a federalization of their nation-states or even the whole region.

Bibliography

Ahmad, Feroz, *The Young Turks and the Ottoman Nationalities. Armenians, Greeks, Albanians, Jews and Arabs, 1908–1918* (The University of Utah Press 2014).

Ateş, Sabri, *Ottoman-Iranian Borderlands. Making a Boundary. 1843–1914* (Cambridge University Press 2013).

Bammarny, Bawar, 'The Legal Status of the Kurds in Iraq and Syria' in Rainer Grote and Tilmann J. Röder (eds.), *Constitutionalism, Human Rights, and Islam after the Arab Spring* (OUP 2016) 475–494.

Baudner, Joerg, 'The domestic effects of Turkey's EU accession negotiations: a missed opportunity for Europe?' in Cengiz Fırat and Lars Hoffmann (eds), *Turkey and the European Union. Facing new challenges and opportunities* (Routledge 2014) 178–194.

Bengio, Ofra, 'The "Other Iraq" after Mosul: What Future for the Kurdish Region?' in Andrea Plebani (ed), *After Mosul Re-Inventing Iraq* (Ledizioni 2017) 69–90.

Bootman, J.C., *The Union of Utrecht: its Genesis and Consequences* in J.C. Boogman and G.N. Van der Plaat, (eds), *Federalism. History and Current Significance of a Form of Government* (Martinus Nijhoff 1980) 5–35.

Caliand, Gérard, *The Kurdish Tragedy* (Zed Books 1994).

Çetinsaya, Gökhan, *The Ottoman Administration of Iraq, 1890–1908* (Routledge 2006).

Deuerlein, Ernst, *Föderalismus. Die historischen und philosophischen Grundlagen des föderativen Prinzips* (Paul List Verlag 1972).

El Abed, Ibrahim, 'The Historical Background and Constitutional Basis to the Federation' in Ibrahim Al Abed and Peter Hellyer (eds), *United Arab Emirates. A new perspective* (Trident Press 2001) 121–144.

Fischer-Tahir, Andrea, 'Widerstand und genozidale Verfolgung in Kurdistan (1968–2003). Akteure, Möglichkeiten und Grenzen, Perspektiven' in Mary Kreutzer and Thomas Schmidinger (eds), *Irak. Von der Republik der Angst zur bürgerlichen Demokratie* (*Ça ira*, 2004).

Fischer-Tahir, Andrea, *Wir gaben viele Märtyrer: Widerstand und kollektive Identitätsbildung in Irakisch-Kurdistan* (Unrast Verlag 2003).

Galip, Özlem Belçim, *Imagining Kurdistan. Identity, Culture and Society* (I.B. Tauris 2015).

Hannum, Hurst, *Autonomy, Sovereignty, and Self-Determination. The Accommodation of Conflicting Rights* (University of Pennsylvania Press 1996).

Haussmann, Melissa, Sawer, Marian and Jill Vickers (eds.), *Federalism, Feminism and Multilevel Governance* (Ashgate 2010).

Henning, Barbara, *Narratives of the History of the Ottoman-Kurdish Bedirhani Family in Imperial and Post-Imperial Contexts. Continuities and Changes* (University of Bamberg Press 2018).

Interview with Hediya Yousef, December 7 2017.

Iraqi Federal Court decision, 113/2017.

Isakhan, Benjamin, 'The Iraqi Kurdish Response to the „Islamic State". Political Leverage in Times of Crisis' in Gareth Stansfield and Mohammed Shareef (eds), *The Kurdish Question Revisited* (Hurst & Company 2017) 437–448.

Jongerden, Joost, 'Elite Encounters of a Violent Kind: Milli İbrahim Paşa, Ziya Gökalp and Political Struggle in Diyarbekir at the Turn of the 20th Century' in Joost Jongerden and Jelle Verheij (eds), *Sozial Relations in Ottoman Diayarbekir, 1870–1915* (Brill 2012) 55–84.

Khoury, Philip Shukry, *Syria and the French Mandate. The Politics of Arab Nationalism, 1920–1945* (Princeton University Press 1987).

Knapp, Michael, Flach, Anja and Ercan Ayboga (eds.), *Revolution in Rojava. Democratic Autonomy and Women´s Liberation in Syrian Kurdistan* (Pluto Press 2018).

Kurdistan Regional Government Unification Agreement, January 21, 2006 <http://cabinet.gov.krd/a/d.aspx?r=24&l=12&a=8891&smap&s=010000>.

Laizer, Sheri, *Martyrs, Traitors and Patriots. Kurdistan after the Gulf war* (Zed Books 1996).

Lundgren Jörum, Emma, *Beyond Syria´s Borders. A History of Territorial Disputes in the Middle East* (I.B.Tauris 2014).

McDowall, David, *A Modern History of the Kurds* (I.B.Tauris 2004).

Osztovics, Christoph, 'Aktuell – Irak' in Katharina Brizić, Agnes Grond, Christoph Osztovics, Maria Six-Hohenbalken and Thomas Schmidinger (eds.), *Wiener Jahrbuch für Kurdische Studien 2017, Band 5. Sprache – Migration – Zusammenhalt: Kurdisch und seine Diaspora* (Praesens Verlag 2017).

Osztovics, Christoph, 'Bedrohung von Außen, interne Spannungen und Parteirivalitäten in Kurdistan – Irak' in Ferdinand Hennerbichler, Christoph Osztovics, Maria Anna Six-Hohenbalken and Thomas Schmidinger (eds), *Wiener Jahrbuch für Kurdische Studien 2015, Band 3. 100 Jahre Völkermord an ArmenierInnen und die KurdInnen* (Caesarpress 2015) 251–254.

Osztovics, Christoph, 'Systemkrisen in Irakisch-Kurdistan' in Katharina Brizić, Agnes Grond, Christoph Osztovics, Maria Six-Hohenbalken and Thomas Schmidinger (eds), *Wiener Jahrbuch für Kurdische Studien 2016, Band 4. Şingal 2014: Der Angriff des „Islamischen Staates", der Genozid an den Êzîdî und die Folgen* (Caesarpress 2016).

Preamble of the Social Contract of the Democratic Federation of Northern Syria.

Saluh, Azad O., *Freies Kurdistan. Die Selbstverwaltete Region Kurdistans. Hintergründe, Entwicklungen und Perspektiven* (Verlag Dr. Köster 2005).

Schmidinger, Thomas, 'Kurdistan: Die Rückkehr der Kurden in die Machtpolitik des Mittleren Ostens' in Horst Schreiber, Monika Jarosch, Lisa Gensluckner, Martin Haselwanter and Elisabeth Hussl (eds.), *Gaismair-Jahrbuch 2016. Zwischentöne* (StudienVerlag 2015).

Schmidinger, Thomas, 'Militärische Expansion mit US-Unterstützung. Aktuelle Entwicklungen in Syrisch-Kurdistan' in Katharina Brizić, Agnes Grond, Christoph Osztovics, Maria Six-Hohenbalken and Thomas Schmidinger (eds.), *Wiener Jahrbuch für Kurdische Studien 2017, Band 5. Sprache – Migration – Zusammenhalt: Kurdisch und seine Diaspora* (Praesens Verlag 2017).

Schmidinger, Thomas, *Krieg und Revolution in Syrisch-Kurdistan. Analysen und Stimmen aus Rojava* (Mandelbaum Verlag 2017).

Schmidinger, Thomas, *Rojava* (Mandelbaum Verlag 2016).

Shairzid, Thomas, 'Von Semele bis zur Anfal-Kampagne. Verfolgung und Widerstand der Assyrerinnen und Assyrer' in Mary Kreutzer and Thomas Schmidinger (eds), *Irak. Von der Republik der Angst zur bürgerlichen Demokratie* (*Ça ira* 2004).

Stansfield, Gareth, 'The Kurdish Experience in Post-Saddam Iraq' in Gareth Stansfield and Mohammed Shareef (eds), *The Kurdish Question Revisited* (Hurst & Company 2017) 355–374.

Tejel, Jordi, *Syria´s Kurds. History, politics and society* (Routledge 2009).

Zedalis, Rex J., *Oil and Gas in the Disputed Kurdish Territories. Jurisprudence, regional minorities, and natural resources in a federal system* (Routledge 2012).

CHAPTER 9

Democratic Confederalism in Syria: The Nation-State, the Kurds, and International Law

Thomas James Phillips

1 Introduction

When the bloody French mandate in Syria finally came to an end in 1946, Syria was 'in many respects a state without being a nation-state, and a political entity without being a political community'.[1] Syria's borders had been, in large part, imposed by European powers[2] and there was a general consensus that the divisions between the States were artificial.[3] To the extent that there was a nationalist movement, it emphasised Arab unity rather than Syrian unity.[4]

This chapter seeks to sketch-out some features of Syria's development into a nation-state, with a particular focus on how that new nation-state reconceptualised the nature of the link between ruler and ruled in a way that grounded the oppression of Syria's Kurds. The chapter will then explain how the Kurds and their allies seek to reconstitute the Syrian State by disaggregating its sovereignty along federal lines. At the same time, this chapter is concerned with how international law legitimised French influence over the early stages of nation-state development in a way that contributed to the later injustices committed against the Kurds, and how international law interfaces with the Kurds' proposed federal model.

Part 1 provides context for the discussion by explaining that ethno-cultural differences in Syria were largely politically irrelevant under the Ottoman Empire. Part 2 explains that post-war international law legitimised French colonial practices in Syria. Those colonial practices, it is argued, instrumentalised the newly emerged minority rights discourse and contributed to (but did not directly cause) the future development of an exclusionary official Syrian

1 Nikolaos Van Dam, *Destroying a Nation: The Civil War in Syria* (IB Tauris 2017) 5.
2 The border between Syria and Iraq was not determined wholly in Europe. *See* Elieuzer Tauber, 'The Struggle for Dayr Al-Zur: The Determination of Borders Between Syria and Iraq' (1991) 23(3) *Int. J. Middle East Studies* 361. The border with Turkey remained uncertain for several years after World War I.
3 John McHugo, *Syria: A Recent History* (Saqi Books 2015) 112.
4 Albert Hourani, *Syria and Lebanon: A Political Essay* (OUP 1946) 96.

 | DOI:10.1163/9789004405455_010

nationalism. Part 3 describes the form of official nationalism that evolved after Syria won its independence, and how that exclusionary nationalism grounded grave abuses against Syria's Kurds. Part 4 describes the Democratic Confederalism project of the Kurds and their allies and its commonalities with some other models of autonomy. Part 5 seeks to analyse the role of international law in the reconstitution of the Syrian State, and some of the ways in which it might validate the claim to a federal model.

II Syria and the Kurds under the Ottoman Empire

Modern-day Syria was an integral part of the Ottoman Empire from 1516 until 1918. Due to its size and diversity, the Empire had to reach *ad-hoc*, non-territorial autonomy arrangements with various religious groups in order to function more-or-less effectively. The political salience of religion was expressed via the *millet* system, which institutionalized and refined some earlier, pre-Ottoman, methods of incorporating non-Muslim religious group into Muslim dynasties. Under the *millet* system, certain religious groups (which sometimes overlapped with ethnic groups) including the Greek, Armenian and Jewish communities were empowered to organise their own existence and take charge of some of their own affairs wherever they resided within the Empire[5] The nature and extent of those powers changed and fluctuated over time due to the unsystematic nature of the system.

While the *millet* system could be described as a form of minority rights protection *avant la lettre,* it is important to bear in mind that *ethno-cultural* differences were not, at that time, of particular political importance. Since the Empire derived its legitimacy, in large part and for most of its history, from religion rather than a claim to represent a particular people or nation, it did not matter whether the ruler shared the language or ethnicity of the ruled.[6] The majority of Syria's population spoke Arabic, but that fact was largely politically inconsequential.[7] Although Kurdish principalities were often repressed by Ottoman authorities, there were no direct threats to Kurdish identity and no attempts to Turkify them.[8] Indeed, as White highlights, it was the evolution of the Ottoman communities into nations that coincided with the evolution of

5 Karen Barkey and George Gavrilis, 'The Ottoman Millet System: Non-Territorial Autonomy and its Contemporary Legacy' (2016) 15(1) *Ethnopolitics* 24.

6 *See* Benjamin White, *The Emergence of Minorities in the Middle East: The Politics of Community in French Mandate Syria* (EUP 2011) Ch. 1.

7 Nikolaos Van Dam, *The Struggle for Power in Syria: Politics and Society Under Asad and the Ba'th Party* (IB Tauris 2011) 2.

8 Jordi Tejel, *Syria's Kurds: History, Politics and Society* (Routledge 2009) 16.

minorities: a development that he describes as a 'traumatic epistemological transformation…'.[9]

The various communities that we would today conceptualise as ethno-cultural minorities because of their cultural differences and numerical inferiority did, of course, exist within the Ottoman Empire. But it was the relatively recent development of the nation-state form, attended by the re-articulation of the relationship between ruler and ruled based on close ties to a particular ethno-cultural majority that gave meaning to the term 'ethno-cultural minority'.[10]

Nationalism only became an animating idea among the educated urban minority in the two decades prior to World War I, and was initially concerned with attempts to preserve the Ottoman Muslim community in the face of expanding European power.[11] Over time, competing nationalisms began to develop – largely in reaction to each other. Turkish nationalism was partly a reaction to pressure from European States and the concomitant secession of many Christian peoples of the Empire. In turn, the emphasis eventually placed upon the Turkish nation began to make Arab nationalism more explicit.[12]

As explained in the next section, Kurdish nationalism was a relative latecomer. Although the presence of a Kurdish population in Syria pre-dates the creation of the Syrian State and the French Mandate[13] they did not constitute a homogeneous group at the beginning of the twentieth century because of their history, lifestyle, geographic origins and settlement.[14] They did not have a common reference point in some kind of shared ethno-cultural minorityhood, rather they were divided into various tribes, sects, villages, and other smaller groups.[15]

II.A *The French Mandate and the Instrumentalisation of Minorities*

As is known, World War I brought about the collapse of the Ottoman Empire and the occupation of Syria by European powers: first the British and then, after their overthrow of the short-lived Faysal government in 1920, the French.

9 Benjamin White, 'The Nation-State Form and the Emergence of "Minorities" in Syria' (2007) 7(1) *SEN* 64.

10 White (n 6) Ch. 1.

11 Albert Hourani, *A History of the Arab Peoples* (Faber and Faber 2013) 309–310.

12 *Ibid.*

13 Michael M. Gunter, *Out of Nowhere: The Kurds of Syria in Peace and War* (Hurst 2014) 8.

14 Jordi Tejel, 'The Kurdish Cultural Movement in Mandatory Syria and Lebanon: An Unfinished Project of "National Renaissance"' in Djene Rhys Bajalan and Sara Zandi Karimi (eds), *Studies in Kurdish History: Empire, Ethnicity and Identity* (Routledge 2015) 161.

15 Tejel, *Syria's Kurds*, 9. The same was true of the majority of the population: Moshe Ma'oz, 'Attempts at Creating a Political Community in Modern Syria' (1972) 26 *Middle East Journal* 389, 393.

The French occupation of Syria derived its legality at the international level from Article 22 of the League of Nations Charter, which inaugurated the Mandates System. As a former part of the Ottoman Empire, Syria's existence as an independent nation-state was provisionally recognised subject to an undefined period of tutelage.

Whereas pre-war international law had been heavily positivist in nature (leaving the internal workings of sovereign States immune from international legal scrutiny) the Mandates System, along with other innovations such as the minority rights treaties, made it possible for international law to lift the veil of sovereignty and access the interior of sovereign States. This major development was occurring at the same time as non-European territories, such as Syria, were beginning to demonstrate that they had the potential to enter the international community as sovereign equals.[16]

The legally sanctioned division of the Arab provinces of the former Ottoman Empire between European powers served to slow their advance to full and formally equal membership of the international community as independent States. In the Syrian context, it was also a method of legitimising French control over the crucial early stages of development of the Syrian nation-state.

Although the imposition of the French Mandate was contrary to the political opinion of the Syrian people, who would have preferred absolute independence,[17] the Mandate was justified (at least for the 'Class A mandates', of which Syria was one) by reference to the principle of self-determination,[18] the idea being that Syria only needed Mandatory assistance until it was able to stand alone.

White argues convincingly that the emergence of minorities in Syria must be understood in the context of the French Mandate due to the interplay of two distinct factors: French policies designed to exacerbate distinctions between communities, and the transition to a nation-state form,[19] which had by then become the norm under the League of Nations.

To begin with the latter, the transition to a sovereign nation-state form did not occur upon the establishment of the French mandate. Although Syria was provisionally recognised as an independent nation under Article 22 of the League of Nations Charter, the Mandates System essentially created a space

16 Antony Anghie, *Imperialism, Sovereignty and the Making of International Law* (CUP 2004) Ch. 3.

17 *See* 'King-Crane Commission Report' (*World War I Document Archive*) accessed 8 January 2018 <https://wwi.lib.byu.edu/index.php?title=The_King-Crane_Report&printable=yes>.

18 Anghie notes that the status of the mandate peoples in Africa and Asia was more uncertain. There, the mandatory powers were required to promote 'self-government': a more ambiguous term. Anghie, *op. cit.*, 121.

19 White, *op. cit.*, Ch. 2.

from which sovereignty was banished, or held in abeyance.[20] The ostensible *raison d'être* of the system was, however, to create the conditions necessary to support a functioning nation-state.[21] It was the decolonisation process that effectively universalised the nation-state form,[22] but the early stages of the transition to that form occurred under French occupation.

As Ma'oz explains, it was not until the French mandate officially ended that Syrian leaders were in a position to embark on the difficult task of achieving national unity,[23] but the future course of that task was partly influenced by the way in which France, under the legitimising umbrella of international law and institutions, sought to exacerbate differences between communities and instrumentalise the newly emerged discourse on minority rights for imperialist ends.

It is widely acknowledged that French policy in Syria sought to divide-and-rule the population in an attempt to counteract growing Arab nationalism. One such policy involved promoting isolated religious minority enclaves.[24] Apart from decreeing a new State of Lebanon in August 1920, the French also created separate States of Damascus and Aleppo and, in 1922, proclaimed the Jabal Druze a separate State under French protection. It was not until 1942 that the Jabal Druze and the separate Alawite State were reunited with the Syrian State.[25]

Part of the French plan was to forestall a widespread sense of Arab nationalism that might threaten their position in Syria and elsewhere by driving wedges between communities based on their religious differences. This policy found some support in the text of the Mandate agreement, which noted, for example, that the Mandatory shall 'encourage local autonomy' (Article 1), and protect religious minorities (Article 8). Indeed, France cloaked its occupation of Syria in the legitimizing language of minority protection, based on the claim that France was the historic defender of Syria's Christians.

Although religious differences rather than ethnic differences were emphasised, the French occupiers employed minority ethnic communities to police the population at large. For example, Kurds were recruited to combat the 1925

20 Susan Pedersen, *The Guardians: The League of Nations and the Crisis of Empire* (OUP 2015) Ch. 7.

21 Anghie, *op. cit.*, 117.

22 Martti Koskenniemi, *The Gentle Civilizer of Nations: The Rise and Fall of International Law 1870–1960* (CUP 2001) 175.

23 Ma'oz, *op. cit.*, 398.

24 Philip Khoury, *Syria and the French Mandate: The Politics of Arab Nationalism, 1920–1945* (Princeton1989) 5.

25 *Ibid.*, 58–59.

Great Rebellion.[26] Given that French rule, despite its earnest attempts to forestall Syrian Arab nationalism, actually provided a stark rallying-point for a kind of anti-imperialist nationalism[27] that would continue well into the post-independence period, those ethnic minority communities were easily singled-out as traitors and potential sources of weakness. The Kurds were again viewed as 'hired agents in the service of powerful foreign enemies of Arabism' after Syria had won its independence:[28] a view that developed under the French Mandate and was then re-shaped to fit new circumstances.

As White points out, the move to reconceptualise distinct communities as minorities (pursuant to international law's newly emerged concern with minorities) began in the 1930s. For France, it contained the possibility of continuing to intervene in Syria's internal affairs after independence had been granted. For some of the communities agitating to be recognised as minorities, it meant the ability to appeal above the Syrian government's head for protection.[29] Again, when Kurdish activists latched onto the new minority rights discourse in an attempt to gain the support of European powers, Syrian nationalists saw it as treachery.[30]

The constant threat of outside interference partly explains why Syria's nascent Arab nationalism came to be tinged by a pronounced paranoia about ethnic minorities. The importance of this dynamic should not be underestimated: Tejel notes that the fear of minority groups being used as pressure points by external powers has been 'one of the constant and undeniable features of the region's modern history'.[31]

French actions in Syria were often legitimized by the League of Nations' PMC. For example, the brutal suppression of the 1925 Great Revolt, which Khoury describes as a 'popular and widespread anti-imperialist uprising with a pronounced nationalist orientation',[32] and which even some within the West

26 Eva Savelsberg, 'The Syrian-Kurdish Movements: Obstacles Rather Than Driving Forces for Democratization' in David Romano and Mehmet Gurses (eds), *Conflict, Democratization, and the Kurds in the Middle East: Turkey, Iran, Iraq, and Syria* (Palgrave 2014) 87.

27 Khoury notes that although nationalism was a growing force during the final years of the Ottoman Empire, 'it was the Mandate system which ensured that nationalism became the overwhelming flavour of the stew'. Khoury, *op. cit.*, 219.

28 Tejel, *Syria's Kurds*, 41–42.

29 White, *Syria's Kurds*, 133.

30 Janet Klein, 'The Minority Question: A View from History and the Kurdish Periphery' in Will Kymlicka and Eva Pföstl (eds), *Multiculturalism and Minority Rights in the Arab World* (OUP 2014) 45–46.

31 Tejel, *Syria's Kurds*, 41–42.

32 Khoury, *op. cit.*, 205.

had begun to see as a war of national liberation[33] resulted in Syrian petitioners to the PMC being told that the choice of Mandatory power was not up for discussion and that the shortest route towards independence was sincere collaboration with France.[34] The PMC also declared that it was permissible for France (in its own interests) to carve-up Syria into smaller States.[35]

Overall, Pedersen argues that the aim of the mandates system was to 'enlist the great powers in a drama of public accountability that would legitimate this form of alien rule before a sometimes critical, newspaper-reading, *Western* public'.[36] In other words, international law provided a fig leaf to mask a method of exploitation that left lasting, deep scars on Syria, as elsewhere.[37]

Having briefly outlined some of the ways in French rule (legitimised by international law) strengthened divisions between communities by instrumentalising the minority rights discourse, it is important to point out that even if Syria had *not* been occupied by France there would still have been political and social pressures driving Syria towards an exclusivist definition of State and nation. The example of Turkey – which was tutored towards the ideal of European civilization by its own, home-grown orientalist,[38] rather than by colonizing European orientalists – and its parlous relationship with Turkey's Kurds serves as a reminder that the process of articulating a new relationship between ruler and ruled along nation-state lines can, and often does, result in exclusionary forms of nationalism. Indeed, the Faysal administration that was overthrown by France was originally called the *Arab*-Syrian government and the Syrian Congress had decided in 1920 to pursue a united Syrian kingdom that would be Arabic in its language and culture.[39] During the Mandate period, the National Bloc adopted a brand of nationalism that emphasised ethno-cultural unity and loyalty to a distinctly Arab nation.[40]

Although there was nothing inevitable about it, the Kurds, who (as the next section indicates) would soon begin to be exposed to their own form of nationalism, and who spanned Syria's borders with Iraq and Turkey, could still have

---

33 Pedersen, *op. cit.*, 147.

34 *Ibid.*, 161.

35 *Ibid.*, 158–159.

36 *Ibid.*, 168.

37 A fuller account of the Mandate System is provided by Anghie, *op. cit.*, Ch. 3.

38 *See* Welat Zeydanlioglu, '"The White Turkish Man's Burden": Orientalism, Kemalism and the Kurds in Turkey' in Guido Rings and Anne Ife (eds), *Neo-colonial Mentalities in Contemporary Europe? Language and Discourse in the Construction of Identities* (Cambridge Scholars Publishing 2008).

39 Ma'oz, *op. cit.*, 395.

40 Khoury, *op. cit.*, Ch. 10.

emerged as 'marked citizens'[41] even without French divide-and-rule policies. The fear of Kurds being used as pressure points by external powers continued post-independence, but did not necessarily rely on the presence of a threatening *European* power. Neighbouring States have frequently taken advantage of each other's Kurdish populations to exert pressure. The late Memed Aksoy called this grim phenomenon the 'Kurdish snare'.[42]

The emphasis on the Mandates System is not an attempt to argue that the brutalisation of Syria's Kurds can be solely attributed to French colonial policies. Nor is it an attempt to identify a simple linear progression from Mandatory rule to the exclusionary character of the Syrian nation-state. This was influenced in complex ways by wider processes of nation-state formation against the backdrop of broader international discourses and regional events. Syrian rulers' prominent roles in the struggle over Palestine and the occupied Golan Heights, and their ability to maintain a kind of forced internal stability (until recently) are also major factors in the development and maintenance of Syria's exclusionary official nationalism.[43] While separate from the events that occurred under Mandatory rule, these events also represent a degree of continuity because they helped perpetuate the anti-imperialist flavour of Syria's nationalism.

Nevertheless, it remains the case that international law legitimised French rule and therefore played an important role in the future development of an exclusionary form of nationalism in Syria. It is hardly surprising that the instrumentalisation of the newly emerged minority rights discourse by imperialist powers should have at least *contributed* to that development.

III Kurds in the Syrian Nation-State

The French occupation of Syria had catalysed an already-growing Arab nationalism as an element of the resistance to imperial rule, but the independent Syria that emerged from the French mandate was, as the introduction to this chapter notes, 'a State without being a nation-state'. Although it had the

41 On 'marked citizens' *see* Klein, *op. cit.*

42 Memed Aksoy, 'The Kurds' 100 year Resistance and the Islamic State' (18 August 2015) *Kurdish Question.* <http://kurdishquestion.com/oldarticle.php?aid=the-kurds-100-year-resistance-and-the-is> accessed 23 January 2018.

43 Auroroa Sottimano, 'Nationalism and Reform under Bashar al-Asad: Reading the "Legitimacy" of the Syrian Regime' in Raymond Hinnesbusch and Tina Zintl (eds), *Syria from Reform to Revolt, Volume 1: Political Economy and International Relations* (Syracuse University Press 2015).

institutions of a nation-state and was recognised internationally as a nation-state, the process of building national unity was just beginning. There was a general consensus that the borders were artificial and, as Van Dam notes, political consciousness stressed pan-Arab ideology and sub-national loyalties at the expense of commitment to the Syrian nation-state.[44]

The new Syrian nation-state was characterised by ethnic and religious diversity. Writing shortly before the outbreak of the 2011 Syrian war, Van Dam noted that Arabic-speakers constituted a majority of 82.5% of the population, and Sunni Muslims constituted a religious majority of 68.7%. The majority of Syria's population (57.4%) consisted of Arabophone Sunnis. Major religious minorities included the Alawis, at 11.5% of the population; Christians, at 14.1% of the population; and smaller communities of Druze, Isma'ilis, Yezidis and others.[45] The largest ethnic minority is the Kurds, the exact size of which is disputed: Kurdish sources claim to represent 12–15% of the overall population and conservative sources claim that they represent around 8% of the overall population.[46]

Some Kurds were present in Syria before Syria's independence and before the French mandate. Others fled to Syria after the 1925 Shaykh Sa'id rebellion in Turkey, which was brutally repressed.[47] Some of those exiled Kurds established the *Khoybun* league, which began to conceptualise the doctrine of Kurdish nationalism in Syria.[48] Thus *Khoybun*, Gunter writes, played 'a constructive role by helping to begin the process of creating or inventing Kurdish nationalism' by 'bringing [Kurds] into belated contact with nationalist concepts already widespread among the Arabs and Turks'.[49]

Although the Kurds are dispersed across Syria, they are also territorially concentrated in certain northern regions. The areas of Afrin, Kobane and Qamishli in northern Syria are mostly Kurdish.[50] The territories lying between those areas contain mixed Arab-Kurdish territories and some non-Kurdish territories.[51] The mostly Kurdish territories are therefore non-contiguous.

---

44 Van Dam, *The Struggle for Power in Syria*, 4–5.

45 *Ibid.*, 1.

46 Harriet Allsopp, *The Kurds of Syria* (2015 IB Tauris) 18.

47 *See* Martin Van Bruinessen, *Agha, Shaikh and State: The Social and Political Structures of Kurdistan* (Zed Books 1992) Ch. 5.

48 Tejel, *Syria's Kurds*, 17.

49 Gunter, *op. cit.*, 11–12.

50 Fabrice Balanche, 'Rojava's Sustainability and the PKK's regional strategy' (24 August 2016) *WashingtonInstituteforNearEastPolicy*.Accessed9January2018<http://www.washingtoninstitute.org/policy-analysis/view/rojavas-sustainability-and-the-pkks-regional-strategy>.

51 *Ibid.*

As McHugo explains, the ideology that most affected Syria during and after 1946 was Ba'athism, which stressed (and still stresses, at least in rhetoric) the extinction of lesser loyalties that contradict Arab unity (which had been fragmented by artificial, externally imposed borders).[52] The First Principle of the Ba'ath Party constitution notes 'The Arabs are One Nation, which has its natural right to live under One State…' and 'The Arab Homeland belongs to the Arabs. They alone have the right to administer its affairs, wealth and running of its potentials'.[53] With its emphasis on secularism, the potential strength of Arab nationalism lay in the possibility of unifying the large Arab nation by overcoming religious differences, such as those exploited under French rule.[54]

The exclusivist emphasis on the Arab nation is clear, but its relationship with the actually existing nation-states created after World War I is less clear. That relationship has developed over time. Zisser notes that throughout the twentieth century Syrian identity oscillated between Arabism and 'Syrianism', with most Syrian leaders searching for a middle-ground that would reconcile the two.[55] By the time of the 1970s, the trend was 'towards difference [between Arab States] and even hostility rather than greater union'.[56]

Despite the *de facto* abandonment of plans for a single Arab homeland, the official line that the State is the exclusive property of its Arab inhabitants has persisted, even though in reality there has been an almost total identification of the State with its leader,[57] who has demonstrated his willingness to brutally oppress *all* segments of Syrian society. Achcar describes pre-2011 Syria as a 'patrimonial State' that was owned by its ruling family[58] – a state of affairs that Syria's patrimonial rulers sought to legitimise via appeals to Arabism.[59]

52 McHugo, *op. cit.*, 117–118.

53 'The Constitution of the Baath Arab Socialist Party' (31 August 2015) *Baath Arab Socialist Party National Leadership*. <http://www.baath-party.org/index.php?option=com_content&view=category&id=307&Itemid=327&lang=en> accessed 18 January 2018.

54 Robin Yassin-Kassab and Leila al-Shami, *Burning Country: Syrians in Revolution and War* (Pluto 2016) 9.

55 Eyal Zisser, 'Who's Afraid of Syrian Nationalism? National and State Identity in Syria' (2006) 42 *Middle Eastern Studies* 179, 183.

56 Hourani, *A History of the Arab Peoples*, 426

57 Zisser, *op. cit.*, 179

58 Gilbert Achcar, *Morbid Symptoms: Relapse in the Arab Uprising* (Kindle edn, Saqi Books 2016) location 187. Also note that Article 8 of the 1973 constitution referred to the Ba'ath Party as 'the leading party in the society and the State'.

59 Roger Owen, *State, Power and Politics in the Making of the Modern Middle East* (3rd edn, Taylor and Francis 2004) 64. As Klein puts it, Arab nationalism became 'a movement of resistance to "colonial" rule and was quickly exploited by rulers and power-seekers … to legitimize their rule or claims to power', Klein, *op. cit.*, 43.

Although their primary concern has been the prolongation and entrenchment of their own power whatever the consequences for Syria's Arabs (who are, under the Ba'ath Party Constitution, supposed to be the sole people administering Syria's affairs), Syria's leaders have also taken concrete action that is consistent with an exclusionary form of Arab nationalism.

The 1973 Syrian Constitution (which was subsequently amended in 2012) stretched the short, tight skin[60] of the Arab nation over the ethnically diverse Syrian population, and so attempted to conceal its heterogeneity. For example, the name of the State is the Syrian *Arab* Republic and Article 1(3) states: 'The people in the Syrian Arab region are a part of the Arab nation', which glosses over the fact that many Kurds consider themselves part of a separate Kurdish nation that transcends the borders imposed after World War I. The insistence on the strict unitary nature of the State, and the exclusionary definition of the nation as consisting solely of the monolithic ethnic majority puts Syria in the same *monistic* category as neighbouring Turkey.[61]

Syria's Kurds, excluded from the definition of the nation, have been able to participate fully in the Syrian State and society only to the extent that they were willing to adopt an Arabic identity.[62] Kurds who refused to commit cultural suicide by surrendering their identities were severely oppressed.

Perhaps the most striking example of the oppression of the Kurds resulted from the 1962 Hasakeh census, which was ostensibly concerned with differentiating between Kurds who had a right to Syrian citizenship and Kurds who had fled to Syria from Turkey and Iraq. Yildiz notes that the inhabitants of al-Hasakeh 'received no prior warning that a census would be conducted, nor were they given any indication of its consequences'.[63] The inhabitants of al-Hasakeh were given a single day to prove that they had lived on the land before 1945, and many deliberately avoided participating in the snap census in order to avoid military conscription.[64] The result was that 120,000 Kurds were classified as *ajanib* (foreigners) and thereby unable to vote, own property or work in government jobs.[65] Since the *ajanib* status was inherited, the number of Kurds affected was approximately 300,000 or more by 2014.[66] A further 75,000 Kurds

60 These are Benedict Anderson's memorable words. Benedict Anderson, *Imagined Communities: Reflections on the Origin and Spread of Nationalism* (Verso 2006) 86.
61 Article 66 of the Turkish constitution declares that 'Everyone bound to the Turkish State through the bond of citizenship is a Turk'.
62 Van Dam, *The Struggle for Power in Syria*, 18.
63 Kerim Yildiz, *The Kurds in Syria: The Forgotten People* (Pluto 2005) 33.
64 *Ibid.*
65 Gunter, *op. cit.*, 2.
66 *Ibid.*

were labelled *maktoumeen* (concealed). They had virtually no civil rights at all, and were worse off than the *ajanib*.[67] An expert report referenced by *International Crisis Group* notes that it was difficult for Kurds rendered stateless to hold legal jobs, go to high school and university, and ride on public busses and sleep in hotels: all activities that required a Syrian identity card.[68]

Another striking illustration of how the Kurds were *othered* is provided by the report of Lt Muhammad Talab Hilal, published confidentially in November 1963. In the report, Hilal likened the Kurds to a 'malignant tumour that had developed in the body of the Arab nation'[69] and proposed that the tumour be excised via the settlement of Arabs in Kurdish areas, displacement of Kurds from their lands, and the denial of Syrian citizenship.

One of Hilal's recommended methods of bringing the Kurdish 'tumour' into remission involved Arabisation: policies designed to assimilate Kurds into the Arab nation. In 1965, a 275km long and 15km wide *cordon sanitaire*, known as the Arab Belt, running along the Turkey-Syria border was planned.[70] In 1973, the policy was implemented by ordering families in Kurdish villages to disperse to the interior regions of Syria, where they would be more remote from the Kurdish population. Arab families who had themselves been displaced by the construction of the Tabqa Dam were moved into areas vacated by Kurds.[71] Furthermore, in 1970 al-Assad blocked the distribution of land in order to avoid creating a Kurdish landowning class. The objective, Balanche notes, 'was to push the Kurdish population to emigrate to the big Syrian cities where it would be more likely to Arabize'.[72]

The mostly Kurdish areas of northern Syria were also deliberately underdeveloped by successive Syrian regimes. Some of the majority Kurdish areas are rich in cotton, wheat and oil: commodities of great importance to Syria as a whole. But the creation of industrial enterprises was long forbidden by the State and the residents of those areas were forced into a situation of economic dependency. As Balanche puts it, resource rich places like Hasakeh 'came to

67 *Ibid.*

68 'Popular Protest in North Africa and the Middle East (VI): The Syrian People's Slow Motion Revolution' (6 July 2011) *International Crisis Group* 20. <https://www.crisisgroup.org/middle-east-north-africa/eastern-mediterranean/syria/popular-protest-north-africa-and-middle-east-vi-syrian-people-s-slow-motion-revolution>.

69 Yildiz, *op. cit.*, 34.

70 Allsopp, *op. cit.*, 25.

71 Yildiz , *op. cit.*, 36.

72 Febrice Balanche, 'From Qamishli to Qamishlo: A Trip to Rojava's New Capital' (8 May 2017) *Washington Institute for Near East Policy*. <http://www.washingtoninstitute.org/fikraforum/view/from-qamishli-to-qamishlo-a-trip-to-rojavas-new-capital> accessed 10 January 2018.

resemble an internal colony forced to feed western Syria with raw materials'.[73] Again, the similarities with neighbouring Turkey[74] are quite striking: there too the Kurdish regions are economically underdeveloped – with the predictable result that many Kurds opt to move to the interior to become a source of cheap labour that can be more easily assimilated into the dominant ethnic group.

Other notable methods of cultural oppression included a *de facto* ban on publications in the Kurdish language;[75] a ban on the teaching of, or teaching in, the Kurdish language – even in private schools;[76] and policies aimed at replacing Kurdish names, business titles, and toponyms with Arabic ones.[77]

Having sketched-out some of the consequences for the Kurdish minority of the official Arab nationalism exercised by the patrimonial Syrian nation-state, the next section will examine how the *Democratic Union Party* (PYD) – which became the dominant party in certain parts of northern Syria during the Syrian war – and associated groups intend to redefine the Syrian State and redistribute its sovereignty in order to salve the wounds inflicted upon the Kurds, and upon others, by the Syrian nation-state.

IV Democratic Confederalism and the Democratic Federation of Northern Syria (DFNS)

When Assad regime forces withdrew from Kurdish areas of northern Syria in July 2012, the PYD's institutions filled the power vacuum, and by November 2013 its armed wings had become the dominant military forces in almost all Kurdish-populated areas.[78] At the time of writing, the PYD's multi-ethnic (but mostly Kurdish) Syrian Democratic Forces (SDF) have liberated areas beyond the Kurdish-inhabited territories (including Raqqa – the former 'capital' of the Islamic State) and established their influence over roughly one third of Syria.

73 Febrice Balanche, 'Rojava Seeks to Break Out in Syria' (12 April 2017) *Washington Institute for Near East Policy*. <www.washingtoninstitute.org/policy-analysis/view/rojava-seeks-to-break-out-in-syria> accessed 10 January 2018.

74 *See* generally Veli Yadirgi, *The Political Economy of the Kurds in Turkey: From the Ottoman Empire to the Turkish Republic* (CUP 2017).

75 Yildiz, *op. cit.*, 114.

76 *Ibid.*, 117.

77 *Ibid.*, 117–119.

78 'Flight of Icarus? The PYD's Precarious Rise in Syria' (8 May 2014) *International Crisis Group*. <www.crisisgroup.org/~/media/Files/Middle%20East%20North%20Africa/Iraq%20Syria%20Lebanon/Syria/151-flight-of-icarus-the-pyd-s-precarious-rise-in-syria.pdf> accessed 11 January 2018.

The PYD is part of the KCK, which is an umbrella organisation encompassing several distinct parties and groups across Syria, Turkey, Iraq and Iran.[79] These organisations have as their common denominator an attachment to 'Democratic Confederalism' as an alternative paradigm to the nation-state.[80]

Democratic Confederalism has been described by its leading theorist – the imprisoned leader of the PKK, Abdullah Öcalan – as 'a non-state political administration or democracy without a state'.[81] It is inspired, in part, by the writings of Murray Bookchin, whose powerful critiques of nationalism and nation-states[82] led to a call for a form of direct democracy. In outline, Bookchin's ideas involve the local self-management of municipalities and (in order to avoid the tendency towards parochialism that could develop from that project) a confederation that transcends the boundaries of the municipality. Within that framework, the means of production would fall under the purview of a local assembly and administrative tasks would be delegated to leaders or collective bodies, provided that they were immediately recallable if they began to abuse their power.[83] In Bookchin's confederalist model, 'policymaking is exclusively the right of popular community assemblies based on the practices of participatory democracy' and 'Power thus flows from the bottom up instead of from the top down'.[84] The flow of power from the bottom up, Bookchin writes, 'diminishes with the scope of the federal council ranging territorially from localities to regions and from regions to ever-broader territorial areas'.[85]

To this emphasis on direct, communal, and confederal democracy as an alternative to the nation-state, the project in Syria adds a strong emphasis on the long-overdue emancipation and empowerment of women.[86]

The Democratic Confederalism project, writes Jongerden, rejects the assumption that the nation-state is the natural social and political form of society[87] and disassociates democracy from nationalism and nation from State.[88]

---

79 *See* generally Seevan Saeed, *Kurdish Politics in Turkey: From the PKK to the KCK* (Routledge 2017).

80 *Ibid.*, 62.

81 Abdullah Öcalan, *Democratic Confederalism* (Transmedia Publishing 2011) 21.

82 Murray Bookchin, 'Nationalism and the "National Question"' (1994) 2(2) *Democracy and Nature* 8.

83 *See* Murray Bookchin, *The Next Revolution: Popular Assemblies and the Promise of Direct Democracy* (Verso, 2015) Chs. 1–2.

84 *Ibid.*, 75.

85 *Ibid.*

86 *See* Abdullah Öcalan, *Liberating Life: Women's Revolution* (International Initiative 2013).

87 Joost Jongerden, 'The Kurdistan Workers' Party (PKK): Radical Democracy and the Right to Self-Determination Beyond the Nation-State' in Gareth Stansfield and Mohammed Shareef (eds), *The Kurdish Question Revisited* (Hurst 2017) 248.

88 *Ibid.*, 252–253.

In its stead, self-determination is conceptualised 'in terms of the right of people to make decisions, to take responsibility for the organisation and regulation of their social, economic, political and cultural affairs (democratic autonomy), and a bottom-up, council democracy for its administration (democratic confederalism)'.[89] In theory then, the aim is not to carve a Kurdish nation-state from an Arab nation-state, or even to carve a Kurdish federal region from an Arab nation-state, but to *banish the nation-state entirely*. If successful, such a project could result in a situation whereby power is not claimed to be exercised on behalf of the majority (with guarantees to protect minorities) but where power is exercised by individuals and local communities in cooperation with each other.

In concrete terms, the original 'Social Contract' of the DFNS (then called *Rojava* – an overtly Kurdish name that was deliberately replaced by the more neutral DFNS) defined itself in its preamble as a 'confederation of Kurds, Arabs, Assyrians, Chaldeans, Arameans, Turkmen, Armenians and Chechens'. The updated version of the Social Contract (unofficially translated into English and published by a prominent journalist with much on-the-ground experience in the DFNS[90]) notes that the DFNS is based on 'democratic self-administrations' (Article 7) and that 'Cultural, ethnic, and religious groups and components shall have the right to name its self-administrations…' (Article 33).

Several observers note that the base level of organisation in the DFNS is the local commune, which federates up to the neighbourhood level, the district level, and finally to a body made up of all district councils. Around this confederal system is built a series of committees focusing on women, defence, economics, politics, justice and ideology.[91]

Although different in some important respects, Democratic Confederalism as expressed in the Social Contract has some things in common with the model of national-cultural autonomy. Like that model, which 'rejects the idea of ethnically or nationally exclusive control over territory',[92] Democratic Confederalism focuses instead on the self-administration of cultural, ethnic and religious groups at the local level. Democratic Confederalism also incorporates some elements of consociational models. For example, according to the most recent

89 Ibid., 254.

90 Wladimir van Wilgenburg, 'Social Contract of the Democratic Federalism of Northern Syria' *Transnational Middle East Observer*. <http://vvanwilgenburg.blogspot.co.uk/2017/03/social-contract-of-democratic.html> accessed 11 January 2018.

91 Michael Knapp, Anja Flach, and Ercan Ayboga, *Revolution in Rojava: Democratic Autonomy and Women's Liberation in Syrian Kurdistan* (Pluto 2016) Ch. 6.

92 Ephraim Nimni (ed), *National-Cultural Autonomy and its Contemporary Critics* (Routledge 2005) 10.

Social Contract the executive councils of the various cantons must adopt a fair representation of peoples, groups and social segments.[93]

There are several notable critiques of the Democratic Confederalist model,[94] and of its implementation (Leezenberg argues that the DFNS actually resembles 'a Leninist one-party statelet' dominated by the PKK[95]). But several first-hand accounts suggest that despite the 'daunting challenges' that undoubtedly face such a radical project,[96] sincere efforts are being made to construct a 'unique system of self-government' springing from 'popular assemblies and democratic councils'. These sincere efforts are said to make possible a form of direct democracy where various ethnic groups can organise autonomously.[97]

Democratic Confederalism does *not* aim to embark on the infeasible task of immediately abolishing States,[98] although it does aim to transcend State boundaries. The PYD also aims to spread the Democratic Confederal model

93 Van Wilgenburg, *op. cit.*, Article 56.

94 David Harvey, for example, writes that in the absence of a 'higher authority' taking policy decisions from the top-down, there could emerge large scale inequality between those living in the more privileged communes and those living in the less privileged communes: David Harvey, *Rebel Cities: From the Right to the City to the Urban Revolution* (Verso 2013) 152.

95 Michael Leezenberg, 'The ambiguities of democratic autonomy: the Kurdish movement in Turkey and Rojava' (2016) 16 *Southeast European and Black Sea Studies* 671. Other academics who have visited the region dispute this characterization: *see* David Graeber, 'No. This is a Genuine Revolution' in Dilar Dirik et. al. (eds), *To Dare Imagining: Rojava Revolution* (Autonomedia, 2016).

96 Incidentally, despite the limited emancipatory potential of some aspects of international law, other aspects present obstacles to the realisation of Democratic Confederalism. The aim to democratise the economy, for example, cuts across the practice of the International Financial Institutions: *see* B.S. Chimni, 'International Institutions Today: An Imperial Global State in the Making' (2004) 15 (1) *EJIL*. For a more recent account, *see* Tor Krever, 'Law, development, and political closure under neoliberalism' in Honor Brabazon (ed), *Neoliberal Legality: Understanding the Role of Law in the Neoliberal Project* (Routledge 2017).

97 'Joint statement of the academic delegation to Rojava' (15 January 2015) *Roar Magazine*. Accessed 12 January 2018 <https://roarmag.org/essays/statement-academic-delegation-rojava/>.

98 As Öcalan explains, peaceful coexistence with the State is possible, subject to a right of self-defence: Öcalan, *Democratic Confederalism*, 32. Bookchin notes that one must expect 'national institutions' to resist and that the democratic confederations, which embody a 'dual power against the state', will either be radicalized by that resistance and 'resolutely face all its consequences', or else they will 'sink into a morass of compromises that absorb it back into the social order that it once sought to change': Bookchin (n 69), 18.

throughout Syria.[99] PYD officials claim that Democratic Confederalism is, in fact, compatible with some form of territorial federalism within Syria. According to one PYD official, it would be desirable to apply a 'geographical federal model rather than a nationalistic one on all of the Syrian territories' which might consist of four federal entities within a newly constituted Syria: 'north, south, coast and desert'.[100]

In summary, Democratic Confederalism is in theory (and, according to several reports, in praxis) an attempt to salve the wounds inflicted upon Syrians by the imposition of the nation-state form. It is, broadly speaking, a project that aims to eventually abolish the nation-state form and the associated concept of minorities by empowering local communities to take charge of their own affairs within a radical confederal network.

V Reconstituting Syria: Some Aspects of the Role of International Law

Christine Bell writes that international law relates to internal conflict with an ethnic component in two ways: human rights abuses are addressed by the application of human rights and humanitarian law standards, and broader issues of 'sovereignty, territory, and access to government which are at the heart of the conflict' are dealt with via international law's self-determination and minority rights provisions.[101] There is a degree of overlap as both self-determination and minority rights are part of the broader human rights framework.

Whereas self-determination in the decolonisation period was the legal mechanism through which, as Koskenniemi puts it, the European State form was 'effectively universalized…as the only form of government that would provide equal status in the organized international community',[102] more modern understandings of self-determination emphasise its *internal* dimensions as well as its *external* dimensions and are therefore more attuned to the problems facing sub-State groups.

99 Si Sheppard, 'What the Syrian Kurds Have Wrought' (25 October 2016) *The Atlantic*. <https://www.theatlantic.com/international/archive/2016/10/kurds-rojava-syria-isis-iraq-assad/505037/> accessed 22 January 2018. Öcalan goes so far as to propose a confederate assembly to oppose the United Nations: Öcalan, *Democratic Confederalism*, 31.

100 Mohammad Bassiki, 'Syrian Kurds focused on federalism' (7 October 2017) *Al-Monitor*. <www.al-monitor.com/pulse/originals/2017/10/syria-federal-state-kurds-turkey-russia.html> accessed 12 January 2018.

101 Christine Bell, *Peace Agreements and Human Rights* (OUP 2003) 32.

102 Koskenniemi, *op. cit.*, 175.

For Bell, the law of self-determination connects peace agreement practice to a 'normative universe'[103] and can operate to essentially blur State sovereignty through the practice of 'hybrid self-determination'.[104] In broad outline, hybrid self-determination consists of procedural and substantive components.

In its procedural aspect, self-determination entails a right of peoples to be heard.[105] In the context of State breakdown and the need to reconstitute such a State, this comes close to what Anaya calls 'constitutive self-determination', which involves individuals and groups being accorded 'meaningful participation, commensurate with their interests, in procedures leading to the creation or change in the institutions of government under which they live'.[106]

In its substantive aspect, self-determination entails a right to 'effective and fair participation in public decision-making and in all public institutions'.[107] This can be implemented through periodic elections,[108] coupled with three frameworks that aim to accommodate the competing demands of the conflict's contenders.[109] *State redefinition* aims at changing the nature of the State through 'articulating a new relationship between people and state'.[110] *Disaggregation of power* addresses the state's internal sovereignty[111] and could involve various forms of territorial, cultural or functional autonomy, as well as human rights mechanisms such as minority rights protection. *Dislocation of power* 'addresses the state's external sovereignty by attenuating it' and involves 'powers of governance that cross state borders and are in some sense shared between more than one state, and/or place international actors at the heart of new arrangements'.[112]

International lawyers have engaged with ethnic and nationalist conflict using broadly similar techniques since the inter-war period, when they sought

103 Christine Bell, *On the Law of Peace: Peace Agreements and Lex Pacificatoria* (OUP 2008) 220.

104 *Ibid.*, Ch. 11.

105 *Ibid.*, 219. *See* also: Jan Klabbers, 'The Right to be Taken Seriously: Self-Determination in International Law' (2006) 28 *HRQ*, 186.

106 James Anaya, 'A Contemporary Definition of the International Norm of Self-Determination' (1993) 3 *Transnational Law & Contemporary Problems* 131, 145.

107 Bell, *op. cit.*, 219.

108 The focus on periodic elections has been critiqued by, *inter alia*, Susan Marks. *See* Susan Marks, *The Riddle of all Constitutions: International Law, Democracy and the Critique of Ideology* (OUP 2003).

109 Bell, *op. cit.*, 105.

110 *Ibid.*, 106.

111 *Ibid.*

112 *Ibid.*, 106–107.

new ways to accommodate nationalism within a newly autonomous international law that was subservient to neither States nor nations.[113]

In the context of the Syrian war, the possibility of using the above frameworks in a future peace agreement is reflected in the Geneva Communique of 30 June 2012, which was adopted by the Secretaries General of the United Nations and the Arab League, the Permanent Members of the UN Security Council, Turkey, Iraq, Kuwait, Qatar, and the High Representative of the European Union for Foreign Affairs and Security Policy (although the Communique notes that a wide range of Syrians were consulted, neither the regime nor the opposition were represented at the meeting[114]). It was endorsed by the UN Security Council in Resolution 2118 on 27 September 2013.

Although the Communique does not set out in advance any particular constitutional model for Syria, it does at least note that the *process* towards a Syrian-led settlement 'must be fully inclusive in order to ensure that the views of all segments of Syrian society are heard in shaping the political settlement for transition'. This emphasises the procedural aspect of self-determination.

The Communique also notes that the *substance* of any political settlement must deliver a transition that 'Offers a perspective for the future that can be shared by all in the Syrian Arab Republic' – not just by the monolithic majority. Whatever form the political settlement takes, it should meet the broad aspiration for a State that is 'genuinely democratic and pluralistic' (para. 8(a)) and it must guarantee the rights of minorities (para. 8(c)). It must also respect the sovereignty, independence, unity, and territorial integrity of Syria (para. 11(a)). The Communique therefore leaves room for some form of federalism to be negotiated in future peace talks.[115]

It is also worth bearing in mind that Syria is bound by various international human rights treaties, including the International Covenant on Civil and Political Rights (ICCPR) and the International Covenant on Economic, Social and Cultural Rights (ICESCR). Those treaties, among others, contain some 'overarching legal categories used to support ethnocultural claims in multiple, and often overlapping ways'.[116] For example, the individual right of members of

113 *See* Nathaniel Berman, '"But the Alternative is Despair": European Nationalism and the Modernist Renewal of International Law' (1992) 106 Harvard Law Review 1792.

114 Van Dam, *Destroying A Nation*, 140.

115 Although polling data suggests that people in both regime and opposition-held areas reject federalism. 'Syria: Opinions and Attitudes on Federalism, Decentralization, and the experience of the Democratic Self-Administration' (26 April 2016) *The Day After*. <http://tda-sy.org/en/category/publications/survey-studies>. Accessed 13 January 2018.

116 Gaetano Pentassuglia, 'Ethnocultural Diversity and Human Rights: Legal Categories, Claims, and the Hybridity of Group Protection' (2015) 6 *The Yearbook of Polar Law* 250, 257–258.

minority groups to use their own language and enjoy their own culture (ICCPR, Article 27) and the closely related rights to equality and non-discrimination (ICCPR, Article 26) have provided the basis for the UN Human Rights Committee's criticism of Syria's discrimination against Kurds and its demand that Kurds should be able to use their own language and enjoy their own culture.[117] Arguments in favour of, for example, mother-tongue education in the Kurdish language could be rooted in particular interpretations of individual human rights norms, based, in essence, on the right to preserve and develop one's culture, and on a thick understanding of equality as requiring (or at least endorsing) positive action to rectify existing inequalities.

Although the rights to culture and equality are *individual* rights, it is possible to link them (and other individual rights) with the *group* right to self-determination by arguing that some kind of autonomy arrangement would be, in a particular context, the most effective way of allowing the group's culture to develop and of allowing the group to re-integrate into the State on more equal terms, and/or the most effective way of meeting other human rights obligations, such as the right to participation (ICCPR, Article 25).[118] Indeed, as Pentassuglia argues, 'there might be circumstances in which autonomy appears to be the only way of implementing existing obligations'.[119] The point, he notes, is that 'human rights norms have the capacity to validate autonomy arrangements'; a capacity that 'does not necessarily or automatically require or presuppose a distinctive right to that effect'.[120]

From a normative angle, it is possible to argue that the legitimacy of the demand for a federal form of internal self-determination in Syria is significantly

117 UNHRC, 'Concluding observations of the Human Rights Committee: Syrian Arab Republic' (9 August 2005) UN Doc CCPR/CO/84/SYR, para 18.

118 The Commentary of the Working Group on Minorities notes that 'the duty of the State to protect the identity of minorities and to ensure their effective participation might in some cases be best implemented by arrangements for autonomy ... The autonomy can be territorial, cultural and local, and can be more or less extensive': UNESC, 'Commentary of the Working Group on Minorities to the United Nations Declaration on the Rights of Persons Belonging to National or Ethnic, Religious and Linguistic Minorities' (4 April 2005) UN Doc E/CN.4/Sub.2/AC.5/2005/2, para 20. Similarly, in his concurring opinion in *Diergaardt et al. v Namibia*, Martin Scheinin noted that 'Some forms of local, regional or cultural autonomy may be called for in order to comply with the requirement of effective rights of participation': UNHRC, *Diergaardt et al. v Namibia* (6 December 2000) UN Doc CCPR/C/69/D/760/1997.

119 Gaetano Pentassuglia, 'Do Human Rights Have Anything to Say about Group Autonomy?' in Gaetano Pentassuglia (ed), *Ethno-Cultural Diversity and Human Rights: Challenges and Critiques* (Brill 2018) 139.

120 *Ibid.*, 140.

augmented by the need to correct the State's past and present injustices.[121] Although international law has not validated or legitimised those injustices and rights violations, it has at least played an important role in validating Syria's exercise of coercive power over the Kurds by recognising it as a sovereign entity.[122] In validating the exercise of coercive power over the entire territory of Syria, international law participated in the creation of the Kurdish minority[123] and has therefore at least indirectly contributed to the injustices suffered by the Kurds and others. Moreover, as explained in Section II, international law legitimised French colonial influence over the initial stages of Syria's transition to the nation-state form and is therefore implicated in the negative consequences that flow from that period of colonialism. If internal self-determination is, as Macklem argues, concerned with promoting a more just exercise of sovereign power,[124] then the claim to some form of federalism (as against arguably more limited individual rights to cultural protection and equality) is significantly bolstered by Syria's history of brutality and rights violations. Broadly speaking, the claim here reflects the view, widely shared among scholars, that self-determination contains remedial aspects and that claims to 'thicker' forms of self-determination (such as federalism) are therefore more legitimate if they might help to overcome injustices that flow from the exercise of sovereign power.

Since the DFNS is, in its present configuration, a very diverse *de facto* entity[125] the ongoing ability of the federal project to engage democratically with the diverse groups that together make up the population of the DFNS, and to gain or maintain their support, will add another important layer of legitimacy. A project that protects the rights of all groups and individuals in the DFNS (as Democratic Confederalism claims to do) clearly has a firmer grounding in international human rights law than an exclusionary Kurdish nationalist project ruling over a majority Arab entity. In this regard, the most recent Social Contract notes that the DFNS shall 'abide by the international declaration of human rights and all related charters of human rights' (Article 17). It also proclaims that cultural oppression shall be considered a crime against humanity

121 *See* Gaetano Pentassuglia, 'Self-Determination, Human Rights and the Nation-State: Revisiting Group Claims through a Complex Nexus in International Law' (2017) 19 *International Community Law Review* 443.

122 *See* Patrick Macklem, *The Sovereignty of Human Rights* (OUP 2015) Ch. 2.

123 *Ibid.*, 104.

124 *Ibid.*, 183.

125 Even before its expansion into majority Arab regions of Syria, the Kurds barely constituted a majority. *See* Fabrice Balanche, 'Arabs in the PYD-Controlled Area' in Patrick Clawson (ed), *Syrian Kurds as a U.S. Ally: Cooperation and Complications* (Washington Institute for Near East Policy 2016).

that gives rise to a legitimate right to resist (Article 20). Concretely, one of the most important ways of allowing cultural groups to thrive involves protecting or promoting their languages, and the Social Contract declares that 'All languages in northern Syria are equal in all areas of life' and that 'Every people shall organize its life and manage its affairs using its mother tongue' (Article 4).

But whatever normative arguments can be advanced for or against federalism within the framework of the Geneva Communique and international law more generally, one must continue to bear in mind that, as McAuliffe puts it, 'the primary concern of conflict principals ultimately remains with strategies that best meet their interests and security needs'.[126] The same rings true for the major external powers presently engaged in Syria – such as Russia, Iran, Turkey, and the USA – who play prominent roles in the stuttering peace negotiations. This is not the place to explore the complex political machinations at work in Syria: suffice it to say that the Kurds have many regional enemies who may have the ability to influence the outcome of any future peace negotiations, no matter what normative arguments can be advanced for a federal arrangement.

VI Conclusions

This chapter has sought to explain how the Syrian regions of the Ottoman Empire evolved into the Syrian nation-state, and how international law legitimised French colonialism which, in turn, contributed to the evolution of an exclusivist form of official nationalism. That official nationalism stretched the short, tight skin of the majority Arab nation over a diverse landscape. French colonial practices were important in that the instrumentalisation of minorities for colonial purposes meant that the Syrian nation-state was born in an anti-imperialist struggle where certain minority groups emerged as 'marked citizens'.

When Syrian leaders were finally free to begin building a political community, they adopted a similar *monist* system to neighbouring Turkey. This involved conceptualising the nation in terms of the dominant ethnic majority and seeking, through various techniques, to assimilate unwanted ethnic others such as the Kurds, who were viewed as threats to the territorial integrity of the State and as potential traitors in the hands of foreign enemies.

126 Padraig McAuliffe, 'The Post-Conflict Security Dilemma and the Incorporation of Ethno-Cultural Diversity' in Gaetano Pentassuglia (ed), *Ethno-Cultural Diversity and Human Rights: Challenges and Critiques* (Brill 2018) 369.

It has also sought to explain how the oppression of Syria's Kurds has its roots in (or has at least been cloaked in the legitimacy of) that exclusivist nationalism. The chapter continued with a description of how some ruling Syrian Kurdish parties and their allies conceptualise a new Syria, eventually without the nation-state form, in order to salve the wounds inflicted upon them. The chapter concluded by considering how international law interfaces with both the process and the eventual outcome of any putative peace negotiations, and how it might validate the claim to a federal model.

International law in its modern form is capable of looking beyond formal State sovereignty and examining the inner workings of States. The right of self-determination, combined with other individual rights, can justify (and might, in some cases, require) the disaggregation of State power and blurring of State sovereignty in order to accommodate sub-state group demands for autonomy. Various factors can augment the legitimacy of the Kurdish claim for a federal Syria, including the need to rectify the State's history of injustice (to which international law contributed in various ways) and the ability of the DFNS to respect, protect and fulfil the rights of the myriad groups and individuals within its boundaries.

Bibliography

'Flight of Icarus? The PYD's Precarious Rise in Syria' (8 May 2014) *International Crisis Group*. <www.crisisgroup.org/~/media/Files/Middle%20East%20North%20Africa/Iraq%20Syria%20Lebanon/Syria/151-flight-of-icarus-the-pyd-s-precarious-rise-in-syria.pdf> accessed 11 January 2018.

'Joint statement of the academic delegation to Rojava' (15 January 2015) *Roar Magazine*. <https://roarmag.org/essays/statement-academic-delegation-rojava/> accessed 12 January 2018.

'King-Crane Commission Report' *World War I Document Archive*. <https://wwi.lib.byu.edu/index.php?title=The_King-Crane_Report&printable=yes> accessed 8 January 2018.

'Popular Protest in North Africa and the Middle East (VI): The Syrian People's Slow Motion Revolution' (6 July 2011) *International Crisis Group* 20. <https://www.crisisgroup.org/middle-east-north-africa/eastern-mediterranean/syria/popular-protest-north-africa-and-middle-east-vi-syrian-people-s-slow-motion-revolution> accessed 10 January 2018.

'Syria: Opinions and Attitudes on Federalism, Decentralization, and the experience of the Democratic Self-Administration' (26 April 2016) *The Day After*. <http://tda-sy.org/en/category/publications/survey-studies> accessed 13 January 2018.

'The Constitution of the Baath Arab Socialist Party' (31 August 2015) *Baath Arab Socialist Party National Leadership*. <http://www.baath-party.org/index.php?option=com_content&view=category&id=307&Itemid=327&lang=en> accessed 18 January 2018.

Achcar, Gilbert, *Morbid Symptoms: Relapse in the Arab Uprising* (Kindle edn, Saqi Books 2016).

Aksoy, Memed, 'The Kurds' 100 year Resistance and the Islamic State' (18 August 2015) *Kurdish Question*. Accessed 23 January 2018 <http://kurdishquestion.com/oldarticle.php?aid=the-kurds-100-year-resistance-and-the-is>.

Allsopp, Harriet, *The Kurds of Syria* (2015 IB Tauris).

Anaya, James, 'A Contemporary Definition of the International Norm of Self-Determination' (1993) 3 *Transnational Law & Contemporary Problems* 131–164.

Anderson, Benedict, *Imagined Communities: Reflections on the Origin and Spread of Nationalism* (Verso 2006).

Anghie, Antony, *Imperialism, Sovereignty and the Making of International Law* (CUP 2004).

Balanche, Fabrice, 'Arabs in the PYD-Controlled Area' in Patrick Clawson (ed), *Syrian Kurds as a U.S. Ally: Cooperation and Complications* (Washington Institute for Near East Policy 2016) 29–38.

Balanche, Fabrice, 'Rojava's Sustainability and the PKK's regional strategy' (24 August 2016) *Washington Institute for Near East Policy*. <http://www.washingtoninstitute.org/policy-analysis/view/rojavas-sustainability-and-the-pkks-regional-strategy> accessed 9 January 2018.

Balanche, Febrice, 'From Qamishli to Qamishlo: A Trip to Rojava's New Capital' (8 May 2017) *Washington Institute for Near East Policy*. <http://www.washingtoninstitute.org/fikraforum/view/from-qamishli-to-qamishlo-a-trip-to-rojavas-new-capital> accessed 9 January 2018.

Balanche, Febrice, 'Rojava Seeks to Break Out in Syria' (12 April 2017) *Washington Institute for Near East Policy*. <www.washingtoninstitute.org/policy-analysis/view/rojava-seeks-to-break-out-in-syria> accessed 10 January 2018.

Barkey, Karen and George Gavrilis, 'The Ottoman Millet System: Non-Territorial Autonomy and its Contemporary Legacy' (2016) 15(1) *Ethnopolitics* 24–42.

Bassiki, Mohammad, 'Syrian Kurds focused on federalism' (7 October 2017) *Al-Monitor*. <www.al-monitor.com/pulse/originals/2017/10/syria-federal-state-kurds-turkey-russia.html> accessed 12 January 2018.

Bell, Christine, *On the Law of Peace: Peace Agreements and Lex Pacificatoria* (OUP 2008).

Bell, Christine, *Peace Agreements and Human Rights* (OUP 2003).

Berman, Nathaniel, '"But the Alternative is Despair": European Nationalism and the Modernist Renewal of International Law' (1992) 106 *Harvard Law Review* 1792–1903.

Bookchin, Murray *The Next Revolution: Popular Assemblies and the Promise of Direct Democracy* (Verso 2015).

Bookchin, Murray, 'Nationalism and the "National Question"' (1994) 2(2) *Democracy and Nature* 8–36.

Chimni, B.S., 'International Institutions Today: An Imperial Global State in the Making' (2004) 15(1) *EJIL* 1–37.

Graeber, David, 'No. This is a Genuine Revolution' in Dilar Dirik et al. (eds), *To Dare Imagining: Rojava Revolution* (Autonomedia, 2016).

Gunter, Michael M., *Out of Nowhere: The Kurds of Syria in Peace and War* (Hurst 2014).

Harvey, David, *Rebel Cities: From the Right to the City to the Urban Revolution* (Verso 2013).

Hourani, Albert, *A History of the Arab Peoples* (Faber and Faber 2013).

Hourani, Albert, *Syria and Lebanon: A Political Essay* (OUP 1946).

Jongerden, Joost, 'The Kurdistan Workers' Party (PKK): Radical Democracy and the Right to Self-Determination Beyond the Nation-State' in Gareth Stansfield and Mohammed Shareef (eds), *The Kurdish Question Revisited* (Hurst 2017) 245–258.

Khoury, Philip, *Syria and the French Mandate: The Politics of Arab Nationalism, 1920–1945* (Princeton 1989).

Klabbers, Jan, 'The Right to be Taken Seriously: Self-Determination in International Law' (2006) 28 *HRQ*, 186–206.

Klein, Janet, 'The Minority Question: A View from History and the Kurdish Periphery' in Will Kymlicka and Eva Pföstl (eds), *Multiculturalism and Minority Rights in the Arab World* (OUP 2014) 27–52.

Knapp, Michael, Flach, Anja and Ercan Ayboga, Revolution in Rojava: Democratic Autonomy and Women's Liberation in Syrian Kurdistan (Pluto 2016).

Koskenniemi, Martti, The Gentle Civilizer of Nations: The Rise and Fall of International Law 1870–1960 (CUP 2001).

Krever, Tor, 'Law, development, and political closure under neoliberalism' in Honor Brabazon (ed), Neoliberal Legality: Understanding the Role of Law in the Neoliberal Project (Routledge 2017) 22–42.

Leezenberg, Michael, 'The ambiguities of democratic autonomy: the Kurdish movement in Turkey and Rojava' (2016) 16 Southeast European and Black Sea Studies 671–690.

Ma'oz, Moshe, 'Attempts at Creating a Political Community in Modern Syria' (1972) 26 Middle East Journal 389–404.

Macklem, Patrick, The Sovereignty of Human Rights (OUP 2015).

Marks, Susan, The Riddle of all Constitutions: International Law, Democracy and the Critique of Ideology (OUP 2003).

McAuliffe, Padraig, 'The Post-Conflict Security Dilemma and the Incorporation of Ethno-Cultural Diversity' in Gaetano Pentassuglia (ed), *Ethno-Cultural Diversity and Human Rights: Challenges and Critiques* (Brill 2018) 337–369.

McHugo, John, *Syria: A Recent History* (Saqi Books 2015).

Nimni, Ephraim (ed), *National-Cultural Autonomy and its Contemporary Critics* (Routledge 2005).

Öcalan, Abdullah, *Democratic Confederalism* (Transmedia Publishing 2011).

Öcalan, Abdullah, *Liberating Life: Women's Revolution* (International Initiative 2013).

Owen, Roger, *State, Power and Politics in the Making of the Modern Middle East* (3rd edn, Taylor and Francis 2004).

Pedersen, Susan, The Guardians: The League of Nations and the Crisis of Empire (OUP 2015).

Pentassuglia, Gaetano, 'Do Human Rights Have Anything to Say about Group Autonomy?' in Gaetano Pentassuglia (ed), Ethno-Cultural Diversity and Human Rights: Challenges and Critiques (Brill 2018) 125–167.

Pentassuglia, Gaetano, 'Ethnocultural Diversity and Human Rights: Legal Categories, Claims, and the Hybridity of Group Protection' (2015) 6 The Yearbook of Polar Law 250–317.

Pentassuglia, Gaetano, 'Self-Determination, Human Rights and the Nation-State: Revisiting Group Claims through a Complex Nexus in International Law' (2017) 19 International Community Law Review 443–484.

Saeed, Seevan, Kurdish Politics in Turkey: From the PKK to the KCK (Routledge 2017).

Savelsberg, Eva, 'The Syrian-Kurdish Movements: Obstacles Rather Than Driving Forces for Democratization' in David Romano and Mehmet Gurses (eds), Conflict, Democratization, and the Kurds in the Middle East: Turkey, Iran, Iraq, and Syria (Palgrave 2014) 85–107.

Sheppard, Si, 'What the Syrian Kurds Have Wrought' (25 October 2016) *The Atlantic*. <https://www.theatlantic.com/international/archive/2016/10/kurds-rojava-syria-isis-iraq-assad/505037/> accessed 22 January 2018.

Sottimano, Auroroa, 'Nationalism and Reform under Bashar al-Asad: Reading the "Legitimacy" of the Syrian Regime' in Raymond Hinnesbusch and Tina Zintl (eds), *Syria from Reform to Revolt, Volume 1: Political Economy and International Relations* (Syracuse University Press 2015) 66–88.

Tauber, Elieuzer, 'The Struggle for Dayr Al-Zur: The Determination of Borders Between Syria and Iraq' (1991) 23(3) *Int. J. Middle East Studies* 361–385.

Tejel, Jordi, 'The Kurdish Cultural Movement in Mandatory Syria and Lebanon: An Unfinished Project of "National Renaissance"' in Djene Rhys Bajalan and Sara Zandi Karimi (eds), *Studies in Kurdish History: Empire, Ethnicity and Identity* (Routledge 2015).

Tejel, Jordi, *Syria's Kurds: History, Politics and Society* (Routledge 2009).

UNESC, 'Commentary of the Working Group on Minorities to the United Nations Declaration on the Rights of Persons Belonging to National or Ethnic, Religious and Linguistic Minorities' (4 April 2005) UN Doc E/CN.4/Sub.2/AC.5/2005/2, para 20.

UNHRC, 'Concluding observations of the Human Rights Committee: Syrian Arab Republic' (9 August 2005) UN Doc CCPR/CO/84/SYR, para 18.

UNHRC, *Diergaardt et al. v Namibia* (6 December 2000) UN Doc CCPR/C/69/D/760/1997.

Van Bruinessen, Martin, *Agha, Shaikh and State: The Social and Political Structures of Kurdistan* (Zed Books 1992).

Van Dam, Nikolaos, *Destroying a Nation: The Civil War in Syria* (IB Tauris 2017).

Van Dam, Nikolaos, *The Struggle for Power in Syria: Politics and Society Under Asad and the Ba'th Party* (IB Tauris 2011).

van Wilgenburg, Wladimir, 'Social Contract of the Democratic Federalism of Northern Syria' *Transnational Middle East Observer*. <http://vvanwilgenburg.blogspot.co.uk/2017/03/social-contract-of-democratic.html> accessed 11 January 2018.

White, Benjamin, 'The Nation-State Form and the Emergence of "Minorities" in Syria' (2007) 7 (1) *SEN* 64–85.

White, Benjamin, *The Emergence of Minorities in the Middle East: The Politics of Community in French Mandate Syria* (EUP 2011).

Yadirgi, Veli, *The Political Economy of the Kurds in Turkey: From the Ottoman Empire to the Turkish Republic* (CUP 2017).

Yassin-Kassab, Robin and Leila al-Shami, *Burning Country: Syrians in Revolution and War* (Pluto 2016).

Yildiz, Kerim, *The Kurds in Syria: The Forgotten People* (Pluto 2005).

Zeydanlioglu, Welat, '"The White Turkish Man's Burden": Orientalism, Kemalism and the Kurds in Turkey' in Guido Rings and Anne Ife (eds), *Neo-colonial Mentalities in Contemporary Europe? Language and Discourse in the Construction of Identities* (Cambridge Scholars Publishing 2008) 155–174.

Zisser, Eyal, 'Who's Afraid of Syrian Nationalism? National and State Identity in Syria' (2006) 42 *Middle Eastern Studies* 179–198.

CHAPTER 10

Legal Background of Autonomy Arrangements in Turkey from Historical Perspectives

Olgun Akbulut

I Introduction

Autonomy discussions in the Turkish legal system are closely linked with discussions on the "concept of minority" and the "rights of minorities". According to almost a century-old policy of Turkey; "*Under the Turkish constitutional system, the word 'minorities' encompassed only groups of persons defined and recognized on the basis of multilateral or bilateral instruments to which Turkey was a party*". "Minority rights" were regulated in accordance with the Treaty of Lausanne of 1923. Under the Treaty, Turkish citizens belonging to non-Muslim minorities fell within the scope of the term "minority". Accordingly, Turkish legislation contained only "non-Muslims" as the beneficiaries of minority rights.[1] Despite the fact that since 1923, very different political parties have come to power, this policy has never changed.

The Treaty of Lausanne, which Turkey relies on in every instance when the protection of minority rights is at issue, was signed in the aftermath of the First World War as a peace treaty between the British Empire, France, Italy, Japan, Greece, Romania and the Serb-Croat-Slovene State on the one side and Turkey on the other.[2] Section III of the Treaty contains Articles 38 to 44, which come under the title "Protection of Minorities". These articles provide minority rights to those defined as *non-Muslim minorities* and are among the few legal provisions from those treaties concluded under the Versailles System of League of Nations which are still applied.

1 United Nations Human Rights Committee, *Consideration of the Reports Submitted by States Parties Under Article 40 of the Covenant-Initial Report of State Parties Turkey* (Report No. CCPR/C/TUR/1, 13 April 2011) 407–410; United Nations Committee on the Elimination of Racial Discrimination, *Consideration of Reports, Comments and Information Submitted by States Parties Under Article 19 of the Convention, Summary Record of the 1914th Meeting* (Doc. No. CERD/C/SR.1914, 02 March 2009) 14; European Commission against Racism and Intolerance, 61 *ECRI Report on Turkey (fourth monitoring cycle)* (Report No. CRI(2011)5, 10 December 2010).

2 "Treaty of Lausanne Between Principal Allied and Associated Powers and Turkey" (signed 24 July 1923) (1924) 28 LNTS Nos. 1, 2, 3, 4, 11–113.

 | DOI:10.1163/9789004405455_011

To ensure consistency with the Lausanne provisions, Turkey ratified both the UN Convention on the Rights of the Child with reservations to Articles 17, 29 and 30 and the International Covenant on Civil and Political Rights (ICCPR) with a reservation to Article 27.[3]

The Lausanne Treaty is widely held to regulate the rights of religious minorities in particular. However, the term "religious minority" is not used in the text of the Treaty, the criteria of religion not having been accepted by the parties to it. Unlike the terms racial, religious and linguistic minorities used in the mother treaty (the Polish Minority Treaty) and the other treaties concluded at the time, the subjects of minority rights in the Lausanne Treaty are only non-Muslim minorities. The Turkish delegation at the Lausanne negotiations actually fought for this change.[4] In other words, the term "minority" as used officially by Turkey, covering non-Muslims as per the Lausanne Treaty, echoes in effect the Ottoman *Millet* system that categorized non-dominant communities on the basis of their religious affiliations.[5] Therefore, Alevis, a sect within Islam and the largest religious minority group in Turkey, were left without minority rights protection under the Treaty.[6]

As I described in my previous works, the Turkish Constitutional Court relied heavily on the Treaty of Lausanne when limiting those political party activities arguing minority rights not only for non-Muslims but for everyone, especially for the Kurds and Alevis.[7]

II An Autonomy Option under the Lausanne Treaty

Until the very last years of the Ottoman Empire, two islands (Imbros and Tenedos) located between Greece and Turkey were part of the Ottoman regional administration in the Dardanelles. During this period, the islands were

3 The reservation made by the Republic of Turkey upon ratification of the International Covenant on Civil and Political Rights reads as follows:

> The Republic of Turkey reserves the right to interpret and apply the provisions of Article 27 of the International Covenant on Civil and Political Rights in accordance with the related provisions and rules of the Constitution of the Republic of Turkey and the Treaty of Lausanne of 24 July 1923 and its Appendixes.

4 *See* C.A. Macartney, *National States and National Minorities* (OUP 1934) 255–257.

5 Thomas Hammarberg (Commissioner for Human Rights of the Council of Europe), *Report following his visit to Turkey on 28 June – 3 July 2009*, Doc. No. CommDH(2009)30 (01 October 2009) 5.

6 *For the details see* Olgun Akbulut & Zeynep Oya Usal, "Parental Religious Rights vs. Compulsory Religious Education in Turkey" (2008) 15 *IJMGR* 432, 434.

7 *See* Olgun Akbulut, "The State of Political Participation of Minorities in Turkey: An Analysis under the ECHR and the ICCPR", (2005) 12 *IJMGR* 375–395.

administered by a governor appointed by the central government. The local Greek populations on the islands were represented in the administrative council of the islands.[8]

Although the islands stayed under Ottoman rule for centuries, the islanders were allowed to retain their Greco-Christian ethnic character. The Greek community maintained eight churches and fifteen priests. The Archbishop of Imbros and Tenedos was located at the provincial capital, Castro (*Kaleköy* in Turkish). The Greek community had ten schools with 1,070 students and 15 teachers in Imbros in 1907. The Turkish population composed one-third of the population.[9]

Following the Greek sea victory in the Balkan wars, the islands came under Greek control in November 1912. Greek control lasted through the First World War. When the Greeks were attacking the Ottoman army in the Dardanelles, they also exerted their dominance over the islands. During the Paris Peace Conference concluded at the end of the war, the Greek leadership offered neutralisation and demilitarisation of the islands in return for retaining sovereignty over them. The British agreed. Imbros and Tenedos remained under British occupation until the Treaty of Sèvres was signed between the allied powers and the Ottoman government on 10 August 1920.[10] The Treaty of Sèvres provided annexation of the islands to Greece. The Ottoman government renounced all its rights and title over the islands in favour of Greece (Article 84 of Sèvres). All parties to Sèvres agreed to demolish and disarm all works, fortifications and batteries on the islands (Article 178/1 of Sèvres). Only Great Britain, France and Italy were allowed to station forces on the islands to guarantee the freedom of the straits of the Marmara Sea (Article 178/4 of Sèvres). Following Sèvres, islanders voted in the general election held on 14 November 1920 in mainland Greece as Greek electors.[11]

In addition to its provisions on renunciation of rights over the islands by the Ottoman government, the Treaty of Sèvres has also created autonomy for predominantly Kurdish areas. A commission sitting in Istanbul composed of three members appointed by the British, French and Italian governments was empowered to draft a scheme of local autonomy for the Kurdish areas (Article

8 Alexis Alexandris, "Imbros and Tenedos: A Study of Turkish Attitudes Toward Two Ethnic Greek Island Communities Since 1923" (Spring 1980) 7 *Journal of the Hellenic Diaspora* 5.

9 Alexandris (n 8) 6.

10 "The Treaty of Peace Between the Allied (The British Empire, France, Italy and Japan) and Associated Powers (Armenia, Belgium, Greece, The Hedjaz, Poland, Portugal, Roumania, the Serb-Croat-Slovene State and Czecho-Slovakia) and Turkey" (signed at Sèvres 10 August 1920) II *The Treaties of Peace 1919–1923* (Carnegie Endowment for International Peace 1924).

11 Alexandris (n 8) 7.

62). The Ottoman government agreed to accept and execute the decisions of the said Commission (Article 63). If the Kurdish people applied to the Council of the League of Nations to show their desire for independence, the Council would decide their fate. The Ottoman government renounced all rights and title over those areas if independence was decided by the Council (Article 64).

The Treaty of Sèvres, which was dictated by the allied forces, aimed to mark the end of Ottoman Empire, one of the losing powers of the First World War. However, the Treaty never entered into force in Greece or the Ottoman Empire. The new government in Ankara rejected the Treaty of Sèvres claiming that it was signed by the Ottoman government which no longer represented the Turkish nation since the establishment of the Grand National Assembly in Ankara on 23 April 1920.

In 1922, things were further complicated. After the Greek defeat by Turkish forces during the national liberation war, the allied powers invited the Ankara government to negotiate another peace treaty which would supersede Sèvres. The new government in Ankara accepted the invitation on the condition that only they, not along with the Ottoman government in Istanbul, would be invited as the sole representative of the newly emerged Turkish state.[12]

The victory strengthened the hand of the Ankara government to eliminate, among others, the possibility of any threat directed to the straits from the northern Aegean Sea. The Turkish delegation used similar arguments as those used by the allied powers during the Sèvres negotiations to guarantee the security of the straits. The problem was again the proximity of the islands to the Straits of the Dardanelles. Imbros is located only eleven nautical miles from the mouth of the Dardanelles, and Tenedos twelve.[13] Therefore, these islands became an issue at the negotiations table of the Lausanne Treaty.

During the Lausanne negotiations, the future of the islands in the Aegean Sea was discussed on 25 November 1922, at the sixth meeting of the Territorial and Military Commission.[14] The Turkish delegation argued that both the British and the Greeks used the islands as bases for aggression against Turkey

12 When the Ankara government was invited to the Lausanne negotiations, the National Assembly was already established on 23 April 1920 and, a new founding constitution of the new state was adopted by the National Assembly on 20 January 1921. Two months after the Lausanne deal was signed, a republic was declared with a constitutional amendment on 29 October 1923.

13 Alexandris (n 8) 5, 9.

14 Sevtap Demirci, *The Lausanne Conference: The Evolution of Turkish and British Diplomatic Strategies 1922–1923* (Dissertation submitted as part fulfilment for the degree of Doctor of Philosophy in International History The London School of Economics and Political Science United Kingdom 1997) 93.

before and during the First World War.[15] Turkey demanded a neutral political existence on both islands. To justify its claim, Turkey argued that these islands were of vital importance to Turkey's territorial security. Against the fact that the Greek population had numerical superiority on the islands, the Turkish delegation reminded all parties of the overwhelmingly Turkish population left in the Balkans after the wars and claimed that, in this particular case, geographic and strategic criteria had priority over demographic factors. They argued that the islands constituted an integral part of Turkish territorial waters, and it was an economic necessity for them to be united with Asia Minor.[16]

As a solution, the allied powers proposed the abrogation of Greek sovereignty on the islands and the establishment of a form of autonomy/local administration under the sovereignty of Turkey. The Turkish delegation accepted the proposal and agreed to grant local self-government to protect the Greek character of the islands.[17] In addition, all the parties to the conference agreed on the demilitarisation of the islands.

Article 14 of the Lausanne Treaty stipulates the agreement as the following:

> The islands of Imbros and Tenedos, remaining under Turkish sovereignty, shall enjoy a special administrative organisation composed of local elements and furnishing every guarantee for the native non-Moslem population in so far as concerns local administration and the protection of persons and property. The maintenance of order will be assured therein by a police force recruited from amongst the local population by the local administration above provided for and placed under its orders.
>
> The agreements which have been, or may be, concluded between Greece and Turkey relating to the exchange of the Greek and Turkish populations will not be applied to the inhabitants of the islands of Imbros and Tenedos.

These islands' special status was further strengthened in another additional protocol, "Protocol Relating to the Karagatch Territory and the Islands of Imbros and Tenedos, Signed by the British Empire, France, Italy, Japan, Greece and Turkey".[18]

15 For a short overview of the war on Dardanelles *see* Sevtap Demirci, "The Dardanelles Campaign and the Contending Strategies for War" (May 2017) 5 *International Relations and Diplomacy* 258, 263–267.

16 Demirci (n 14) 93–94; Alexandris (n 8) 10.

17 Alexandris (n 8) 12; Demirci (n 14) 93.

18 <\www.mfa.gov.tr/xv_-protocol-relating-to-the-karagatch-territory-and-the-islands-of-imbros-and-tenedos_.en.mfa> accessed 25 August 2018.

Together with Article 4 of the Protocol, the implementation of the Lausanne provision on the islands were linked to the withdrawal of the Greek military presence. Article 4 of this Protocol reads:

> The withdrawal of the Greek troops and authorities from the islands of Imbros and Tenedos shall be carried out as soon as the Treaty of Peace signed this day shall have been ratified by the Greek and Turkish Governments. As soon as this withdrawal has taken place, the stipulations of Article 14 of the said Treaty [Lausanne Treaty, OA] shall be applied by the Turkish Government.

Turkey also granted amnesty and guaranteed the personal security of the islanders. Article 5 of the Protocol reads:

> ... no inhabitant of the islands mentioned in paragraph IV shall be disturbed or molested in Turkey under any pretext whatsoever on account of his military or political conduct or any assistance of any kind given by him to a foreign power signatory of the Treaty of Peace signed this day or to the nationals of such powers.
>
> Full and complete amnesty shall be granted to all the inhabitants of the territory and islands mentioned in the preceding paragraph for all crimes and offences, whether political or under the ordinary law, committed before this day.

As a result, islanders became under Turkish sovereignty as new citizens of the new republic.

Along with the Lausanne Treaty, Turkey and Greece also signed another treaty (30 January 1923) concerning the exchange of Greek and Turkish populations. The idea was to limit the minority protection of the Treaty to small groups by creating a new nation state with homogenized population groups. To reach this target, population exchange aimed at mutual exclusion of the largest ethnic and religious minority groups from the post-World War I nationalized lands of Greece and Turkey.[19]

According to the "Convention Concerning the Exchange of Greek and Turkish populations Signed at Lausanne, January 30, 1923", the Government of the

19 Elif Babül, "Claiming a place through memories of belonging: Politics of recognition on the island of Imbros" (2006) 34 *New Perspectives on Turkey* 47, 48.

Grand National Assembly of Turkey and the Government of Greece agreed on Article 1 which reads:

> As from the 1st May, 1923, there shall take place a compulsory exchange of Turkish nationals of the Greek Orthodox religion established in Turkish territory, and of Greek nationals of the Moslem religion established in Greek territory.
>
> These persons shall not return to live in Turkey or Greece respectively without the authorisation of the Turkish Government or of the Greek Government respectively.[20]

Article 2 of this Convention provides exceptions for two groups: a) The Greek inhabitants of Constantinople, b) The Moslem inhabitants of Western Thrace.

The main treaty, Lausanne, provided other exceptions along with these two places: Imbros (Gökçeada in Turkish) and Tenedos (Bozcaada in Turkish), two islands located in the north-east of the Aegean Sea.

Lausanne and its additional protocol referred to above created an administration for the islands with self-governing powers despite the fact that the government in Ankara had sovereignty over these territories.[21]

First of all, islanders will have their own "special administrative organisation".

Secondly, the personal security and property of the islanders are put under the responsibility of their own local administration.

Thirdly, islanders will secure their own order with a police force composed of islanders themselves.

Fourthly, de-militarisation of the islands further aimed at the protection of the identity of the islands by creating a vacuum out of a potential Turkish-Greek military tension.

Lastly, a new page was opened for the islanders with a full and complete amnesty granted to all the inhabitants of the islands for all crimes and offences committed during the war years.

All of the above proved that the central government in Ankara was not seen as the sole protector of the identity of the islands. Therefore, it was the inhabitants of the islands with a distinct identity who would secure their own characteristics.

---

20 <www.mfa.gov.tr/lausanne-peace-treaty-vi_-convention-concerning-the-exchange-of-greek-and-turkish-populations-signed-at-lausanne_.en.mfa> accessed 25 August 2018.

21 As we know from the judgements of the Permanent Court of International Justice that central government enjoys full sovereignty over the autonomous regions. *See Lighthouses in Crete and Samos* (Judgment) 1937 PCIJ Series A/B No 71.

III Domestic Law Giving Effect to the Lausanne Treaty

Prior to the Lausanne negotiations, the new Ankara government declared its first constitution in 1921. The 1921 Constitution in Article 11 stipulated that local provinces in Turkey were to have full autonomy in the areas such as health, education, culture, farming, economy, development, and administration of foundations and welfare grants. The National Parliament was empowered to enact an autonomy law. The historic papers of the Parliament prove that the aim behind the autonomy arrangement in the Constitution was to build local governments in the lands inhabited by Kurds.[22] It was defined as the implementation of a part of the Kurdish policy developed by the Ministry of Council.

It was even considered constitutional when the Turkish delegation in Lausanne proposed demilitarisation and administrative autonomy for the islands under Turkish sovereignty. Interestingly, in the same years Finland proposed autonomy for the Åland islands in return for keeping its sovereignty over the islands.[23]

A general autonomy law giving effect to Article 11 of the 1921 Constitution was never enacted but, in order to make Article 14 of the Lausanne Treaty part of domestic law, the Turkish Parliament enacted Law No: 1151 in 1927 under the title *"On the regulation of the local administration of the islands of Imbros and Tenedos"*.[24] The law has 22 provisions.

The Law underlined the special administration on the islands, but linked the administration on the islands with the Çanakkale governorship, a nearby city on the coast of the mainland (Article 1). Not only law enforcement officers but also other civil servants will be employed from among the inhabitants of the islands (Articles 2 and 16). All expenses, including the salaries of the civil servants, of the islands would be paid from the special budget of the islands (Article 10).

The central administrative body of the islands is the Islands' Council. The Council is composed of ten members which are elected by and from among the islanders. The Council is responsible for administering daily issues (Articles 3 and 5). Although the members are elected, it is not clear whether the Council has legislative powers. All the legislation of the central government, as long as it is in compliance with the autonomy status, has binding effects on the islands

22 Murat Sevinç, Dinçer Demirkent, *Kuruluşun İhmal Edilmiş İstisnası – 1921 Anayasası ve Tutanakları* [*Neglected Exception of the Foundation – 1921 Constitution and the Minutes of the Preparatory Meetings*] (Iletisim 2017) 37–48.

23 *See* Chapter 3 in this volume by Sia Spiliopoulou Åkermark.

24 Official Gazette (No: 638, Series: 3, Vol. 8, 20.07.1927) 983.

(Article 19). The Council is the body to prepare the budget of the islands. The budget, however, has to be approved by the Ministry of Interior upon a positive decision by the Çanakkale governorship (Aricle 11). The Council works together with the administrator appointed by the central government. When they deem it necessary, both the central government and its governor can call an extraordinary meeting of the Council (Article 4).

The identifiable local executive branch of the central government on the islands is the administrator. The administrator carries out a similar function to the governors, presidents, prime ministers or ministers in other autonomous regions elsewhere in the world.[25] The administrator is responsible for the execution of the central organ's laws and decisions on the islands. He/she works with a personnel employed from among the islanders (Article 15). The administrator is empowered to apply Çanakkale governorship in case of illegality in the actions of the Council. On the basis of the decisions of the governorship, the Ministry of Interior as the upper power in the hierarchy, can annul the decisions of the Council (Article 7). Additionally, if the Council ceases its work, the Ministry has the right to annul the Council, which will be reformed/re-elected (Article 8). The administrator is the responsible body for public expenses using the budget of the island administration. Çanakkale governorship's administrative authority does not extend to the islands (Article 18). Its powers are limited by the self-governing status of the islands.

The Law also touches upon the issue of minority identity. Greeks are considered a religious minority in that their religious institutions will be administered by their own organisations. Therefore, according to the Law, the schools of the Greek population will be administered by the local administration and their properties will be transferred to local administration (Article 13). Together with Article 14, education in the mother tongue in these schools is prohibited. Article 14 only allows teaching of the mother tongue in those schools outside the ordinary school hours as a language course. Unlike the general expenses of the schools, the expenses for these additional language (and also religion) courses will be paid by the minority group.

Apart from the faith and culture based institutions, the Lausanne minorities in Turkey also have special institutions such as hospitals and clinics. These institutions, together with their properties, are also transferred to local administration by the Law (Article 13).

Does the above legal basis qualify the islands as an autonomy?

25 Hurst Hannum, Richard B. Lillich, "The Concept of Autonomy in International Law" (1980) 74 *AJIL* 858, 861.

Autonomies in the world are designed in response to the needs of the ethnic, linguistic and religious characteristics of the group and region. It is widely accepted that the term autonomy is a general legal term which has to be given a concrete content.[26] However, there are certain minimal elements that are needed to define a region as an autonomous one.

Above all, autonomy is about de-concentrated powers and internal self-determination to create a space for people not regulated by the central government. For that reason, autonomous entities in general have an elected legislative organ that operates as the main local authority.[27] This organ enacts laws in order to implement autonomy law and regulate areas specifically left to the entity. The Law on Imbros and Tenedos established an elected organ (Council), but this organ is framed as an executive organ with decision making powers. The organ is not enacting laws but making decisions and implementing them.

Executive organs representing the central government have been established on Imbros and Tenedos. The powers of these organs, as listed above, are in parallel with the powers of similar organs in other autonomous regions.

The judicial organs on Imbros and Tenedos form part of the central judicial authority. Surveys on autonomous regions in the world rarely point to courts totally separated from the central judicial authority.[28]

In many cases, local police forces are framed as part of the governmental powers of the autonomous region.[29] The police force regulated by domestic law on Imbros and Tenedos follows this line of administrative structure.

In addition, cultural affairs, healthcare, education and religious services are generally considered areas under the responsibility of autonomous regions. This is also the case with Imbros and Tenedos. Institutions operating in these areas during the Ottoman Empire were transferred to the local governing authorities together with their properties. However, their relationship with the area of the cultural characteristics of the islands and islanders was weakened. The law imposed the central governments' curriculum on the schools in the islands.

Both national and international legal documents on Imbros and Tenedos do not specifically focus on issues such as ownership of land, natural resources,

26 Hans-Joachim Heintze, "On the Legal Understanding of Autonomy" in Markku Suksi (ed), *Autonomy: Applications and Implications* (Kluwer 1998) 8.

27 *See* Markku Suksi, *Sub-State Governance through Territorial Autonomy: A Comparative Study in Constitutional Law of Powers, Procedures and Institutions* (Springer-Verlag 2011) 7; Hannum/Lillich (n 25) 865.

28 Hannum/Lillich (n 25) 869–872.

29 Hannum/Lillich (n 25) 875–876.

foreign relations, financial and economic institutions which are deemed important to protect the distinct characteristics of the autonomous entities.

The local self-governing arrangement for Imbros and Tenedos, as it is formulated in international and domestic legal documents, is equipped with the powers which are enjoyed by the majority of the autonomous regions in other parts of the world. Despite its shortcomings, the Imbros and Tenedos administration meets the minimum threshold to be considered as a *sui generis* autonomous region.

IV Imbros and Tenedos under Republican Turkey

The legal background of the autonomy arrangement in Imbros and Tenedos does not overlap well with the historical developments on the islands from an implementation perspective.

In order to follow the changes on the islands, one should start with looking at the population movements to and from the islands. In 1923, the population of Greeks on the islands was estimated to be 8,500. The population census of 2000 showed only 200 Greeks and 8,000 Muslims.[30]

The self-administration of the Greek Orthodox community in Imbros and Tenedos never came into existence.[31]

Only from 1950 onwards was the Greek language taught at schools in Imbros and Tenedos.[32]

The relatively easy years after 1950 did not last long. First, the Turkish-Cyprus conflict disturbed the islanders, which resulted in a gradual decline of the Greek population. The growing intensity of the Turkish-Cyprus conflict caused more Greek islanders to leave their territory. Hence 1964 marked an important year in terms of the high number of departures by Greeks from the islands. Second, an immediate policy of Turkification was started by the Turkish government: populations from all around Turkey were moved to and provided living opportunities on the islands. The government declared special credit opportunities and agricultural aid to encourage people to settle on Imbros. The same year, agricultural lands were expropriated and a military base

30 Babül (n 19) 50 and fn. 11. No official data for the ethnic groups is available since 2000 because, the census data of the following years did not contain information about the number of different ethnic groups.

31 Spyridon Sfetas, "The Legacy of the Treaty of Lausanne in the Light of Greek-Turkish Relations in the Century: Greek Perceptions of the Treaty of Lausanne" (2015) 46 *Balcanica* 195, 208.

32 Sfetas (n 31) 210.

constructed on the island. Two years later, the government established a farm for agricultural production together with an open prison on the southwest coast of Imbros. In 1970, the Greek name of the island "Imbroz" was changed to a Turkish name "Gökçeada". The Greek names of districts and villages on the islands were replaced with Turkish ones.[33]

With the removal of restrictions on visitation to the islands, the 1990s witnessed a boom in tourism.[34] Since then, the islands have represented one of the nearest tranquil spots for the inhabitants of metropolitan Istanbul. Tenedos, with its historic architecture of the city center with Greek origins and vineyards on the outskirts, has attracted many Istanbulians for a visit, which has helped the islands' economy to grow.

During the 2000's, Turkey was liberalising its law to adopt European Union *acquis* and fulfil the Copenhagen criteria aiming for full membership in the EU. The process was supposed to give possibilities for the islanders to seek the implementation of Lausanne provisions and domestic law on the islands. However, this has not been the case. Liberalisation policies have barely touched upon the rights of the minorities in the country. Greeks living in Istanbul received their confiscated property after its return was ordered by the European Court of Human Rights. Usage of the Kurdish language in media and election campaigns and teaching Kurdish as a foreign language to Kurdish people at schools became possible. However, the islanders received no benefit from these new laws.

V Concluding Remarks: Autonomous Status of the Islands Today and in the Future

For a sound analysis of the legal status of the islands a starting point should be the validity of the League of Nations minority treaties, treaty provisions and the protection system after the establishment of the United Nations.

On 2 March 1948, the Economic and Social Council of the United Nations requested the Secretary-General to study the question whether and to what extent the treaties and declarations relating to international obligations undertaken to combat discrimination and to protect minorities should be regarded as being still in force, at least in so far as they would affect the states' rights and

33 Babül (n 19) 50, 52 and fn. 17. Today, old Greek names are given to restaurants and hotels to remember the Greek past of the islands.

34 Babül (n 19) 56.

obligations, the existence of which would be independent of their guarantee by the League of Nations.[35]

According to the report of the Secretariat, an international obligation remains valid so long as there is no cause for its removal. Accordingly, the absence of the obligation cannot be presumed; it is essential to establish the fact which caused its removal, such as the expiry of its period of validity or the disappearance of the object of the obligation. The report analysed seventeen League of Nations treaties under these principles.[36]

The general conclusion of the report stands on the legal principle of *rebus sic stantibus* (Latin: "things standing thus").[37] According to the authors, if the problem is regarded as a whole; there can be no doubt that the whole minorities protection regime was, in 1919, an integral part of the system established to regulate the outcome of the First World War and create the League of Nations. One principle of that system was that only certain states that had been newly reconstituted or considerably enlarged should be subject to obligations and

---

35 Economic and Social Council Resolution No. 116 C (VI) (2 March 1948).

36 *See* United Nations Economic and Social Council, *Study of the Legal Validity of the Undertakings Concerning Minorities* (Commission on Human Rights – Sixth session, E/CN.4/367, 7 April 1950).

37 "The concept of *rebus sic stantibus* (Latin: "things standing thus") stipulates that, where there has been a fundamental change of circumstances, a party may withdraw from or terminate the treaty in question". *See Encyclopedia Britannica*, <www.britannica.com/topic/rebus-sic-stantibus> accessed 26 August 2018.
The principle later codified in Article 62 of the 1969 Vienna Convention on the Law of Treaties (adopted 23 May 1969, entered into force on 10 January 1980). Article 62 under the title "Fundamental change of circumstances" read as follows:

1. A fundamental change of circumstances which has occurred with regard to those existing at the time of the conclusion of a treaty, and which was not foreseen by the parties, may not be invoked as a ground for terminating or withdrawing from the treaty unless:
   (a) the existence of those circumstances constituted an essential basis of the consent of the parties to be bound by the treaty; and
   (b) the effect of the change is radically to transform the extent of obligations still to be performed under the treaty.
2. A fundamental change of circumstances may not be invoked as a ground for terminating or withdrawing from a treaty:
   (a) if the treaty establishes a boundary; or
   (b) if the fundamental change is the result of a breach by the party invoking it either of an obligation under the treaty or of any other international obligation owed to any other party to the treaty.
3. If, under the foregoing paragraphs, a party may invoke a fundamental change of circumstances as a ground for terminating or withdrawing from a treaty it may also invoke the change as a ground for suspending the operation of the treaty.

See 1155 UNTS 18232 (1980) 331–353.

international control in the matter of minorities. However, the authors continued, this whole system was overthrown by the Second World War. All the international decisions reached since 1944 have been inspired by a different philosophy; namely, the idea of a general and universal protection of human rights and fundamental freedoms. Within this new UN system special provisions in favour of certain minorities are still conceivable, but the point of view from which the problem is approached is essentially different from that of the League of Nations system. For the authors, it would be difficult to maintain that the authors of the peace treaties would have adopted that attitude if they had supposed that the engagements assumed in 1919 respecting the treatment of minorities would remain in force for the states which do not fall within the category of ex-enemy states. The report concluded that between 1939 and 1947 circumstances as a whole changed to such an extent that, generally speaking, the system should be considered as having ceased to exist.[38]

What about Lausanne? The report deals with the Lausanne Treaty under a separate chapter on peace treaties imposing obligations with regard to minorities on defeated states. With the reasoning that Turkey did not participate in the Second World War, Lausanne is analysed separately under this chapter.

The report based its decision regarding Lausanne on two points. Firstly, the reports argues that, since the authors of the treaty of peace with the defeated States considered that the minorities protection regime had ceased to exist for states defeated in the Second World War, the Lausanne Treaty continue to exist because Turkey was not among the states that entered the Second World War. Yet, there has been no new treaty since the Treaty of Lausanne affecting minorities and related questions. Secondly, the report stresses that Turkey's national and other minorities did not endanger the security of the state and the political regime and the international situation of Turkey has remained as it was before the Second World War. Hence, the report concluded that circumstances have not materially altered as far as Turkey is concerned. Although it is considered that all obligations concerning the treatment of minorities are now no longer valid, the obligations undertaken by Turkey have retained their validity.[39]

The conclusions of the report were, to a great extent, welcomed in the legal literature. Some argued that the cold war affected its conclusions, but nevertheless the findings are found to be legally sound.[40]

38 (n 36) 70–71.

39 (n 36) 56–57.

40 *See* Shabtai Rosenne, "Rebus sic stantibus and the Minorities Treaties: An Afterword" (1982) 12 *Israel Yearbook on Human Rights* 334; Patrick Thornberry, *International Law and the Rights of Minorities* (OUP 2001) 53–54.

In addition to the findings of the above UN report, in 1977 at an international seminar organised by the UN on the human rights of minorities, the Turkish delegation declared that in contrast to the fate of other minority treaties of the League of Nations, the minority provisions of Lausanne are still alive and enforced.[41] In fact, the views expressed by the Turkish representative during the seminar reflect the policy of Turkey concerning Lausanne. Since the establishment of the Republic in 1923, the Turkish political and legal establishment strongly stood behind Lausanne and the Treaty has been seen as the founding international legal instrument of modern Turkey. All the high courts in Turkey placed Lausanne at the top of the hierarchy of legal norms in the Turkish constitutional system.[42] Apart from the question of to what degree the Lausanne minority provisions are implemented, the Lausanne provisions have enjoyed a privileged position also because only a limited number of groups (non-Muslim minorities) are the subject of minority rights in Lausanne. In other words, Turkey's largest ethnic group, Kurds, and the largest religious group, Alevis, have been left outside Lausanne protection as being Muslim. Therefore, Turkey relies on Lausanne in every instance when the protection of minority rights is at issue and, proudly declares the treaty as a living historical document.[43]

Occasionally leading political figures in Turkey have attacked some Lausanne provisions concerning the Iraqi-Turkish border or the numerous islands and islets close to the Turkish coastline left to Greece, but no policy developed over the course of almost a century has argued that Lausanne has become old-fashioned. Therefore, it can be concluded that with all its provisions starting from the Ottoman debt, the borders of Turkey and extending to minority regulations as well as Article 14, the Lausanne Treaty has been and continues to be legally enforced in Turkey without interruption. So far no argument has been put forward concerning the validity of Article 14.

Moreover, domestic law from 1927 on the autonomy of Imbros and Tenedos is listed in official records under the existing domestic laws in Turkey.[44] Yet again, no policy argument has been heard concerning its validity. Both Article 14 of Lausanne and the domestic autonomy law are typical *dormiunt leges*

41 Boris Vishinski (ed), *United Nations Seminar on the Promotion and Protection of Human Rights of National, Ethnic and Other Minorities (Ohrid, Yugoslavia 25 June–8 July 1974)* (Macedonian Review Editions 1977) 27.

42 For details *see* Akbulut (n 7) 379, 383.

43 Although the Lausanne Treaty does not list the beneficiaries of minority rights set out in the Treaty, they are only granted to three religious groups: Greek Orthodox, Armenian Christians and Jews.

44 *See* Law No. 1151 on <www.mevzuat.gov.tr/Kanunlar.aspx> accessed 26 August 2018 (On the link "mevzuat" stipulates "existing legal rules" and "kanun/lar" means "law/s)".

(sleeping laws). However, *dormiunt leges aliquando nunquam moriuntur* (The laws sometimes sleep but never dies).[45]

Hence, Article 14 of Lausanne and Law No. 1151 are the legal basis for autonomy on Imbros and Tenedos, if the islanders wish to argue their implementation even today. A new rapprochement between Greece and Turkey, Turkey's closer relationship with the liberal world and the development of multiculturalist policies in the country mean this might be the right time to do so. They may enable the islanders to smoothly shift towards enjoying autonomy on Imbros and Tenedos.

Bibliography

Akbulut, Olgun, "The State of Political Participation of Minorities in Turkey: An Analysis under the ECHR and the ICCPR", (2005) 12 *IJMGR*.

Akbulut, Olgun & Aktoprak, Elçin (eds), *Autonomy as a Model for Minority Self Government: From Theory to European and Middle Eastern Perspectives* (Brill 2019).

Akbulut, Olgun & Usal, Zeynep Oya, "Parental Religious Rights vs. Compulsory Religious Education in Turkey" (2008) 15 *IJMGR*.

Åkermark, Sia Spiliopoulou, "The Multiple Paths to Territorial Autonomy: Examples and Conceptual Underpinnings", in Olgun Akbulut and Elçin Aktoprak (eds), *Autonomy as a Model for Minority Self Government: From Theory to European and Middle Eastern Perspectives* (Brill 2019).

Alexandris, Alexis, "Imbros and Tenedos: A Study of Turkish Attitudes Toward Two Ethnic Greek Island Communities Since 1923" (Spring 1980) 7 *Journal of the Hellenic Diaspora*.

Babül, Elif, "Claiming a place through memories of belonging: Politics of recognition on the island of Imbros" (2006) 34 *New Perspectives on Turkey*.

Demirci, Sevtap, *The Lausanne Conference: The Evolution of Turkish and British Diplomatic Strategies 1922–1923* (Dissertation submitted as part fulfilment for the degree of Doctor of Philosophy in International History The London School of Economics and Political Science United Kingdom 1997).

Demirci, Sevtap, "The Dardanelles Campaign and the Contending Strategies for War" (May 2017) 5 *International Relations and Diplomacy*.

Encyclopedia Britannica, "rebus sic stantibus", <www.britannica.com/topic/rebus-sic-stantibus> accessed 26 August 2018.

45 <https://dictionary.thelaw.com/dormiunt-leges-aliquando-nunquam-moriuntur/> accessed 25 August 2018.

European Commission against Racism and Intolerance, 61 *ECRI Report on Turkey (fourth monitoring cycle)* (Report No. CRI(2011)5, 10 December 2010).

Hammarberg, Thomas, (Commissioner for Human Rights of the Council of Europe), *Report following his visit to Turkey on 28 June–3 July 2009*, Doc. No. CommDH(2009)30 (01 October 2009).

Hannum, Hurst & Lillich, Richard B., "The Concept of Autonomy in International Law" (1980) 74 *AJIL*.

Heintze, Hans-Joachim, "On the Legal Understanding of Autonomy" in Markku Suksi (ed), *Autonomy: Applications and Implications* (Kluwer 1998).

Macartney, C.A., *National States and National Minorities* (OUP 1934).

Official Gazette of Turkey (No: 638, Series: 3, Vol. 8, 20.07.1927).

Permanent Court of International Justice, *Lighthouses in Crete and Samos* (Judgment) 1937 PCIJ Series A/B No 71.

Rosenne, Shabtai, "Rebus sic stantibus and the Minorities Treaties: An Afterword" (1982) 12 *Israel Yearbook on Human Rights*.

Sevinç, Murat & Demirkent, Dinçer, *Kuruluşun İhmal Edilmiş İstisnası – 1921 Anayasası ve Tutanakları [Neglected Exception of the Foundation – 1921 Constitution and the Minutes of the Preparatory Meetings]* (Iletisim 2017).

Sfetas, Spyridon, "The Legacy of the Treaty of Lausanne in the Light of Greek-Turkish Relations in the Century: Greek Perceptions of the Treaty of Lausanne" (2015) 46 *Balcanica*.

Suksi, Markku, *Sub-State Governance through Territorial Autonomy: A Comparative Study in Constitutional Law of Powers, Procedures and Institutions* (Springer-Verlag 2011).

Thornberry, Patrick, *International Law and the Rights of Minorities* (OUP 2001).

"Treaty of Lausanne Between Principal Allied and Associated Powers and Turkey" (signed 24 July 1923) (1924) 28 LNTS Nos. 1, 2, 3, 4.

"Treaty of Peace Between the Allied (The British Empire, France, Italy and Japan) and Associated Powers (Armenia, Belgium, Greece, The Hedjaz, Poland, Portugal, Roumania, the Serb-Croat-Slovene State and Czecho-Slovakia) and Turkey" (Sévres Treaty) (signed 10 August 1920) II *The Treaties of Peace 1919–1923* (Carnegie Endowment for International Peace 1924).

United Nations, Economic and Social Council, *Study of the Legal Validity of the Undertakings Concerning Minorities* (Commission on Human Rights – Sixth session, E/CN.4/367, 7 April 1950).

United Nations, Committee on the Elimination of Racial Discrimination, *Consideration of Reports, Comments and Information Submitted by States Parties Under Article 19 of the Convention, Summary Record of the 1914th Meeting* (Doc. No. CERD/C/SR.1914, 02 March 2009).

United Nations, Human Rights Committee, *Consideration of the Reports Submitted by States Parties Under Article 40 of the Covenant-Initial Report of State Parties Turkey* (Report No. CCPR/C/TUR/1, 13 April 2011).

United Nations, Economic and Social Council, Resolution No. 116 C (VI) (2 March 1948).

"Vienna Convention on the Law of Treaties 1969" (adopted on 23 May 1969, entered into force on 10 January 1980). 1155 UNTS 18232 (1980).

Vishinski, Boris (ed), *United Nations Seminar on the Promotion and Protection of Human Rights of National, Ethnic and Other Minorities (Ohrid, Yugoslavia 25 June–8 July 1974)* (Macedonian Review Editions 1977).

<https://dictionary.thelaw.com/dormiunt-leges-aliquando-nunquam-moriuntur/> accessed 25 August 2018.

<www.mevzuat.gov.tr/Kanunlar.aspx> accessed 26 August 2018 (Turkish Law No. 1151).

<www.mfa.gov.tr/xv_-protocol-relating-to-the-karagatch-territory-and-the-islands-of-imbros-and-tenedos_.en.mfa> accessed 25 August 2018.

<www.mfa.gov.tr/lausanne-peace-treaty-vi_-convention-concerning-the-exchange-of-greek-and-turkish-populations-signed-at-lausanne_.en.mfa> accessed 25 August 2018.

CHAPTER 11

Unpacking the 'Democratic Confederalism' and 'Democratic Autonomy': Proposals of Turkey's Kurdish Movement

Cengiz Gunes

1 Introduction

The political settlement in the Middle East following the demise of the Ottoman Empire resulted in the division of Kurdistan – the historic homeland of the Kurdish people – among the states of Iraq, Iran, Syria and Turkey, and the Kurdish question has been an important political and security concern in the region ever since. The Kurds resisted the new states that came into being in a series of revolts but their attempts have ultimately failed. In Turkey, the category of universal national rights was assigned only to the Turkish nation, and the Kurds' subsequent articulations of their group-specific demands were considered illegitimate.[1] Nevertheless, Kurdish political activists determinedly continued their advocacy of Kurdish rights and their nascent movement began to attract the attention of the Kurdish public from the late 1960s onwards. The subsequent repression that the Kurdish political activists experienced, especially during the military regime between 1971 and 1974, led to their radicalisation and their efforts led to the establishment of Kurdish left-wing groups or clandestine political parties in the mid-1970s.[2] However, except the Kurdistan Workers' Party (PKK), which was one of these parties that was established in this period, the Kurdish political parties and groups were crushed by the repression by the military that the coup of 12 September 1980 unleashed.

The PKK's initial political programme was structured around the objective of unifying the Kurds in an independent and socialist republic and from 1984 onwards, it began its guerrilla campaign.[3] However, the revolutionary

1 Derya Bayır, *Minorities and Nationalism in Turkish Law* (Ashgate 2013) 145–154.

2 For a detailed discussion *see* Cengiz Gunes, *Kurdish National Movement in Turkey: From Protest to Resistance* (Routledge 2012) 65–80.

3 For a detailed discussion *see*: Cengiz Gunes, 'Explaining the PKK's Mobilization of Kurds in Turkey: Hegemony, Myth and Violence', (2013) 12(3) *Ethnopolitics* 247; Cengiz Gunes, 'Kurdish Mobilisation in Turkey during the 1980s and 1990s' in Gareth Stansfield and Mohammad Shareef (eds), *The Kurdish Question Revisited* (Hurst and Co. 2017).

 | DOI:10.1163/9789004405455_012

overthrow of the Turkish state that the PKK's insurgency sought to achieve began to seem unlikely from the mid-1990s onwards and as a result the PKK began to emphasise the need for a political solution to the conflict and the Kurdish question. In order to facilitate a political solution to the conflict, it declared three ceasefires during the 1990s. In 1999, after its leader Abdullah Öcalan was captured by Turkey, the PKK began to undergo a more radical ideological transformation that has significantly altered the movement's long-term objectives and the demands for the Kurds.[4] In this period, Öcalan was able to direct the PKK's ideological transformation through the texts he produced as part of his legal defence submitted to the Turkish and European courts that heard his case and through his instructions via his lawyers.

The democratic solution that Öcalan's defences seek to develop aims at a radical transformation of the whole of the Middle East through the development and deepening of democracy. In formulating his new proposals, Öcalan draw upon a diverse number of radical intellectual traditions including 'the libertarian social ecologist Murray Bookchin, feminist political theorists, such as Judith Butler, and leftist Foucauldians and critical Marxists'.[5] Currently, the PKK's democratic solution is conceptualised around the interlinked proposals of 'democratic confederalism' and 'democratic autonomy'. Democratic confederalism is developed as a project of national self-determination for the Kurds but does not involve the creation of a separate Kurdish state. Democratic autonomy aims at realising Kurdish self-governments in the existing states with a Kurdish population.

The other major political movement that represent the Kurds in Turkey is the pro-Kurdish democratic movement, which came into being when the People's Labour Party (HEP) was established on 7 June 1990, and has been represented by various political parties since then. Due to the nature of the political demands it has been raising, such as the constitutional recognition of the Kurdish identity, it has been facing severe repression and is considered as a political outsider. The pro-Kurdish parties were represented in the Turkish parliament during the early 1990s and from 2007 onward but the state repression resulted in the closures of several of the pro-Kurdish political parties during 1990s and 2000s. The current representative of the pro-Kurdish political movement at the national level is the Peoples' Democratic Party (HDP), which

4 Ahmet Hamdi Akkaya and Joost Jongerden, 'Confederalism and Autonomy in Turkey: The Kurdistan Workers' Party and the Reinvention of Democracy' in Cengiz Gunes and Welat Zeydanlıoğlu (eds), *The Kurdish Question in Turkey: New Perspectives on Violence, Representation and Reconciliation* (Routledge 2014) 186.

5 Klaus Happel, 'Introduction' in Abdullah Öcalan, *Prison Writings: The Roots of Civilisation*, Klaus Happel (transl.) (Pluto Press 2006) xv.

was founded in October 2012. In the general election held on 7 June 2015, the HDP managed to win 13.1 per cent of the popular vote and secure 80 seats in the parliament in Ankara. However, in the repeated election on 1 November 2015 there was a reduction in the HDP's vote but despite that it still managed to obtain 10.75 per cent of the popular vote and 59 seats in the parliament.[6] It won 11.7 per cent of the popular vote and 67 seats at the most recent general election held on 24 June 2018. There are several smaller political parties, such as the leftist Hak-Par (Rights and Freedoms Party) and the Islamist Hüda-Par (Free Cause Party), that aspire to represent the Kurds in Turkey but so far, they have not managed to win sufficient votes in either the parliamentary or the local elections.

This chapter seeks to unpack the democratic confederalism and democratic autonomy proposals that the Kurdish movement in Turkey has been developing during the 2000s. It examines the key texts through which these proposals have been articulated and aims to reflect the Kurdish movement's understanding and interpretation of these concepts. It first charts the development of Öcalan's democratic solution to the Kurdish question before moving on to a discussion on the PKK's ideological transformation and the emergence of democratic confederalism and democratic autonomy as its principal political demands for the Kurds in Turkey. Öcalan's and PKK's approach has had an impact on the wider Kurdish movement in Turkey and for this reason the final section of the chapter offers an examination of the democratic autonomy proposals developed by the pro-Kurdish democratic movement and other Kurdish representative organisations, such as the Democratic Society Congress (DTK).

II Öcalan's Democratic Solution to the Kurdish Question

Abdullah Öcalan has been the main figure in the PKK from the early days of the movement and has been involved in drafting its key texts. He was born in the Şanlıurfa province in 1948 and was a student at Ankara University's Faculty of Political Science during the early 1970s when he led the formation of the group that later established the PKK. In July 1979, Öcalan moved to Syria and then to Lebanon where efforts to transform the PKK into a guerrilla movement were intensified. He was based in Syria until 9 October 1998 when he was forced out by Turkish military pressure and threat of attacking Syria if it continued to host him. His attempts to find shelter in Greece, Russia and Italy

6 For a detailed discussion *see*: Gunes, *Kurdish National Movement in Turkey*, 152–175; Cengiz Gunes, 'Turkey's New Left' (2017) 107 *New Left Review* 9.

were unsuccessful and he was captured in Nairobi, Kenya by Turkish intelligence agents, with support from the CIA and Israel's Mossad, on 15 February 1999. Öcalan's first articulation of the democratic solution was during his court trial that started on 31 May 1999 and ended on 29 June 1999. He was found guilty of 'founding and leading a terror organisation' and sentenced to death but his sentence was commuted to life imprisonment and he has been held at a high-security prison on the island of İmralı in the Marmara Sea ever since.[7] He was kept in solitary confinement until 2009 and his communication with the external world was severely restricted. During the 2000s, his lawyers were able to visit him most weeks. However, in the past decade, for long periods of time, his lawyers were prevented from visiting him and their last visit took place on 27 July 2011. During the dialogue process between the state and the PKK and Öcalan that began in January 2013, a delegation comprised of three HDP MPs was able to regularly visit him and their last visit was on 5 April 2015. Since then his brother, Mehmet Öcalan was able to visit him twice, on 11 September 2016 and on 12 January 2019.

Rather than being a legal response to the charges listed on the public prosecutor's indictment, the defence Öcalan presented centred on ending the violent conflict between the PKK and the Turkish state.[8] There were previous occasions during the 1990s when Öcalan and the PKK stressed the suitability and acceptability of a framework whereby Kurds obtained their group rights within Turkey. These were often expressed as part of moves to facilitate the development of a political solution to the conflict and the clearest indication came on 17 March 1993 when, in a press conference to announce the PKK's unilateral ceasefire, Öcalan stated that a solution based on the recognition of Kurds' democratic rights and identity within Turkey could be acceptable.[9] Similar calls were made during the declaration of subsequent ceasefires in August 1995 and September 1998.

During his trial, Öcalan called for the re-organisation of the relations between Kurds and the state in Turkey on the basis of equality and freedom and rejected the separatist approach his movement had previously taken. He reinterpreted the solution to the Kurdish question on the basis of deepening of democracy and called for measures to address the Kurdish demands within a

7 In 2002, the democratisation reforms carried out for increasing harmony with the EU law (Law no. 4771) Turkey abolished the death penalty for peace time offences. In 2004 it was removed for war time offences as well (Law no. 5218). The last time death penalty was carried out was in 1984.

8 Abdullah Öcalan, *Savunma: Kürt Sorununda Demokratik Çözüm Bildirgesi* (Mem Yayınları 1999), 16.

9 A. Kadir Konuk, *PKK'nin Tek Taraflı ilan Ettiği Ateşkes ve Yankıları* (Agrı Yayınları 1993) 34.

democratic Turkey.[10] Öcalan also made frequent references to the historical periods in which Kurds and Turks cooperated and argued that this common history offered an example of partnership that can be emulated in the modern period and be the basis of future coexistence and cooperation of Kurds and Turks within a democratic republic. The option of establishing a separate Kurdish state in the region, Öcalan argued, did not have a material basis and faced multiple difficulties. He also stressed that the accommodation of Kurdish rights through territorial autonomy and federation offer only a partial solution as Kurdish population is dispersed in Turkey. Thus, citing the peculiarity and the deep-rooted nature of the relations between the Kurds and Turks, including their historical alliance that resulted in the establishment of the republic, Öcalan argued that a solution within the democratic system is the only viable option:

> The democratic solution option, in generally as well as in the case of the Kurdish question, is the only option. Separation is neither possible nor required. The interests of the Kurds definitely lie in a democratic union with Turkey. If the democratic solution is duly implemented, it would be a more successful and realistic model than autonomy and federation.[11]

This initial articulation of the democratic solution to the Kurdish question conceived of it in the following terms: respecting Turkey's territorial integrity, democratisation of the republic, the removal of the prohibitions in front of Kurdish language and culture, abandoning the military approach to the management of the Kurdish question and paving the way for the participation of illegal political organisations, such as the PKK, in formal politics. Öcalan expanded on his democratic solution proposals through the defences he submitted to the European Court of Human Rights (ECtHR) in 2001 that considered his appeal. His defence was published as a two-volume book in the end of 2001.[12]

The first volume offered an analysis of global historical developments and focuses on the emergence and evolution of class-based societies, which he traced back to the Sumerian civilisation in Ancient Mesopotamia. The second volume focussed more specifically on the solution of the Kurdish question and Öcalan called for a comprehensive democratisation of the republic and to end of state's approach of denying the existence of the Kurdish national identity in

10 Öcalan, *Savunma*, 22.

11 *Ibid.*, 32. All the quotes from Turkish language texts are author's own translation.

12 Abdullah Öcalan, *AIHM Savunmaları: Sümer Rahip Devletinden Demokratik Cumhuriyete* (Mezopotamya Yayınları 2001).

Turkey, which he argued would be the best course of action to prevent Kurdish separatism.[13] He proposed a 'nation of Turkey' as an inclusive identity for all citizens and argued that such a framework would be a major step on the direction of the democratic solution: 'All that is necessary is loyalty to the democratic system, to renounce the chauvinist fascist claims and for each group [in Turkey] to experience its cultural identity and education without denying the formal system'.[14]

In 2004, Öcalan submitted another defence text to the ECtHR that expanded on his democratic solution and was published as a book in the same year titled *Bir Halkı Savunmak* (Defending a Nation).[15] In this new text, the issue of the formal legal status of the Kurds and Kurdistan within the existing states gained more emphasis. Here, Öcalan proposed a framework whereby the 'people's own democratic administration in Kurdistan' will co-exist with the 'state as the general public authority'.[16] This framework required a significant roll-back in the power and authority of the state in Turkey to enable the development of people's democratic rule. Öcalan proposed a model inspired by delegative democracy where Kurds would choose delegates as their representatives:

> As the national state cannot be a solution to the national problem in Kurdistan, the congressional regime remains the most appropriate solution. Since the people [of Kurdistan] will not accept the old slave life under any circumstance and it is clear that the search for the national state carries the danger of deepening the existing deadlock, the most appropriate instrument of the democratic solution is the People's Congress.[17]

Kurdish people would be involved in the overall management of their democratic rule and be responsible for holding their representatives to account. For Öcalan, the democratic solution is not only about obtaining Kurdish rights within the existing states but also seen as a project to democratize the Kurdish society:

> The democratization of Kurdistan is beyond a legal problem and a comprehensive societal project. It involves the excluded segments forming, institutionalizing, managing and overseeing their economic, social and political will against the segments that deny the determination of the

13 *Ibid.*, 171.
14 *Ibid.*, 172–173.
15 Abdullah Öcalan, *Bir Halkı Savunmak* (Weşanên Serxwebûn 2004).
16 *Ibid.*, 402–403.
17 *Ibid.*, 420–421.

> people's identity and destiny. It is a continuous process. Elections are only one of the vehicles used for determining people's will. The democratization of Kurdistan essentially requires the functional organization of and action by the people. It is a democratic process extending from the local village and city communes, to the city councils, to the municipalities and up to the people's congress. It expresses a dynamic political life.[18]

Öcalan continued to elaborate on his democratic solution during the second half of the 2000s and the early years of the 2010s. From March 2005 onwards, Öcalan began to describe the solution to the Kurdish question in terms of democratic confederalism and in subsequent years expanded on his ideas in his five-volume book titled *Demokratik Uygarlık Çözümü* (The Democratic Civilisation Solution).[19] In Öcalan's analysis, the nation-state is described as an institutional framework of capitalist modernity and 'democratic nation' is offered as an alternative. Drawing on Benedict Anderson's definition of the nation as an imagined community, Öcalan defined a nation as 'a community of people who share a common mindset' and the democratic nation model as 'the model of nation that curbs and excludes exploitation and oppression'.[20] This description is based on a pluralist understanding of national community and sees the democratic nation as being capable of representing different collective identities and groups.[21] Furthermore, Öcalan links the drive to establish a nation-state to capitalism and sees it intimately connected to the extraction of profit. He argues that for socialists the main solution for national questions must be a democratic nation, which is 'a common society created by individuals and communities with their own free will'.[22] Thus for Öcalan, the democratic solution to national questions essentially involve:

> ...being a democratic nation and the community constructing itself as a democratic national community. It is neither becoming a nation through the state nor abandoning the right to be a nation; it is the community exercising its right to build itself as a democratic nation.[23]

18 *Ibid.*, 403.

19 The first three volumes were first published in July 2009, the fourth volume was published in July 2010 and the final volume was published in December 2012. They were republished as a set in June 2015 (Abdullah Öcalan, *Demokratik Uygarlık Çözümü*, Amara Yayıncılık 2015).

20 Abdullah Öcalan, *Demokratik Uygarlık Çözümü* (*Fifth Volume*), 52.

21 *Ibid.*, 53.

22 *Ibid.*, 427, 461, 469–470.

23 *Ibid.*, 469.

In addition, the democratic modernity project that Öcalan espouses is motivated by the realisation of a wider notion of emancipation, including eliminating economic inequality and achieving gender equality. Both democratic confederalism and democratic autonomy are seen vital parts of developing a social economy, increasing gender equality and ecological sustainability in the region. Öcalan often described his theorisation as a paradigm shift and argues his 'democratic, ecological and gender liberationist' political project will achieve the peaceful coexistence of all of the social and cultural groups in the Middle East.

III The PKK's Ideological and Organisational Transformation

During the first half of the 2000s, Öcalan – through his lawyers – was able to send detailed instructions to the PKK and guide the process of organisational change and renewal of the movement, which he argued was necessary for the development and implementation of the democratic solution to the Kurdish question. In addition, the texts Öcalan produced throughout the 2000s have been used by the PKK and the other representative organisations it established to develop new proposals for the resolution of the Kurdish question in Turkey. This began during the PKK's Seventh Congress held in January 2000, where, in tandem with Öcalan's calls for a democratic solution, the decision to transform itself into a movement that used democratic means was taken. The Central Committee report submitted to the congress stressed that in the democratic era, class struggles, national conflicts and various other societal problems, finds their solution without the need or use of violence:

> ...without any doubt this era is one of democracy and freedom. The stage that awaits us will be filled with struggles emerging from contradictions based on differences pertaining to class, gender, environment and development, and with the aim of furthering democracy and freedom.[24]

The PKK's ideological and strategic transformation involved the establishment of new representative political organisations whose objective was to develop the democratic solution to the Kurdish question. As part of its new strategy, in May 2000, the PKK reorganised its guerrilla forces into a defence force, the People's Defence Forces (HPG). While it stated that the use of violence in the

24 PKK, *Dönüşüm Süreci ve Görevlerimiz* (Weşanên Serxwebûn 2000) 21–22.

past was necessary to break the hegemony of Turkish nationalism and the traditional Kurdish classes over the masses, in the current era, political means were the fundamental form of struggle. The concept of 'legitimate defence' was introduced to characterise the new military strategy, which enabled the PKK's capacity to carry out an armed campaign should the democratic political solution fail or the movement come under attack. Furthermore, keeping the military capacity was seen as necessary for self-defence and to ensure the long-term safety and existence of the movement because the region continues to remain unstable and that the possibility of attacks against the PKK were highly likely.[25] In April 2002, during its Eighth Congress, the PKK declared that it ceased all political activity and the Kurdistan Freedom and Democracy Congress (KADEK) was established as its successor.

The KADEK's programme conceptualised the solution to the Kurdish question within the development of democracy and as the equal and free development of the Kurdish people in the region: 'The solution to the Kurdish question, before anything else, involves making the Kurdish society democratic and free and progressing on such a basis to reach the era of democratic civilisation'.[26] The solution to the Kurdish question was envisaged through systemic change across the states in the Middle East with a Kurdish population and without the need to alter the existing state boundaries:

> The KADEK's solution to the Kurdish question is based on the democratic transformation of the existing states in their present boundaries and without aiming at their overthrow. In line with this view, it calls upon, firstly the Republic of Turkey, and all the other concerned states, which have left the Kurdish question without a solution and envisage denial and destruction, to overcome such outworn policies and accept the rights of the Kurdish people that have been recognised by the international norms.[27]

Kurdish national unity was conceived within the Democratic Middle Eastern Union and was seen as a natural result of the democratisation process the KADEK sought to bring about. It was argued that the democratisation of the existing state system would enable the Kurds to express their identity and culture and cultivate the conditions for Kurds to realise their national unity

25 PKK, *PKK VI. Ulusal Konferansına Sunulan Politik-Örgütsel Rapor* (Weşanên Serxwebûn 2001) 33–34.

26 Mahsum Şafak, *KADEK Kuruluş Kongresi (PKK VIII Kongresi Belgeleri)* (Mem Yayınları 2002) 208.

27 *Ibid.*, 179.

through developing closer ties and relations between Kurdish communities in Iraq, Iran, Turkey and Syria and without the need of establishing a Kurdish state. The widespread democratisation was needed in Kurdish society and seen as a precursor to solving the Kurdish question and the democratisation of the states:

> Developing democracy and liberty within the internal structure of the Kurdish society will accomplish an important part of the democratic solution to the Kurdish question and create an environment and force for its full resolution. The rest will be resolved with the democratisation of the states and societies in which parts of Kurdistan are located in.[28]

The KADEK's existence was relatively short lived as it was abolished to make way for the Kurdistan People's Congress (Kongra-Gel) in November 2003. The establishment of Kongra-Gel was needed because the KADEK continued to be strongly associated with and was seen as an extension of the PKK, which made it difficult to fulfil its role in developing the democratic solution to the Kurdish question and extend its appeal.[29] In terms of the political programme, objectives and discourse, there were remarkable similarities between the KADEK and the Kongra-Gel, with the realisation of the democratic solution to the Kurdish question being the Kongra-Gel's primary objective. It perceived the democratisation of the region and the solution to the Kurdish question to be intertwined and argued that one cannot develop without the other:

> The democratic restructuring of the Middle East cannot be realised without the solution of the Kurdish question on the basis of democratic unity and freedom. Also, without creating a democratic Middle East, we cannot talk about the success and assurance of a resolution.[30]

A notion of democracy that recognises and promotes the rights and demands of all of the groups within the society is demanded by the Kongra-Gel: 'Democracy cannot be seen as a tool to further the interest or domination of a class, nation, ethnic or religious group. It is a political regime in which every group has the right to self-expression regardless of their power'.[31] It argued that the

28 *Ibid.*, 209.

29 Kongra Gele Kurdistan (Kongra-Gel), *Program, Tüzük ve Kararları* (Weşanên Serxwebûn 2004) 25.

30 *Ibid.*, 83.

31 *Ibid.*, 90.

democratic solution of the Kurdish question required the recognition of Kurdish identity and all of the associated national rights at the state level:

> The democratic solution will be achieved within the framework of constitutional citizenship of Turkey, by realising full democracy in the areas of governance and life, obtaining constitutional assurances to protect Kurdish identity, through the recognition of all of the rights that are accepted for Turkish identity, language and culture for Kurdish identity, language and culture, and by creating freedom in every domain.[32]

The Kongra-Gel also conceives of Kurdish unity within the democratic unity of the Middle East. Such a unity will allow amicable relations between Kurds and neighbouring nations to develop and strengthen the ties and solidarity between Kurdish communities from different parts of Kurdistan.[33] The KADEK was made up of exclusively the PKK members but the Kongra-Gel includes more Kurdish political actors. For example, the former Democracy Party (DEP) MP and the member of the Kurdistan National Congress (KNK), Zübeyir Aydar, was elected as Kongra-Gel's leader. This was seen as a necessary step to internalise democracy within the organisation and de-centralise the movement.

In 2005, the PKK was re-established and its new party programme described the 'democratic solution' to the Kurdish question as its main political objective, the central tenet of which was described as the 'democratic transformation' of the current state system in the Middle East into federal and confederal entities. In the PKK's programme, the Kurds are described as one of the main actors of democratisation in the region:

> As Kurdish democracy develops and resolves the Kurdish question, the democratic transformation of the society in the Middle East will be ensured. The progress of Kurdistan towards a democratic confederation will lead to the democratization of the Middle East and its democratic confederal unity.[34]

The PKK maintained its objective of reconstituting the Kurds as a nation but emphasised that this did not involve the creation of a Kurdish nation-state.[35] Furthermore, it argued that the proposed Kurdish confederal entity would neither challenge the established and internationally recognised borders nor

---

32 *Ibid.*, 103–104.

33 *Ibid.*, 106.

34 PKK, *Program ve Tüzüğü* (Weşanên Serxwebûn 2005) 68.

35 *Ibid.*, 13.

resort to nationalism or establishing a nation-state. While the construction of a Kurdish nation-state is seen by the PKK as unnecessary, the central focus for its political activities has been on developing democratic confederalism as an administrative framework for Kurdish self-rule in the Middle East.

IV Kurdish Unity through Democratic Confederalism

The proposal for democratic confederalism was first introduced by Öcalan in March 2005 and was proposed as an alternative to a Kurdish nation-state. It seeks to organise Kurdish communities across the Middle East and to unite Kurds without creating a Kurdish nation-state. Although it has similarities to a number of existing autonomy proposals, such as cultural autonomy, it has aspects that differ significantly and as a result much effort has gone into providing clear descriptions of it in the PKK's political discourse. One of the earliest descriptions of democratic confederalism provided by the PKK conceived of it in terms of deepening democracy and described it as a system to spread democracy to the grassroots levels. It was seen as a unifying framework for the different social and political organisations that represent the different segments of Kurdish society:

> The democratic confederal organization allows the Kurdish people to undertake many activities in the social, economic and cultural fields by themselves. With this structure, the potentials of the Kurdish people in these fields are uncovered and vitalized. This level of democratization of the Kurdish people and the energy it emits plays a major role in bringing about the solution of the Kurdish question.[36]

An article published in the PKK's monthly magazine *Serxwebûn* provided the following definition:

> Democratic confederalism is a system based on democratic institutionalization starting from the grassroots. To bring democratic confederalism into existence is to organize the society from the level of the neighbourhood and village communes to neighbourhood and provincial councils and to establish a people's congress to represent their common will.[37]

36 PKK, 'Demokratik Konfederalizm Devletsiz Özgürlükcü ve Demokratik Yaşamdır' [2005] 280 Serxwebûn 20.

37 PKK, 'Demokratik Özerklik ve Özerk Demokratik Kürdistan' [2007] 312 Serxwebûn 26.

Hence, democratic confederalism seeks to organise the Kurds as a nation and obtain their national rights within the existing states in the Middle East within a democratic confederal structure to bring together all of the local and regional level Kurdish self-governing communities. It adopts an inclusive approach towards the ethnic and cultural groups in Kurdistan and seeks to also be their representative body: 'The Confederation is the general name of the political, social organization in Kurdistan. It is not only solely for the Kurds but includes everyone living in Kurdistan'.[38] Democratic confederalism is proposed as an alternative to the nationalist and statist solutions and is based on the promotion of fraternity and democratic unity of the nations and furthering democracy in society. The proposed Kurdish confederate entity is seen as necessary for organising the Kurdish communities across the Middle East within a non-state democracy and is seen as capable of providing Kurds political representation at the international level. As an entity, it will exist and operate across the states that have a Kurdish population but crucially without attempting to change the established and internationally recognised borders.

During the Kongra-Gel's third general assembly meeting in May 2005, the KCK (Koma Civakan Kurdistan – the Union of Kurdistan Communities) was established and it is designed as a pan-Kurdish entity to put into practice the democratic confederalism proposals that Öcalan formulated. Initially it was known under the name *Koma Komalan Kurdistan* (The Council of Associations of Kurdistan, KKK) but in May 2007 it took the name KCK and has been known as such since then. In the Preface to the KCK constitutive document, the KCK Contract, Öcalan described it as 'the people's non-state based democratic system':

> Democratic Confederalism is based on recognition, protection and the freedom of expression of all cultural beings. It takes its basic principle to be the democratic solution of the Kurdish question, the recognition of Kurdish identity on all levels and the development of Kurdish language and culture.[39]

Öcalan describes this model as a framework to obtain Kurdish self-determination but interprets the principle of national self-determination to mean

38 PKK 'Demokratik Konfederalizm Bir Toplumsal Organizasyondur' [2005] 283 Serxwebûn 14.

39 KCK, *KCK Sözleşmesi*, <https://code.google.com/p/bookstorer/downloads/detail?name=KCK%20S%C3%B6zle%C5%9Fmesi.pdf> 2.

building national representative institutions rather than strictly establishing a nation state for the Kurds:

> I understand the right to self determination of nations in the following way: it is the right to build its democracy and non-state self-government. It is the right of the non-state groups/communities to create their model to discuss and solve their own problems at the level of villages, neighbourhoods and cities...Our goal is not to establish a state but a democracy.[40]

The KCK Contract resembles a constitution and provides detailed description of the democratic confederal system in Kurdistan, the principles upon which it is built and the rights of its members or citizens, including the freedom of belief, speech, assembly and the right to participate in the political life of their communities. It also recognises group identities and their collective rights such as the citizens' right to receive education in their mother tongue.

Subsequently, in the fifth volume of *The Democratic Civilisation Solution*, Öcalan describes the KCK as the medium for the *democratic solution* of the Kurdish question and argues that it would overcome the pitfalls of the state-oriented approach:

> The KCK is a concrete expression of democratic solution of the Kurdish Question and is different from traditional approaches. It does not see the solution from obtaining a share of the state. Even in the sense of autonomy, it is not in pursuit of a state for the Kurds. It does not aim at a federal or confederal state and does not see that as its own solution. Its basic demand from the state is to recognise that the Kurds have a right to self-government by their free will, and that they do not hinder Kurds from becoming a democratic national community.[41]

As an entity, it is a bottom-up structure seeking to organise Kurds in self-governing communities at the local level (neighbourhood or village) which will be connected upward to higher self-governing entities at the city, region and national levels. Öcalan perceives that the Kurdish self-governments in the existing states would come into being through a political struggle and via a constitutional framework. He believes that the KCK's existence and long-term viability requires recognition by the existing states and their consent for their Kurdish populations to organise in self-governing communities. However,

40 *Ibid.*, 8.

41 Öcalan, *Demokratik Uygarlık Çözümü*, 469.

given the current difficulties that the Kurds face in obtaining the recognition of their identity and national rights, Öcalan argues that the Kurdish communities should have the determination to create and defend their democratic autonomous authorities.[42] In order to further elaborate the relations between the Kurds and the existing states, the democratic autonomy proposal is developed, which I discuss below.

V Democratic Autonomy

In 2005, democratic autonomy also entered the lexicon of Kurdish movement and it is a part of Öcalan's overall democratic solution to the Kurdish question. When described in general terms, it refers to the autonomy of national and religious identities, their right to preserve their differences and originality and obtain their freedom.[43] More specifically in the Kurdish context in Turkey, it concerns the nature of the relationship between the Kurds and the Turkish state and seeks to accommodate Kurdish rights and demands within Turkey's territorial integrity: 'Democratic autonomy is about the Turkish state and the Kurds agreeing a new contract for their unity. It is the establishment of a democratic political union instead of a union based on force and assimilation'.[44] It is seen as a way of limiting the power and authority of the central state. An important step in this direction involves the recognition of Kurdish identity and cultural rights:

> A fundamental characteristic of democratic autonomy is that the Turkish state accepts the constitutional recognition of the national identity of the Kurdish people. Together with the recognition of national identity, it is necessary to remove all obstacles in front of the Kurdish language and cultural development and to enable Kurdish to become a language of education.[45]

In addition, empowerment of local government is demanded as part of a general decentralisation and democratisation of state structures. As part of this decentralisation, the right of the Kurdish communities to create their self-governments and organise themselves through a network of local and regional

42 *Ibid.*, 466.

43 PKK, 'Demokratik Konfederalizm', 22.

44 PKK, 'Demokratik Özerklik', (2007) 301 *Serxwebûn* 57.

45 *Ibid.*

councils is demanded. These representative councils will have responsibility on solving societal problems in areas that does not directly concern the state.[46] The state's recognition of Kurdish rights should include the freedom of assembly to allow Kurds to freely express their collective identity and establish political parties. However, Kurdish democratic autonomy should not be restricted to the areas in which the Kurds constitute the majority of the population and have a historic presence but to the Turkish majority areas too in order for the Kurds who have migrated to these regions to enjoy and benefit from it.[47]

The Diyarbakır based Democratic Society Congress (DTK) is another Kurdish representative organisation that is associated with the development of democratic autonomy proposals and it is an important political actor in the majority Kurdish populated areas that campaigns for realising democratic autonomy. The DTK was formally established in October 2007 to politically organise Kurds and develop and implement the democratic autonomy proposals that Öcalan has been developing. The DTK is an umbrella organisation that brings together civil society groups, trade unions, political parties and many local Kurdish political actors based in the Kurdish-majority regions. During 2010 and 2011, it held many meetings where Öcalan's ideas were discussed in detail and a more detailed democratic autonomy framework was developed.[48] The DTK's democratic autonomy framework embodies the principle of decentralisation, grassroots democracy and people organising themselves in local councils and actively taking part in debating issues and decision-making at the local level and electing delegates to represent the local council in higher representative bodies such as the district, province and regional levels. It 'aims to organize Kurdistan society in eight dimensions: Political, Legal, Self-Defense, Social, Economic, Cultural, Ecology and Diplomacy, and to build political autonomy and to build Democratic Autonomous Kurdistan'.[49]

The DTK sees itself as the representative body for the Kurds in Turkey and the main vehicle for the implementation of Kurdish democratic autonomy in Turkey.[50] It seeks to organise Kurdish society within a democratic and autonomous administrative body. The lowest level administrative body is the

46 *Ibid.*

47 Cengiz Gunes and Çetin Gürer, 'Kurdish Movement's Democratic Autonomy Proposals in Turkey' in Ephraim Nimni and Elçin Aktoprak (eds) *Democratic Representation in Plurinational States: The Case of Kurds in Turkey* (Palgrave MacMillan 2018) 168.

48 DTK, *Kürt Sorununun Çözümü İçin Demokratik Özerklik* (Aram 2012).

49 DTK, 'Demokratik Toplum Kongresi Bileşenlerince Hazırlanmış Olan, Demokratik Özerk Kürdistan Modelinin Taslak Sunumu', <http://bianet.org/files/doc_files/000/000/179/original/demokratiközerklik.htm>.

50 *Ibid.*

commune which is usually comprised of the residents of a village or a street in the urban context. The neighbourhood council is the higher level representative body that offers representation to communes as well as people representing different ethnic and political groups, followed by the district council. It is also a representative body for the local, district and provincial councils and citizens' assemblies that were established in the Kurdish-majority regions since 2005. In addition to aspiring to represent the Kurdish community, it has sought the inclusion of representatives of the different ethnic and religious groups, such as the Syriac community, that are historically based in the Kurdish-majority regions.

The DTK seeks to be a platform where the societal problems are discussed and solutions are developed. In this respect, it seeks to include the different segments of society in the solution of the problems as well as voicing their specific problems and issues that have been pushed aside and marginalised. The DTK has a number of commissions that are tasked with developing solutions in specific areas of social life, such as language and education, gender equality and legal disputes. The DTK has also incorporated a form of customary justice into its practices and seeks to solve the legal disputes and disagreements that individuals face, such as blood feuds and land disputes.[51] The DTK operates a co-chair system and a number of well-known Kurdish political figures, such as Ahmet Türk, Hatip Dicle, Selma Irmak and Aysel Tuğluk, who have been active in the pro-Kurdish political parties in the past three decades have acted as its co-chairs.

During the second half of the 2000s, the pro-Kurdish political parties also began to appropriate the democratic autonomy proposals into its political demands. This started with the DTP during its second party congress in 2007 when it accepted the democratic autonomy as a framework to accommodate Kurdish rights in Turkey. It argued that extensive reform of Turkey's political structure was needed, and its democratic autonomy proposals envisaged decentralisation of power and the establishment of between twenty and twenty-five self-governing regions in Turkey. These regions would bring together two or three existing provinces that have dense social, cultural and economic relations and would have a regional parliament and administration, which will make decisions relating to matters of education, culture, social services, agriculture, environment etc. The decision on matters relating to policing and legal services would be jointly decided by the central government and regional assemblies and those that pertain to foreign affairs, finance and

---

51 Çetin Gürer, *Demokratik Özerklik: Bir Yurttaşlık Heterotopyası* (Notabene 2015) 298.

national security will be conducted by the central government.[52] It argued that such a decentralised framework would enable the participation and representation of citizens in the decision-making processes and greatly contribute to the advancement of democracy in Turkey. In order to enable the participation and representation of all of the ethnic and national groups in Turkey, a more inclusive definition of nationality in Turkey's constitution was needed. Such steps, it argued, would facilitate the development of the democratic solution of the Kurdish question in Turkey.[53]

The DTP was closed-down by Turkey's Constitutional Court in December 2009. The Peace and Democracy Party (BDP) became the main representative of the pro-Kurdish democratic movement in Turkey. The BDP also advocated the need for a more inclusive and pluralist notion of national identity and citizenship and demanded that the collective rights of the Kurdish people, including education in the Kurdish language, needed to be recognised and protected by the constitution. Furthermore, the BDP's party programme argued that decentralisation in Turkey's political system was needed to solve the Kurdish question and listed the implementation of the recommendations of the Council of Europe's *European Charter of Local Self-Government* in Turkey among its key political objectives. It argued that such a framework will empower the local communities and administrations and thereby will be a major step towards deepening democracy in Turkey.[54] In September 2011, at its second party congress, the BDP began to use 'Democratic Autonomy' to describe its proposals for reform of Turkey's political system and solution of the Kurdish question. It had significant similarities with the DTP's democratic autonomy proposal and proposed the decentralisation of Turkey's centralist political and administrative structure and creation of twenty to twenty-five self-governing regions that would exercise extensive autonomy. It argued that such a framework was needed to strengthen democracy and pluralism in Turkey.[55]

The current representative of the pro-Kurdish movement, the HDP, also advocates the accommodation of Kurdish rights within a democratic autonomy framework. Similar to its predecessors, the HDP also proposes a decentralised

52 DTP, *Demokratik Toplum Partisi'nin Kürt Sorununa İlişkin Demokratik Çözüm Projesi* (2008) 11.

53 *Ibid.*, 12.

54 BDP, 'Barış ve Demokrasi Partisi Programı', accessed at: <https://bdpblog.wordpress.com/parti-programimiz/>.

55 BDP, 'Democratic Özerklik Projesi', accessed at: <https://bdpblog.wordpress.com/2011/05/04/demokratik-ozerklik-projesi/ >.

political system for Turkey to break the domination of the centre over the regions and develop models of local self-governance to meet the needs of different minority groups to protect and develop their culture and identity. HDP's democratic autonomy proposal seeks to decentralise power to autonomous and self-governing local and regional administrations, but does not specify how many of such regions would be created in Turkey.[56] Such decentralisation of the state in Turkey is proposed to empower local administrations, ensure citizens' direct participation in the decision-making processes at the local, regional and national levels and to develop socio-economic policies that address the needs of the whole of society in Turkey. Additionally, it purports that such a decentralised and democratic framework can address the demands of the Kurdish minority for autonomy and will pave the way to a peaceful solution for the Kurdish conflict.

Democratic autonomy is not only a proposal that can be used for the accommodation of Kurdish rights in Turkey but an ongoing process of organising the Kurdish society politically and culturally at the grassroots level and mobilising them for political action to realise Kurdish self-rule irrespective of whether the state recognises or not. The state however, has interpreted these developments as a challenge to its authority and took measures to repress it. Starting in April 2009, thousands of Kurdish political activists of the pro-Kurdish democratic movement were arrested on charges of involvement in building Kurdish state-like institutions with the aim of destroying Turkey's national unity and territorial integrity.[57] In the summer 2015, declarations of democratic autonomy in various town and cities of Kurdish-majority region in Turkey were made, including Diyarbakır and Şırnak and the districts of Cizre and Nusaybin, which involved local armed youth groups affiliated with the PKK digging trenches and preventing police access. This brought about a violent reaction from the state and resulted in significant loss of life large material destruction in especially Sur district in Diyarbakır's old city and Şırnak. In addition, through the use of decrees, the government has appointed district and provincial governors as trustees to replace the democratically elected mayors. This process began on 11 September 2016 and so far 94 of the town and city councils that the pro-Kurdish party controls have been taken over by the state and the majority of the mayors have been arrested.

56 HDP, *Büyük İnsanlık-Bizler Meclise* (Ankara 2015) 10.

57 Derya Bayır, 'The role of the judicial system in the politicide of the Kurdish opposition' in Cengiz Gunes and Welat Zeydanlıoğlu (eds), *The Kurdish Question in Turkey: New Perspectives on Violence, Representation and Reconciliation* (Routledge 2014) 33.

VI Conclusions

Democratic solution to the Kurdish question has been a project in development with gradually a more coherent programme emerging. Öcalan has been at the heart of this project and his ideas were originally expressed within the context of transforming Turkey's centralised and nationalist authoritarian political system to become a democratic republic that was more responsive to the rights and demands of all its citizens and recognised the ethno-cultural differences within it. Subsequently, Öcalan has expanded and developed his ideas and introduced the concepts of 'democratic confederalism' and 'democratic autonomy' as proposals to accommodate Kurdish rights in Turkey. He believes the solution of the Kurdish question through the construction of a Kurdish nation-state will deepen the current Kurdish conflicts rather than resolve it and proposes a solution on the basis of the democratisation of society and states. His proposals call for the existing states to recognise Kurdish identity and the rights of the Kurdish people. He proposes the Kurdish communities to establish their self-governments and organise themselves as a national community within the existing state borders.

The PKK and the pro-Kurdish political parties in Turkey used Öcalan's ideas to develop their own democratic autonomy proposals. While there are similarities between the PKK's and HDP's proposals, there are also significant differences. For the PKK, the objective is to organise the Kurds as a national community in each of the states the Kurds are based and it envisions a pan-Kurdish non-state entity in the form of the KCK. It conceives of a solution to the Kurdish question in the Middle East in terms of decentralised federal entities. This is proposed as a system that is the most suitable for the overcoming the current stalemate by developing a fairer and freer society in the region in which values of gender equality and environmental sustainability can take root. Moreover, by creating a loosely united confederal entity the new proposed political structure will neither challenge the established and internationally recognised boundaries nor resort to nationalism or establishing a nation-state. For the HDP and the other pro-Kurdish parties before it, the proposals are developed as a framework to decentralise Turkey's political structure, which it sees as necessary to rebuild the existing state-society relations on the basis of democracy pluralism and recognition of group rights of different national, ethnic and religious communities in Turkey.

Overall, Öcalan's democratic solution has triggered a significant transformation in the PKK as well as Turkish politics. Throughout the past decade numerous organisations have been set-up that represent the Kurdish society and seek to institute democratic autonomy in Turkey. The past two decades also witnessed a significant reduction in the violent incidents between the PKK and the state security forces in Turkey and although the violence returned after 2004, its intensity was far less than the violence of the 1990s. The return of the pro-Kurdish parliamentary opposition in 2007 enabled the Kurds to raise their demands and contribute to the public debate on the Kurdish question. The Kurds used the democratic space to organise and build pressure on the state to carry democratisation reforms. However, the lack of any concrete steps to meet the Kurdish demands together with the AKP's growing authoritarianism has reversed the positive developments since the summer of 2015. In this period, we have witnessed a process of re-securitisation of Turkey's Kurdish question and the government's reliance on the use of the force on a massive scale to dismantle the pro-Kurdish opposition and repress any form of Kurdish dissent.

Bibliography

Akkaya, Ahmet Hamdi and Joost Jongerden, 'Confederalism and Autonomy in Turkey: The Kurdistan Workers' Party and the Reinvention of Democracy' in Cengiz Gunes and Welat Zeydanlıoğlu (eds), *The Kurdish Question in Turkey: New Perspectives on Violence, Representation and Reconciliation* (Routledge 2014) 186–214.

Bayır, Derya, *Minorities and Nationalism in Turkish Law* (Ashgate 2013).

Bayır, Derya, 'The role of the judicial system in the politicide of the Kurdish opposition' in Cengiz Gunes and Welat Zeydanlıoğlu (eds), *The Kurdish Question in Turkey: New Perspectives on Violence, Representation and Reconciliation* (Routledge 2014) 21–46.

BDP, 'Barış ve Demokrasi Partisi Programı', accessed at: <https://bdpblog.wordpress.com/parti-programimiz/>.

BDP, 'Democratic Özerklik Projesi', accessed at: <https://bdpblog.wordpress.com/2011/05/04/demokratik-ozerklik-projesi/>.

DTK, *Kürt Sorununun Çözümü İçin Demokratik Özerklik* (Aram 2012).

DTK, 'Demokratik Toplum Kongresi Bileşenlerince Hazırlanmış Olan, Demokratik Özerk Kürdistan Modelinin Taslak Sunumu', <http://bianet.org/files/doc_files/000/000/179/original/demokratiközerklik.htm>.

DTP, *Demokratik Toplum Partisi'nin Kürt Sorununa İlişkin Demokratik Çözüm Projesi* (2008).

Gürer, Çetin, *Demokratik Özerklik: Bir Yurttaşlık Heterotopyası* (Notabene 2015).

Gunes, Cengiz, *Kurdish National Movement in Turkey: From Protest to Resistance* (Routledge 2012).

Gunes, Cengiz, 'Explaining the PKK's Mobilization of Kurds in Turkey: Hegemony, Myth and Violence', (2013) 12 (3) *Ethnopolitics* 247–267.

Gunes, Cengiz, 'Kurdish Mobilisation in Turkey during the 1980s and 1990s' in Gareth Stansfield and Mohammad Shareef (eds), *The Kurdish Question Revisited* (Hurst and Co. 2017) 187–198.

Gunes, Cengiz, 'Turkey's New Left' (2017) 107 *New Left Review* 9–30.

Gunes, Cengiz and Çetin Gürer, 'Kurdish Movement's Democratic Autonomy Proposals in Turkey' in Ephraim Nimni and Elçin Aktoprak (eds) *Democratic Representation in Plurinational States: The Case of Kurds in Turkey* (Palgrave MacMillan 2018) 159–175.

Happel, Klaus, 'Introduction' in Abdullah Öcalan, *Prison Writings: The Roots of Civilisation*, Klaus Happel (transl.) (Pluto Press 2006).

HDP, *Büyük İnsanlık-Bizler Meclise* (Ankara 2015).

KCK, *KCK Sözleşmesi*, <https://code.google.com/p/bookstorer/downloads/detail?name=KCK%20S%C3%B6zle%C5%9Fmesi.pdf>.

Kongra Gele Kurdistan (Kongra-Gel), *Program, Tüzük ve Kararları* (Weşanên Serxwebûn 2004).

Konuk, A. Kadir, *PKK'nin Tek Taraflı ilan Ettiği Ateşkes ve Yankıları* (Agrı Yayınları 1993).

Öcalan, Abdullah, *Savunma: Kürt Sorununda Demokratik Çözüm Bildirgesi* (Mem Yayınları 1999).

Öcalan, Abdullah, *AİHM Savunmaları: Sümer Rahip Develtinden Demokratik Cumhuriyete* (Mezopotamya Yayınları 2001).

Öcalan, Abdullah, *Bir Halkı Savunmak* (Weşanên Serxwebûn 2004).

Öcalan, Abdullah, *Demokratik Uygarlık Çözümü* (Amara Yayıncılık 2015).

PKK, *Dönüşüm Süreci ve Görevlerimiz* (Weşanên Serxwebûn 2000).

PKK, *PKK VI. Ulusal Konferansına Sunulan Politik-Örgütsel Rapor* (Weşanên Serxwebûn 2001).

PKK, *Program ve Tüzüğü* (Weşanên Serxwebûn 2005).

PKK, 'Demokratik Konfederalizm Devletsiz Özgürlükcü ve Demokratik Yaşamdır' [2005] 280 Serxwebûn.

PKK, 'Demokratik Özerklik ve Özerk Demokratik Kürdistan' [2007] 312 Serxwebûn.

PKK 'Demokratik Konfederalizm Bir Toplumsal Organizasyondur' [2005] 283 Serxwebûn.

Şafak, Mahsum, *KADEK Kuruluş Kongresi* (*PKK VIII Kongresi Belgeleri*) (Mem Yayınları 2002).

Index

Accommodation vii, ix, 64, 68n, 69n, 70, 72, 81, 135, 145, 146n, 147, 150, 151, 189n, 199, 250, 263, 264
Åland Islands vii, viii, xiii, 25, 38, 38n, 78, 84, 86, 87, 88, 89, 89n, 90, 96, 97, 98, 98n, 99, 99n, 100, 100n, 101, 101n, 102, 103, 104, 105, 235
Anti-colonialism 183
Austria xii, xiii, 41n, 52, 54n, 61, 69, 69n, 76, 83n, 86, 107, 108, 136, 137, 156, 157, 158, 159, 171, 183

Basque Country ix, xii, xiii, xiv, 107, 110, 110n, 112, 116n, 120, 120n, 123, 123n, 124, 127, 133, 134, 135, 137, 138, 139, 140, 140n, 141, 142, 143, 144, 145, 146, 146n, 147, 148, 149n, 150, 151
Belgium 51, 52, 74, 77, 83n, 107, 108, 117n, 130, 136, 230n, 244

Canada viii, 4n, 10, 13, 31, 74, 75, 83, 84, 86, 87, 88, 89, 92, 93n, 94n, 95n, 101, 102, 103, 104, 105, 113, 113n, 114, 129, 183
Catalonia ix, xii, 3n, 5n, 13, 29, 31, 120n, 133, 134, 135, 138, 139, 140, 140n, 141, 142, 143, 144, 145, 146, 146n, 147, 148, 149, 150, 153, 174n
Citizenship 15, 35n, 40, 41, 41n, 42, 45n, 58n, 60, 61, 63, 71n, 75, 81, 91, 118n, 129, 211, 211n, 212, 256, 263
Climate change viii, 109, 109n, 110, 110n, 115, 116, 117n, 119, 120n, 121, 121n, 123, 124, 125, 127, 128
Colonialism 4, 7, 11, 50, 80, 183, 221, 222
Confederalism x, 201, 202, 213, 214, 214n, 215, 216, 216n, 217, 217n, 221, 226, 246, 247, 247n, 248, 252, 253, 257, 257n, 258, 265, 266
Consociationalism 52, 54n, 162n, 171n, 181
Cultural autonomy xiii, 24, 52, 54n, 61, 64, 69, 163, 163n, 167, 178, 188, 189, 215, 215n, 220n, 226, 257

Decentralization ix, 133, 136, 137, 139, 197, 219n, 223
Democratic Federation of Northern Syria (dfns) ix, x, 183, 194, 196, 197, 197n, 200, 213
Demoi 54, 55, 55n, 56, 57, 58, 59
Denmark viii, 11, 77, 83, 84, 84n, 87, 90, 91, 101, 102, 103, 104, 137
Diversity ix, xii, xiii, xiv, 23, 48, 49, 57n, 61, 64, 70, 72, 78, 80, 107n, 109n, 116n, 126, 127, 133, 134, 135, 136, 138, 140, 154, 155n, 173, 174, 174n, 179

Environmentalism vii, viii, 106, 117, 118, 118n, 127, 129
European Union (eu) 50, 51, 52, 55, 57, 57n, 58, 59, 86, 98n, 99, 99n, 104, 107, 107n, 108, 110, 113, 115, 116, 118, 120n, 123n, 126, 129, 145n, 151, 164n, 168n, 171, 182, 187n, 198, 219, 239, 249n

Faroe Islands viii, 84, 84n, 86, 87, 89n, 90, 90n, 91, 91n, 101, 102, 103, 104
Federation viii, ix, 22, 83, 84, 84n, 85, 86, 88, 92, 95n, 102, 121n, 183, 187, 190n, 196, 198, 200, 213, 250
Finland viii, xiv, 25, 38n, 64, 65, 65n, 66, 66n, 67, 70, 72, 74, 78, 81, 82, 83, 83n, 84, 87, 88, 89, 89n, 90, 96, 97, 98, 99, 99n, 100, 100n, 101, 102, 103, 104, 105, 137, 235
France viii, 9, 11, 33, 34, 34n, 47, 47n, 59, 66, 69n, 75, 84n, 188, 191, 205, 206, 207, 228, 230, 230n, 232, 244

Germany 58, 58n, 75, 83n, 86, 107, 108, 136
Greece 68, 69, 74, 77, 185, 228, 230, 230n, 231, 232, 233, 234, 242, 243, 244, 248
Greenland xi, 3, 3n, 10, 29, 84, 84n, 86, 87, 91n

Human rights vii, x, xi, xiv, 3n, 4n, 5, 5n, 6, 6n, 7, 8, 9, 10, 10n, 11n, 12, 13, 16, 17, 20, 21, 22, 22n, 23, 25, 26, 26n, 27, 28, 29, 30, 37, 41, 42n, 43, 45, 46, 46n, 47, 48, 49, 56, 60, 61, 62, 63, 79, 80, 83n, 109n, 192, 195, 195n, 197, 198, 217, 217n, 218, 219, 219n, 220, 220n, 221, 221n, 222n, 224, 225, 226,

Human rights (cont.)
227, 228n, 229n, 239, 240n, 241, 241n, 242n, 244, 245, 250

Identity 19, 23, 24, 35n, 44, 45, 58, 61, 68, 69n, 70, 71n, 81, 118n, 125n, 127, 134, 134n, 139, 146, 147, 150, 151, 152, 155n, 156, 167, 178, 179, 180, 185n, 199, 202, 203n, 210, 210n, 211, 212, 220n, 226, 227, 234, 236, 247, 249, 250, 251, 252, 254, 256, 258, 260, 261, 263, 264, 265
Imbros 229, 230, 230n, 231, 232, 232n, 233, 233n, 234, 235, 237, 238, 239, 242, 243
Independence 3n, 4, 4n, 5, 6, 8, 10, 11, 12, 13, 14, 15, 16, 17, 18, 28, 30, 31, 51, 66, 68, 74, 75, 84n, 91, 117, 118, 144, 145, 145n, 146, 146n, 147, 148, 149, 150, 151, 183, 185, 188, 194, 202, 204, 206, 207, 208, 209, 219, 231
Indigenous 3, 4, 5, 7, 8, 9, 12, 13, 16, 17, 18, 20, 21, 21n, 22, 23, 25, 26, 27, 28, 29, 30, 36, 38, 38n, 39, 42, 49, 49n, 50, 51, 52, 52n, 53, 53n, 54, 56, 59, 60, 61, 79, 114, 118
International law XIII, 3, 3n, 4, 4n, 5, 6, 7, 8, 9, 9n, 12n, 15, 17, 21n, 22n, 25, 28, 29, 30, 31, 32, 38n, 49, 49n, 50, 53, 59, 60, 61, 62, 62n, 63, 72, 72n, 73, 73n, 74, 81, 82, 116n, 144, 145n, 151, 157n, 201, 202, 204, 205, 205n, 206, 207, 208, 216n, 217, 218, 218n, 219, 219n, 221, 221n, 222, 223, 224, 225, 226, 236n, 241n, 244
Iraq VII, IX, XIV, 154n, 180, 181, 183, 185, 186n, 188, 189, 191, 193, 193n, 194, 195, 196, 197, 198, 199, 200, 201n, 206n, 207, 211, 213n, 214, 219, 223, 226, 246, 255
Italy XII, 4n, 10, 30, 69, 71, 71n, 72, 76, 81, 136, 137, 154, 154n, 156, 157, 157n, 158, 158n, 161n, 172, 181, 184, 228, 230, 230n, 232, 244, 248

Kurdistan XIII, 4n, 30, 185n, 186, 187, 189, 189n, 191, 191n, 192, 192n, 193, 193n, 194, 194n, 195, 195n, 196, 197, 197, 197n, 198, 199, 200, 209n, 214n, 215n, 225, 227, 246, 247n, 251, 252, 254, 255, 255n, 256, 257n, 258, 259, 261, 261n, 266, 267
Kurdistan Region of Iraq (KRG) IX, 183, 191, 192, 193, 194, 196, 197

Language rights X, 159n, 163, 167, 168n, 181
Lausanne Treaty X, 229, 231, 232, 233, 235, 241, 242, 242n
League of Nations 38n, 64, 73, 74, 77, 77n, 78, 82, 204, 205n, 206, 226, 228, 231, 239, 240, 241, 242

Minority rights XI, XII, XIII, XIV, 20, 22n, 23, 25, 30, 70n, 79, 81, 154n, 179n, 180, 195, 201, 202, 204, 205, 206, 206n, 207, 208, 217, 218, 225, 228, 229, 242, 242n
Multinational IX, 57, 57n, 61, 124, 133, 134, 134n, 152

Nation-state VII, VIII, 35n, 36, 37, 38, 40, 41n, 52, 55, 56, 57, 60, 71, 72, 73, 80, 134, 196, 197, 198, 201, 203, 203n, 204, 205, 207, 208, 209, 210, 213, 214, 214n, 215, 217, 221, 221n, 222, 223, 225, 226, 227, 252, 256, 257, 265
Nationalism VIII, XI, XII, XIII, 32n, 40n, 42n, 44, 54n, 60, 61, 63, 64, 70, 71, 71n, 72, 80, 81, 106, 107n, 117, 117n, 118, 118n, 125n, 127, 128, 129, 130, 134, 134n, 147n, 148, 152, 183, 187, 199, 202, 203, 205, 205n, 206, 206n, 207, 208, 208n, 209, 210, 210n, 211n, 213, 214, 214n, 219, 219n, 222, 223, 224, 225, 226, 227, 246n, 254, 257, 265, 266
Non-territorial autonomy VII, X, 28, 50, 69n, 70, 81, 202, 202n, 224

Ottoman Empire 66, 72n, 76, 183, 184, 185, 186, 187, 201, 202, 203, 204, 206n, 213n, 222, 227, 229, 231, 237, 246

Palestine IX, 12, 35n, 50, 61, 183, 190, 208
Pluralism XI, 55, 57n, 61, 134n, 143n, 152, 263, 265
Power-sharing 79, 158, 160, 163, 164, 170, 170n, 171n, 178, 180, 181
Proportionality 163, 163n, 165n, 167, 170, 178

Rojava IX, X, 183, 187n, 194, 194n, 195, 195n, 196, 197n, 199, 200, 209n, 212n, 213n, 215, 215n, 216n, 217n, 223, 224, 225, 226

Sami 21n, 25, 30, 52
Scotland 13, 86, 110, 110n, 130
Self-determination VII, VIII, IX, X, XIII, 3, 4, 4n, 5, 5n, 6, 6n, 7, 8, 9, 9n, 10, 11, 11n, 12, 13, 14, 15, 16, 17, 18, 19, 20, 20n, 21, 21n, 22, 22n, 25, 26, 27, 28, 29, 30, 31, 32, 33,

34, 35, 37, 38, 38n, 41, 49, 50, 51, 52, 53, 54, 54n, 58, 59, 61, 68n, 76, 76n, 77, 78, 81, 82, 139, 142, 142n, 143, 143n, 144, 147, 147n, 149, 149n, 152, 153, 156, 158, 158n, 159, 177, 181, 183, 184, 189n, 199, 204, 214n, 215, 217, 218, 218n, 219, 220, 221, 221n, 224, 225, 226, 237, 247, 258
Self-rule 257, 264
Separation 9, 11, 13, 14, 67, 72, 97, 148, 160, 173, 175, 178, 250
South Tyrol IX, XII, 4, 4n, 10, 30, 70, 154, 154n, 155, 155n, 156, 156n, 157, 157n, 158, 158n, 159, 159n, 160, 160n, 161, 161n, 162, 162n, 163, 163n, 164, 164n, 165, 165n, 167, 167n, 168, 168n, 169, 169n, 170, 170n, 171, 171n, 172, 173, 174, 174n, 175, 175n, 176, 176n, 177, 178, 178n, 179, 179n, 180, 181, 182
Sovereignty 4, 15, 16, 26, 28, 29, 32, 34, 36, 36n, 37, 38, 38n, 39, 48, 49, 49n, 50, 51, 52, 52n, 53, 54, 56, 58, 60, 61, 63, 68, 68n, 69, 73, 73n, 74, 74n, 76, 76n, 77, 78, 81, 82, 83, 83n, 85, 113, 113n, 114, 114n, 115, 116, 125, 125n, 126, 129, 137, 139, 142, 142n, 143n, 144, 145, 145n, 146, 146n, 147n, 148, 149, 150, 151, 152, 153, 189n, 199, 201, 204, 204n, 205, 213, 217, 218, 219, 221n, 223, 224, 225, 230, 232, 233, 234, 234n, 235
Spain VIII, IX, XII, 51, 52, 106, 107, 107n, 108, 110, 112, 115, 115n, 116, 119n, 123, 123n, 124, 124n, 125, 125n, 126, 129, 131, 133, 134, 134n, 135, 136, 136n, 137, 137n, 138, 139, 140, 144, 145, 145n, 147, 148, 149, 151, 152, 153
Sub-state VIII, XIV, 83, 84, 85, 85n, 86, 87, 88, 90, 92n, 102, 103, 104, 106, 107, 108, 109, 110, 110n, 113, 116, 118, 119, 120, 121, 122, 124, 126, 130, 187, 188, 217, 223, 237n, 244
Sustainable development VIII, 106, 113, 115, 117, 117n, 119, 119n, 120n, 121, 122, 123, 124, 125, 126, 128, 130
Syria VII, IX, XIV, 183, 187, 187n, 188, 191, 194, 195, 195n, 196, 197, 197n, 198, 199, 200, 201, 201n, 202, 202n, 203, 203n, 204, 205, 205n, 206, 206n, 207, 208, 208n, 209, 209n, 210, 210n, 211, 211n, 212, 212n, 213, 213n, 214, 215n, 217, 217n, 219, 219n, 220, 221, 221n, 222, 223, 224, 225, 226, 227, 246, 248, 255, 262
Sweden VII, XI, 65, 67, 75, 77, 78

Tenedos 229, 230, 230n, 231, 232, 232n, 233, 234, 235, 237, 238, 239, 242, 243, 245
Territorial autonomy VII, VIII, IX, X, XIV, 22n, 24, 27, 28, 31, 50, 62, 63, 64, 68, 69n, 70, 72, 73, 78, 79, 80, 81, 85n, 86, 104, 133, 135, 141, 150, 202, 237, 243, 244, 250
Titular nation 36, 36n, 38, 40, 43, 58
Treaty of Sèvres 186, 230, 231
Turkey VII, X, XI, XII, XIII, 75, 187, 187n, 188, 195, 198, 201n, 206n, 207, 207n, 209, 211, 212, 213, 213n, 214, 214n, 216, 217n, 219, 222, 224, 225, 226, 227, 228, 228n, 229, 229n, 230n, 231, 232, 233, 233n, 234, 235, 236, 238, 239, 241, 242, 243, 244, 245, 246, 246n, 247, 247n, 248, 248n, 249, 249n, 250, 251, 253, 254, 255, 256, 260, 261, 261n, 262, 263, 264, 265, 266, 267

Unitary state 83, 84, 133, 137, 186, 187, 188, 189
United Arab Emirates (UAE) IX, 183, 190, 190n, 198
United Nations (UN) 3, 5, 6, 7, 10, 11, 12, 15, 16, 21, 22n, 30, 31, 53, 53n, 54, 61, 110, 119, 121, 122, 157, 158, 182, 217n, 219, 220n, 226, 228, 239, 240n, 242n, 244, 245
Unites States of America (USA) 15, 183, 184, 191, 222

Wales XIII, 110, 110n, 117, 120, 120n, 130

Printed in the United States
By Bookmasters